THE CAMBRIDGE COMPANION TO
ANCIENT ETHICS

The field of ancient Greek ethics is increasingly emerging as a major branch of philosophical enquiry, and students and scholars of ancient philosophy will find this Companion a rich and invaluable guide to the themes and movements which characterized the discipline from the Pre-Socratics to the Neo-Platonists. Several chapters are dedicated to the central figures of Plato and Aristotle, and others explore the ethical thought of the Stoics, the Epicureans, the Skeptics, and Plotinus. Further chapters examine important themes that cut across these schools, including virtue and happiness, friendship, elitism, impartiality, and the relationship between ancient eudaimonism and modern morality. Written by leading scholars and drawing on cutting-edge research to illuminate the questions of ancient ethics, this volume will provide students and specialists with an indispensable critical overview of the full range of ancient Greek ethics.

CHRISTOPHER BOBONICH is C. I. Lewis Professor of Philosophy at Stanford University, and has published extensively on Plato and Aristotle. He is the author of *Plato's Utopia Recast: His Later Ethics and Politics* (2002), co-editor of *Akrasia in Greek Philosophy: From Socrates to Plotinus* (2007), and editor of *Plato's "Laws": A Critical Guide* (Cambridge University Press 2010).

OTHER VOLUMES IN THE SERIES OF CAMBRIDGE
COMPANIONS

(continued after index)

The Cambridge Companion to
ANCIENT ETHICS

Edited by Christopher Bobonich
Stanford University, California

CAMBRIDGE
UNIVERSITY PRESS

CAMBRIDGE
UNIVERSITY PRESS

University Printing House, Cambridge CB2 8BS, United Kingdom

One Liberty Plaza, 20th Floor, New York, NY 10006, USA

477 Williamstown Road, Port Melbourne, VIC 3207, Australia

4843/24, 2nd Floor, Ansari Road, Daryaganj, Delhi – 110002, India

79 Anson Road, #06–04/06, Singapore 079906

Cambridge University Press is part of the University of Cambridge.

It furthers the University's mission by disseminating knowledge in the pursuit of education, learning, and research at the highest international levels of excellence.

www.cambridge.org
Information on this title: www.cambridge.org/9781107053915
DOI: 10.1017/9781107284258

First published 2017

Printed in the United Kingdom by Clays, St Ives plc

A catalogue record for this publication is available from the British Library.

ISBN 978-1-107-05391-5 Hardback
ISBN 978-1-107-65231-6 Paperback

Contents

Contributors

Julia Annas is Regents Professor of Philosophy at the University of Arizona. She is the author of *An Introduction to Plato's Republic* (1981), *The Morality of Happiness* (1993), *Platonic Ethics, Old and New* (1999), and *Intelligent Virtue* (2011).

Christopher Bobonich is C.I. Lewis Professor of Philosophy at Stanford University. He is the author of *Plato's Utopia Recast: His Later Ethics and Politics* (2002). He has edited *Plato's Laws: A Critical Guide* (Cambridge University Press 2010) and co-edited with Pierre Destrée *Akrasia in Greek Philosophy: From Socrates to Plotinus* (2007).

Luca Castagnoli is Associate Professor of Ancient Greek Philosophy at the Faculty of Philosophy of Oxford University and a Stavros Niarchos Foundation Fellow at Oriel College. He is the author of *Ancient Self-Refutation* (Cambridge University Press 2010) and the editor of *The Cambridge Companion to Ancient Logic* (forthcoming).

David Charles is Professor of Philosophy at Yale University. He is the author of *Aristotle's Philosophy of Action* (1984) and *Aristotle on Meaning and Essence* (2000), and the editor of *Definition in Greek Philosophy* (2010).

Daniel Devereux is Professor of Philosophy at the University of Virginia. He is the author of numerous articles on the ethics and metaphysics of Plato and Aristotle, and is the co-editor of *Biologie, logique et métaphysique chez Aristote* (1990).

Corinne A. Gartner is Assistant Professor of Philosophy at Wellesley College. She has published several articles on ancient moral psychology.

Margaret Graver is Aaron Lawrence Professor of Classics at Dartmouth College. Her publications include *Stoicism and Emotion* (2007) and *Cicero on the Emotions: Tusculan Disputations 3 and 4* (2002). Together with A.A. Long, she has recently published a complete annotated translation of Seneca's letters (2015).

Terence Irwin is Professor of Ancient Philosophy in the University of Oxford and a Fellow of Keble College. He is the translator and editor of Plato's *Gorgias* (1979) and Aristotle's *Nicomachean Ethics* (1999), and his other publications include *Aristotle's First Principles* (1988), *Classical Thought* (1989), *Plato's Ethics* (1995), and *The Development of Ethics*, in three volumes (2007–09).

Rachana Kamtekar is Professor of Philosophy at the University of Arizona. She works in ancient philosophy, primarily on ethics, politics, and moral psychology. She has edited *Critical Essays on Plato's Euthyphro, Apology and Crito* (2004), *The Blackwell Companion to Socrates* (along with Sara Ahbel-Rappe, 2006), and *Virtue and Happiness: Essays in Honour of Julia Annas* (2012). She is the author of *Plato's Moral Psychology* (forthcoming).

Richard Kraut is the Charles E. and Emma H. Morrison Professor of Humanities at Northwestern University. He is the author of *Socrates and the State* (1984), *Aristotle on the Human Good* (1989), *Aristotle: Political Philosophy* (2002), and *How to Read Plato* (2008).

André Laks retired from the University of Paris-Sorbonne in 2011 and is Professor of Ancient Philosophy at the Universidad Panamericana, Mexico, D.F. His publications include *Le Vide et la haine. Eléments pour une histoire archaïque de la négativité* (2004), *Médiation et coercition. Pour une lecture des 'Lois' de Platon* (2005), *Introduction à la 'philosophie présocratique'* (2006), *Histoire, Doxographie, Vérité. Etudes sur Aristote, Théophraste et la philosophie présocratique* (2007), and *Diogène d'Apollonie. La dernière cosmologie présocratique* (2008). He is the coauthor with Glenn W. Most of *Early Greek Philosophy*, Loeb Collection 9 vol. (2016) (also available in French: *Les débuts de la philosophie grecque* (2016)).

Jessica Moss is Professor of Philosophy at New York University. She is the author of *Aristotle on the Apparent Good: Perception, Thought, Phantasia and Desire* (2012).

Dominic J. O'Meara is Professor Emeritus of Philosophy at the University of Fribourg. His publications include *Pythagoras Revived: Mathematics and Philosophy in Late Antiquity* (1989), *Plotinus: An Introduction to the* Enneads (1993), and *Platonopolis: Platonic Political Philosophy in Late Antiquity* (2003).

David Sedley was formerly Laurence Professor of Ancient Philosophy 2000–14, and remains a Fellow of Christ's College. His publications include *The Hellenistic Philosophers* (with A.A. Long, 1987), *Lucretius and the Transformation of Greek Wisdom* (1998), *Plato's Cratylus* (2003), *The Midwife of Platonism: Text and Subtext in Plato's Theaetetus* (2004), and *Creationism and Its Critics in Antiquity* (2007).

Frisbee Sheffield is Affiliated Lecturer in the Faculty of Classics at the University of Cambridge and a Bye-Fellow of Girton College. She is the author of *Plato's Symposium: The Ethics of Desire* (2006) and the co-editor of *Plato's Symposium: Issues in Interpretation and Reception* (with D. Nails and J. Lesher, 2006), *Plato's Symposium* for Cambridge Texts in the History of Philosophy (with M.C. Howatson, 2008), and *The Routledge Companion to Ancient Philosophy* (with J. Warren, 2014).

Katja Maria Vogt is Professor of Philosophy at Columbia University. Her publications include *Skepsis und Lebenspraxis* (1998, paperback with new material 2015), *Law, Reason, and the Cosmic City: Political Philosophy in the Early Stoa* (2008), *Belief and Truth: A Skeptic Reading of Plato* (2012), and numerous articles in her fields. She is the editor and co-translator of Diogenes Laertius's report on *Pyrrhonian Skepticism* (2015).

David Conan Wolfsdorf is Professor of Philosophy at Temple University. He is the author of *Trials of Reason: Plato and the Crafting of Philosophy* (2008) and *Pleasure in Ancient Greek Philosophy* (2013), and the editor of *Early Greek Ethics* (forthcoming).

Raphael Woolf is Reader in Philosophy at King's College London. He is the author of *Cicero: The Philosophy of a Roman Sceptic* (2015) and translator of Cicero's *De Finibus* (with Julia Annas, Cambridge University Press 2001) and Aristotle's *Eudemian Ethics* (with Brad Inwood, Cambridge University Press 2013).

Acknowledgments

I would like to thank all of the contributors who wrote new essays for this volume and graciously complied with various requests during the editing process. Hilary Gaskin was a model of patience and helpfulness from the beginning of this volume to its completion. I would also like to thank Huw Duffy for all his work in putting together the volume's bibliography. Needless to say, any remaining errors are my own responsibility. Finally, I would like to thank my wife, Karen, and our furry daughter, Sophie, for their understanding and support throughout this project.

Introduction

Christopher Bobonich

Few contemporary cosmologists feel the need to take into account Thales' speculation that all is water, nor do modern medical researchers survey Galen before starting their own experiments. But there are aspects of ancient thought that retain more than an historical interest. (This is not meant, of course, to diminish the intrinsic importance of being of historical interest.) Accompanying the resurgence of work in metaphysics from the 1970s onwards, there has been renewed interest in Aristotle's metaphysics. In epistemology, quite recently the *Meno*'s old question of what, if anything, makes knowledge more valuable than true belief has sparked new inquiry.

But it is in ethics that the relevance of ancient philosophy is greatest and has longest been recognized. G. E. M. Anscombe's justly famous 1958 article "Modern Moral Philosophy" convinced many philosophers that ancient virtue ethics can be a competitor of, or at least teach valuable lessons to, modern moral philosophy.[1] Virtue ethics, drawing primarily on Aristotle, is now a flourishing contemporary research program. So we hope that this volume will be of particular interest to philosophers working on contemporary ethics, along with those more focused on ancient philosophy.

So far I have mentioned Plato and Aristotle as inspiring contemporary interest, but there is a great deal to ancient philosophy besides these two towering figures. Since the 1970s, there has been an explosion of work on the Hellenistic philosophers (the Epicureans, the Skeptics, and the Stoics) as well as the Neo-Platonist tradition, and research on the Pre-Socratics has grown ever more philosophically sophisticated. A primary aim of this volume is to acquaint the reader with the full breadth of ancient philosophical ethical thinking and recent research on it. Thus we have included chapters on the Pre-Socratics, Socrates, Plato, Aristotle, the Epicureans, the Stoics, the Skeptics, and the Neo-Platonist tradition, especially its greatest figure, Plotinus.

We begin with a chapter by André Laks on the Pre-Socratics (Chapter 1). It has sometimes been thought that it was Socrates who first made ethics, as opposed to the study of nature, a matter of philosophical reflection. In this chapter, Laks focuses on the relations between ethics

and physics in Pre-Socratic thought and distinguishes three relevant possibilities: correspondence, separation, and tension. Correspondence thinkers believe that we can read off, using the natural world as a model, how
we are to behave. Separation theorists deny that knowledge of the world
can give us any practical knowledge. Finally, theorists who see a tension
between ethics and physics find various complex difficulties for humans
in trying to base their lives on the order of the cosmos.

This chapter also raises two more general issues that will turn up
in several of our other contributions. First, what counts as part of ethics?
Is ethics simply concerned with how we treat each other or is it broader
in scope? Do its requirements go beyond various sorts of self-
improvement in character to include knowledge of the natural world?
Second, if the study of nature is part of ethics, broadly construed, what
does this suggest about the kind of knowledge needed by a good person?
As we shall see, even on views that keep ethics and natural philosophy
more widely separated, an important issue is the relation between the
kind of knowledge needed to succeed in the study of nature and the kind
of knowledge needed to be a good person.

In Chapter 2, David Conan Wolfsdorf considers our evidence for
the views of the historical Socrates. Careful examination of these sources
leads Wolfsdorf to the conclusion that we can only establish some "general features of Socrates' ethics but not its details." We have good
grounds for thinking that ethics and political philosophy were central
to Socrates' philosophy, that it was informed by his experience of the
divine, and that argumentation was fundamental to it. More specifically,
we also have good reason to think that Socrates' ethics was eudaimonistic and that he held that knowledge was responsible for living well. But,
Wolfsdorf argues, our evidence will not take us beyond this point.

The next set of chapters consists of essays on virtue and happiness,
ethical psychology, and love and friendship first in Plato (see Chapter 3
by Daniel Devereux, Chapter 4 by Rachana Kamtekar, and Chapter 5 by
Frisbee Sheffield) and then in Aristotle (see Chapter 6 by David Charles,
Chapter 7 by Jessica Moss, and Chapter 8 by Corinne Gartner). They are
followed by chapters on Epicurean ethics in general (see Chapter 9 by
Raphael Woolf), the Stoics on virtue and happiness (Chapter 10 by Katja
Maria Vogt), and the Stoics on ethical psychology (Chapter 11 by
Margaret Graver). Given their topical overlap, I shall focus on some of
the common philosophical issues that our authors discuss. Virtue and
happiness are the two central notions in Greek ethics. Although different
thinkers and schools have different conceptions of them, the following is

a rough first approximation. A virtue (*aretê*) is an excellent feature or characteristic and things other than humans can have them. Virtues are the features that make something a good instance of the kind of thing it is: a knife possessing the virtues of a knife (say, sharpness and durability) is a good knife and a horse possessing the virtues of a horse (say, speed and endurance) is a good horse. Moreover, being a good instance of the kind of a thing one is involves performing well the activities that are characteristic of one's kind; for example, a good horse runs well and a good knife cuts well. Thus one basic way that virtue makes its possessor good is by enabling it to perform its characteristic activities well. So some central questions here include the following.

(1) What features (e.g. of reason, of the emotions and of the desires) make a human being a good human being; that is, what virtues are there? What are the characteristic activities of human beings and how do the virtues enable their possessors to perform them well?
(2) Since virtue is an excellence, does it require the excellence of our rational capacity, that is, knowledge? If so, what kind of knowledge is required? Practical or theoretical? Might some appropriate form of true belief suffice for a lower grade of virtue?
(3) How many virtues are there and what are the relations among them? In particular, is it possible to have one virtue without having the rest? Or do the virtues come in a package such that if one has one virtue, one has them all? If one cannot have one virtue without having them all, is this because all the virtues are identical or are they interentailing without being identical?

The exact details of various philosophers' conceptions of happiness (*eudaimonia*) are often intricate, but etymologically and in its earliest uses, being happy (*eudaimôn*) meant being well off with respect to divine forces (*daimones*). In philosophical writers, being happy is understood as living a kind of life that is overall best for the person in question. A number of important questions arise here.

(1) What is the relation between being virtuous and acting virtuously and being happy? Greek philosophers differ over the precise relations between happiness and virtue, but agree that they are intimately connected. Is virtue necessary for happiness, sufficient for happiness, or is it identical with happiness?
(2) Are the virtues and virtuous activity only instrumentally good insofar as they bring about the distinct end of happiness? (As we shall see, this

is the Epicurean position.) Or are they good in themselves insofar as they are constituents of happiness and thus are aimed at with no further end in view? Does this capture what we mean by the idea that virtue is good in itself? Is virtue more or less valuable than virtuous activity?

(3) If happiness is not identical with virtue, then happiness will have other constituents. What are these constituents? Do they include, for example, (at least some kinds of) pleasures? Do they include the happiness of some other people? What is the place of philosophical contemplation?

(4) It is often thought that Greek ethicists are rational eudaimonists; that is, they think that insofar as I am rational, I pursue everything else for the sake of my own happiness while I always pursue my own happiness for its own sake. As we shall see, some of our authors reject this assumption. But if Greek ethics is eudaimonist, is it too egoistic to be an acceptable ethical theory? This issue is relevant to the chapters on love and friendship as well as those by Julia Annas (Chapter 14) and Richard Kraut (Chapter 15).

The chapters on ethical psychology are a reflection of the fundamental role that psychology plays in Greek ethical philosophy. Perhaps the most famous question in Greek ethics is "How should I live?" (e.g. Plato, *Gorgias* 500BC). This includes, but is much broader than, the question of what actions I should perform. Deciding how I should live requires determining not only what goals I should adopt, but also what desires and emotions I should have (including what sorts of attitudes I should have to family, friends, and fellow citizens). Some of the main questions that arise here include the following.

(1) What are the basic kinds of human motivations and can they be divided into rational and non-rational kinds? What distinguishes rational and non-rational motivations? What are desires and emotions? What is the nature of reason and how do theoretical and practical reason differ?

(2) Can desires and emotions overcome reason so that the agent acts contrary to her rational judgment of what is best?

(3) What are good sorts of desires and emotions to have and what is it that makes them good? Does their value lie only in being instrumentally productive of right action and avoiding psychic turmoil or can they have some further non-instrumental value?

(4) What is pleasure and what role does it play in the happy life?

As I have noted above, one's attitudes towards others are an important part of what kind of person one is, and the notions of love (*eros*) and friendship (*philia*) play a much more significant role in ancient ethics than in modern morality. Some of the questions that our authors explore here include the following.

(1) What is friendship and what does it involve? Does it, for example, require aiming at the happiness of my friend for her own sake? Does it require that I have a correct conception of her happiness?

(2) If rational eudaimonism is true, then cultivating and maintaining friendships will only be rational if doing so optimally conduces to my happiness. Does the requirement that my friendship with you benefit me undermine the idea that I should aim at your happiness for its own sake? What are the benefits of friendship? Do they accrue to the one who loves, the one who is loved or to both equally?

(3) Is friendship such a demanding relationship that I can only have a few friends? Or might it extend more widely, say, to my fellow citizens? What, if any, is the relation between friendship and my general attitudes of concern for other people?

As we shall see, *eros* plays a much larger and more significant role in Plato's ethics than in Aristotle's. Insofar as Plato thinks of *eros* as a desire for the beautiful or the fine (the *kalon*) that is ultimately to be identified with our desire for our own happiness, its relation to interpersonal love seems problematic. One of the central questions pursued in Sheffield's chapter is how *eros*, so understood, is compatible with, or even requires, friendship understood as interpersonal love.

We have also included chapters on two philosophical schools, the Skeptics and the Neo-Platonists, who are less frequently seen as essential parts of the Greek ethical tradition. These chapters, by Luca Castagnoli (Chapter 12) and Dominic J. O'Meara (Chapter 13), demonstrate why such an omission is a mistake. Castagnoli explores the argumentative strategies used by Academic and Pyrrhonian skeptics in ethics, the sorts of conclusions they reached, and the relation between the skeptics' views on ethics and the rest of their skepticism. Ancient skepticism, as the reader will see, aimed to undermine not just knowledge, but also belief, and Castagnoli shows how the skeptics tried to reply to the "inactivity" charge that such a life without beliefs would lead to paralysis or random or inhuman behavior. Finally, at least in the Pyrrhonian tradition, skepticism was seen as a way of life that answers the old ethical question of how I should live. In particular, skepticism seemed to the Pyrrhonian to be the only way of life capable of giving a person what we are all seeking, that is, tranquility (*ataraxia*). Castagnoli examines why the Pyrrhonians think this, what a skeptical way of life would be like, and what problems a skeptic would face in trying to live her skepticism.

It has sometimes been thought that the Neo-Platonist tradition in late antiquity had little concern with the sorts of ethical issues that occupied their predecessors. Its focus on metaphysics and the goal of achieving some sort of union with the transcendental principle of the One or the Good might seem to leave little room for day-to-day practical ethical issues or even substantial concern for others. In his chapter, Dominic J. O'Meara (Chapter 13) argues that this is a misconception. In particular, he shows that, although some of their answers are quite different, the Neo-Platonists engaged deeply with the sorts of questions about the nature of happiness and of virtue, their relation, and the roles of pleasure and concern for others that are so important to previous philosophers.

The volume closes with several thematic chapters on central topics that cut across philosophical schools. In Chapter 14, Julia Annas considers the relations between the eudaimonism of ancient ethical systems and modern morality. Annas focuses on some of the main contrasts that scholars have seen between ancient eudaimonism and modern morality. In particular, she examines two of the most fundamental criticisms of ancient eudaimonism made from the point of view of modern moral theories: that is, that eudaimonism is too egoistic and that it does not provide enough action guidance to agents. In answering these objections, Annas shows how eudaimonism's response depends not just on one or two of its characteristic claims, but on some of its deep and systematic features. The result, Annas argues, is that eudaimonism is radically distinct from modern moral theories and that recent attempts to graft part of eudaimonism onto such modern theories are likely to fail.

In Chapter 15, Richard Kraut sees greater agreement between ancient theories and modern morality, at least on the key issue of impartiality. It is a central feature of much modern moral thought that morality requires some sort of impartiality in one's dealings with others. It has also often been held that ancient ethics attaches little importance to impartiality. Kraut argues that this view about ancient ethics is mistaken. He holds that the Stoics endorse an extremely robust form of impartiality, as does Plato. Aristotle endorses a strong form of impartiality with respect to one's fellow citizens and may, arguably, be open to its extension in the direction of Plato and the Stoics. The Epicureans, however, are an exception and extend a sort of impartiality only to their friends. Such impartiality is enabled by the fact that, according to Kraut, most ancient ethical philosophers were not rational eudaimonists. (The reader will notice that Kraut disagrees here with Annas and several other contributors to this volume.)

In Chapter 16, I examine the old complaint that ancient ethics is too elitist; that is, it restricts the possibility of virtue and happiness to too narrow a group of people. I argue that we do find a radical form of elitism in middle-period Plato (around the time of the *Republic*). Plato here restricts the possibility of virtue and happiness to philosophers; non-philosophers cannot be either virtuous or happy and their lives are deeply undesirable. The fundamental problem of non-philosophers is that they cannot grasp basic value properties and thus cannot value what is good or fine because it is good or fine. This inability is grounded in Plato's middle-period epistemology, metaphysics, and psychology. I argue that these views change in his later period and that Plato thus comes to think that non-philosophers are capable of doing significantly better with respect to virtue and happiness. Turning to Aristotle, we find that at times he claims that any normal Greek male is capable, with the appropriate habituation and education, of becoming virtuous and happy. I consider some ways in which other of Aristotle's views may lead him to restrict this thesis.

In Chapter 17, David Sedley argues that Plato and Aristotle share a common goal for human life, that is, "becoming godlike." But in becoming like god, what, exactly, is it that we become? Sedley argues that for both Plato and Aristotle (although the story for Plato is more complicated) the relevant respect in which we are to become godlike is by leading a purely intellectual life. For both, the purely intellectual life is happier than any life devoted to ethical or political activity. Even if the contemplative philosopher engages in ethical activity, such ethical activity does not form any part of what it is to lead a godlike life. Aristotle's gods lack the ethical virtues, but as Sedley shows the question is more complex for Plato. The other important respect in which humans can become godlike is immortality and Sedley explores the relation for both Plato and Aristotle between contemplation and attaining, in some way, immortality.

In "Horace and Practical Philosophy" (Chapter 18), Terence Irwin takes up, in the case of Horace, what is a general and highly practical problem facing the student of ancient ethics (including, perhaps, some of the readers of this volume): ancient philosophers offer advice about how to live one's life, but can an individual actually profit from it? Irwin focuses on three worries. First, schools differ in the advice that they give. So we have to make decisions about basic matters of philosophy, but few of us have the ability to weigh all the relevant arguments. Second, the recommendations of these philosophers often differ radically from common sense. Thus by adopting them, we run the risk of alienation from our society. Third, if these ethical philosophies require constant self-examination, we may find them too demanding or simply unattractive. Horace, Irwin argues, deals with these questions implicitly even if not explicitly. Irwin considers what Horace's answers to these worries might be and how these answers relate to Horace's claim not to adhere to any of the philosophical schools, but to follow different schools in different circumstances.

Although the authors of these chapters disagree on many points, it is our common hope that they do not fully satisfy your curiosity about ancient ethics, but rather that they encourage you to go back to the ancient texts themselves.

NOTE

1. Anscombe (1958). This article has been reprinted in many places.

I Origins

1   What Is Pre-Socratic Ethics?

André Laks

Is there something such as "Pre-Socratic ethics"? If we take "Pre-Socratic" in a chronological sense, and "ethics" in a non-theoretical sense, the answer cannot be anything but positive. For archaic litera-ture – Homer and Hesiod, Lyric poetry and Drama – most of which falls "before Socrates," is full of ethical situations, ethical views, and ethi-cal debates, which not only constitute a well-represented object of study for classicists but have also attracted the attention of contem-porary philosophers.[1] Moreover, a great number of ethical precepts are attributed to a series of important figures (most of them historical, although some display mythical features) called the "Sages"[2] – pronouncements that can be compared in some respects to oriental sapiential literature. But if "Pre-Socratic" is taken in a more restricted – and technically more usual – sense to refer to the group of thinkers who have come to be known as the "Pre-Socratic philosophers," the answer to the question of whether there is a "Pre-Socratic ethics" turns out to be somewhat more complex. This is mainly owing to the fact that Socrates, from early on, was thought of as the one who, according to a well-entrenched formula, "introduced ethics" (in the sense of ethical theory) into philosophical discourse.[3] The problematic status of Pre-Socratic ethics is made textually visible by two documents, very differ-ent in kind, but both crucial for a history of early ethics. First, it is striking that one does not find, in the dialectical and doxographical sections of Aristotle's *Nicomachean Ethics*, expositions or discussions of Pre-Socratic ethical theories comparable to that which we find in his physical and metaphysical works – an absence that is more significant in that a famous passage in *NE* 7. 1 (1145b2–7) explicitly reflects about the good use of "reputable views" (*endoxa*) for philosophical inquiry. Also highly suggestive is the manner in which Arius Didymus, in the introduction to his exposition of Stoic ethics, jumps directly from venerable Homer, who gets credit for having Ulysses say that the end of human life is happiness,[4] to those whom he calls, by contrast, "the philosophers," a group in which the only "Pre-Socratic" quoted, namely Pythagoras, features only as an honorific ancestor of Socrates and Plato.[5]

Modern scholarship has corrected the picture in important ways. Charles Kahn's article "Pre-Platonic ethics" is a case in point.[6] Plato, and not Socrates, constitutes here the historiographical divide, and what Kahn gives us is a general presentation of Greek moral ideas from a period before Plato, starting with Homer and including poets and historians as well as Sophists and philosophers, up to Socrates. The presentation is structured by topics rather than by authors, as we are mainly dealing with views rather than doctrines. More precisely, we learn about archaic views about two questions – the question of happiness and the good life and the question of justice. Nevertheless, the leading thread in both sections is to present the development of archaic moral views as a preparation for some basic features of Socrates' ethics. Thus Kahn, following a scheme frequently found in histories of archaic ethics, depicts the progressive abandonment of the Homeric heroic ideal and so-called "competitive" excellence in favor of an internalized conception of virtue and the good, and an increasing awareness about "collaborative" virtues, a development which goes together with the growing importance given to the soul, *psuchê*, as the directing organ of moral life.[7] By the same token, he traces different Pre-Socratic views about law (*nomos*), namely its relationship to "nature" on the one hand and to justice on the other hand – two topics which we know had been hotly debated throughout the fifth century, in particular but not exclusively by the Sophists. And all these debates understandably serve as a background to Plato's dialogues – think, for example, of Socrates' discussion with Callicles in the *Gorgias* – and to Socrates himself, who then stands not as the one who "introduced ethics" but rather as one who, at the end of an already long story, transformed in some spectacular way an extremely important heritage.

Since Kahn's contribution is extremely valuable, I simply refer readers to it concerning a number of topics that, crucial as they may be, I shall here touch on only marginally – such as the Sophists' views about man, virtue, and justice. For in the present chapter, I wish to raise a question of a different nature and to switch attention from the *content* of archaic ethical views to the *function* the reference to ethics – or absence thereof – played for the development of early Greek philosophy.

It will be useful at this point to return briefly to the notion that Socrates "introduced ethics." This idea can be traced back to Plato's *Apology* and Xenophon's *Memorabilia*; both authors insist, in a clearly apologetic context, that Socrates "never" dedicated himself to the study of celestial phenomena.[8] These texts can be considered as providing the first steps towards a disciplinary distinction between distinct philosophical fields – a distinction that seems to have been first conceptually formulated by Xenocrates (a first-generation pupil of Plato).[9] Now the notion that philosophical subfields were not always differentiated, and that a process of differentiation had to take place in order for the Greeks – and for us – to speak about "ethics" (as opposed to "physics") has immediate implications for our talk of "Pre-Socratic ethics." One might, indeed, raise two questions in this respect: First, if physics and ethics were not yet differentiated, this surely implies the possibility (although not the necessity) that what we call "ethics" and "physics" were co-present in Pre-Socratic thought; second, we can ask about the manner in which the process of differentiation between physics and ethics took place before Socrates re-oriented an already existing set of questions in a totally new direction.

There are good reasons, indeed, to cast doubt on the succession story, derived from ancient doxographical sources, according to which ethics "succeeded" physics. As a matter of fact, some prominent interpreters such as Werner Jaeger, Rodolfo Mondolfo, and Jean-Pierre Vernant have defended the idea that the world was first thought to be the semblance of the institutions of the city.[10] Admittedly, we classify "institutions" and "the city" as "politics," not as "ethics." But, to begin with, the division between politics and ethics is not going to lead us very far before Plato – it is highly significant that Socrates himself claims in the *Gorgias* to be the only true politician because he cares for the souls of his fellow citizens.[11] Moreover, once we begin to look a bit harder, we realize that Pre-Socratic thinkers in general, including those who arguably dedicate themselves to doing "pure physics" (or, for that matter, pure metaphysics) have something to say, either explicitly or implicitly, about "ethics" and about the status of ethical reflection. In other terms, there certainly is, if not a formally identifiable "ethics," at least an "ethical dimension" of Pre-Socratic cosmo-ontologies that we would be well advised not to ignore in our appreciation of Pre-Socratic philosophy.

I shall proceed typologically and consider three possible relationships between "ethics" and "physics" – an approach that, far from precluding chronological considerations, makes them perhaps even more interesting.

(1) Some theories are based on the idea of a tight intertwining and
    correspondence between human action or institutions and the
    cosmos. This kind of theory is probably the most familiar one –
    indeed, it is the one on which the Jaeger-Mondolfo-Vernant approach
    relies. It is important to stress from the outset that these

"correspondence" theories are not descriptive, but normative or prescriptive, thus they already presuppose a difference between the physical world and the "world" of human action even if, or rather precisely because, they may aim to overcome or abolish this difference. The individual outlook of such theories may differ widely, as will become clear by comparing three cases – Philolaus, Parmenides, and Xenophanes.

(2) Some theories presuppose the necessity of *separating* two kinds of approach, one physical and one moral. Two complementary trends can be identified here: on the one hand, theories that implement this separation by concentrating on the world or the conditions of the possibility of its knowledge (these would include "pure" cosmologists such as Anaximenes, Anaxagoras, and Diogenes of Apollonia, but also dialectically oriented thinkers such as Melissos and Zeno); on the other hand, they include theories that concentrate on human excellence and the city – Protagoras being the one we know the most about. The case I shall consider here, however, is that of Democritus, which is especially interesting because Democritus seems to have registered in his *own* work this disciplinary separation of physics and ethics.

(3) Some theories point to some kind of *tension* between ethics and physics, which I shall illustrate by reference to Anaximander and Empedocles, two interesting figures to compare, because of their respective chronology – the former still an archaic thinker, and the latter a more modern, "classical" one.

It should be clear that the classification proposed here and the trichotomy on which it relies (correspondence, separation, and tension) have no claim to exhaustiveness. They point, rather, to directions and tendencies, which means that they can accommodate exceptions and overlappings, like Weberian ideal-types. Thus, I shall barely mention a number of important thinkers, such as, for example, Heraclitus or Antiphon,[12] and I leave it to the reader to test whether the tools I offer here are of any help in supporting or modifying available interpretations of their contribution to ethical theory.[13]

I   CORRESPONDENCE

The basic idea is here a rather simple one, namely that the cosmos is a model, which is or rather can be made transparent, so that what we should do and how we should behave (institutionally as well as individually) can be read off an adequate account of how the world is organized.

Philolaus

At the end of Plato's *Gorgias* (507E–508A), left with no other argument against Callicles, the most brilliant advocate of the "right of nature" as "the right of the stronger,"[14] Socrates famously refers to the doctrine of "the wise":

> Yes, Callicles, wise men claim that partnership and friendship, orderliness, self-control and justice hold together heaven and earth, and gods and men, and that is why they call this universe a *world order* [emphasis added, *kosmos*], my friend, and not an undisciplined world-disorder. I believe that you don't pay attention to these facts, even though you are a wise man in these matters. You've failed to notice that proportionate equality has great power among both gods and men, and you suppose that you ought to practice getting the greater share. That's because you neglect geometry.[15]

Doubts have been recently cast against the traditional identification of "the wise" with the Pythagoreans.[16] But the joint mention of equality, friendship, community, and geometry clearly points in this direction, even if some of these terms also find significant echoes in other thinkers, such as Anaximander, Heraclitus, or Empedocles. Now, the Pythagoreans are a rather fuzzy category, and there is probably more than one way to illustrate Plato's general report by reference to specific names. I shall focus here on a statement by Philolaus, according to which "The first thing fitted together, the one in the middle of the sphere, is called 'Hearth' (*Hestia*)."[17] G. Betegh observes, aptly, that "This novel idea [i.e. that of the so-called 'central fire'] is fully motivated by metaphysical and physical considerations and finds its place in the framework of Pre-Socratic cosmological speculations; yet, at the same time, it incorporates, and thereby reinterprets, elements of the religious tradition... By putting the Hearth at the center of his astronomical system, Philolaus immediately conveys the image that the cosmos is one large household populated by relatives."[18] What should be stressed in the present context is that Philolaus' "immediate," that is, non-explicit, "reinterpretation" of a religious tradition that has deep social and political implications possesses an obvious *axiological* value. By pointing to *Hestia* as the ultimate reality around which his cosmological system is constructed, Philolaus not only projects on the universe a fundamental social structure, but he also legitimates this social structure as being the fundamental constituent of a universal order. It is interesting to compare Philolaus' implicit "cosmological ethics" (as we may dub it) with a well-known feature of ancient Pythagoreanism, namely the existence of a large set of Pythagorean moral and religious precepts (*symbola*) indicating "what should be and should not be done."[19] Examples of such precepts are: "Don't stir the fire with a knife, don't step over a yoke, don't sit down on a bushel, don't eat a heart, don't help to unload a burden but to load it, always keep your bed-clothes tied up ... don't urinate turned towards the sun, don't walk outside the highway," among others.[20] It is probable that these recommendations were originally sheer taboos; but there is also some evidence that these taboos were fairly early rationalized in the light of cosmological considerations, while the world order was itself interpreted as a moral order.[21] The full picture is lost, but we have a trace of this endeavor in Aristotle's report in the *Posterior Analytics* that the Pythagoreans say that thunder comes about in order to frighten those (the dead) who live their post-mortem lives in Tartar.[22] If so, both Philolaus and older Pythagorean precepts testify, each in its own very special way, to the existence of a strong connection between what the world is and the manner in which we should act and behave.

Parmenides

Pythagorean "cosmological ethics" may cast some light on the ethical implications of a thinker such as Parmenides. For although Parmenides is a distinctively non-ethical thinker, in the sense that he does not develop ethical views, a number of "ethical" (religious or social) notions and figures appear in his ontological-cosmological poem. This is true of its proem, whose overall setting and particulars are filled with references to religious views and practices. But it is also true of the body of the poem, most notably in its first, ontological part. The central notion, which is present both in the proem and the first part, is that of *Dikê*, i.e., justice. In the proem, "justice" guards the house of the divinity, but also gives access to it (28B1.14); and according to the anonymous divinity who welcomes the brilliant youth to her home, "justice" and lawfulness (*themis*) are the ultimate forces which have driven him in his journey (B1.26); in the poem's second part, justice is said to "maintain" being in its chains and prevents its being generated and destroyed (B8.14f.). There are interesting differences, but also subtle correlations, between these three occurrences of the term "justice." Some of the differences are obviously related to the difference between the two contexts. Justice in its first occurrence is retributive (*polupoinos*); the second is an intellectual and emotional quality or disposition; the third occurrence (in the second part of the poem), finally, represents some kind of metaphysical necessity.

But how are we to understand the relationship between justice as a social concept and this "metaphysical" necessity? There are in fact two possible readings of the data: either that real justice, properly conceived of, is just that, metaphysical necessity, or that metaphysical necessity is but an aspect of a broader concept – one which is crucially rooted in human institutions, as was the case with Philolaus' *Hestia*. Now, it is more difficult to settle the matter in Parmenides' case than it was with Philolaus, because Parmenides' poem does not develop moral-religious concerns in the way the Pythagorean tradition does, even if Parmenides is reported to have had a Pythagorean teacher (Ameinas) and came in the long run to be described as a Pythagorean.[23] In any case, two things might incline us in favor of reading Parmenides' poem in an ethical perspective.[24] First, some testimonies, the source of which must have been Speusippus' *On Philosophers*, say that Parmenides acted as an extremely successful legislator of his native town Elea, so much so that its citizens apparently maintained the habit until Plutarch's time to "swear an oath to the magistrates every year to respect Parmenides' laws."[25] It is certainly fascinating to think that the "metaphysician" Parmenides could serve as a legislator to Elea in the same way that Protagoras – the resolutely social thinker – did in Thurioi.[26] Less anecdotally, there certainly is an ethical import–at least at the individual level – in the initiatic process of the extraordinary youth whose distinctive qualities make him deserve the attention of the divinity. Only an elevated character is worthy of learning about truth and falsehood.

Xenophanes

Compared to Philolaus' and, even more, Parmenides' cases, the situation is much clearer when it comes to Xenophanes.

Xenophanes' theological views are presented in his epic hexameters. They are characterized by his well-known fight against anthropomorphism, as represented by Homer and Hesiod. God, or gods, is or are not "like" us in any respect. The (not fully developed) chain of thought

runs as follows: common morality condemns theft, adultery, and deception – and rightly so. It may be difficult for human beings to respect these
prohibitions, and in fact they often are not respected. But it is insane to
attribute to gods this kind of behavior, as Homer, to whom Greeks owe
their education, and Hesiod did.[27] God is a standard. We then find the
reformatory features corresponding to these general views in
Xenophanes' elegiac work. What shall we say about the gods, what
shall we do to honor them? What we shall *not* do is to tell stories about
Centaurs or Titans, says Xenophanes in the first of his two preserved
elegies.[28] But we also have some positive recommendations as to how to
behave towards them, i.e. with piety. "Purification" is the key term here,
and it is not by chance that the epithet "pure" appears in the very first
line of the elegy, applied to the floor of the room where a banquet – a
fundamental institution of Greek social life – is going to take place. This
reform extends to other domains. Most notable is Xenophanes' down-
grading of sportive competition – another central item of Greek social
morality – in his second elegy as being useless to the city ("For this does
not fatten the city's store-chambers").[29]

Xenophanes' importance for the development of a philosophical
ethics is obvious, since books 2 and 3 of Plato's *Republic* basically
consist in an elaboration and rewriting of Xenophanes' moral theology.
But what is interesting from the perspective I am developing here are the
two following points: first, that the formal duality that governs
Xenophanes' poetic production (epic hexameters on the one hand,
elegiac distichs on the other hand) anticipates in some way the much
later division between physics and ethics (with theology providing a
bridge between the two) – and second, that this duality points to the
existence of an intelligible articulation between the two domains of
human actions and of cosmo-theological explanations – a correspondence that is facilitated by the resolutely theological orientation of
Xenophanes' cosmological poem.

2   SEPARATION

Might not the history of early Greek philosophy be construed as a series
of differentiated answers to the split originally opened up, long before
Socrates, by Xenophanes – not to speak of Hesiod?[30] The result would be
that what happened philosophically in the course of the late sixth and
fifth century was not the thriving of a cosmo-ontological paradigm to be
succeeded by another one (be it Socratic or more generally Sophistic), but

rather an intricate and often implicit debate about the relationship between different fields of human activity.

Looking at things that way may help us get a better sense of what the relationship between Anaxagoras and Protagoras, his younger contemporary, might be.[31] Anaxagoras was considered from very early on to be a typical "philosopher of nature" (Sextus Empiricus calls him a "most naturalistically oriented" thinker),[32] whereas Protagoras is the first of the so-called "Sophists." Indeed, a very striking feature of Anaxagoras' treatise is that it is devoid of any reference, metaphorical or not, to socio-political notions such as the ones we encounter in Philolaus or Parmenides (and which also were prominent in Anaximander's thought, as we shall see in a moment). But if we consider things from the angle suggested above, we realize that Protagoras' concentration on human excellence (aretê) and socio-political questions such as education and law, on the one hand, and Anaxagoras' approach to cosmo-ontological questions, on the other hand, represent two complementary ways of responding to the kind of approach represented by thinkers like Parmenides or, for that matter, Anaximander.[33] Certainly, there were other pure cosmologists before and after Anaxagoras, such as the earlier Anaximenes and the later Diogenes of Apollonia. But this only suggests that an ongoing debate between ethical and non-ethical cosmologies took place – this is one of the aspects that make "ethics" an important factor in the development of early Greek philosophy.[34]

The correspondence tradition, as appears from what I said earlier, was not monolithic in any way. Xenophanes and Philolaus have very different ways of articulating, both in form and content, the question of the relationship between man and the world. But both of them are united not only by the question – which remains unformulated as such – of what the relationship is between what is and how we are to behave, or, in modern terms, between "is" and "ought," but also by a common attempt to establish a definite link between the two. By the same token, Protagoras and Anaxagoras, who seem simply to have nothing to do with one another, are linked at a deeper level by their agreement that there is no point trying to link ontology with ethical theory, that "ethics" and "physics" are two independent fields of inquiry.[35] Socrates, of course, could build on this differentiation and engage, like Protagoras, on the side of "ethics" against an Anaxagoras – without too much success, it can now be added, since already with Plato (from the *Phaedo* onwards) the coupling of "physics" and "ethics" makes a striking comeback which will remain, globally speaking, a constant of ancient thought.[36]

An interesting side question is whether what I have dubbed "pure" (that is non-ethical) cosmology may have by itself some kind of *ethical* import. There are two ways in which that might be the case.

The first one is that by restricting sharply the object of their investigation to the study of the "world" (its genesis, its present state, its future), pure cosmologists contribute to the formation of an "ethics of the expert" (to take up another Weberian notion) – the idea, that is, that looking for truth must not be open to other considerations than research itself. This idea, however, does not seem to have been available to the Pre-Socratics (and probably wasn't to the Ancients in general). On the other hand, it is fairly clear that the question of the ethical import of "theoretical" knowledge was recognized as such already in Pre-Socratic times, even if it appears to have been raised on stage rather than in philosophical treatises. Aristophanes' *Clouds* is our main testimony in this respect.[37] But a famous fragment of Euripides that reads as a direct response to the charges that are leveled in Aristophanes' play against the moral dangers of natural investigation summarizes well the debate:

> Happy the man who, having attained
> The knowledge deriving from inquiry,
> Aspires neither to trouble for his fellow-citizens
> Nor to unjust deeds,
> But observes immortal nature's
> Unaging order, where it was formed,
> In what way, and how.
> Never to men like this does the practice /Of shameful
>   actions come near.[38]

The idea here is not that the universe provides us with a paradigm for living (this would be the strong version of an ethical cosmology). The point, which is weaker but for this reason perhaps more effective, is rather that the sheer fact of studying how the world came to be, and actually is, is incapable of generating bad conduct (as engaging in politics, one is tempted to surmise, might well do). Euripides might be specifically thinking of Anaxagoras, who we know was prosecuted for impiety some twenty-five years before Socrates.

Democritus

Whereas the contrast between Anaxagoras and Protagoras is significant, there is, as I said above, at least one "Pre-Socratic" thinker who illustrates within his own work the independence of ethics vis-à-vis physics, namely Democritus. For physics and ethics in Democritus seem to run parallel: there is no apparent bridge between the way the world is constituted and the question of how man should conduct his life.

We are fortunate that a catalogue of Democritus' works has survived. Although this catalogue certainly includes some inauthentic titles, it nevertheless gives us a fair idea of Democritus' encyclopedic spirit, which makes of him a distinctively "modern" mind – a predecessor of Aristotle's own encyclopedic writings. In this catalogue, we find a section specifically devoted to his ethical writings, such as *On the Disposition of the Sage, On what happens in Hades, On Manly Excellence,* or *On Contentment,* and we know from other sources he had written a book titled *On Well-Being.* Even more importantly, a great number of Democritus' ethical fragments have been transmitted (although some of them must be spurious). One striking feature of these fragments is that they have in general the form of "maxims" that are more often than not reminiscent of Greek wisdom literature.[39] And this means that the form of exposition of Democritus' ethics, at least as far as it has reached us, is different from that of his physical doctrines – a situation comparable, *mutatis mutandis,* to what we have encountered in Xenophanes.

Many of these maxims are of a prudential nature, which is in accordance with their gnomic form. One central idea is that the soul must control the desires, bodily and otherwise, and that the goal of life is contentment, well-being, and serenity. The global picture that emerges from the maxims and doxographical reports is simple enough. A good summary is provided by Diogenes Laertius 9.45: "The goal is contentment (*euthumia*), which is not the same thing as pleasure, as some have understood it, misinterpreting it, but the state in which the soul lives in serenity and equilibrium, without being disturbed by any fear, superstition, or other affection. He calls this well-being (*euestô*) and many other terms."[40]

One question which arises concerning Democritus' ethics is that of its originality or depth – the maxims often give the impression of being commonsensical – even if, on the other hand, they contain a number of features which strongly recall "Socratic" – not to mention Epicurean – ethics. But the main question here is about whether any kind of relationship can be established between Democritus' ethics and his atomistic physics. This does not appear to be the case, even if we were to think (as I do not) that the beginning of fragment B191 – the longest piece we have from Democritus – says something about the atomic structure of the soul in different emotional states.[41] This disturbing parallelism-without-encountering is borne out by a passage in Epicurus' *On Nature* which clearly targets Democritus: "The first people to have advanced satisfactory causal explanation ... forgot themselves, even though on many points they brought great relief, in attributing the cause of everything to necessity and what is spontaneous."[42] The implied criticism is that if Democritus had had a moral theory in conformity with his physical theory, as required by Epicurus (among others), he should have denied that the soul can do anything by itself in order to regulate its desires, which is exactly the contrary of what Democritus claims in his ethical maxims. But what I think is interesting in Democritus' case, from the point of view I am developing here, is precisely that it implies the recognition, no less profound than any kind of articulation, of the idea that the two domains of ethics and physics are in some important respect *independent* of one another.

3   TENSION

In the two last cases I shall discuss, the leading intuition is that physics and ethics do belong together (contrary to what is assumed, each in his own manner, by Anaxagoras, Protagoras, or Democritus), but that their relationship is one of tension, rather than correspondence.

Anaximander

I shall first consider here Anaximander, which might come as a surprise, since he is often considered as the first thinker to have put forward not only the idea of a "natural law" (which might well be the case in some sense),[43] but also and more specifically that of an ethically binding natural law, one that makes the well-ordered city an image of a cosmos, regulated by a principle of equilibrium, justice, and, on the specific version made popular by G. Vlastos and J.-P. Vernant, of equality.[44] But I think that attributing to Anaximander this idea of a binding natural law relies on a biased reading of the available material.

The main piece of evidence – which is, admittedly, thin – comes from Simplicius' commentary on Aristotle's *Physics*:

Anaximander of Miletus ... said that the principle and element of
beings is the unlimited ... He says that it is neither water nor any other
of what are called elements, but a certain other unlimited nature from
which come about all the heavens and the worlds in them. And the
things out of which birth comes about for beings, into these too their
destruction happens, *according to obligation: for they pay the penalty*
(dikê) and retribution to each other for their injustice (adikia)
according to the order of time.[45]

On one reading of this passage – which is the traditional reading – what
Anaximander is doing is explaining in politico-ethical terms the great
cyclical schemes which characterize cosmic life: days turn to night and
night to days, seasons to seasons and rainy days to sunny ones. These
changes are the result of a continuous fight between the two basic constituents that the world comes from, the hot and the cold (we know this
from other testimonies). Physical processes are taken to result from
things "causing injustice" to one another and then "being punished" in
due time for their transgressive behaviors. Now is this not the way a city
functions, too, or rather should function in order to secure stability?

The problem with this reading, however, is that Anaximander's
cosmos, taken as a whole, does *not* obey a cyclical scheme at all. Cosmic
cycles, which are of fundamental importance for human life (both biological and political), are nothing more than a certain moment of a fundamentally *entropic* process whereby the equilibrium between the
constituent parts of the world, and finally the elements themselves, will
be dissolved back into the infinite, according to a model that J. Mansfeld
has aptly described as "dissipative."[46] But if so, is it not obvious that men
and cities should better *not* act in accordance with the universe? To
speculate about what Anaximander's positive ethics may have looked
like is probably idle. But it should at least be clear that there is a problem
in taking him as a correspondence theorist in the sense indicated above.

From a formal point of view, it is highly probable that Anaximander
wrote in the same way as Philolaus (or for that matter as Parmenides),
which means that he inscribed his views about the relationship between
city and the world *within* his cosmological explanations without developing an independent "ethical" argument. By contrast, Empedocles, the
second representative of the tension I wish to consider, follows a
"Xenophanean" model (much more perspicuously than was the case with
old Xenophanes) by bringing into play two related but independent stories
in order to speak about the relationship of cosmic life and human behavior.

Empedocles

Although there are many disagreements among interpreters about the general structure and many details of Empedocles' cosmic story, there is little doubt that this story had a cyclical outlook involving four so-called "roots" (the future Aristotelian quasi-"elements" of air, fire, earth, and water) and two forces, Love and Discord. Love and Discord are arch-enemies, whose everlasting fight determines different phases of the cycle. Love's total domination means that the roots are completely mingled in a further divinity called *Sphairos*, the Sphere. But *Sphairos* is not an everlasting god; it is periodically destroyed by Discord, which separates again what Love has previously unified. When Discord in turn comes to its full power, the roots are once more separated. There are two main points to be made here. The first is that the alternation of Love's and Discord's domination is determined by a factor that Empedocles calls "the revolution of time" – which Aristotle took (rightly) to be a way of expressing "necessity."[47] The second is that Love's and Discord's domination, in spite of their opposition, yields the same result from the point of view of all the compounds of which the world is made: in both cases they are dissolved and hence disappear.

Now men are part and parcel of this "natural" world. Its story is their story. But they also are alien to it. For this story reaches back to times when they did not yet exist – no more than other mortal species – and encompasses a future when they will have disappeared, like everything else. And this story does not tell anything about the manner in which men must conduct their short-lived lives – a silence that is the more striking in that the forces which are acting in the world are called Discord and Love, which are the two main motivations when it comes to *human* behavior. This question, I take it, is the topic of *another* story, which relates the way in which failed divinities (the so-called "demons")[48] can recover their lost state of blessedness – a story that is meant to supply precisely the moral teaching that is so blatantly absent from the cosmic story.[49] Indeed, this second story includes a description of the kind of life that would result from acting in conformity with Love rather than with Discord. Significantly, it concentrates on the question – which is fundamental for the self-understanding of Greek political communities – of sacrifice. An ethics and politics of Love would be in the first place one that would ban animal sacrifice, whose life is the life of fallen divinities, and would consequently prohibit the consumption of meat to which it is tightly linked.[50] But not spilling animal blood is only a first step to not spilling blood in general. In Empedocles' ideal community, there is no Zeus, no Kronos, no Poseidon, and above all no Ares nor warlike shouting (Kudoimos).[51] Empedocles' *Purifications* is, in fact, "a project of universal peace."[52]

Empedocles' ban on animal sacrifice may imply an indirect critique of Xenophanes' more limited reforming endeavors concerning simple *banquets* and Olympic games. But the main point for me here is that, far from ever *entailing* how men should shape their life on the sole basis of the cosmic story, the cosmic story goes in a different direction than its demonic counterpart. For Love may well be the condition for the reconstitution of a blessed god: the price to be paid for such a reconstitution is, as I said, the *destruction* of everything else, including men and human communities. The *Purifications*, by contrast, militates for the *preservation* of life, human and otherwise. In spite of the obvious analogies between the cosmic and the demonic stories, physics and ethics in the end *diverge*. The tension between the two stories may be best grasped by reference to the status of the two cycles, cosmic and demonic. The cosmic cycle, in the sense of the return of some special state of the "cosmos," or rather of "what is," repeats itself in principle an infinite number of times. This repetition amounts to saying that the fight between Love and Discord is itself eternal, that it will never be settled by the victory of one of the opponents. Things are different in the case of the demonic cycle, which is informed by the structure of punishment. The punishment itself consists in an exile of the divinity, whose "folly" has prompted him or her to shed blood. The cycle corresponds to the time it takes for the punishment to be completed. But it does not imply repetition – indeed, automatic repetition would clash with the very logic of punishment. Rather, punishment restores an order that persists, unless it is broken anew. Accordingly, Necessity is not the name of the force that prompts the divinity to commit the crime, but that of the retributive power that castigates it. Nothing tells us that the crime *must* of all necessity be committed. The cosmic and demonic cycles are very different in this respect. In the one case there will necessarily be cycle and repetition; in the other case it is necessary that there be a cycle, under certain conditions. We need not assume that Empedocles read Aristotle's *Analytics* to claim that he grasped the difference between absolute and hypothetical necessity. This divergence, as I see it, echoes in a much more articulated way the tension between "ethics" and "physics," which was already implied in the more archaic "dissipative" model of Anaximander.

CONCLUSION

The interpretation I have sketched by reference to some Pre-Socratic thinkers such as Philolaos and the Pythagoreans, Xenophanes, Anaxagoras, Democritus, and Empedocles relies on some notions ultimately derived from sociology rather than philosophy. One of them is the Weberian concept of *differentiation* – the question being how and for what reason the philosophical discipline as such came to produce its objects, among others those subdisciplines which we are still somehow working with: dialectic, physics, ethics. Another such concept is that of a *field* (in the sense the word has in physics, that is a "field of forces"), in the way made popular by Pierre Bourdieu – a "field" being constituted by the group of features in relationship to which an individual situated in the field in question has to position himself in order to acquire a distinctive profile. In the present case, what I have suggested is that the triad of correspondence, autonomy, and tension, applied to physics and ethics, to the cosmos and human behaviors, constitute such a field and help us understand what different Pre-Socratic thinkers actually did when they engaged in their work. I would only add that this approach, which is not a standard one, perhaps makes the Pre-Socratics better to think with than we might first be inclined to suppose. For the question about the fundamental status of ethical thought and its autonomy vis-à-vis the natural sciences is still with us.

NOTES

1. Adkins (1960), Nussbaum (1986), Williams (1993).
2. On the Seven Sages, cf. Martin (1993).
3. D.L. 2. 16; Cic., *Tusc.* 5.4.10.
4. *Od.* 9.5–6.
5. Arius Didymus in Stobaeus, *Anthology*, vol. II, p. 49.8–50.10. Wachsmuth.
6. Kahn (1998).
7. On competitive vs. collaborative virtues, cf. Adkins (1960).
8. Cf. Plato *Ap.* 18AB, 19AC, Xenophon's *Mem.* 1.1.11. See also Plato *Phd.*, 96A–99D.
9. Fragm. 1 Heinze (= S.E., *Adv. Math.* 7.16).
10. Jaeger (1936), vol. I 160ff., Mondolfo (1956), 223–55 (esp. 239ff.), Vernant (1962).
11. *Gorgias* 521C–522D.
12. On Heraclitus, cf. Bolton (1989) and Sider (2013); on the Sophists, see Kerferd's (1981) classic study.

13. Unless otherwise indicated, translations of Pre-Socratic authors and other archaic texts are taken from Laks and Most (2016).

14. Callicles, perhaps a Platonic creation, reflects in any case one important trend within the so-called "sophistic" movement, one that is opposed to a Protagorean view about law and society.

15. Trans. D. Zeyl, in Cooper (1997).

16. Huffman (2013a), for example, thinks that "the wise" encompasses a large group of theorists (252–53).

17. 44B7 DK.

18. Betegh (2014) 162–63 (with reference to the notions of "connectedness and friendship" in the *Gorgias* passage).

19. For an overview on Pythagorean *symbola* or *akousmata*, cf. Thom (2013).

20. This comes from a fragment of Aristotle's work on the Pythagoreans quoted by Diogenes Laertius at 8.16 (my translation).

21. This point is developed in Huffman (2013b).

22. *An. Post.* 2.11 94b33–34.

23. Cf. the expression "the Pythagorean and Parmenidean life" found at the beginning of the Hellenistic *Table of Cebes*.

24. One of the very few attempts in this direction that I have come across is Evans' (1970) unpublished dissertation (a reference I owe to Sider (2013)). The thesis is summarized on p. 202: "It is because Being combines within itself these characteristics of the just, the necessary and the ordained that there lives a hope of achieving a reasoned agreement among men." Independently, see also Bollack (2006) (for instance 63 and the entry "éthique" in the index).

25. Plut. *Adv. Col.* 32. 1126a10–11 (28 A12 DK); cf. D.L. 9. 23 (28 A1 DK) "And he is said to have established laws for the citizens, as Speusippus says in his *On Philosophers*."

26. D.L. 9.50.

27. Cf. 21B11 DK: "Homer and Hesiod have attributed to the gods all things/That among men are sources of blame and censure/Thieving, committing adultery, and deceiving each other." For Homer as educator of the Greeks, see B 10 DK. Xenophanes might or might not have attributed to Hesiod the same role.

28. 21 B1.21–22 DK. Note the occurrence of the word *aretê*, i.e. (moral) excellence, in the preceding line.

29. 21B2.13–22 DK.

30. The *Theogony* gives a systematic picture of how the world is; the *Works and Days*, of right behaviors. Not unexpectedly, the two poems cross in the story of Prometheus.

31. Ca. 500/428 for Anaxagoras; Protagoras was probably some twenty years younger (ca. 484–14).

32. S. E. *Adv. Math.* 7.90.

33. See below, pp. 22–3. I mention here the older Anaximander and not Philolaos, who probably belongs to the next generation.

34. The papyrus of Derveni, which has attracted much attention since its first (unofficial) publication in 1962, is an interesting testimony about this debate, although the columns that are crucial in this respect are poorly preserved.

35. The Sophists Hippias of Elis, whose polymathy, reaching from astronomy to genealogy and craftsmanship, has been very deeply (and plausibly) construed as the expression of a conciliatory politics (cf. Brunschwig 1984), and Antiphon, a most acute critic of law who we know was also engaged in cosmological problems, would represent other ways to deal with the ongoing differentiation of knowledge.

36. This is even true for Aristotle, although things are certainly more complicated in his case.

37. On the relationship between Aristophanes' *Clouds* and Pre-Socratic philosophy cf. Laks-Saetta Cottone (2013).

38. Fr. 910 Snell. Coming most probably from Euripides' *Antiope*, explicitly referred to by Plato in the *Gorgias* in the discussion between Socrates and Callicles about the respective merits of the theoretical and the practical life represented by the two brothers, Amphion and Zethos.

39. On Democritus' ethical sayings and their relation to gnomic tradition, see Natorp (1893).

40. 68A1, see further B140, A 167, A169, etc.

41. On this question, see Warren (2002), 62–3; Demont (2007), 183–84. Here is the relevant passage: "For contentment (*euthumia*) comes about for human beings from the moderation of enjoyment and proportion (*summetria*) in life. Lacks and excesses tend to change [scil. into one another] and to produce great movements in the soul. Of souls, those that move for large distances [or: intervals] are neither well balanced (*eustathees*) nor contented. Therefore you must hold your thought (*gnômê*) to what is possible and be satisfied with what is present."

42. Epicurus, *On Nature, Lib.* 25 (41 Laursen, *Cron. Erc.* 27, 1997).

43. Cf. Kahn (1994), 183–93 ("this oldest formula of natural law," 191, commenting on Anaximander 's formula – see below – "the order of time").

44. Cf. Vlastos (1995a), 74–82).

45. I have italicized the words that are likely to go back to Anaximander.

46. Mansfeld (2011), see esp. 10: "things will come to an end ... for both physical and moral reasons, as a compensation for their violent beginnings" (25).

47. Aristotle, *Phy.* 8.1.252a5–10.

48. From *daimôn*, which in pre-Platonic Greek often refers to an anonymous (and obscure) "divinity," which often is a personal divinity.

49. Whether this second story was related in an independent poem called the *Purifications* or is part of a single poem is not essential; the main point is whether one thinks that there are two different stories, as I do.

50. This prohibition has certainly some Pythagorean background, even if the Pythagorean diet did *not* imply vegetarianism, at least at the beginning.

51. 31B128 DK.

52. So aptly the subtitle of Bollack's (2003) edition of the *Purifications*.

2 The Historical Socrates

David Conan Wolfsdorf

I THE SOCRATIC PROBLEM

Viewed as the first philosopher to have made ethics his central concern and ethics itself the central concern of ancient philosophy, Socrates has long held a special place in the history of Western ethical philosophy.[1] But the enormity of Socrates' influence sharply contrasts with the complete lack of direct evidence for his philosophy. Socrates did not commit his thought to writing. Attempts to recover the content of his philosophy must use such evidence as exists in the writings of others. The main sources that have been used include Old Comedy, principally Aristophanes' *Clouds*; the literature of the Socratic writings (*Sokratikoi logoi*), principally Plato's and Xenophon's;[2] and testimony scattered throughout Aristotle's corpus. These sources are problematic in various ways. Hence the attempt to recover Socrates' philosophy is justly described as "the Socratic problem."[3]

Old comics tend to caricaturize. In *The Clouds* Aristophanes presents Socrates as a pseudo-philosophical type, a man with corrupt values, his comically exaggerated features agglomerated from various historical individuals.[4]

The Socratic writings are usually treated as our most important source. But there is broad consensus among leading scholars today that the norms of the genre of Socratic literature recommended creative and personal adaptation and expression rather than strict historical fidelity. Disparities in significant detail between Plato and Xenophon corroborate this point.[5] Moreover, as I have argued in work on Plato's early dialogues, the characters named "Socrates" in these writings are not strictly trans-textually identical. Rather, from dialogue to dialogue Plato uses Socrates in various ways for various purposes, albeit in similar ways and for similar purposes.[6] Xenophon does the same.[7] I infer that other writers of Socratic literature either also did so or at least felt free to. In sum, various authors used a character called "Socrates" to explore and advance philosophical thought of their own, albeit philosophical thought

Thanks to Joel Yurdin for discussing this chapter with me and suggesting a number of subtle improvements.

variously indebted to and inspired by the historical Socrates as well as variously informed by and engaged with one another.

In Anglophone scholarship, the most significant recent attempt to solve the Socratic problem is Gregory Vlastos' argument that a set of Plato's dialogues, regarded as his earliest, represents a coherent body of philosophical thought, distinct from the thought of Plato's middle dialogues, and that the philosophy of Plato's early dialogues represents the thought of the historical Socrates.[8]

Today most leading scholars of Socrates and the Socratic writings reject Vlastos' argument for various reasons. Here, for instance, is the gist of Louis-André Dorion's criticism: Plato uses the character Socrates in both early and middle dialogues. So Plato does not hesitate to put views, which Vlastos acknowledges are not the historical Socrates', in the mouth of his character Socrates. So why think that the views of Socrates in Plato's early dialogues are the views of the historical Socrates? Vlastos' response is that Plato's representation of Socrates in the early dialogues agrees, on several important points, with Aristotle's and Xenophon's representations of Socrates. But Vlastos "grossly" overestimates the agreement between Xenophon and Plato. For instance, in sharp contrast to Plato's Socrates, Xenophon's Socrates never professes ethical ignorance. More generally among the ten theses Vlastos cites as distinguishing Plato's early from his middle Socrates, Xenophon's Socrates and Plato's early Socrates agree only on two. Moreover, these two are negative theses: that Socrates did not develop a metaphysical theory of separate Forms and that Socrates did not maintain a tripartite theory of the *psuchê*.[9]

Aristotle arrived in Athens as a teenager in 367 BCE. His earliest testimony would then have been composed more than a half-century after Socrates' death. This testimony has largely been discounted on the grounds that Aristotle typically does not distinguish between the views of the historical Socrates and those of a character Socrates in a given Socratic writing.[10] Moreover most of the claims Aristotle attributes to Socrates can be recovered from Plato's Socratic dialogues.[11]

In view of the great influence that Socrates had on the history of ancient ethical philosophy and on the history of Western ethical philosophy broadly, these evidentiary problems yield a disappointing result: We can plausibly grasp a few very general features of Socrates' ethics, but not its details. Moreover, the general features are ones that we would probably grasp prior to careful examination: that ethics was central to Socrates' philosophy, that Socrates' philosophy was somehow informed by his alleged experiences of divinity, that Socratic ethics was eudaimonistic, that

Socrates viewed the soul and more precisely knowledge of some kind as centrally responsible for living well, and that some form of reasoned argumentation was central to Socrates' philosophy. On the other hand, it requires some expertise to confirm and clarify these claims and to explain why others as well as more detailed proposals are unwarranted or merely speculative.

2   ETHICS AND THE SCOPE OF SOCRATES' PHILOSOPHY

(1a)   Ethics was central to Socrates' philosophy.[12]

No one would doubt this, but what justifies (1a)? One reason is the prominence of related claims among ancient testimonies as early as Aristotle, claims for which there is no serious contradictory evidence. Above I said that Aristotle's testimony can largely be discounted; I did not say that it can wholly be discounted. In a few passages Aristotle clearly takes himself to be describing the historical Socrates. Some of these remarks, in conjunction with other evidence, can be used to corroborate certain claims about Socrates.

A second reason justifying (1a) is that ethics is central in most extant Socratic writings, including Plato's, Xenophon's, and the fragments of Aeschines. In addition, evidence regarding lost Socratic writings suggests that ethics was central to their content too.[13]

This is one way Socratic literature can be used to make plausible claims about the historical Socrates' philosophy: If there is uniformity or if there are at least prominent trends in the content of the surviving literature or of what we know about the genre, and if this uniformity or prominent content is not contradicted, then it is reasonable to accept that such content derives from the historical Socrates.[14]

(1a) does not exclude other topics from prominence in Socrates' philosophy. But consider one of Aristotle's testimonies. The context is Aristotle's account of the various philosophical contributions of his predecessors. Clearly then Aristotle takes himself to be making a claim about the historical Socrates:

> And when Socrates, busying himself with ethical matters (ta êthika) rather than nature as a whole ...[15]

This testimony supports (1a), but suggests further that:

(1b)   The focus of Socrates' philosophy excluded natural philosophy.

Content from some of Plato's writings corroborates this aspect of Aristotle's claim.[16] Perhaps Aristotle's claim principally derives from these Platonic texts. But support for (1b) also derives from testimony pertaining to other Socratics' disregard of natural philosophy.[17]

Granting (1b), political concerns are also prominent in the Socratic writings. Generally, the distinction between ethical and political philosophy is not sharp in the Socratic writings. A central reason for this is that personal and civic identity in the Classical Greek polis were intimately related. The citizenry of Athens was relatively small, about thirty thousand men, and politics was broadly inclusive and involved direct representation.[18] Concerns with the relation between personal welfare and the welfare of the city-state are prominent in the Socratic writings.[19] In fact, Aristotle himself remarks in a passage from *Parts of Animals*, in which he is also clearly talking about the period of Socrates' historical activity:

> By the time of Socrates, [the study of explanation in nature] had advanced; but in this period inquiry into nature (*to zêtein ta peri physeôs*) ceased, and those engaged in philosophy turned their attention to useful excellence and political excellence (*tên chrêsimon aretên kai tên politikên*).[20]

Hence:

(1c) Political philosophy was also central to Socrates' philosophy.

Additionally there is compelling evidence that in pursuing philosophy Socrates took himself to be influenced in some form by divinity. In Plato's and Xenophon's writings this influence is referred to as "*to daimonion.*" As Walter Burkert has explained, the Greeks thought of a *daimôn* not substantively as a divinity, but as a mode of divine presence or influence. In other words, a *daimôn* is a way that divinity makes itself or its power present.[21] Given that Socrates' experiences of divinity were significant to his philosophical life, it is plausible that:

(1d) Divinity also played an important role in Socrates' philosophy.

I suppose that the role of divinity in Socrates' thought was intimately related to his ethics and political philosophy. There are numerous reasons for thinking so. Among them, religion pervaded most aspects of ancient Greek private and civic life.[22] A signal example of the influence of divinity on Socrates' ethics and politics is the way the *daimonion* influenced his practical decisions in private and public spheres. For instance, Xenophon writes that "in accordance with the forewarnings of the *daimonion*, Socrates counseled many of his companions to do this or not to do that."[23]

More direct confirmation of (1d) comes from the fact that the topic of divinity variously features in Plato's and Xenophon's Socratic writings as well as in Aeschines', Euclides', and Antisthenes'.[24]

Further support for (1d) can be derived from Socrates' trial: Socrates was of course prosecuted for impiety. Granted this, I underscore that throughout my discussion I marginalize the trial of Socrates as evidence for the content of his philosophy. Even if we could establish Meletus', his associates', and the jurors' motives for prosecuting and condemning Socrates, this would only clarify hostile and popular conceptions of Socrates. Further evidence would then be needed to corroborate the accuracy of those conceptions. In the present case, however, whatever Socrates' views of divinity, the fact that he was tried for impiety, in conjunction with the other evidence I have cited, corroborates (1d).

One further consideration bears on the scope of Socrates' philosophy. There is compelling evidence that in pursuing philosophy Socrates took a special interest in method. Consider one further passage from Aristotle in which again he clearly takes himself to be describing the historical Socrates:

> Socrates busied himself with the ethical excellences (*êthikas aretas*) and of these was the first to seek to define the universal (*peri toutôn horizesthai katholou*) ... For there are two things that one may rightly attribute to Socrates: epagogic arguments (*epaktikous logous*) and definition of the universal (*to horizesthai katholou*).[25]

Below I will examine Aristotle's attribution of these particular methodological concerns.[26] Presently I introduce them to draw attention to any concern with method that Socrates might have had. Note that I use "method" here broadly to refer to epistemology as well as rational inquiry and argumentation. For convenience I will refer to such methodology by the term Plato and Aristotle use: dialectic (*dialektikê*).[27] I suggest, then, that:

(1e)   Dialectic too was central to Socrates' philosophy.[28]

In proposing (1e), I presume that the role that dialectic played in Socrates' philosophy differed from the roles of ethics, politics, and divinity as follows. Ethics, politics, and divinity were topical foci. I presume that dialectic was also a topical focus.[29] But dialectic also played a formal and epistemological role in the practice of Socratic philosophy itself.

In addition to Aristotle's testimony, support for (1e) derives from the methodological concerns featured in Plato's and Xenophon's Socratic writings as well as testimonies suggesting that other Socratics were especially concerned with dialectic.[30]

In sum, I propose that the following accurately describes the general scope of Socrates' philosophy:

Ethics, political philosophy, and divinity were central to Socrates' philosophy. Dialectic was central too, both topically and instrumentally.

3   SOCRATES' CONCEPTION OF HIS PHILOSOPHY

There is no compelling evidence that Socrates conceived of his philosophy as inquiry into *ta êthika*. The association of that phrase with ethics was principally due to the influence of Aristotle's character (*êthos*)-centric conceptualization of ethics. The term "*êthos*" and its cognates are relatively rare in Xenophon's Socratic writings. At least until his last work, *Laws*, they are also relatively rare in Plato's corpus. Moreover, the idea that *êthos* has a principal place within ethics is informed by a certain conception of the soul and its parts or faculties. But we have no compelling evidence regarding the historical Socrates' view of the structure of the *psuchê*.[31]

It is more plausible that one way Socrates conceived of his philosophy was as inquiry into the good (*to agathon*).[32] With respect to ethics specifically, Socrates was concerned with the human good.[33] Observe that the phrase "the human good" obscures an important distinction between "the goodness of a human" and "that which is good for a human." I presume that Socrates took an interest in both, for both topics are engaged in the surviving Socratic writings as well as in what we know of the contributions and ideas of the Socratics whose writings do not survive. For example, the topic of *aretê* (excellence)[34] is, at least pre-theoretically, a matter of the goodness of a human, whereas freedom, health, pleasure, wealth, and political status are popular Greek views of what is good for a human. The thesis that *aretê* itself is good for a human – which we encounter in a number of Socratics – is, in turn, a substantive and indeed contentious one.

It may be wondered whether Socrates' concern with the human good included a more abstract interest in the good per se. By "the good per se" I mean to refer, at least as a theoretical possibility, to that which various good things share in virtue of which they are good. For instance,

Dissoi Logoi, a philosophical text presumably composed in the late fifth century, contains a discussion of whether the good is unified.[35] Then again, Socrates' concern might have been more narrowly focused on the nature of good citizenship and leadership. Indeed, these topics are prominent in various Socratic writings. As such they indicate one significant way that ethics and political philosophy might have been integrated in the historical Socrates' thought.

Presumably Socrates was interested in all three: the good per se, the human good, and good citizenship and leadership. On the other hand, it is doubtful that he regarded a description such as *"to agathon"* or *"to andros agathon"*[36] as definitively identifying the unifying concern of his philosophy. For instance, assuming Socrates conceived of his philosophy as unified in some way, reasonable alternatives might include: care for the soul, political science, the art of leadership, civic education, or service to the divine.[37]

In *Memorabilia*, Xenophon characterizes Socrates' philosophy this way:

> His own conversations always concerned human affairs (*ta anthrôpina*). He inquired into the nature of piety and impiety, excellence and badness, justice and injustice, sound-mindedness and madness, courage and cowardice, state and statesman, government and governors, and everything else that he thought someone truly noble (*kalon*) should know, or that anyone ignorant of would deserve to be called servile.[38]

Xenophon hereby suggests that Socrates pursued knowledge that a *kalon* person should have. Perhaps Socrates conceived of such knowledge as *sophia*. If so, he might have conceived of his activity simply as a pursuit of *sophia*, perhaps even as *philosophia*. In fact, Livio Rossetti has argued that Socrates and the Socratics were the first to define their intellectual activity as *philosophia*.[39] Whether or not we accept this thesis, it is likely that Socrates and in turn the Socratics took themselves to be involved in inquiry into a form of *sophia* that they regarded as distinctive and especially important, and that they thereby appropriated the term *"philosophia"* and were subsequently responsible for an influential conception of it.

In short, there are various plausible ways that Socrates could have conceived the ethical facet of his philosophy or his philosophy as a whole. We cannot determine whether he privileged one over others.

4   EUDAIMONISM

From the fourth century, Greek ethical philosophy is, without exception or perhaps with one exception, eudaimonistic.[40] Since Socrates was executed at the beginning of the fourth century, it is questionable whether his ethical thought was eudaimonistic.[41] Eudaimonism is the view that the supreme value and hence orienting point of ethics is living a good life. Observe that under this description eudaimonism may include aspects of both construals of the human good.

I have suggested that insofar as he was concerned with ethics, Socrates took himself to be concerned with the human good. It may therefore be questioned whether Socrates' ethical thought was eudaimonistic. If so, a distinct question is whether Socrates actually spoke prominently of *eudaimonia*. And if so, another question is whether Socrates thought of this condition in its etymological sense, namely as being under a good divine influence. The following considerations lend some support to positive answers to these three questions.

First, the term *"eudaimonia"* and its cognates are common in Plato's Socratic writings and in Xenophon's *Memorabilia*. *"Eudaimonia"* also in occurs in a fragment of Aeschines.[42] Testimony also suggests its use by Antisthenes.[43] Second, in its common usage in fifth-century Athens, *"eudaimonia"* is understood in its etymological sense.[44] Furthermore, whether or not Socrates viewed his own life as an example of *eudaimonia*, the fact that he took his philosophy to be informed by his experience of the *daimonion* and the prominence of divinity within his ethical thought suggests that Socrates would have conceived of a good human life as *eudaimôn* in an etymological sense.

The following, somewhat speculative consideration lends further support to the preceding conclusions. Elsewhere I have argued that both Socrates and the Socratics took a special interest in Hesiod's *Works and Days*. In particular, the Encomium to Work (vv. 287–319) and Prodicus' adaptation of it in *The Choice of Heracles* influenced how they framed and conceptualized some of their fundamental ethical concerns.[45] When I advanced this argument, I did not draw a connection with eudaimonism under that description. However, the ethical concerns in question are eudaimonistic: What is the place of pleasure in a good human life? And to what sort of work should one devote oneself? In fact, in Xenophon's paraphrase of Prodicus' *Choice*, each of the two paths of life offered to Heracles is characterized as *"eudaimonia."*[46] Finally, it is noteworthy that Hesiod's poem concludes with the first attested use of the word "*eudaimôn.*"[47]

In sum, I suggest that Socrates' ethics was eudaimonistic and, probably, that it was self-consciously so.

5   PSUCHÊ, EXCELLENCE, AND WISDOM

From the Archaic period into the fifth century, the word "*psuchê*" was principally used to mean "life" or "vital spirit." But in the second half of the fifth century some philosophers appropriated the word to mean something like "soul."[48] According to this usage the *psuchê* was regarded as in some sense a substantial unity, contrasted with the body, and responsible for a range of what we now call "psychological" capacities and functions. This conceptual development was momentous for the history of ethics, for the *psuchê* thereby came to be viewed as a personal power governing or shaping one's life.

Among fifth-century philosophers, it is widely believed that:

(3a)   Socrates used "*psuchê*" to mean "soul."

Indeed, it is widely believed that:

(3b)   *Psuchê*, conceived as soul, was central to Socrates' ethics.

Decisive evidence for (3a–b) is actually difficult to find. Weak evidence for (3a) derives from two instances of "*psuchê*" in Aristophanes' *Clouds*.[49] David Claus notes that "remarkably, [these uses] attribute *sophia* to the *psuchê*, an association that, with the exception of Heraclitus B 118 and the Gorgianic *Helen*, is original to this play."[50]

An alternative approach to (3a–b) proceeds by way of Socrates' interest in the *aretai* (excellences). Recall Aristotle's testimonies:

> Socrates busied himself with the ethical excellences ...
> [In Socrates' time,] those engaged in philosophy turned their attention to useful excellence and political excellence.

Among the things Aristotle has in mind when he speaks of "ethical excellences" and "useful excellence and political excellence" are traits such as courage, justice, and self-control. Given earlier remarks, it should be clear that Socrates would not have conceived of these *aretai* as "*êthikai*"; however, he might well have viewed them as "*politikai*." For convenience, I will refer to them as "practical excellences." That

Socrates examined some practical excellences and considered their importance for *eudaimonia* is corroborated by the fact that they are so treated in Plato's and Xenophon's Socratic writings and by testimony that they were so treated in the works of other Socratics, in particular Aeschines and Antisthenes, but also Aristippus.[51]

Furthermore, there is compelling evidence that Socrates held one of the following theses:

(4a)   The practical excellences are a single thing, namely, a form of practical knowledge.

(4b)   The practical excellences are forms of practical knowledge.

(4c)   Practical knowledge of some kind is only partly constitutive of practical excellence.

For convenience, I will hereafter refer to the practical knowledge constitutive of practical excellence as "wisdom."

The evidence for Antisthenes suggests a commitment to (4a).[52] Testimony attributes (4a) to Euclides.[53] (4a) and (4b) are developed, albeit ultimately aporetically, in several of Plato's Socratic dialogues.[54] Relatedly, in a fragment from Phaedo's *Zopyrus*, the character Socrates claims to have cured his psychological defects by means of reason (*ratione*).[55] (4a) or (4b) seems to be expressed in a passage of Xenophon's *Memorabilia*.[56] However, Dorion has compellingly argued that (4c) is Xenophon's position.[57]

(4a–c) are, in turn, to be distinguished from the following thesis:

(4d)   Wisdom is not necessary for some aspects of human excellence.

For example, by the value they place on bodily strength and wellness, both Xenophon and Antisthenes commit to (4d).[58]

Given Socrates' interest in the nature of certain practical excellences, given his view that wisdom is at least central to human excellence, and assuming that Socrates conceived of wisdom as a condition of the *psuchê*, understood as soul, it can be inferred that concern with the soul as such was central to Socrates' ethics.

However, it must be emphasized that the assumption that Socrates conceived of wisdom as being a condition of the soul is the weakest premise in this argument. It would certainly have been possible for Socrates to take the pursuit of practical excellence to be central to his ethics and to identify practical excellence with wisdom, without conceiving of practical excellence or wisdom as conditions of the *psuchê* as such.

Perhaps the strongest evidence that Socrates used "*psuchê*" to mean "soul" comes from consideration of the prominence of "*psuchê*" as so used in Plato's early dialogues. Some of these dialogues were almost certainly composed in the decade immediately after Socrates' death. If Socrates did not use "*psuchê*" to mean "soul," then the fact that Plato does so without fanfare or special explanation itself requires explanation.

6   WISDOM, SKEPTICISM, AND EUDAIMONIA

Given these conclusions, I want to raise several questions for Socrates' ethics, some of which I believe we cannot answer for lack of evidence.

What did Socrates take wisdom to consist in? This question may be analyzed as conjoining two others: What was Socrates' conception of the dispositional epistemic attitude constitutive of wisdom? And what was his conception of the content of wisdom? Regarding the former, in Plato's and Xenophon's Socratic writings, wisdom is often examined in relation to forms of technical or craft knowledge (*technê*).[59] A familiar question in Platonic scholarship in particular is whether wisdom is a *technê* or rather whether *technê* analogies are merely used to explore ethical epistemology. *Technê* analogies are also employed in fragments of Aeschines' *Miltiades* and *Alcibiades*.[60] Aristotle also mentions that Aristippus favorably contrasted *technai* with mathematics, insofar as the former concern themselves with things that are good and bad.[61] Hence I infer that in examining the nature of wisdom, Socrates himself employed *technê* analogies. The fact that he did is itself a remarkable and ingenious contribution to ethical epistemology. Taken in conjunction with the way I have argued that Hesiod's *Works and Days* informed his ethical thought, Socrates' employment of the *technê* analogy suggests that he at least entertained the idea that one's life is a work or product (*ergon*) of which one is the craftsman.[62] That said, we do not know just what Socrates concluded from such considerations.

However he conceived of wisdom, did Socrates take himself to have achieved it? Here the Socratics' presentations markedly diverge. Plato portrays Socrates as a subtle ethical-epistemological skeptic.[63] In his one remark on this subject, Aristotle claims that Socrates viewed himself as a skeptic.[64] In a fragment from Aeschines' *Alcibiades*, the character Socrates also appears to express skepticism:

And so although I knew no instruction (*mathêma*) that I could teach to anyone to benefit him, nevertheless I thought that in keeping company with Alcibiades I could, through loving him, make him better.[65]

In striking contrast, Xenophon consistently attributes wisdom to Socrates and repeatedly portrays Socrates as beneficently applying it to his friends. Likewise, Antisthenes appears to present a doctrinal rather than aporetic conception of Socratic philosophy.[66] I suggest, then, that it is unclear whether Socrates took himself to possess wisdom.

Precisely how did Socrates understand the relation between wisdom and *eudaimonia*? For instance, did he take there to be a logical relation between the two, such that the former is necessary or sufficient for the latter? Alternatively, did he conceive of the relation as causal? Relatedly, assume that, among conditions of the soul, wisdom alone is required for *eudaimonia*. Are other factors also required, in particular bodily or environmental conditions? In considering this question, observe that from its earliest usage in the Archaic period through the fifth century, *eudaimonia* was associated with a life or at least an extended period of life of ample pleasure.[67] Above I mentioned that central to the influence of Hesiod's *Works and Days* and Prodicus' *Choice of Heracles* on Socrates and the Socratics' ethical thought was a concern with the place of pleasure in the good life. The Socratics' views on this topic are various and contradictory. I infer, then, that Socrates himself took a serious interest in the place of pleasure in the good life. But what place he accorded to pleasure, we don't know.[68]

Finally, since *eudaimonia* is understood to involve divine favor, the idea that *eudaimonia* also centrally depends on wisdom appears paradoxical. To what extent do humans determine their lives, and to what extent does the divine? One solution may lie in the idea that wisdom is the very thing that may be favorable to the divine. If Socrates engaged this question, how did he respond to it? Moreover, how would his conception of the *daimonion* feature in his response?

7 METHOD

Above I referred to Socrates' philosophical method as "dialectic." I now consider some alleged features of it: *elenchus*, definition, and *epagôgê*.

Something called "*elenchus*" has traditionally been viewed as characteristic of Socrates' philosophical method. Basically, *elenchus* involves the exposure of inconsistency in an interlocutor's set of beliefs pertaining to some (typically) ethical topic. Inconsistency in turns indicates lack of pertinent wisdom. *Elenchus* may be humiliating for the interlocutor, but it may also serve to engender a philosophical motivation.[69] In numerous passages in Plato's and Xenophon's Socratic writings, Socrates' interlocutor is exposed as ignorant and such exposure is shameful and painful. In some cases the exposure also inspires philosophy.[70] Aeschines' *Alcibiades* and *Aspasia* include examples.[71]

Granted this, I resist identifying Socrates' method with *elenchus* and thereby limiting his method to it. Given his intellectual or dialectical facility, surely Socrates often exposed ignorance in his interlocutors. Moreover, such episodes surely struck his associates as memorable and philosophically significant.[72] But presumably Socrates also spent time with his associates cooperatively inquiring into ethical topics and problems.[73]

Note further that however prominently *elenchus* featured in Socrates' philosophical practice, the significance of doxastic consistency and more precisely coherence that *elenchus* entails suggests precisely this as a key feature of dialectic: Doxastic coherence must have been a governing norm of Socrates' dialectic.[74]

Recall now that Aristotle attributes definition of the universal (*katholou*) and epagogic arguments to Socrates. The term *"katholou"* is Aristotelian. But we may simply consider whether it was a prominent feature of Socrates' inquiries to pursue questions of the form "What is *F*?" where "*F*" stands for some ethical kind. The character Socrates pursues definition as such in a number of Plato's Socratic dialogues and occasionally uses the term *"horos"* (definition) and its cognates. Xenophon also attributes such pursuits to Socrates.[75] There is no evidence of definitional inquiry in Aeschines' fragments. On the other hand, Antisthenes took serious interest in definitions as well as in theory pertinent to definitions.[76] The weight of evidence therefore suggests that Socrates himself pursued questions of the form "What is *F*?" This is another major contribution Socrates made to the history of philosophy and to ethical philosophy in particular.

In considering Aristotle's attribution of *epagôgê* to Socrates, let's first clarify what Aristotle takes *"epagôgê"* to mean. The term is standardly translated as "induction" and therefore understood to refer to a form of inferential reasoning where information not contained in the premise set is derived from it. Precisely how Aristotle views such reasoning is controversial. Scholars have mainly focused on *Prior Analytics* 2.23, Aristotle's most sustained discussion. Recently, however, John McCaskey has argued that the very interpretation of Aristotelian *epagôgê* as induction is misguided and that this error is precisely the result of too narrow a focus on the *Prior Analytics* passage. Drawing on uses of "*epagôgê*" throughout Aristotle's corpus, McCaskey concludes that Aristotle and his philosophical contemporaries understood *epagôgê* as a form of argumentation in which a concept or the meaning of a general term is elucidated through comparison (*parabolê*).[77] For example:

> In medicine (*technê* 1), the doctor (*technikos* 1) is one who knows how to solve medical (*technê* 1-specific) problems.
>
> In architecture (*technê* 2), the architect (*technikos* 2) is one who knows how to solve architectural (*technê* 2-specific) problems.
>
> etc...
>
> Therefore, a *technikos* is one who knows how to solve *technê*-specific problems, hence has *technê*-specific knowledge.[78]

I doubt that in every instance Aristotle understands and employs "*epagôgê*" in this way. But my point here does not require such a strong thesis. Rather, as McCaskey emphasizes, *epagôgê* so understood is a signal feature of Socratic dialectic in Plato's early dialogues;[79] and so it is reasonable to conclude that when he attributes the introduction of *epagôgê* to Socrates, this is what Aristotle means.

Examples of epagogic argumentation also occur in Xenophon. There is also an instance in Aeschines' *Aspasia*, which Cicero, our source, explicitly identifies as a case of *inductio*, and which employs a *technê* analogy.[80] Based on the employment of epagogic arguments in these various Socratic writings, in conjunction with Aristotle's testimony, I infer that epagogic argumentation was a feature of Socrates' dialectic. Furthermore, the use of the *technê* analogy in the epagogic argument in Aeschines' *Aspasia*, as commonly features in instances of epagogic argumentation in Plato's and Xenophon's Socratic writings, suggests that Socrates deployed the *technê* analogy particularly in conjunction with *epagôgê*. Finally, confirmation of Aristotle's attribution of epagogic argumentation to Socrates further confirms the correctness of his attribution of definitional inquiry to Socrates.

8   SPECULATIVE CONCLUSION

As I noted at the beginning of this chapter, the primary reason the Socratic problem exists is that Socrates never committed his philosophy to writing. But why didn't he? It is doubtful that Socrates was illiterate. In any case – and although his intense devotion to philosophy seems to have ultimately reduced him to poverty – if Socrates had wanted to create philosophical compositions, he had wealthy friends who would have gladly paid for scribes. Since many of Socrates' philosophical contemporaries composed works, I assume that Socrates himself chose not to. This fact itself deserves consideration. Moreover, I suggest that such consideration should go hand-in-hand with consideration of the following question: Why did ethics become central to Socrates' philosophy at all? The answers I offer here are speculative, but certainly plausible.

Socrates' adult life coincided with the apex and subsequent defeat of the Athenian Empire. I conjecture that in the course of his life, perhaps especially in the last decades of the fifth century, Socrates became deeply concerned with Athens' imperial culture and with the ethical and political values of his fellow citizens. I suggest, then, that Socrates' practice of philosophy principally had a political goal. Socrates wanted to motivate his fellow Athenians and their sons to become good citizens and good political leaders. In pursuing philosophy himself, then, Socrates was driven by a sense of patriotism as well as the belief that his objective was divinely sanctioned.

Furthermore, Socrates believed that pursuit of his goal could be effective only through personal dialectical engagement. The reason for this relates to Socrates' epistemic or centrally epistemic conception of human excellence. Socrates appreciated that the ethical and political opinions and discursive habits of his contemporaries were complex and diverse, varied in subtle as well as unsubtle ways. Moreover, such opinions tend to be deeply held, anchored in forms of life as a whole. Consequently identification, exposure, and adjustment or extirpation of such opinions is a challenging task.[81] Different interlocutors require different strategies of dialectical engagement, and the same interlocutor may require different strategies at different stages in his intellectual development. Contrast a written work, which literally says the same thing to every reader, yet inevitably impacts diverse readers in diverse ways; and at the same time is unable to respond to, let alone dialectically engage with, these diverse responses.

Socrates believed he possessed a level of dialectical skill effective to motivate at least some of his contemporaries to cultivate excellence by pursuing wisdom.

NOTES

1. Socrates was not the only philosopher of his day to examine ethical questions. All of the sophists did, as did other philosophers such as Democritus. But Socrates pursued ethical philosophy in a powerful and unique way.
2. For an overview of the Socratics, cf. Döring (2010) 24–47.
3. Cf. Dorion (2010) 1–23; Waterfield (2013) 1–19. For a collection of responses to the problem, cf. Patzer (1985).
4. Cf. Patzer (1993) 72–93; Patzer (1994) 50–81; Konstan (2010) 75–90.
5. Cf. Dorion (2010).
6. Cf. Wolfsdorf (2004a) 15–41.
7. Cf. Gera (2007) 33–50.
8. Vlastos (1991) esp. 45–106.
9. Cf. Dorion (2010), esp. 14–16, and n.38 with references to Bandini and Dorion (2000).
10. Cf. Chroust (1952) – although I believe its conclusions are too extreme; Deman (1942); Gigon (1959). For a recent, more charitable treatment of Aristotle's testimony, cf. Smith (forthcoming).
11. While Aristotle surely read many *Sokratikoi logoi* other than Plato's, in his surviving writings he has nothing to say about any particular others. Among other Socratics, he mentions Aristippus twice (*Meta.* 996a32, 1078a33) and Antisthenes several times (*Top.* 104b21, *Meta.* 1024b32, 1043b24, *Pol.* 1284a15, *Rhet.* 1407a9). For a recent discussion of Aristotle's conception of the *Sokratikoi logoi*, cf. Ford (2010) and Ford in Goldhill (2008) 29–44.
12. By "Socrates' philosophy" I mean Socrates' mature philosophy. Plausibly, when he began to engage in philosophy the problems that preoccupied Socrates were those central to Pre-Socratic philosophy. The autobiographical section of Plato's *Phaedo* (96a–102a) is consistent with this point. I see no way of identifying when ethics became a central focus of Socrates' philosophy.
13. This evidence is assembled in *SSR*. Some of this material is translated in Boys-Stone and Rowe (2013). In particular, cf. *SSR* IV A 166, 167. On Antisthenes, most likely the oldest of the Socratics, cf. Brancacci (2015); Prince (2015). On Aeschines, cf. Lampe (2015b).
14. Consider the following problem. In some Platonic dialogues Socrates is the central philosophical protagonist; but the central content of those dialogues is not ethical,

for example, *Cratylus* and *Theaetetus*. If the centrality of ethical content is a necessary condition of membership in the genre of Socratic literature, then appeal to this literature to justify (1a) is circular. Assuming a familiar view of Plato's literary chronology, one way around this problem is to restrict Plato's Socratic writings to Plato's early dialogues. The idea, familiar enough, would then be that later in his career, Plato's thought developed in directions beyond the scope of Socrates' philosophy.

15. *Meta.* 987b1–2 (I cite the continuation below); cf. 1078b17; Xen. *Mem.* 1.1.2, 1.4.1, 4.7.2–8.

16. *Ap.* 19AD; *Phd.* 96A-102A.

17. *SSR* IV A 166, 167, 169. Cf. Xen. *Mem.* 1.1.11–16, 4.6.2–8. Cf. PBerol inv. 21213 r (*CPF* I.1***, 1999, 771–3). Antisthenes' *On Nature* needn't be an exception. Arguably, its content concerned distinctions between natural and conventional views pertaining to ethical and political topics. Cf. *SSR*, vol. 4, nota 25.

18. Cf. Hansen (1991) 86–124.

19. Cf. Brickhouse and Smith (1994) 137–75; Ober (2010) 138–78; Pangle (1994) 127–50; McNamara (2009). The names of political figures in the titles of other Socratic writings include: Aeschines' *Militiades, Aspasia, Alcibiades* (*SSR* VI A 22); Aristippus' *Artabazus, Advice to Dionysios* (*SSR* IV A 144); Euclides' *Alcibiades* (*SSR* II A 10); Antisthenes' *Cyrus, Apasia, Alcibiades*, and *Archelaus* (*SSR* V A 41). On Antisthenes' political philosophy, cf. Prince (2015).

20. 642a29–31.

21. Burkert (1985) 179–81.

22. Cf. Parker (1996) esp. 152–217; Mikalson (1983). (In fact, from the Pre-Socratics to Late Antiquity, there is scarcely a philosopher who does not engage the topic of divinity in some form.)

23. *Mem.* 1.4.

24. For Aeschines, cf. Mallet (2013) 225–32. For Euclides, cf. Brancacci (2005b) 143–54. For Antisthenes, cf. *SSR* V A 179–182 and Brancacci (1985/6). For Xenophon and Plato, cf. Destrée and Smith (2005) and McPherran (2010) 111–37.

25. *Meta.* 1078b18–29. Cf. "[And Socrates] ... was inquiring, among these [ethical matters], into the universal and was the first to focus his mind on definitions" (987b1–4).

26. This will require consideration of what Aristotle means by "*epagôgê.*"

27. Aristotle uses the word in the *Metaphysics* passage in question. The earliest surviving occurrences of the word are in Plato. However, the titles *Peri tou dialegesthai* and *peri dialektou* are listed among Antisthenes' writings (*SSR* V A 41). Cf. Xen. *Mem.* 4.5.12. On Aristotle's own conception of dialectic, cf. Evans (1977); Beriger (1989).

28. To be clear, Plato and Aristotle understand dialectic differently from one another, and Plato's own conception of dialectic develops through his corpus. So from Socrates to Plato to Aristotle, there is a development of the idea and of the theory of dialectic. The word "*dialektikê*" itself derives from the verb "*dialegesthai*" meaning "to engage in discussion." "*Dialektikê*" is short for "*dialektikê technê*" (the art of discussion) and thus already marks a significant development. Cf. the phrase "*technê logôn*" (art of words or speech) at Xen. *Mem.* 1.2.31–34; *Dissoi Logoi* 8.3–9; Plato *Phdr.* 266C3ff.

29. Support for this claim derives from the importance of epistemological and argumentational topics in the works of various Socratics. I return to this point below.

30. On Aristippus, cf. Lampe (2015a) 57–63; Dorandi (2015). On Antisthenes, cf. Brancacci (1990); Prince (2015). For Euclides, cf. *SSR* II A 3, 34. For a recent discussion of Socratic dialect in Xenophon, cf. Patzer in Gray (2010) 228–56; Natali in Judson and Karasmanis (2006) 3–19. For a review of recent interpretations of Socratic method in Plato's Socratic dialogues, with particular focus on the *elenchus*, cf. Wolfsdorf in Bussanich and Smith (2013) 35–65.

31. In saying this I do not at all mean to deny that Socrates was interested in kinds and characters of individuals.

32. Cf. Patzer (2012). Cf. Plato *Ap.* 29B8–9.

33. Cf. Plato *Ap.* 38A1–6.

34. The word "*aretê*" is a nominalization of the superlative adjective "*aristos*" (best). Just as there are many kinds of goodness, there are many kinds of excellence. Common translations of "*aretê*" as "virtue" mislead insofar as they identify *aretê* with ethical excellence specifically.

35. 90 DK, 1.1–17. Cf. Plato *Prot.* 333D8–334D6; Xen. *Mem.* 3.8.1–4. Note that one of Antisthenes' works has the title *On Good* (*SSR* V A 41).

36. Cf. Plato *Prot.* 325A2.

37. Cf. A. Brancacci's claim that Antisthenes conceived of his ethical program as *epistêmê tôn prakteôn* ((2005b) 9). Cf. the phrases "*paideia anthrôpôn*" and "*epimeleia heautou*" in Aeschines' *Miltiades* (*SSR* IV A 79) and *Alcibiades* (*SSR* VI A 50).

38. 1.1.16; cf. Bandini and Dorion (2000) n.44.

39. Rossetti (2010) 59–70.

40. Cf. Tsouna (2002) 464–89; Lampe (2015a) 92–100.

41. For eudaimonism in Plato's Socratic dialogues, cf. Bobonich (2010b) 293–332. Cf. O'Connor (2010) 48–74.

42. Fr. 35.47 Dittmar. Cf. Them. *De Virt.* 34.10–35.9.

43. Cf. *SSR* V A 134.11; Prince (2015).

44. Cf. De Heer (1969) esp. 59–67.

45. Wolfsdorf (2008). On Antisthenes in relation to Prodicus' *Choice of Heracles*, cf. Prince (2015).
46. *Mem.* 2.1.26, 29, 33.
47. 826–28.
48. Cf. Claus (1981); Huffman (2009) 21–43.
49. *Nub.* 94, 414–15.
50. Claus (1981) 157; cf. Moore in de Luise and Stavru (2013) 41–55.
51. For Aeschines, cf. *SSR* VI A 16; fr. 8.24 Dittmar. For Antisthenes, cf. the titles *On Justice, On Courage, On Law or Republic* (*SSR* V A 41); cf. *SRR* V A 77, 92, 103, 132, 134; and Prince (forthcoming)a. For Aristippus, cf. Lampe (2015a) 57–63, and note the work entitled *Aretê* among Aristippus' writings (*SSR* IV A 144).
52. *SSR* V A 134; cf. Prince (2015).
53. *SSR* II A 30, 32.
54. Namely, *Protagoras, Charmides, Laches,* and *Republic I*. (Aristotle repeatedly attributes (4b) to Socrates: *EN* 1116b4, 1144b14; *EE* 1216b3, 1229a12, 1230a4; cf. *MM* 1182a15, 1183b9, 1190b21, 1198a10. However, in these cases Aristotle appears to be thinking of Plato's Socrates.)
55. Cic. *TD* 4.80 (= fr. 7 Rossetti); cf. Boys-Stone (2004) 1–23.
56. 3.9.5–7.
57. Dorion (2012) 455–75; cf. Morrison (2010) 227–39.
58. For Antisthenes, cf. "Those who intend to become good must exercise their body with physical exercises and their soul with *logoi.*" (*PKöln* 66 II 2, *CPF* I 1*, 1989, 237) Cf. *SSR* V A 163.
59. For Plato, cf. Balansard (2001); Roochnik (2007). For Xenophon, cf. Parry in *SEP*.
60. *SSR* VI A 80, 48; cf. Kahn in Vander Waerdt (1994) 87–106, at 90–91.
61. *Meta.* 996a32-b1 (= *SSR* IV a 170).
62. Cf. Plato *Charm.* 165C4–166A2, 171D1–172A8, 173C7–174B10.
63. Cf. Wolfsdorf (2004b) and (2004c). It is worth noting here that Antisthenes composed an epistemological work on the distinction between belief and knowledge in four books (*SSR* V A 41.40).
64. *SE* 183b7.
65. *SSR* VI A 53.
66. Cf. Brancacci (2015); Prince (2015).
67. Cf. De Heer (1969) *passim*.
68. Cf. Lampe (2015a) 31–35.
69. For Socratic *elenchus* in Plato's Socratic dialogues, cf. the reference in n.26.
70. For *elenchus* in Xenophon's *Memorabilia*, cf. Bandini and Dorion (2000) CXVIII-CLXXXII. Cf. also Morrison in Gray (2010) 195–227.
71. Cf. Kahn (1994).
72. Cf. Plato *Ap.* 23C2–5.

73. In Wolfsdorf (2003), I argue that in Plato's Socratic dialogues this is actually Socrates' prevailing attitude.

74. Cf. the topic of *homonoia heautôi* in Antisthenes in Brancacci (2011); Prince (2015).

75. Cf. *Mem*. 1.2.41–46, 50; 3.9.4–10; 3.14.2; 4.2.13–22, 25–29; 4.4.11–25; 4.5.1–11; cf. Patzer (2010) 234–45.

76. *SSR* V A 147–59 and vol. 4, nota 34, 327–9; cf. the competing interpretations of Brancacci (1990) and Prince (2015). And cf. Gili (2013) 321–28.

77. McCaskey (2007) 345–74; cf. Cajolle-Zaslawsky (1990) 365–87.

78. The example is adapted from McCaskey (2007) 364–5, he in turn appropriating it from Vlastos' (1991, 267–8) discussion of Plato *Ion* 540b-d. At *Rhet*. 1393b4–8 Aristotle cites a related argument and claims that it represents the sort of comparisons (*parabolai*) Socrates used.

79. Cf. McPherran (2007).

80. *SSR* VI A 70.

81. Pertinent to these facts is the topic of *polytropia* (versatility and adaptability), arguably central to Socratic dialectic, which I have not had space to consider here. Cf. Lévystone (2005).

II Plato

3 Virtue and Happiness in Plato

Daniel Devereux

I VIRTUE AND HAPPINESS IN THE SOCRATIC DIALOGUES

Socrates on the Virtues

In the *Apology*, Socrates defends his way of life, explaining to the jury that he spends his days discussing the virtues and related topics. He believes that knowledge of the nature of the virtues is of paramount importance in understanding how we ought to live our lives. In the short "Socratic" dialogues, Plato depicts Socrates examining and refuting definitions of particular virtues offered by his interlocutors. His examinations are guided by certain key assumptions. For example, he assumes that virtues are inherently fine or admirable qualities; if a proposed definition implies that a virtue is in some situations *not* fine or admirable, this is taken as a sufficient reason to reject the account. Again, Socrates on a number of occasions objects to the common tendency to define a virtue in terms of certain patterns of behavior (e.g. "courage is standing firm in battle"); he wants his interlocutor to see that a virtue is an internal source of behavior, not the behavior itself. In this respect, he views the virtues as similar to arts or crafts. It would sound a bit odd to say, e.g. that "carpentry is making furniture"; carpentry is the knowledge of how to make furniture – it is an "internal" capacity which enables one to make furniture.

Socrates sees a further similarity between virtues on the one hand, and arts and crafts on the other. In the *Apology*, he reports that among the various people he interviewed, only the craftsmen were justified in claiming to possess knowledge or expertise. An expert weaver, for example, knows how to produce fine textiles, and she can explain the techniques she uses: she can teach others how to do what she does. Socrates implies that someone who claims to possess a virtue should have a similar ability to explain. In other words, virtues require the possession of knowledge in the same way that arts and crafts do. In the *Laches*, this knowledge requirement is related to the assumption that a virtue is

I am grateful to Doug Reed for extensive discussion of virtue and happiness in the *Republic* and *Phaedo*.

inherently fine or admirable. Socrates points out that courage cannot be simply equated with endurance, for in some cases it would be unwise to hold out or endure, and such endurance would be the opposite of admirable. He suggests that a more promising account of courage would be: "endurance combined with wisdom or knowledge." Similar reasoning could be used to show that each of the virtues must involve a kind of wisdom or knowledge.

Scholars sometimes speak of Socrates' "craft analogy," meaning by this that Socrates views the virtues as analogous to crafts. Some of the sophists held that the virtue which they claimed to teach *is* an art or craft (*technê*). And there are passages in the Socratic dialogues which treat virtues as crafts (not just analogous to crafts). In the central argument of the *Protagoras*, Socrates contends that there is an "art of measurement" which enables its possessor to accurately weigh the goods and evils in any course of action, and to choose the best available option. He then argues that a courageous person, possessing such an art, will always choose the appropriate act in a situation calling for courage. Because of its generality (encompassing all "goods and evils"), the art of measurement would guarantee that one would choose the appropriate action in situations calling for temperance, justice, piety, etc.; in other words, possession of this art would guarantee virtuous action in general.

In view of these considerations, it seems that Socrates might agree with the sophists in holding that virtue *is* an art or craft. On the other hand, the sophists accepted the common view that arts are teachable, and thus if virtue is an art it must be teachable. (As self-proclaimed teachers of virtue, they of course had a self-serving motive to claim that virtue is an art.) Socrates, however, argues in several places that virtue is not teachable. We might take this to imply that he had doubts about the claim that virtue is an art, *or* that he had misgivings about the common view that an art, as such, must be teachable.[1] Another problem for the view that virtues are arts comes to light in the *Hippias Minor*. Arts seem to be capacities for opposites; e.g. an expert in medicine is more able to cure than a non-expert, but also more able to cause sickness. Experts can misuse their knowledge of an art to bring about bad results. If a virtue is an art, then it could be misused to bring about a bad result, e.g. a just person might misuse her justice to bring about a bad result; but surely this can't be right.

All in all, the Socratic dialogues reveal a certain ambivalence towards the view that virtue is an art or craft; on the other hand,

Socrates seems committed to the view that the virtues require a certain kind of knowledge or wisdom. Another issue on which Socrates seems ambivalent is the relationship holding among the individual virtues. If we focus on his claim in the *Protagoras* that there is an art of measurement which guarantees that one will choose the best action in any given situation, it would seem that all the virtues could be reduced to this one form of knowledge. For if a virtue like courage is the inner source of courageous action, and if the art of measurement is the source of courageous action, then it seems that courage – as well as the other virtues – can be equated with the art of measurement. This result seems to accord with the particular arguments in the *Protagoras* for the unity of the virtues: e.g. the conclusion of the argument for the unity of temperance and wisdom is that "they are one [thing]" (333B); and Socrates later concludes that "according to this argument courage would be wisdom" (350°C).

The arguments in the *Protagoras* seem to support a "strict unity" view of the relationship holding among the virtues, i.e. the virtues are identical to each other and consist in knowledge of the art of measurement. On the other hand, in the *Laches*, another Socratic dialogue, Socrates pretty clearly commits himself to the view that each of the virtues is a distinct part of a whole (198A, 190CD); in other words, there are distinct accounts for each of the virtues, and they are not identical to each other. Socrates' view in the *Laches* is still intellectualist in that "knowledge of good and evil" is viewed as both necessary and sufficient for each of the virtues.[2] As we shall see, in the *Republic* this strong intellectualist view is no longer maintained, and the unity of the virtues also comes into question.

Virtue and Happiness

In several passages in the Socratic dialogues, Socrates makes the strong claim that anyone who possesses the virtues is guaranteed a happy life.[3] However, it is unclear how he understands the relationship between virtue and happiness: does he regard virtue as an instrumental means to happiness, or is there a closer relationship – virtue being identical to, or a part of, happiness? Socrates investigates the nature of happiness in the *Euthydemus*, and it will be helpful to give a brief summary of his discussion.

Socrates begins with the common belief that to be happy is to possess an abundance of goods such as wealth, health, power, and status, and the virtues of justice, temperance, courage, and wisdom (278E9–279C). He then points out that possession of these goods is not sufficient: even if we have all of these goods we will not be happy unless we benefit from them, and this means that we must *use* them (280BD). Moreover, we must use them rightly, that is, wisely, for if goods are used *un*wisely they will result in more harm than good. Happiness and "doing well" will therefore consist in the wise use of such goods as wealth, health, power. Wisdom turns out to be the key to happiness (280D–281B). Indeed, Socrates goes on to argue that, strictly speaking, wisdom is the only real good. For if a real good is something we are *always* better off having, wisdom seems to be the only thing that qualifies; someone who lacks wisdom would not be better off with wealth or power, or any of the other things on the list of "goods," for if these things are used unwisely (as they can be), they turn out to be harmful rather than beneficial. Happiness, then, will consist in the wise use of assets; one must apparently have some assets to use wisely,[4] but the most important factor is wisdom.

The view that happiness consists in a certain kind of *activity* (the wise *use* of assets) is standard in the Socratic dialogues: happiness is equated with *doing* well or *living* well in a number of passages (see e.g. *Charmides* 172A, 173D, *Crito* 48B, *Gorgias* 507BC, *Republic* 1, 353D–354A). Given the distinction between possession and use (*hexis* and *chrêsis*), happiness falls on the side of use. Wisdom (or virtue; cf. 282D–283B), on the other hand, falls on the side of possession: wisdom/virtue is something which may be used, but it is not the use itself. This distinction allows for some clarification of the relationship between virtue/wisdom and happiness. Since they are different types of entities (belonging to different "categories," as Aristotle would say), they cannot be identical. And if a part of an activity must be an activity, then virtue/wisdom cannot be a part of happiness. Can we say that happiness is a product of virtue/wisdom? The relationship between the two seems different from the relationship between a craft and its product. Once the carpenter's table is finished, its *continued* existence does not depend on the carpenter's skill; the existence of the activity which is happiness, on the other hand, cannot exist independently of the wisdom/virtue of the good person. In this respect, the relationship between wisdom/virtue and happiness is closer to the relationship between the carpenter's skill and his skillful activity; just as the skill of the carpenter is manifested in the activity of building a cabinet, so wisdom/virtue is manifested in the wise use of assets, i.e. the activity which is constitutive of happiness.

2 THE "MIDDLE" DIALOGUES

The Phaedo

With the introduction of the theory of Forms in the *Phaedo*, there are striking changes in the conceptions of happiness and virtue. Along with the innovation of "separate," transcendent Forms, the *Phaedo* introduces the notion of the "true philosopher" as one who turns away from the world of everyday experience and seeks knowledge of Forms through the use of pure intellect and reasoning. The highest – perhaps the only true – form of happiness is the philosopher's intellectual "communion" with the Forms. Such communion is hindered in this life by the soul's connection to the body and its needs and desires; only at death does the philosopher's soul, having been purified by virtuous living and intellectual inquiry, attain full-fledged wisdom and happiness (66E). While the philosopher's soul is united to the body, he or she is able to partake of wisdom and happiness, but not in their fullest, most complete, forms.[5] The other virtues aside from wisdom, e.g. temperance, courage, justice, have a subordinate, instrumental role in the life of the philosopher. Wisdom is the philosopher's aim and goal, and the other virtues are cultivated and exercised for its sake: the virtues have the function of "purifying" the soul by separating it from the body, thus enabling it to achieve wisdom or knowledge of Forms.

Thus we see two noteworthy differences between the *Phaedo*'s conception of the philosopher's virtue and happiness and the conception of virtue and happiness characteristic of the Socratic dialogues. According to the Socratic conception, happiness does not consist in purely intellectual, contemplative activity: it consists in a life of virtuous activity, i.e. activity in accordance with justice, temperance, courage, and wisdom. Virtuous activity, insofar as it is constitutive of happiness, is desired for its own sake. In the *Phaedo*, by contrast, the virtuous activity of the philosopher is not constitutive of her happiness, and is apparently not desired for its own sake; it is desired for the sake of wisdom or philosophical enlightenment. We might say that one of the Socratic virtues, wisdom, is singled out as the end, and the other virtues are regarded as means to that end; but wisdom now has a contemplative, other-worldly dimension which it did not seem to have in the Socratic dialogues. It also seems that philosophers who are not yet wise may possess true forms of courage, temperance, and justice – a significant modification of the "unity of virtue" doctrine of the Socratic dialogues.

The *Phaedo* also differs from the Socratic dialogues in distinguishing between "true" or genuine virtue attainable by philosophers, and an inferior, "counterfeit" form of virtue attainable by non-philosophers. Non-philosophers who possess the counterfeit forms of justice, temperance and courage perform the same sorts of actions as philosophers with genuine virtues; it is for this reason, presumably, that counterfeit virtues may be mistaken for the real thing. The chief factor which distinguishes counterfeit from true virtue is motive: the philosopher performs virtuous actions for the sake of wisdom while the non-philosopher performs the same sorts of actions for the sake of bodily pleasure and the avoidance of pain (68B–69C). The non-philosopher forgoes immediate pleasures in order to avoid greater pains in the future, and chooses courageous actions to avoid the painful consequences of cowardly action, e.g. public disgrace (68D, 82C). The seemingly virtuous non-philosopher calculates that temperate, just and courageous actions will lead to an overall balance of bodily pleasure over pain, and chooses such actions for this reason.[6] The philosopher chooses similar actions, but *only* because they promote the end of wisdom; the fact that such actions lead to a greater balance of pleasure over pain plays no role in her motivation.

Non-philosophers who are virtuous view their (counterfeit) virtues as instrumentally valuable for their consequences: the pleasures obtained and the pains avoided. Nothing is said about these virtues being valued for their own sake. But philosophers apparently also value their true virtues for the sake of consequences: wisdom and intellectual enlightenment. Again, nothing is said about the philosopher's justice, temperance, and courage being valued for their own sake. As we shall see, in the *Republic* these virtues *are* regarded as valuable for their own sake as well as for their consequences, and they must be valued as such by their possessors.

Corresponding to the inferior form of virtue available to non-philosophers, there is an inferior form of happiness. Consider someone who consistently acts in accordance with justice, temperance, and courage, but not with a view to the attainment of wisdom. Such people have what Socrates calls "demotic and political" virtue (82AB), and they are "the happiest" of those who are not philosophers and "go to the best place" after death. Towards the end of the dialogue, in the myth describing the fate of souls in the afterlife, Socrates indicates that all of those who have lived virtuous lives "ascend to a pure abode"; some of these are philosophers and some are not; only the philosophers escape the cycle of reincarnation (114BC). Thus some non-philosophers, who have an inferior form of virtue, nevertheless live meritorious lives and are rewarded in the afterlife; their lives have a certain kind of genuine value. This should indicate that when Socrates says that those who have this inferior form of virtue are "the happiest" of the non-philosophers, he means that they do enjoy a form of happiness, though not the highest form.[7] Since all non-philosophers are tied to the body and its needs and desires, the happiness of those with "demotic" virtue will at least involve the measured enjoyment of bodily pleasures as an important element.

The Republic

The main argument of the *Republic* is aimed at showing three things: (i) what justice and injustice are, (ii) that justice is valuable for its own sake as well as for its consequences, and (iii) that the life of a just person is better and happier than the life of an unjust person – even one who is never caught and punished. Socrates' argument depends on an analogy between a city and an individual: since we attribute justice to cities as well as to individuals, he suggests it might be easier to determine what justice is in the larger thing, and then look to see if it is the same quality in an individual. He proceeds to "construct in speech" an ideal city, a city which *as a whole* is as happy as can be; for it is plausible to suppose that in such a city one would be most likely to find justice (420BC). Another supposition guiding Socrates' search is that a city which is *happy as a whole* is one which is well governed (420BC, 421A). This in turn suggests that those governing the city must be best suited for the task, and must receive the best possible training for their task. The ideal city will therefore be constituted of different groups or classes, and it will have an extensive program of education for the future rulers.

Socrates distinguishes three classes within the ideal city. The largest class consists of those who provide for the material needs of the city: farmers, artisans, and tradesmen – the "Producers." The other two classes are made up of the Rulers and their "Auxiliaries"–a permanent military force. Both Rulers and Auxiliaries receive a common education in "music and gymnastic," which is designed to promote the virtues of courage, temperance, and justice (386A–392C). The ruling class receives further education in mathematics and philosophy, an education which aims at the virtue of wisdom, the chief prerequisite for being a good ruler.

The three classes making up the ideal city have different natural aptitudes and interests. When Socrates says that the ideal city is happy *as a whole*, he means that each class will have a share of happiness; the constitution and laws are aimed at the common good of all, not at maximizing the happiness of one class (e.g. the class of Rulers) at the expense of others. Socrates notes that it would not be surprising if the Rulers turned out to be the happiest in the city; but this should not be the aim of the constitution and laws (420B, 421BC). Given their natural differences, what happiness consists in for each class will presumably be different, e.g. the happiness of the Philosopher-Rulers will not be the same as that of the productive class. As Socrates puts it: "as the entire city develops on a proper foundation, each class will partake of happiness in a way suitable to its nature" (421C).

Later in the *Republic*, Socrates twice refers back to this passage in Book 4 (419–21). In Book 5, when describing the benefits and honors enjoyed by the Auxiliaries (see 468A8), he concludes that they have a finer and better life than the victors at Olympia who were honored and supported by their home cities; and he points out that their share of happiness is clearly greater than that of the Producers mentioned at the beginning of Book 4 (466AB; cf. 419A). Socrates refers back to the passage at 419–21 again in Book 7. After describing the ascent of the philosophers to knowledge of the Form of the Good, and stipulating that they must return to the cave to perform their duties as Rulers, Socrates is met with the objection that it would be unjust "to compel them to live a worse life when they are capable of living a better" (519D). Socrates reminds his interlocutors that their original aim was not to maximize the happiness of one class at the expense of others, but to maximize the happiness of the city as a whole. The philosophers are understandably reluctant to give up, even temporarily, their supremely happy life of contemplation outside the cave (519BC; cf. 516C, 518AB, 521A): their lives would be happier if they could – without injustice to their fellow citizens – avoid returning to the cave. However, since they spend most of their adult life in philosophy (520D, 540B), their lives are happy; and, as Socrates predicted (420B), they are clearly the happiest class within the city.

The life of Philosopher-Rulers in the ideal city of the *Republic* is similar to that of the philosophers in the *Phaedo*, but there are two differences. First, Socrates seems more optimistic about the possibility of achieving full knowledge of Forms in the *Republic*. In the *Phaedo*, philosophers welcome death because only then will they attain complete wisdom; the philosophers in the ideal city of the *Republic* do not have to wait for death to achieve this goal. In this respect, the philosophers of the *Republic* seem to have happier lives. Second, because of the special circumstances of the ideal city, the Philosopher-Rulers must spend a significant portion of their lives in non-contemplative, practical activity, whereas there is no such constraint on philosophers in the *Phaedo*. In this respect, the philosophers of the *Phaedo* seem to have the advantage. These differences, however, may not reflect changes in Plato's views but rather the fact that one dialogue considers what the philosopher's life would be like in an ideal city while the other assumes non-ideal circumstances.

We noticed earlier that Socrates distinguishes two grades or levels of happiness in the *Phaedo*: the happiness of the philosopher, which consists in a life of intellectual inquiry and contemplation, and the happiness of those who practice the "demotic" virtues. The *Phaedo*, like the *Republic*, distinguishes between two types of non-philosophers, "money-lovers" and "honor-lovers," corresponding to Producers and Auxiliaries respectively. However, the *Phaedo* does not distinguish between two corresponding (inferior) types of happiness and virtue in the way that the *Republic* apparently does. The happiness of those who practice the demotic virtues in the *Phaedo* seems similar to the happiness of the Producers in the *Republic*.[8] But as we shall see in a moment, the happiness and virtue of the *Republic*'s Auxiliaries has no parallel in the *Phaedo*.

Although the *Republic* does not discuss what sort of virtue might be possessed by the Producers, it seems likely that they have the "demotic" virtues of the *Phaedo*, i.e. the inferior forms of temperance and justice (see the reference to "demotic" virtue at 500D). Insofar as "doing one's own" is identified as a form of justice – an outward manifestation (433AE) – it seems that the Producers have a sort of justice. Also, given the fact that they willingly obey the commands of their rulers and conform to the laws of the city (431E9–432B), it seems that they must have a kind of temperance – the sort of temperance possessed by some non-philosophers in the *Phaedo*. It is clear, on the other hand, that Producers ("money-lovers") do not have the counterfeit form of courage possessed by some honor-lovers in the *Phaedo*, for it requires courageous action and a fear of dishonor which is stronger than a fear of death (cf. 68BD with 82BC). And like the demotically virtuous of the *Phaedo*, the Producers are probably motivated by bodily pleasure and pain.

As we noted earlier, the future Auxiliaries and Rulers of the *Republic* receive a comprehensive education in music and "gymnastic" (physical training). This education is aimed primarily at instilling the virtues of courage, temperance, and justice (386A–392C) – but not wisdom: the higher education leading to knowledge of the Form of the Good is reserved for the future Rulers (522A). If, as we argued, the Producers in the ideal city have the demotic virtues of temperance and justice, we might wonder if the temperance and justice of the Auxiliaries are the same as those of the Producers. Since the Auxiliaries' virtues result from their extensive education in music and gymnastic, we might expect them to be different from the virtues of the Producers. One key difference lies in the Auxiliaries' attitude towards the virtues and their motivation to perform virtuous actions. Their musical education instills in them an appreciation of, and attraction to, that which is beautiful and noble (*kalon*). In concluding his discussion of music, Socrates points out that those who have received this education will have a finely attuned judgment of (objective) moral properties and their fineness – both in individuals' characters and actions, and in portrayals in literary works (401C–402D). Towards the end of Book 4, Socrates argues that just and virtuous *actions* are valuable and choiceworthy insofar as they produce and maintain the corresponding *states* within the soul (444C–445B); and the value he attributes to these states consists in their being "a kind of health and *beauty* and fine condition of the soul" (444DE) – i.e. the value referred to here is tied to the kind of things they are, not to their potential beneficial consequences.[9] The Auxiliaries, as appreciators of beauty and fineness, are attracted to justice and the other virtues *for their own sake*, and not simply for their consequences.

The pseudo-virtuous money-lovers and honor-lovers of the *Phaedo* are motivated by bodily pleasure and pain, and because of this Socrates calls their virtue "slavish" (69B). We suggested earlier that the Producers in the *Republic* have the "demotic" forms of temperance and justice; if so, their virtue would be "slavish" for the same reason. On the other hand, Socrates does not mention bodily pleasure and pain as motivations of Auxiliaries' virtuous actions, nor does he refer to *their* virtues as slavish.[10] According to the passages we have considered, the motivation of those educated in music (the Auxiliaries and Rulers) is tied to the intrinsic beauty and fineness of the virtues. The Auxiliaries may also be motivated by certain beneficial consequences of the virtues: if a happy life is such a consequence, then this would of course be one of their reasons for valuing the virtues.[11] But Socrates nowhere mentions bodily pleasure and pain as motivating factors.

The following objection might be raised at this point. In his argument for the superior pleasure of the just life in *Republic* 9, Socrates distinguishes three types of people in terms of their dominant motivations – money-lovers, honor-lovers, and lovers of learning – and three corresponding types of life. He then argues that the life of the lovers of learning is the most pleasant of the three lives (581C). We noticed that the same three types of people are mentioned in the *Phaedo*. Corresponding to these three types in the *Republic* are the Producers, the Auxiliaries, and the Rulers. The objection is that the Auxiliaries, as honor-lovers, are motivated by "external" incentives: by the honors they receive for acting justly and courageously, not by the intrinsic fineness and nobility of such action. However, this objection overlooks the fact that the Auxiliaries, in contrast with the honor-lovers considered in *Republic* 9, are given an education in music, which, as we have seen, produces in them a love of what is fine and noble for its own sake – their natural character as honor-lovers is refined and ennobled by their education in music.

Although the virtues of the Auxiliaries are genuine and not counterfeit, they are still inferior to the virtues of the Philosopher-Rulers since the former are based on right opinion whereas the latter are based on knowledge of Forms. Even though the Auxiliaries, through their musical education, are generally able to make correct judgments about virtuous (and vicious) characters and actions (401C–402D), the judgments of the Philosopher-Rulers are more accurate because of their knowledge of the Forms of the virtues (520C). In the *Phaedo*, the virtues of non-philosophers are regarded as sham or counterfeit, "having nothing sound or true in them," while the virtues of philosophers are called "true virtue" (69AC). In the *Republic*, instead of the distinction between "true" and "counterfeit" virtue, we find a distinction between "complete" and "incomplete" (or "perfect" and "imperfect" virtue).[12] The justice, temperance, and courage of the Auxiliaries are genuine virtues – they are not "counterfeit" or "slavish" – but they fall short of perfect virtue to the extent that they are not based on knowledge of the Forms of the virtues and the Form of the Good.[13]

The *Republic* thus presents a more complex account of types of virtue and corresponding forms of happiness than we find in the *Phaedo*. In the *Phaedo*, there is one type of virtue and happiness available to non-philosophers, and another type available to philosophers. In the *Republic*, in addition to the two types in the *Phaedo*, there is a third type of virtue and happiness available to non-philosophers: the virtue and happiness of the Auxiliaries. A further point of difference is that in the *Republic* Socrates holds that in order to be just, one must "love" justice for its own sake, and not simply for its consequences (cf. 358A with 361C). We have seen that the "musical" education elaborated in Books 3 and 4 is designed to instill the virtues of courage, temperance, and justice, but also an appreciation of the intrinsic beauty and fineness of these virtues. Thus both Auxiliaries and Philosopher-Rulers are motivated, at least in part, by a love of justice and the other virtues for their own sake. In the *Phaedo*, on the other hand, Socrates says that the philosopher pursues the other virtues for the sake of wisdom; he does not say that a just person must love justice for its own sake, nor does he anywhere indicate that the "true" virtues apart from wisdom are valuable for their own sake. Here again, however, it is possible that this difference relates to the different aims of the two dialogues: in the *Phaedo*, Socrates emphasizes the instrumental value of the other virtues in relation to wisdom as part of his explanation of why the philosopher welcomes death: the "purified" soul of the philosopher, once separated from the body, will at last be able to attain wisdom. We do not need to suppose that the sole value of "true" justice and temperance in the *Phaedo* is their contribution to wisdom.

Before leaving the *Republic*, we should note a couple of gaps or unclarities in Socrates' arguments for the value of justice. In Book 9, he concludes his discussion of tyranny and the tyrant's life with the claim that the life of the perfectly just person is happiest, while the life of the most unjust, the tyrant, is the most miserable. Socrates then offers two arguments for the claim that the perfectly just person's life is the most pleasant. How these two arguments are related to the first is left unclear: Are they meant to be additional arguments for the superior happiness of the just person's life, or are they meant to show that the just person's life is better not only in being happier but also in being pleasanter? This unclarity raises the general question: How does Socrates understand the relationship between happiness and pleasure? Does he think that pleasure is an essential component in a happy life, or does he think that one could have a happy life even if it was not a pleasant life? If he believes that pleasure is an essential component of happiness, does he believe that all pleasures, or only some, can contribute to happiness? As we shall see, these questions are taken up and answered in the *Philebus* and *Laws*, both of which were written after the *Republic*.

A further "gap" in Socrates' argument in the *Republic* relates to one of the demands made by Glaucon in Book 2. He asks Socrates to show that a just person who is regarded as unjust and suffers extreme persecution still has a better and happier life than any unjust person (361B–362A). Socrates' argument does not take up this challenge. He considers instead the lives of just people who are recognized as just, and who live in very favorable circumstances. Furthermore, in his arguments for the superior pleasure of the just person's life, the pleasures he appeals to are derived from philosophical activity, not from the exercise of justice itself. What he needs to show, one might object, is that the just person *qua* just (not *qua* philosopher) has a pleasant life. As we shall see, these matters of "unfinished business" in the *Republic* are taken up in the *Laws*. The *Philebus* and *Laws* undoubtedly contain modifications of certain views argued for in the *Republic*, but these later dialogues may also be seen as filling in gaps and clarifying points in the earlier dialogue.

3   THE "LATE" DIALOGUES

The Philebus

The *Philebus* is a notoriously difficult dialogue, and our discussion will be limited to parts which are relevant to the nature of happiness and its relationship to the virtues. The dialogue consists of an inquiry into the constituents making up the ideally best life for a human being. Surprisingly little is said about the virtues apart from wisdom; and since Socrates' concern is with the best possible life, there is no discussion of sub-optimal forms of virtue and happiness, as there is in the *Phaedo* and *Republic*. The focus is mainly on the relative contributions of pleasure and wisdom/knowledge to the best life. The best life, which involves a mixture of pleasure and wisdom, is referred to at different points as "the good" and as "happiness" (11D, 20CD, 22D).

Socrates begins by arguing that a life of pleasure which includes no wisdom or knowledge would not be a happy life; likewise, a life which includes knowledge, wisdom, or intellect but no pleasure would not be happy. So the best life must include both pleasure and knowledge or wisdom. The thesis which Socrates then sets out to defend is that wisdom, knowledge, and related intellectual powers (e.g. true opinion and memory) are more akin to "the good" than pleasure, and therefore intellect's contribution to happiness is greater than pleasure's. In order to show this, it is necessary to distinguish the various types of pleasure and knowledge, and then determine which types of pleasure and which types of knowledge should be included in the mixture making up the best life. The typologies of pleasure and knowledge take up most of the dialogue, and the discussion of different kinds of pleasure is especially rich and detailed (31B–55C). I will simply summarize some of the results.

One major division of pleasures is between those which are in one way or another mixed with pain, and those which are "pure," i.e. do not involve any mixture of pain. Some mixed pleasures, called the "greatest," are characterized by their vehemence and intensity, and are prized by the enemies of moderation and self-restraint – characters like Callicles in the *Gorgias* (45C, 47B, 63D, 65C). Other mixed pleasures are moderate and allied with a temperate way of life (45DE). Among pure, unmixed pleasures, some are associated with sense perception, and some with the activity of the soul by itself (51A–52B). Examples of the pure pleasures of perception are the sight of simple, beautiful shapes and colors, or the hearing of simple beautiful sounds. Examples of pure "psychic" pleasures are those associated with knowledge and learning, and those derived from the activities of the virtues (63E, 52AB, 12D). Socrates argues that these pure pleasures are the truest and "most pleasant," even if not the "greatest" or most vehement (52D–53°C).

After distinguishing the different types of pleasures, Socrates draws distinctions among different types of knowledge. The main division is between pure and mixed forms of knowledge, corresponding to the division between pure and mixed pleasures (57AB). "Pure" forms of knowledge are distinguished by two chief factors: their *aim* is knowledge and truth for its own sake, and their *objects* are abstract, eternal, and unchanging. Mixed forms, on the other hand, aim at things distinct from the knowledge itself, and they are concerned with things subject to change; they are mixed in that they involve elements related to pure forms of knowledge, i.e. the use of measurement and calculation (55D–56C). Examples of the mixed forms are music, medicine, house-building, and ship-piloting. As for examples of pure forms of knowledge, Socrates first makes a distinction between pure and impure forms of arithmetic, geometry, measurement, and calculation: the pure are concerned exclusively with abstract, unchanging objects, and aim at knowledge for its own sake, while the impure have a practical aim and are "applied" to things subject to change. The different branches of pure, "philosophical," mathematics belong to the class of pure forms of knowledge, as does the master-science of dialectic (57A9–58D).

Once these distinctions are made, Socrates proceeds to specify the types of pleasure and knowledge which should be included in the best life. But in doing so, he introduces a further question: Which factors or elements are the *cause* of the goodness of the best life? This cause is now designated "the good" (64C).[14] As for the types of knowledge to be included in the mixture, it is agreed that both pure and impure forms should be mixed in. On the other hand, only some pleasures should be included. The first to gain admission are the pure, unmixed pleasures of perception and intellect, and those that accompany the virtues (62E, 63E–64A). It is also agreed that the "moderate" mixed pleasures, which are necessary ingredients in a healthy, measured way of life, should be included (61D–62E). All other mixed pleasures, i.e. those that accompany vice and folly, must be excluded.

At this point, Socrates surprisingly insists that another element, "truth," must be included in the mixed life (64AB). Here, it seems clear, he is taking up the question: What is the cause of the goodness of the best life? Two additional causal elements are specified: beauty and proportion. The latter two are connected to virtue (64E: "For measure and proportion manifest themselves everywhere as beauty and virtue"), while truth is linked to intellect and wisdom (64D–65D). These three elements form a kind of trinity: a triune cause of the goodness and beauty of the best life (65A).

Since there are three causal elements in addition to pleasure and knowledge, it turns out that there are five components of the best life. Socrates lists the five as follows: (1) the mean, measure, and the "fitting"; (2) proportion, beauty, completeness, and sufficiency; (3) intellect, wisdom, truth; (4) the other forms of knowledge and true opinion; (5) pure unmixed pleasures (66AC). The original contenders, pleasure and wisdom, are included, but only wisdom is a cause of the goodness of the best life; pure pleasures are a *part* of such a life, but are not causes of its goodness. And the "greatest" pleasures advocated by Philebus are excluded on the ground that they are incompatible with a happy life.

We noted earlier that the moral virtues, e.g. justice and temperance, are hardly mentioned in the *Philebus*; and it is striking that "virtue" is not listed as a constituent of the best life. However, as we noted above, Socrates indicates a close connection between virtue, on the one hand, and measure, proportion, and beauty on the other. In the light of this connection, it is plausible to suppose that virtue *is* included in the second causal element.

Since the *Philebus* is concerned with the ideally best life, it is understandable that it does not consider whether virtue and wisdom are sufficient for happiness – i.e. whether the wise and virtuous person has a happy life even in extremely unfavorable circumstances. The dialogue, on the other hand, does give a careful and sophisticated treatment of the relationship between pleasure and happiness. In this regard, we may see the *Philebus* as providing clarification of a puzzling feature of the arguments in *Republic* 9: how the two pleasure arguments are related to the preceding argument for the superior happiness of the just life. The *Philebus* indicates that certain kinds of pleasure contribute to happiness, but their contribution is not as important as several other factors. The *Philebus* also claims that there are "pure" pleasures accompanying virtuous activity – a claim that seems absent from the *Republic*. The *Laws*, as we shall see, develops this claim and uses it to argue that a just person *qua* just has a happier and more pleasant life than any unjust person.

The Laws

We will conclude our discussion of virtue and happiness with a few brief remarks about Plato's views in his latest work, the *Laws*. The *Laws* has a practical and political orientation which sets it apart from the *Philebus*. It is not a "theoretical" investigation of the best life, but the development of a plan for a new city-state on the island of Crete – a plan which is expressly said to fall short of the ideal (739CE, 807BC). The main speaker is a visitor from Athens, the "Athenian Stranger." In the course of the Athenian's lengthy discussion, he offers a number of claims and arguments concerning wisdom, virtue, happiness, and pleasure. Perhaps because of the practical orientation, the Athenian's conception of wisdom is more down to earth than Socrates' conception in the *Republic* and *Philebus*. Wisdom is not "pure" knowledge of eternal and immutable beings, but the agreement or harmony between an individual's "right reason" and his feelings of pleasure and pain (689DE, 696C).[15] Agreement between reason and pleasures and pains is also central to the Athenian's understanding of virtue (653AC). The first stage in the acquisition of virtue is the development of a child's affective responses so that he or she is pleased and pained by the right sorts of things: pleased by the truthful, the just, the temperate, and in general by what is fine and noble, and pained by the opposite qualities. In the second stage, the students acquire "right reason," which serves to guide their conduct and give rational grounding to their well-formed affective responses. Taking pleasure in what is fine and noble is thus essential to both virtue and wisdom.

The Athenian's conception of wisdom is clearly broader than the conception we find in the *Republic* and *Philebus*: this wisdom is not the preserve of a select few – not the special virtue of philosophers.[16] Since wisdom is a harmony of reason and passions, it is naturally tied to temperance and justice. Temperance and justice are inextricably linked (696C), and it seems that one could not have wisdom without temperance and justice, and vice versa. Although there is a form of courage which is compatible with intemperance, injustice, and lack of wisdom (696BE, 661DE), this courage is "qualified" and "partly enslaved"; "free" and unqualified courage requires temperance and the other virtues (635CD; cf. Irwin (1995), 343).

The Athenian's view that taking pleasure in what is fine and noble is essential to the virtues implies that a virtuous person takes pleasure in acting virtuously (and would be pained to act otherwise). The Athenian uses the link between pleasure and virtue in arguing for the superior pleasure and happiness of the virtuous person's life. He concedes that the pleasures sought by the unjust, licentious person are distinguished by their intensity and vehemence (the "greatest" pleasures of the *Philebus*); the pleasures of the temperate, just life are "tame" by comparison (734AC). But the pains involved in the licentious life are also more intense than the pains of the temperate, just life. Moreover, the pains of the licentious life exceed the pleasures "in magnitude, number and frequency," while the pleasures of the just and temperate life exceed its pains. Thus the just person's life is pleasanter than the unjust person's, and also superior in nobility and correctness; for all these reasons, the just person's life is happier (734D).

This argument makes it clear, as did the *Philebus*, that certain kinds of pleasures contribute to the happiness of a happy life. And there is at least an attempt to show that the life of a just person *qua just* is happier than the life of an unjust person; in other words, there is an attempt to answer one of Glaucon's challenges which Socrates failed to address in the *Republic*. Of course, we may still have doubts about how effective the argument is in meeting Glaucon's challenge: Does it really show that the just person's life *in the most unfavorable circumstances* is still happier than any unjust person's life? Does it make good on its claim that the pleasures of the just person's life always exceed its pains? Perhaps not. But the *Laws* does bring out, as the *Republic* did not, that the just person's commitment to justice in the face of great misfortune may be a source of inner satisfaction, even joy.

NOTES

1. For arguments against the teachability of virtue, see *Protagoras* 319A–320B, and *Meno* 89D–96C; cf. *Euthydemus* 282C.
2. See Devereux (1992).
3. See e.g. *Gorgias* 507C, 508AB; *Republic* 1, 353E–354A.
4. See 280CD: the craftsman cannot "do well" unless he has tools and materials to work with. The question whether, according to the *Euthydemus*, possession of "assets" is necessary for happiness has been debated recently by scholars; see e.g. Irwin (1995) 52–65; Brickhouse and Smith (1994) 103–23; Jones (2013).
5. At 81A Socrates suggests that a philosopher is only happy after death; but the experience after death can be approximated by "practicing death" in this life.
6. At 82B Socrates calls the virtues of non-philosophers "demotic," and says that they are acquired through habituation "without philosophy and understanding [*nous*]." "Demotic" virtue seems to designate the kind of virtue that most people (the *demos*) can attain; it is similar to Protagoras' conception of "political" virtue: see *Protagoras* 322E–323B.
7. For arguments against the view that non-philosophers can attain a kind of happiness, see Bobonich (2002) 14–42.
8. Against our argument that the Producers in the ideal city enjoy a kind of happiness, it might be objected that the description of their lives in the allegory of the cave portrays them as the opposite of happy (514A–517A). We should note, however, that the allegory is specifically concerned with the cognitive status of the different classes (514A); while the cognitive status of the Producers may be abysmal, Socrates indicates, as we have seen, that they derive a genuine satisfaction and kind of happiness from their way of life in the ideal city.
9. He thus satisfies Glaucon's second demand: to show that justice is valuable for its own sake and not simply for its consequences. See Devereux (2004) for further argument for this claim.
10. At 430BC, the courage of the Auxiliaries is distinguished from a somewhat similar disposition which is called "slavish": this is perhaps a further indication that the courage of the Auxiliaries is different from the counterfeit courage possessed by (some) honor-lovers in the *Phaedo*.
11. For defense of the claim that Socrates regards happiness as a consequence of justice (or virtue), see Devereux (2004).
12. See e.g. 360E, 361D, 543C–544A (cf. 541B), 545A, 548D, etc.
13. Cf. Kamtekar (1998).
14. Earlier at 22D Socrates noted that neither intellect nor pleasure turns out to be the good, but one or the other might be the cause of the good. "The good" is here understood as the well-mixed life of pleasure and wisdom. The same conception of

the good seems to be invoked at the beginning of the mixing process (60B–61A), but at 61B Socrates speaks of the good as something present *in* the well mixed life; and at 64C–65A he clearly shifts to understanding "the good" as the cause of the goodness of the well-mixed life.

15. Cf. *Statesman* 309E for a similar "political" conception of wisdom. For discussion of wisdom in the *Laws*, see Bobonich (2002) 194–200; Irwin (1995) 350–53.

16. Towards the end of the *Laws*, the Athenian sketches a program of "higher" education, and stipulates that these "higher" studies will be undertaken by those who will hold the highest offices in the state (964A–968B). He speaks of certain "elders" in the new state who have completed these studies as "outstandingly wise" (965A); their special wisdom consists in part at least in a philosophical understanding of the virtues, as well as of cosmology and theology; their wisdom is not simply a "harmony of right reason and passions." The *Laws* thus seems to imply a distinction between what might be called "political" and "philosophical" wisdom.

4   Plato's Ethical Psychology

Rachana Kamtekar

I   INTRODUCTION

Plato is the first philosopher in the Western tradition from whom we
have a more-or-less integrated account of the soul, according to which
one and the same entity, the *psuchê*, is the source of the movements of
living things in general and of human action in particular, the bearer of
our moral character, and the subject of our various cognitive and affective experiences and activities. This chapter traces the development of
Plato's psychology through the dialogues, focusing on topics that are
especially relevant to our ethical lives. Because the account to follow
diverges from the mainstream account of the development of Plato's
psychology, I should say a couple of words at the outset to explain why.
In the mainstream account, in the early dialogues Socrates espouses an
intellectualist psychology according to which because we desire our own
good, we always and only (are motivated to) do what we believe best
secures that good (Santas 1966, Penner and Rowe 1994). Recently some
qualifications have been suggested to the mainstream account, viz., we
have non-good-directed or non-rational motivations but our virtue and
vice depend only on our good-directed or rational motivations (Devereux
1995), or we have non-rational motivations but they effect action only
via their influence on our beliefs about what is best (Brickhouse and
Smith 2010). Then (according to the mainstream account and its var-
iants), starting with the *Republic*, in order to account for akratic action
and animal behavior, Plato allows that non-rational motivations exist, or
can produce actions on their own, or are after all relevant to our virtue
and vice.

I reject this account for three reasons. First, the only argument for
the psychological thesis that we always do what we believe is the best of
the things we can do is found in the *Protagoras*, where Socrates argues,
on the (everywhere else rejected) assumption that pleasure is the good,
that it is impossible for the one who knows that one thing is best to
choose another thing because it is more pleasant – which is far from
a general argument against the possibility of akratic action, and hardly
a sufficient argument to establish the psychological thesis. Second, this

psychological thesis is neither necessary nor sufficient for a key ethical claim it is supposed to ground, namely that no one does bad or unjust things willingly. Third, since Plato is well aware of the phenomenon of akratic action when he writes the *Protagoras*, and since he there offers an intellectualist account of it as ignorance empowering appearances, it would have to be dissatisfaction with that account that motivates the admission of non-rational motivations to account for akratic action (or to count as relevant to character assessment). But the mainstream account does not explain why Plato is now dissatisfied with this account and how the admission of non-rational motivations addresses his dissatisfaction.

While I cannot here argue in detail against the mainstream view,[1] I can sketch an alternative account of Plato's ethical psychology – of the problems it addresses and the intellectual motivations for the directions it takes – that I believe makes better philosophical sense of Plato's texts in their intellectual context. Section 2 below considers two early[2] dialogues (*Protagoras*, *Gorgias*) for what I'll call their implicit psychology – Socrates' claims about what must be true of the soul for his interlocutors' teaching programs to succeed. Section 3 explains why "we always do the best of the things we can do" does not provide a psychological grounding for "no one does wrong or is bad willingly" and suggests an alternative. Section 4 explains why Plato divides the soul, and section 5 why the spirited part is a distinct part of the soul. Finally, section 6 draws out the ethical implications of our soul's being immortal and having an afterlife that is a consequence of our present life.

2   IMPLICIT PSYCHOLOGY

In Plato's *Protagoras*, the eponymous sophist claims that he makes his students successful in domestic and public affairs (319A, 328B, cf. 357E). Although Protagoras himself thinks that human nature contains diverse and overlapping motivational sources (e.g. confidence can come from courage, knowledge, passion, or madness, and courage itself comes from nature and good upbringing [351A, cf. 325D, 326C]), which would seem to have the potential to come into conflict, Socrates reasons that if virtue, the success-maker, is teachable, it must be knowledge, and knowledge must be the master in the soul (352CD) – so our psychology must be such that we always do what we believe is best (358C–360D). Now Protagoras' description of the teaching of virtue by providing a receptive soul with models of the virtuous and vicious to internalize, and punishing souls that do not learn in order to straighten them out

(325D–326D) suggests that even though the soul has a natural capacity for justice and respect, the content of justice and respect are provided by the (variable) models of virtue in the environment, literature, and the law, before which the soul is passive. And here, even as he supplies Protagoras with a psychology that, if true, could ground Protagoras' claims to teach virtue, Socrates introduces an anti-Protagorean element. If Protagoras' expertise is to secure success, it must be an expertise for measuring (*metrêtikê technê*) goods and evils, and be authoritative over the power of appearance (*tou phainomenou dunamis*) in us (356D–357A). Socrates models this measuring art on optics, the expertise for determining sizes of visible objects on the basis of measured distance and apparent size. (In the visual case, the contrary-to-measurement appearance persists even after the measurement has been made, but perhaps that is too slender a basis on which to suppose that it persists even in the ethical case.) A measuring expertise holds out the prospect of correcting what appears (e.g. in laws, literary models) rather than taking appearances to be the criterion of reality (as the historical Protagoras seems to have argued; see Fragment 1 D-K; *Theaetetus* 152A, 166C, 167C) – but this is just what Protagoras needs, if he is to be able to teach what he says he does.

In the *Gorgias*, the rhetor boasts that his expertise in persuasive speaking empowers its possessor over others (452DE), even over other experts in the subject at hand; for example, he claims that he is more effective than his doctor brother in getting patients to follow the medical regimen prescribed for them (456AC). This echoes the boast that the historical Gorgias makes about the power of persuasive speech in his *Encomium of Helen*, that it belongs to persuasive speech to be able to make any impression it wishes on the soul of its audience (13). In the *Gorgias*, Socrates describes an area of the soul in which appetites are found (*tês ... psuchês touto en hôi epithumiai eisi tugchanei*), which is easily persuaded, and, in the souls of fools, not easily satisfied (493AB); this seems to concede that Gorgias' expertise does indeed have the power Gorgias claims – but only over one part, the worst part, of the soul. For Socrates contrasts these appetites with the wishes we have only for good things and for the actions by which we obtain these good things (466D–468E). Correlated with the two kinds of desire are, on the one hand, types of expertise that aim at the good of their object with knowledge of how to produce it, as e.g. legislation and medicine aim at and know how to produce the good of the soul and body, and, on the other hand, examples of pseudo-expertise that care nothing about the good but aim at pleasure instead (e.g. as sophistry aims to please the soul and cookery to please the body) on the basis of experience (464A9–465E). Since the historical Gorgias himself says that it is people's lack of memory, understanding, and foresight that makes them so impressionable (*Encomium* 11), presumably possession of these powers would enable one to resist persuasion. Further, to be an expert in persuasive speech, Gorgias would have to have some grip on the truth about both his subject matter and the causes of persuasion to audiences (a point developed by Socrates in the *Phaedrus* [260A–262A, 270E–271B]).[3]

In these dialogues Socrates is not opposing his own intellectualist psychology to Protagoras' and Gorgias' irrationalist psychology as much as he is drawing attention to their simultaneous reliance on and denial of the active powers of reason. If the Socrates of the early dialogues is an "intellectualist" it is not because he denies (the existence or direct motivational efficacy or relevance to virtue of) non-rational motivations, but because of the attention he pays to the truth-tracking elements in our practical pursuits.

3 WHY NO ONE DOES WRONG OR BAD THINGS WILLINGLY

I claimed above that "we always and only (are motivated to) do what we believe is the best of the things we can do" is neither necessary nor sufficient for "no one does wrong willingly" (that the former is Socrates' basis for the latter is argued in Santas 1964). To see that it is not sufficient, consider this example: I pursue an MBA because it seems to me to promise an interesting and lucrative career of my choosing, but in fact, the MBA only narrows my horizons. To be sure, I pursued the MBA in ignorance of its consequences, but how does this ignorance make my pursuit of it *unwilling*? I wasn't impeded from doing what I believed best, after all. One explanation is that I wanted the interesting and lucrative career for the sake of which I pursued the apparent good of an MBA, and the MBA undermined my successful pursuit of that desire. But that explanation would make my pursuit of the MBA unwilling, whether or not we always and only (are motivated to) do what we believe is the best of the things we can do.

To see that "we always and only (are motivated to) do what we believe is the best of the things we can do" is not necessary for the unwillingness of doing wrong or being bad, consider that the *Republic*, *Timaeus*, and *Laws* allow for the possibility of an agent acting contrary to his belief about what it is best to do (e.g. out of appetite) but still maintain that we are in bad conditions (e.g. believing falsehoods, or having intemperate characters) unwillingly and that we do wrong unwillingly.

In fact, many of Socrates' and Plato's contemporaries regard at least some cases of wrongdoing as unwilling, due to the sort of misfortune that overstrains human nature (e.g. Simonides says a man can't help but be bad when misfortune knocks him down [*PMG* 542, discussed at *Protagoras* 339A-347A, cf. *PMG* 541]; Hippias excuses Achilles' not keeping his word on the grounds that he was compelled by the plight of the Greek army [*Hippias Minor* 370DE]; Gorgias' *Encomium of Helen* raises the question of the limits of this kind of excusing argument). A sophistic position about justice described by Glaucon suggests a general account of unwillingness. According to this position, all who practice justice do so unwillingly (*akontes*), as something necessary rather than good, and from a lack of power to do injustice with impunity. This is because every nature desires to outdo others and get more and more, but is led by law and force to honor fairness (*Republic* 358C-359C). In other words, our just behavior is unwilling because justice and law compel us to act contrary to our natural impulse to go for what is good for us. The idea that what is unwilling is what is contrary to our natural impulses has intuitive appeal and can account for the judgments of bad and shameful actions as compelled by circumstances that overstrain human nature. Plato seems to experiment with different versions of this idea across the dialogues: in the *Gorgias*, Socrates takes it up to argue that unjust actions are unwilling because they are undertaken to secure the agent's (naturally desired) happiness but in fact undermine that end; in such cases the agent does not do what he wants to do but rather does what he does not want to do and so acts unwillingly (467D-479E, cf. 509DE); in the *Republic* he argues that we unwillingly acquire false beliefs about the most important things (382A, 413BD); in the *Timaeus*, Timaeus argues that no one is bad willingly, and our begetters and nurturers are responsible for the folly or madness that is our vice (86B-87B). In all these cases the warrant for calling something unwilling is its contrariety to the good that is our natural end. And there are dialogues where contrariety to the good that we desire is invoked to deny that we desire anything that is in fact bad – no matter if we believe it to be good or go after it in our pursuits (*Meno* 77D-78A, *Symposium* 205E-206A).

But the sophistic idea is obviously too simple, and Plato shows one reason why in the *Laws*: the Athenian argues that although all injustice is unwilling, and a voluntary act cannot come from an involuntary state of soul, the law must nevertheless distinguish between voluntary and involuntary actions because it needs to correct the voluntary wrongdoer. His solution is to count the same act as voluntary qua injurious and involuntary qua unjust (860D–862D; for a discussion of this see Schofield 2012a), but this is an unstable answer. More generally, the problem is that even if "unwilling" captures something about our relationship to actions and conditions which are contrary to the good at which we naturally aim, it also fails to capture something important, namely, the sense in which some of those actions are still *our* actions and some of those conditions are due to our actions. In the next section I argue that soul-division is what allows Plato to capture both these insights.

4   SOUL-DIVISION

Probably the psychological contribution for which Plato is best known is the tripartite soul. I break this contribution down into two parts: in this section, I argue that rather than to allow for the existence/motivational efficacy/relevance to virtue of non-rational or non-good-directed motivations, Plato divides the soul in order to establish the attributability to the agent of non-good-obtaining motivations. In section 4, I provide a rationale for why the soul consists of, in addition to a part whose desires come from the body and a part whose desires come from its own reasoning, a third part which doesn't reason but desires whatever the reasoning part does.

In *Republic* IV, after affirming that cities come to have characteristics such as spiritedness and love of learning from the spirited and learning-loving individuals in them, Plato's Socrates raises a "hard" (*chalepon*) question (which is still hard today, even though we have at our disposal empirical techniques to measure the involvement of the different functionally specialized areas of the brain in a given activity):

> do we do each of these things with the same [part] or do we do them with three different [parts]: Do we learn with one [part], anger with another, and with some third desire the pleasures of food, drink, sex, and however many pleasures are akin to them? Or, whenever we go after something, do we do so with the whole of our soul in each case? These things will be hard to distinguish in a way that is worthy of our argument.   *(436AB)*

To establish that the soul is not a "one" but a "many," Socrates argues on the basis of a principle of opposites, according to which:

> Principle of Opposites: The same thing (*t'auton*) won't do or suffer opposites, at the same time (*hama*) in the same respect (*kata t'auton*), in relation to the same thing (*pros t'auton*); if these things happen [viz., the doing or suffering of opposites in the same respect in relation to the same thing at the same time], we'll know it/there is not [one and] the same thing (*t'auton*) but many (*pleiô*). (436B, cf. 436E–437A)

The first argument runs as follows:

(1) We can have opposite psychological attitudes towards one and the same thing (437BC).

(2) For example, a person who is thirsty wants to drink. Insofar as he is thirsty, the thirsty person wants only to drink: if he wants hot or cold drink, or good or bad drink, we have to assign to him another desire, for hot or cold or good or bad, that "qualifies" his thirst (437DE).

(3) But sometimes a thirsty person refrains from drinking, for example, if the drink is bad for him.

(4) In the thirsty person who refrains from drinking a bad drink, the opposite attitudes, "have a drink!" and "refrain from drinking!" can't belong to one and the same thing [by the Principle of Opposites], so there must be something else in the soul of the thirsty person apart from the desire to drink – another part that "bids them not to drink" (439 C).

(5) The desire to drink arises from a bodily condition (439 C).

(6) The desire to refrain from drinking arises from calculation (439 C).

(7) Therefore, in the soul there is a part that desires on the basis of bodily conditions (let us call it "the appetitive part") and another part that desires on the basis of reasoning (call it "the reasoning part") (439D).

(Plato does not use the word "part" [*meros*] in this argument, but uses instead expressions like "that which thirsts," "that which reasons," or "the reasoning"; it is English that requires a noun in addition, and "part" seems to be an appropriately bland candidate.)

In the course of making this argument Socrates pauses to address an objection:

> let no one clamor at us being uninvestigative, [saying] that (*hôs*) no one desires (*epithumei*) drink but rather good drink, nor food but good food,

for (*gar*) everyone desires good things, so that (*oun*) if thirst is a desire, it will be a desire for good drink or whatever, and similarly with the others. (438A)

Although some readers have taken Plato here to be asserting that some desires may be good-independent, i.e. for their natural object rather than for the good (Kahn 1987, 85; Irwin 1995, 206), and others have taken him to be asserting that since all desires are for things qua good, desires must be distinguished by their natural objects (Carone 2001, 118–19), in my view he is doing neither, but instead blocking the following inference:

(a) It is our nature to pursue our good.
(b) This drink is contrary to that good.
(c) Therefore, we cannot desire this drink.

This is the inference discussed in section 2 above, from our desire for our real good to our non-desire for things that impede it (and hence, if our actions do obtain those impeding things, to our having acted unwillingly). The conclusion that we are "many," i.e., that we have multiple independent sources of motivation, shows why (c) doesn't follow. This isn't the whole story, however, because (as I'll argue in a moment) Plato seems to take on the burden of explaining why we are able to sometimes desire and go after things that are in fact contrary to our good.

But first, to fill out this sketch of the rationale for a divided soul, let us turn to a different argument for dividing the soul in *Republic* X, one relying not on conflicting desires but conflicting beliefs.

(1) The same magnitude appears through sight not to be equal close up and far off; the same sticks look bent in the water and straight outside it ... (602 C).
(2) Measuring, counting, and weighing help us so that the apparent large or small (etc.) doesn't rule in us but the calculated and measured or weighed does (602D).
(3) Calculating, measuring, and weighing are the work of reasoning (602D).
(4) Often after the reasoning part has calculated, the opposites (viz. to the apparently large or small)[4] appear to it (*toutôi*, the reasoning part) (602E2–4).
(5) The same thing can't believe opposites about the same thing at the same time (602E).

(6) The thing that believes contrary to measurement can't be the same as the thing that believes in accordance with measurement (these are pro and con attitudes towards one and the same thing) (603A).

(7) That which believes in accordance with measurement is the best thing in us.

(8) That which opposes it is one of the inferior things in us (603A).

The *Republic* arguments share a structural feature that clearly answer one question left undecided from the *Protagoras* and *Gorgias*: in each case, there are multiple simultaneously coexisting psychic origins of the soul's activities which make it possible for it to come into conflict with itself. One would hope that virtue at least reduces conflict, but the character of some of these origins – bodily conditions such as thirst and visual appearances of size – make it seem likely that conflicts can never be eliminated entirely (as at least seemed possible in the *Protagoras*). However, the point is not conflict, but multiplicity. This point is confirmed in the *Phaedrus*, where even the gods (who are not akratic or in any way conflicted) have divided souls, the parts of which are a charioteer and two obedient horses; but the forward motion of the horses is distinct from the steering action of the charioteer, and presumably both are needed for a god to be efficacious. If we think back to the initial division of the soul in *Republic* IV from this perspective, we are reminded that the initial characterization of the soul-parts was functional. It was just the difficult task of determining the independence of these functions of the soul that required an argument from psychic conflict.

The *Timaeus* gives a very different kind of argument for the separateness of soul-parts: in the course of explaining how the natural world is a product of intelligence and necessity, Timaeus explains that, for the world to be as perfect or as like the Living Thing Itself as possible, it must contain all the kinds of living things (39E–40A). But this requires the embodiment of rational souls, the result of which is that the soul comes to experience sense-perception, which arises from forceful affections; desire mixed with pleasure and pain; and fear, anger, and however many other affections are consequent upon sense-perception and desire (42AB). Later, Timaeus explains that when the lesser gods take up the task of embodying our souls, they build a mortal soul, containing terrible but necessary (*anangkaia*, 69C9) affections – pleasure, pains, boldness, fear, anger, and expectation. These are the simply necessary consequences of embodiment. But when Timaeus speaks of the gods constructing the mortal type of soul "as necessary" (69D5, *anangkaiôs*) – housing (*proôikodomoun*) the soul in the body; mixing (*sunkerasamenoi*) and putting together (*sunethesan*) the mortal soul; combining (*sunkerasamenoi*) desire and sense-perception with pleasure, pain, daring, fear, etc. – he seems to be describing designing activities, and he gives as their aim to stain the rational soul only as much as necessary (*mê pasa ên anangkê*, 69D7). This suggests that the construction of the mortal soul (as opposed to the existence of non-rational motivations) is hypothetically necessary, necessary given the good end of reason being in charge (70B) but also being able to contemplate (contra Johansen 2008, 147–49, who restricts hypothetical necessity to the construction of the body). The gods are said to do a number of things in order to secure the conditions for reason to be able to be in control and to contemplate. They locate the mortal soul in the trunk, separated from the head by a neck. They divide the trunk into two sections, housing the superior spirited part nearer the head so it can listen to reason and, along with reason, restrain the appetitive part by force (*biai*, 70A5) whenever it won't willingly obey (*peithesthai hekon etheloi*, 70A7) reason's orders and reasoning. They put the heart near the spirited part so that it can, through the blood vessels, ready all the parts of the body for action if the spirited part "boils over" upon learning that the appetites are suffering or doing something wrong. They put the lungs near the heart to cool it down when overheated by anger or fear – so that it labors less and so is better able to help spirit serve reason (perhaps because the heating up/ pounding is not useful to/is in excess of the sensitization). They put the appetitive part of the soul – which has appetites for things that the body needs and is necessary if there are going to be mortal animals – in the lower part of the trunk, tying it down here to "live at its trough" in order to keep it from disturbing the reasoning part. Since the appetitive part is unable to understand reason's orders, or, even if it understands them, to take care (*melein*, 71A5), they construct the liver as a surface to be stamped by the power of thought (*hê dunamis tôn dianoêmatôn*) from intelligence (*ek nou*) which reflects back visible images.

The suggestion here is that it is better for us that the soul be partitioned, because locating non-rational parts at some distance from the rational part and enabling them to perform at least some of their functions on their own allows the rational part to do its contemplative work in peace – while still remaining in charge. Were reasoning to be required for every act of appetition or anger, it would be deprived of the leisure to observe and understand the movements of the heavenly bodies and so to bring the soul into order. But although this arrangement is optimal, sometimes creatures will go after something that is not good for them: an unhealthy drink that quenches their thirst, for example. We can assume that it was not possible to design a self-contained system for restoring the body's balance of wet and dry that would at the same time be sensitive to health and other considerations.

The teleological argument for soul-division is not entirely independent of the empirical arguments of *Republic* IV and X – in addition to showing that it is best for soul-parts to function independently it has to be established that they do (otherwise there might be some constraint one overlooked). But the empirical arguments also aren't entirely independent: we can't tell, for example, whether the lesson of cases of psychic conflict is that souls are permanently divided, no matter what their moral character or whether this is a feature only of non-virtuous souls (Whiting 2012). That it is better that they should be so offers a complementary argument.

5   WHY IS THERE A SEPARATE SPIRITED PART?

Plato uses the conflict arguments of the *Republic* and the teleological arguments of the *Timaeus* to argue not simply for a divided soul but specifically for a tripartite soul. While it is fairly easy to distinguish two kinds by the source of their desires or beliefs – calculation for the reasoning part, bodily conditions for the appetitive – Plato is not explicit about the source of so-called spirited (*thumoeides*) motivations. Is it our social nature (Cooper 1984, Burnyeat 2006)? The need to restrain the unlimited appetites inevitably generated by embodiment (Brennan 2012)? Or reason's conception of what is good or fine (Irwin 1995, Singpurwalla 2013)?

The question about the source of spirited motivations may seem narrow, but in the *Phaedrus* Socrates recommends investigating simple natures by asking, "what do they do and by what are they affected?" (270CD). So as we examine Plato's arguments for a third, spirited part of the soul, let us see what we can glean about the source or cause of spirited motivations.

To show the independence of the spirited kind in the soul in the *Republic*, Socrates applies the principle of opposites to a story about Leontius, who desired to look at some corpses but also felt angry about doing so, and after some struggle, opened his eyes wide and simultaneously cursed them for looking (439E–440A). Socrates says that Leontius' case establishes that anger sometimes makes war against appetite, and that often when appetite forces someone contrary to rational calculation, that person reproaches himself and gets angry with that in him that's doing the forcing (440AB). Finally, he says that the spirited part *never* cooperates with the appetites to do what reason has decided must not be done (440BD). The reason for this is that the spirited part is by nature an auxiliary of the reasoning part unless it has been corrupted by a bad upbringing (441A).

One may be forgiven for thinking that the last statement qualifies the previous one, so that in a corrupt person, the spirited part opposes the reasoning. But we have two reasons to think otherwise: first, the corrupted characters described in *Republic* VIII and IX are people whose reasoning parts are in the service of their appetitive or spirited parts; second, an auxiliary (*epikouros*) is an auxiliary to someone in charge, and so in corrupted people, people ruled by parts other than their reasoning part, it is not possible for the spirited part to be an *auxiliary* to the reasoning part, even if it always goes along with the reasoning part's conception of the good. So Socrates' initial claim stands: the spirited part always sides with the reasoning part, whether the reasoning part is in charge or subservient to another part. And we don't see a case of the spirited part persisting in an attitude after reason has decided against that attitude.

This account of the spirited part of the soul explains distinctive features of its treatment in the *Republic*. First, the case of opposition between the reasoning and spirited parts involves reason opposing spirit, not vice versa: Odysseus restrains his angry impulse to kill his maidservants because he has calculated it is better to wait to kill them (441B). Second, the gymnastic and musical education aims to make the spirited part optimally tense (ready to act) and relaxed (flexible) (410C–11E) rather than obedient. Third, courage is the virtue due to the spirited part's preservation of the wise person's *knowledge* about what to fear and what not to fear (442C), not just the preservation of whatever beliefs about the fearful one happens to hold. Finally, the puzzling bipartition of the *Republic* X arguments falls into place: the division there is between a part that opposes or is indifferent to the reasoning part and the part that reasons and/or forms its beliefs in accordance with reasoning. On this way of dividing up the soul, the spirited part – being the part that is ready to obey the law wherever it leads (604B) – would fall on the side of the reasoning part.

Plato's characterization of the tripartite soul in the *Phaedrus* confirms this account. Here, the spirited part is represented as an obedient horse, as noble, a lover of honor with modesty and respect, a friend of true opinion, driven by commands and reason alone (253E–54A).

By contrast, the appetitive part is represented by a lusty and deaf horse which has to be beaten into obedience.

The teleological perspective of the *Timaeus* explains why it is good to have a reason-receptive part such as spirit: given the goal of freeing reason up so that it can contemplate in peace, it helps to have a spirited part close enough to reason to hear it and respond with force when necessary (70AB).

This way of dividing up the soul, into a reasoning part, a part that does not reason itself but always follows reason, and a part that responds to bodily conditions, may not seem to divide psychological nature at the joints (as does, say, the division of the soul into rational, social, appetitive parts). But there are reasons to think that the division is insightful even if not intuitive. First, it is a remarkable fact that some of our passions are responsive to reasons, even in opposition to pains and pleasures. To take an easy example: step on my toe and I will not only feel pain but also anger at you; indicate that it was an accident, and my anger will abate even though my pain does not. Second, if our good is an intellectual condition, then the psychological functions that get us to that condition (calculation, contemplation, truth-seeking) should not be lumped together with their effects (what the spirited part is ready to do) when those effects don't get us to that good intellectual condition.

6   IMMORTALITY AND THE AFTERLIFE

Although Socrates says in the *Apology* that he does not know whether death will be the end of him or his soul will live on and be transferred to another place (40C–41C), in a number of other dialogues (e.g. *Phaedo, Republic, Timaeus, Phaedrus, Laws* X) he or another main speaker argues that the soul is immortal and will live an afterlife that is a consequence of its present life.

Plato's accounts of the soul's afterlife have been under-appreciated by scholars, who for the most part assume that they are simply stories of reward or punishment for virtue or vice (e.g. Annas 1982). In fact (as I argue in greater detail in Kamtekar 2016), there are two kinds of afterlife consequences: reward or punishment by a god for the sake of our improvement (or, if we are incurable, for the improvement of others), and the choice (*Republic* 617E, *Phaedrus* 249B) or desires (*Phaedo* 81DE) or opinions (*Phaedrus* 248B) that lead us to be reincarnated into an animal body that is well suited to our character or preferred type of ethical life: The gluttonous are reincarnated as donkeys, the criminal as wolves or hawks or kites, the behaviorally virtuous as bees, ants, or other social insects (*Phaedo* 81E9–82B); those who study the heavenly bodies using only their eyes but not their minds are reborn as birds; those whose interests are only bodily are reborn as land animals with elongated heads since they do not engage in rational thought and many legs to draw them closer to the earth; and so on (*Timaeus* 91D–92C).

Plato is careful to separate the responsibility for these two kinds of consequences. The fact that the god's treatment of our souls aims to improve them gives us confidence in the justice and goodness of the cosmos as a whole, and the fact that our reincarnation is an expression of our character gives us a way to see our souls, now, for what we are becoming by our way of life. The lesson of the afterlife accounts, as Socrates makes explicit in the *Republic*'s myth of Er, is that because we ourselves choose our lives, the most important thing of all is to learn how to make the best choice, caring only for justice and injustice, and determining how external things like wealth, beauty, and public office, in combination with each other and a given state of soul, contribute to living justly or unjustly (618C–19B). It is noteworthy that this lesson stands whether or not we believe the afterlife accounts themselves.

NOTES

1. But I do in my *Plato's Moral Psychology* (forthcoming, Oxford University Press).
2. I follow a relatively uncontroversial grouping of the dialogues into three groups, designated early, middle, and late, by their stylometric proximity to or distance from Plato's uncontroversially late work, the *Laws*. Kahn (2003) summarizes the findings of the best stylometric research.
3. Our reasoning power's connection to the truth receives a fuller articulation in the *Republic*, according to which,

   Education isn't what some people declare it to be, namely, putting knowledge into souls that lack it, like putting sight into blind eyes ... [Rather,] the instrument with which each learns is like an eye that cannot be turned around from darkness to light without turning the whole body ... Education takes for granted that sight is there but that it isn't turned the right way or looking where it ought to look, and it tries to redirect it appropriately ... [T]he other so-called virtues of the soul are akin to those of the body, for they really aren't there beforehand but are added later by habit and practice. However, the virtue of reason seems to belong above all to something more divine, which never loses its power. (*518BE*)

4. Following Lorenz (2006), 68 which follows Adam (1902), Appendix II to Book X.

5   Plato on Love and Friendship

Frisbee Sheffield

One of the great strengths of Plato's philosophy is that reflections on the nature of goodness are grounded in an appreciation of what is distinctive about human life. Though the dialogues sometimes lead us into unfamiliar territory in their articulation of an ideal of godlikeness, discussions of the human good are grounded in reflection upon our passions, desires, and loves, and the philosophical life is characterized as the culmination, and satisfaction, of those desires. Nowhere is this clearer than Plato's continued preoccupation with *eros* – passionate desire, or love. Plato wrote one dialogue (the *Symposium*) devoted to *eros*, another in which it is a central theme (the *Phaedrus*), and characterized the philosopher in terms of *eros* in several works. The dialogues are also concerned with *philia*, another kind of love, often used to characterize bonds of affection between family and friends. The *Lysis* is devoted to discussion of *philia*, it is a theme of the *Phaedrus*, and its continued significance can be seen in the role of *philia* in binding together the city in Plato's political works (*Republic, Politicus, Laws*).

Exploring these features highlights significant strands of Plato's ethical thought. Attending to *eros* highlights a strand in Plato's thinking about virtue in which, like other ancient ethical theorists, he does not focus solely on the articulation of rules for good action, but on the characterization of the agent and the development of virtue (Annas: 1993). Since what we love shapes the course and nature of our lives, the concern with the good life inevitably involves clarifying what it is good for us to care about and to love (*eros*). Though the discussions of *eros* are primarily agent centered, Plato's reflections on *philia* (friendship) provide the groundwork for an account of other-directed care and concern, which mitigates the depersonalized and abstract picture sometimes drawn of the contemplative philosopher.

I would like to thank James Lesher and the editor of this volume for comments on this chapter.

I   EROS, BEAUTY, AND PHILOSOPHY

One reason why *eros* mattered for Plato is that it mattered to the historical Socrates. There was a long-standing association between Socrates
and *eros*, which can be seen in the tradition of *Sokratikoi logoi*.[1] In these
works it is a defining characteristic of Socrates that he is disposed to form
erotic attachments with the young, and this is part of the distinctive way
in which he educates. In the *Alcibiades* of Aeschines, for example,
Socrates claims to have improved Alcibiades "because of his love
(*eros*)."[2] Given that at least one of Plato's goals in the dialogues is to
celebrate the character of Socrates, however distinctive his own characterization turned out to be, it is not surprising that *eros* is a theme of his
works and that Plato draws, in particular, on the relationship between
Socrates and Alcibiades, which had a significant, and largely negative,
impact on how Socrates was perceived by his peers.

Relationships between an older male lover (*erastês*) and a younger
male beloved (*eromenos*) had an important educational dimension
among members of the Athenian elite during the fifth and fourth
centuries in particular. Feelings of desire and, at best, concern for the
welfare of one's partner were employed for the socially productive end of
furthering the education of the young at institutions such as the Greek
symposium (drinking party). This goes some way towards explaining
Plato's interest in *eros*. Those dialogues in which *eros* is prominent,
Alcibiades I, Lysis, Symposium, and *Phaedrus*, show an overriding interest in education.[3] In these works Plato builds on existing erotic practices
and revises them in accordance with his novel goals for education. Since
part of what it is to be a proper lover-cum-educator is to know about the
sorts of things that might benefit another, and to offer guidance about
how to attain them, pederasty and philosophy walk hand in hand for
Plato.

Plato did not just inherit pederastic practices as a context for
education, however; he integrated them into the heart of his philosophical project by arguing that *eros* for another person can be a propaedeutic
to philosophical activity. This can be seen in the "ascent-passage" of the
Symposium, where "loving boys correctly" (211B5–6) leads to reflection
on the grounds and nature of the attraction, and prompts investigation
into the qualities that make beautiful bodies and souls into attractive
instances of their kind. The love of beautiful boys is a "step" towards
appreciation of beauty (*to kalon*) in a more abstract and general sense
(211B5–D1). In the *Phaedrus*, love for a beautiful youth can provide

a stepping-stone to contemplation of a purely intelligible beauty (257A3–B6). In the *Republic*, the end of education is *eros* for beauty (403C). The relationship between *eros* and the *kalon* was axiomatic for the Greeks, and a repeated feature of Plato's accounts of *eros* (*Symposium* 204BC, *Republic* 402D, *Timaeus* 87D7–8, *Phdr*. 250E1). Though the *kalon* is a difficult term to translate, both "the beautiful" and "the fine" capture much of its sense, where the range is broader than the superficial, or cosmetic, appearance of a thing.[4] To call something *kalon* was to appraise the object and to suggest that it had a relationship with the good (*to agathon*). Since the *kalon* had a connection with the appearance of a thing, and the good of a thing, one way to capture this connection is to say, with Kosman (2010: 355), that "it is the mode of the good that shows forth; it is the splendor of the appearance of the good." Attendance to beauty, then, can be indicative of our conception of value in a broader sense, and visual perceptions of beauty can highlight where we see value to reside in the world. As such, visual beauty can provide initial conceptions of the fine and the noble, and reflection on our notions of beauty can contribute to the formation of an embryonic moral sense.[5] The axiomatic role of the *kalon* in Plato's scheme of values, shown by the central role given to the *kalon* in the attainment of virtue and happiness in the *Symposium*, the *Phaedrus*, and the educational program of the *Republic* goes some way towards explaining the use to which Plato puts *eros*. One reason why *eros* matters is because the *kalon* matters to Plato, and our natural responsiveness to beauty – *eros* – can be used as a way into the good life. The love of embodied beauty is one way, a very basic way for Plato, in which our orientation to value is made manifest. As such, it can be a productive starting point for ethical reflection.

The relationship between *eros* and beauty also explains the sense in which philosophy itself is an *erotikos* activity (*Phd*. 66E2–4, 67E5–68A2, 68A7–B6, *Symp*. 204BC, *Rep*. 485B, 490B, 501D2, *Phdr*. 252C–253B). In the *Symposium* it is argued that since *eros* is concerned with beauty, and wisdom is one of the most beautiful things, Eros personified is necessarily a philosopher (204B2–3). Wisdom is desired because it is *one of the most beautiful things*. The superlative suggests a correlation between the degree of perceived beauty in the object and the *eros* experienced for that object. With this in place, the argument is that *eros* is concerned with the beautiful (204B3); the more beautiful the object, the more *eros* desires that object; wisdom is one of the most beautiful things (B2–3); therefore *eros* is, in the highest degree, a lover of wisdom. The notion that wisdom is an object of erotic attraction is no mere metaphor. Though philosophical *eros* is not sexual in any sense, it is truly *erotikos*, properly speaking, and not in some transferred sense; for all *eros* is concerned with beauty (e.g. *Symp.* 206E). The fundamental experience of *eros* is a desire for beauty, the most basic expression of which is sexual *eros* for embodied beauty, where this is simply one of its common forms. Given the range of phenomena designated *kalon* – bodies, souls, cultural practices, and so on – there will be a range of objects to which *eros* can respond. Many passages in Plato associate the highest objects of wisdom – the intelligible forms – with beauty; this is not just a property had by the form of beauty (*Cratylus* 439C; *Euthydemus* 301A; *Laws* 655C; *Phaedo* 65D, 75D, 100B; *Phaedrus* 254B; *Parmenides* 130B; *Philebus* 15A; *Republic* 476B, 493E, 507B).[6] Given that *eros* is, for Plato, the name of that specific desire for beauty, and the notion that wisdom and its objects are among the most beautiful things, we can appreciate why one can have *eros* for forms. Philosophical *eros* would not emerge were one to consider wisdom simply, though perhaps rightly, to be the highest good; it emerges specifically and properly when one comes to desire wisdom *as one of the most beautiful things*. Socrates' "erotic art" (*Symp.* 177D8–9, *Phdr.* 277C, 257B) consists in his ability to make people see the beauty of wisdom – not just its goodness, or its centrality in the good life, but its *beauty*; for all *eros* is concerned with beauty (*Symp.* 206E). Socrates' art would not be *erotikos* were it to argue us into the pursuit of philosophy by reasoned argument about its goodness; it is *erotikos* insofar as it encourages a desire for wisdom by making apparent, in a variety of ways, its beauty. This is dramatized in the *Symposium*, which opens with Socratic devotees and closes with the bemused Alcibiades, who is torn between rage at his rejection and longing for the man who is a supreme object of beauty and love for him. Socrates' wisdom and virtue (222A) is so manifest in his character and life that this "splendor" makes him an object of erotic attention for Apollodorus (172C) and Alcibiades (217C5), despite the fact that, according to pederastic conventions, the older lover was supposed to pursue the younger beloved. The aesthetic dimension of the dialogues also exemplifies this art, as Plato portrays wisdom, in the character of Socrates, alluring images of the philosophical life, and the engaging dramatic form of the works, as one of the most beautiful things. Plato uses our natural responsiveness to the *kalon* to cultivate a specific – *erotikos* – response to wisdom.

2 THE SYMPOSIUM: EROS, EUDAIMONIA, AND THE DIVINE

The nature, aim, and activity of our response to the *kalon* are explored in the *Symposium*.[7] *Eros* is a desire of a specific kind. When someone experiences *eros*, there is something the agent wants, and this is something she lacks (either now or in the future: 200E3–5). But *eros* is more than a lack and longing; it involves cognitive components, specifically an evaluative judgment of its object as beautiful (201A8–10, B6–7, C4–5, 202D1–3, 203D4), which makes it a desire amenable to philosophical reflection and analysis. Socrates' difficulty in clarifying *why* we pursue beauty highlights the need for such reflection. Significantly, given what our ultimate aim will turn out to be, he begins by substituting "good" for "beauty" to clarify the aim of *eros* before he is able to explain our persistent attraction to beauty. It seems obvious to Socrates that when we desire some *good* thing we do so because we think it will make us happy. This is the ultimate aim of desire because:

> One no longer needs to go on to ask "And what reason does the person who wishes to be happy have for wishing it?" Your answer seems complete. *(Symp. 205A2–3; trans. Rowe)*

This desire for happiness (*eudaimonia*) is unpacked as a desire to possess good things for oneself forever (206a11–12), a desire later exposed as an aspiration towards the immortal and happy state of the gods, who possess good and beautiful things forever (202C6–7, 207A1–3). This is not an alternative to the idea that we desire *eudaimonia*; the immortal gods are the ideals towards which we aspire in our attempt to secure *eudaimonia*.[8] The notion that happiness is the aim of *eros* relates the *Symposium* to a range of dialogues in which Socrates argues that all desire relates to a single ultimate end, which is the desire for happiness (see *Gorgias* 466A, 468E, *Meno* 77AB, *Euthydemus* 278E–282C, 288C–292E).[9] And the fact that our attempts to secure happiness are explored here as an aspiration towards the immortal and happy state of the gods relates this account of *eros* to those works in which the ethical ideal is to become like god, something which also plays a role in the account of *eros* in the *Phaedrus*. Indeed, *eros*' function is to serve as an intermediary between men and the gods towards whom we aspire (*Symp.* 202E–203A). Why *eros* is an appropriate engine of action for our aspiration to the divine is an interesting question.

The intensity and enthusiasm that characterize *eros* are related to this aim. The objects it pursues as valuable are desired as goods that matter to us in a particular kind of way, as things whose pursuit, above all else, are thought to make life worth living and bring us closer to the state of the gods. When something is pursued with *eros*, it is valued as supremely beautiful and perfect, and, as such, standing in some relationship to the divine (204C4, *teleon kai makariston*). A beautiful person, or thing, may be misleading in this role, but the point is that when that person or thing is pursued with *eros*, it is thought to be capable of satisfying the desire for a divine state of *eudaimonia*. Seeing *eros* as a specific mode of valuation of this kind allows us to appreciate why *eros* is an appropriate response to have towards wisdom and its objects. There are many arguments in the dialogues designed to show that wisdom is that without which, above all else, life is not worth living (*Apol.* 29DE; *Euthyd.* 281E2–282A6, *Symp.* 211D1–2). If so, it will not be enough to have just *any* desire for wisdom; any other desiring relation to the object will expose one as having the wrong view about the value of wisdom, namely that it is lower in value than its true ranking, and thereby indicate that one does not value wisdom in the proper way. Attending to the significance of the pursuit of wisdom in terms of *eros* indicates something about the kind of value wisdom is for Plato and the role he wants it to play in our lives.

Since *eros* involves this specific valuation, it also has a specific mode of activity. Someone with *eros* does not just want to gaze at the value of the desired object, or come to possess it in the sense in which one wants to get a piece of property. Nor does one desire to care for the object in such a way that the beloved object is benefitted; it is seen as perfect and blessed (204C4–5). *Eros'* characteristically productive work – reproduction in beauty (206C) – is designed to reproduce the value of the desired object for the agent himself, and in that way to create something which promises to bring his *own* life closer to that of the blessed gods. *Eros* for bodily beauty manifests itself in the attempt to capture that value by the production of physical offspring, thought to provide "memory and happiness for all time to come" (208E4–5); *eros* for a beautiful city or soul might issue in an attempt to capture that value by the production of fine poems or speeches, thereby securing an honorable life as a poet or educator for their producers (208C3, 209B). Such productive activity is the way in which mortal creatures like ourselves try "to have a share in" the divine (*athanasias metechei*, 208B5).

What Plato offers here is nothing less than a psychology of creativity; *eros* is a fundamental urge to self-creation and our relentless pursuit of beauty a drive to reproduce the value we see in the world and capture it in a life of our own, as parents, poets, legislators, or philosophers.[10] The heights towards which Plato leads us in this account, in the so-called "ascent of love," can be appreciated in light of this distinctive aim and activity. For if a stable and secure state of happiness is the real end of *eros*, and its creative effects are designed to secure that end, this has an impact on the way to practice love most effectively; or so Socrates will argue. Here is the suggested practice:

> This is what it is to approach love matters, or to be led by someone else in them, in the correct way: beginning from these beautiful things here, one must always move upwards for the sake of that beauty I speak of, using the other things as steps from one to two and from two to all beautiful bodies, from beautiful bodies to beautiful activities, from activities to beautiful sciences, and finally from sciences to that science, which is science of nothing other than beauty itself, in order that one may finally know what beauty is, itself.   (Symposium *211-D1; trans. Rowe*)

The ascent describes a desiring agent moving beyond sensible examples of beauty that change over time, are subject to change and decay, and are beautiful in one respect and not in another, towards a beauty whose nature is pure, changeless, and divine (211E), and the source of value for its various manifestations. Why beauty of this kind is required draws on complex metaphysical theses Plato explores elsewhere, which concern the instability of value in the sensible world. Their significance here is that the attainment of success (*aretê*) and happiness (*eudaimonia*) is dependent on the creative environment in which one chooses to be creative: "grasping an image one gives birth to an image, but grasping the truth, he gives birth to truth" (212A). If creative endeavor is had in an environment whose beauty changes over time, is subject to change and decay, and which is beautiful at one time and not at another, the products of these encounters will carry those hallmarks and not secure stable and secure happiness. A fine and beautiful person may hold out the promise of fine offspring, but those children may not, after all, provide "a name for all time." Poems, or laws, designed to capture the value of beautiful youths, or cities such as Athens or Sparta, might not exhibit anything of enduring value to secure an honorable life for their producers if the cities and souls that occasion those productions reflect a partial and fragile glimpse of value. Our creative activities carry both the marks of the environment in which they are produced and the efforts of their producers; and these are related. Finding the right kind of creative environment is just what the ascent addresses in its urge to explore the range of phenomena that exhibit value. If we want to love and pursue what is really and not just apparently beautiful ("not an image, but the truth"), in order to produce something really and not just apparently good, then we must *understand* beauty, see it for what it really is, and this, for Plato, just is to cultivate the intellectual excellence of soul that leads to contemplation of an intelligible form of beauty.

How exactly this satisfies our desire for happiness remains a controversial question.[11] One thing is clear: understanding beauty is not something separate from the experience of *eros*; it manifests its proper expression. Cognitive engagement with beauty is the way in which one comes to be in the creative environment of the genuinely beautiful and, given the nature of the object in question, contemplation of the object is how we come "to have intercourse with it." This activity is still, in other words, an expression of that *eros* for beauty, but where the object is so radically re-conceived, so will the activity by which we encounter it. There is not *eros* on the one hand and rational activity on the other; philosophy is the perfection of that *erotikos* drive to secure happiness through productive work (now conceived philosophically) in beauty (conceived intelligibly). In this way Plato connects his ideals to our deepest desires and concerns; philosophy is characterized as the expression of what we all really want. That *eros* for beauty that characterizes all human beings has its roots in the sensible and its proper expression in the intelligible. The beauty of the body is a way in which the intelligible world shows its presence in the sensible, and if we pursue beauty as promiscuously and as reflectively as the ascent urges, then our attraction to beauty can lead to the divine form (211E3). Since the motive force of our sensitivity to that is *eros*, it is full of productive potential, the best "co-worker" with human nature (212B3), and appropriately characterized as a *daimon*, a central meaning of which is "guardian spirit."

3   THE EROTIC PHILOSOPHER IN THE REPUBLIC

The picture turns darker in the *Republic*, however. Though philosophers are, again, *erastai* of the truth (485B, 501D, 611E), and no city will flourish unless its rulers cultivate an *eros* for philosophy (499BC, cf. 485A10–D5), the tyrant is also characterized in terms of *eros* (572B–576C), and *eros* is classed with appetites in some places (*Rep.* 436AB, 439D).[12] One might wonder, then, whether the account of *eros* in the *Symposium* has been subject to modifications and developments, in light, perhaps, of the division of the soul in the *Republic* (and *Phaedrus*).[13] One need not draw this conclusion. The desire for happiness requires specification, which leaves room for a variety of expressions, but the characteristic features of *eros* as a specific desire term seem appropriately applied to both types. The philosopher and the tyrant are both marked by the passion of their desires (*aplêstia*, "insatiability" used of the philosopher (475C), and of the tyrant (578A)). For both, *eros* provides a strength of focus that "maketh the man" by marginalizing other desires and concerns. Those who wish to transform a youth into a tyrant implant an *eros* in his soul, to act "as a leader" of his desires (572B–576C). The single overriding aim (519C), what Scott (2007: 140) has termed "tunnel vision," emerges in the soul with *eros*.[14] *Eros* subordinates other desires under its rule; it manifests a degree of commitment to a set of desires and concerns (it functions as a "leader"), and as such it provides the unity required of an emergent personality. The phenomenology of *eros* seems appropriate to both types, as it does for anyone who chooses to fixate upon a central object of concern in their pursuits.[15]

The import for the development of the philosophical character is borne out in the "hydraulic metaphor" of desires (485DE): if desires incline strongly in one direction, then like a stream that is not diverted, the strength of the flow will be strong and steady, weakening the force of other inclinations. Philosophers have temperance because there is no strength in bodily desires; they possess broad-mindedness (*megaloprepeia*) because they are insatiable in their appetite for learning (486A8–10); they are orderly and so not unjust (486B6–8). Compare the *Symposium*, which explores how someone with *eros* for the form of beauty disdains the body and, as a result of *eros* for the "wide sea" of beauty, has no "small-mindedness" (*smikrologia*, 210D2). As scholars have noted, the hydraulic metaphor plays a role in the argument for the philosopher's fitness for rule; *eros* is part of an emphasis on the dispositional properties of a person that have a bearing on the acquisition and maintenance of knowledge.[16]

Some scholars (Demos (1964), Kraut (1973), Irwin (1995)) have seen further significance in the *Republic's* use of *eros*. Irwin (1995: 312), for example, argues that the characteristic activity of *eros* explored in the *Symposium* – its generative power – is a source of benevolence, whose presence diffuses the puzzle of why the philosopher is concerned not only with his own contemplation and happiness, but returns to rule: *eros* involves "the desire to express and extend the traits one values about oneself and embody them in other things" (Irwin 1995: 309).[17]

The *Republic* does strikingly recall the *Symposium's* account of *eros* for the form of beauty:

> It is only when he uses this part of his soul to get close to and be intimate with what really is, so engendering understanding and truth, that he finds knowledge, true life, nourishment, and relief from the pains of the soul's childbirth. (490B with *Symp.* 211E–212A)[18]

The issue concerns just what is being recalled. In the *Symposium*, the aim of *eros'* productive work is to secure some good for the producer himself (206A11), which may or may not involve a desire to embody it in other things, depending on how one conceives of the relevant goal.[19] What seems clearer is that *eros* is the attitude of loving whatever one sees as valuable in such a way that one wants to reproduce the value of the object for oneself, in order to secure *eudaimonia*. This fits well with the *Republic*. The philosopher imitates the forms in his productive work (*Rep.* 500C), and reproduces their value in his own soul by "engendering understanding and truth." Since compulsion of some kind is required to put what he sees there in the souls of others (500D, 519C), the productive work of *eros*, its imitative expression, cannot be identified with other-directed activity; nor does it seem to require, or to motivate, it. Generative *eros* surely is, benevolent it need not be.

4   FROM EROS TO PHILIA: THE PHAEDRUS

Eros has ranged far from the interpersonal, then. Though Socrates in the *Symposium* describes how to go about "loving boys correctly" (211B5–6, cf. *Republic* 403C), the proper object of *eros* there (as in the *Republic*) is a form, and not a person (*Symp.* 211E, *Rep.* 490B). The marginal role of other persons has led to charges of "cold-hearted egoism" (Vlastos 1981a). But, as Socrates explained, it is a semantic and a philosophical confusion to think that *eros* centrally refers to interpersonal love; it refers, more broadly, to anything we make a central object of concern in our pursuit of happiness (205D). If happiness is the aim of *eros*, and our pursuit of beauty is determined by that aim, it is not just a semantic confusion to think that *eros* centrally refers to love for individuals, but a deeply misguided idea to think that a person can satisfy our aspiration for good things and happiness, or that they are the proper objects of *eros*. If we respect the focus on human aspirations quite broadly conceived, then Socrates' move away from individuals as the focus of a happy human life is laudable. We want persons to figure in our conception of a happy life, to share a happy life, but to be the proper objects of our happiness, to be that on which our happiness depends, is not only a heavy burden for an individual to carry, but a limited view of the rich possibilities for human aspiration. That is one reason Socrates welcomes a more expansive encounter with things considered to be of value in the "ascent."

Criticisms concern not just the fact that Socrates encourages a broader view of *eros*, but that he does so in a way that appears to demean the value of other persons. This concern is addressed in Plato's *Phaedrus*, arguably a rich, though neglected, resource for an account of *philia*.[20] Though it has long been recognized that *philia* is where one should turn for an account of interpersonal relations, Plato's exploration of this topic in the aporetic *Lysis* has left a mixed response. Though this dialogue's influence on Aristotle's account of *philia* can hardly be doubted, it is clearer when developing puzzles about friendship than it is when offering suggestions for a positive account.[21] Here the *Phaedrus* delivers. Though the expressed subject of all three of the speeches is *eros*, each is concerned with whether *eros* is compatible with *philia* (231B79–C7, 232D1–4, 232D7–E2, 233A1–4, 237C6–8, 253C5, 255B5–7), in order to show how others are benefited by loving relationships, the assumption being that it is in a relationship of *philia* that other-directed care and concern comes to the fore. By developing a theory of *philia* alongside an account of *eros*, Plato shows how loving relationships are part of broader evaluative commitments, which inform and determine the development of those relationships.[22] In this way Plato suggests that an understanding of *eros* is the beginning, not the end, of interpersonal love.

Each speech outlines a specific kind of *philia*, grounded in the larger desires of the relevant parties, which determine the nature of the friendship in each case. A relationship with someone dominated by a desire for pleasure "does not come with goodwill (*eunoia*); it is like an appetite for food, for the purpose of filling-up" (241C6–D1). What is pleasing to such a person is what does not resist him (232C5–E2, 238D5–E5, 239BD), so he deprives the beloved of family, friends, and possessions, to increase dependency. When satisfied, such a person is "compelled to default," so the association is likely to be fleeting (232E6). Goodwill is restricted because it is shown only insofar as the other provides pleasure; the other's good is not promoted if it is inconsistent with that. A second kind of friendship is explored between "honor lovers," which is based on an exchange of pledges (256D); this suggests some mutual advantage for both. Though this couple spend their lives as friends, their *philia* is not as great as philosophical types (256A6–D3); they are subject to occasional pulls of appetite, which suggests they, too, sometimes use the other as an instrument of their own pleasure. Given the pitfalls of this kind of instrumental concern spelt out in the previous case, we can see that here, too, goodwill will be restricted as a result of the desire to use the other "for the purpose of filling up."

The best kind is contrasted with this kind of instrumental concern. It occurs between those who are alike in respect of a shared orientation towards wisdom and virtue, and who build a relationship of equality and reciprocity in which the other is a genuine end of care and concern. It is characterized by goodwill (*eunoia*, 255B4, 256A3), an absence of envy (*pthonos*, 253B7), and the sharing of a life together "of one mind" (*homonoêtikon*, 256B1). The other is loved not because of some pleasure or advantage for the lover, but because of his good and beautiful nature (*phusin*, 252E3, 255B). A love of wisdom grounds the interest in qualities of the soul, which is where the other's good resides. This leads to benefits for the other both because it is *his* nature, rather than some benefit for the lover himself that forms the focus of the care and concern in this case, but also because it is his *nature*, and this is where the good of the other is cultivated best. A philosophical disposition enables the friend to appreciate the value of the other: an awareness of the intelligible beauty the other "images" encourages him to treat these qualities with "reverence and awe" (254E). A desire to investigate the grounds and nature of the attraction allows him to explore and enable their full expression (254B). An appreciation of the value of those qualities for their own sake prevents the instrumental concern that characterized the first two friendships; the other is treated as if he was "equal to the gods" (252D, 255A2) and his good nature is honored and promoted (252E1). The beloved sees himself reflected in the admiring gaze of the lover "as if in a mirror" (255D), and as the lover cultivates the philosophical disposition that attracts him to the other (252E5), he brings his own philosophical nature into sharper focus (252E–253B). The recognition of a shared good nature, and a shared orientation towards virtue and wisdom, allows them to lead a life together, structured around the pursuit of these goals, in a way that brings happiness to both.

The best kind of friendship is one in which another is loved, and their good promoted, "for their sake."[23] Though the other would not be loved if he were not good, that does not entail that it is not for his sake that he is loved.[24] Friendship does not stem from self-concern in this case; it is grounded in an appreciation of the other's good nature, and it is for the sake of the other's good that one acts to benefit him. Insofar as Plato describes a shared life of virtue and mutual benefit, though, self-interest and concern for the other's good are not clearly distinct normative perspectives. This will disappoint some.[25] Appreciating the relationship between *eros* and *philia* shows the value of this approach, however. If interpersonal relationships are considered within the broader perspective of the life one wants for oneself, there is less tension between one's own goals and the demands of a relationship. The relationship can have the stability and endurance of a lifetime partnership because the other is part of a broader life goal. And since the primary goal of both parties is shared (wisdom), they can each see clearly what the other's goal is, and appreciate its value in the proper way. Insofar as this desire for wisdom is constitutive of the life worth living for each, an ability to see the value of wisdom is a crucial part of being able to appreciate the value of the other's life and support its orientation. The moral psychology within which Plato's account of interpersonal relationships is rooted here also diminishes the taint of egoism. For to love another for their own sake – for the sake of their characteristic goodness – *and* for the sake of one's own happiness, is not also to love the other because of desires that are selfish, spontaneous, and inclination-based, and which, as such, diminish the value of other directed concern.[26] It is to love another for their sake and for the sake of a rationally grounded desire for genuine value, something which is deliberately and actively cultivated through the leading of a certain kind of life, and whose value rests on reasons independent of the fact of the agent's desiring them. This desire can ground true friendship precisely because it is rational both for oneself and for the like-minded other and, as such, it can provide a basis for other-directed concern.

5 PHILIA: BROADER SCOPE AND POLITICAL BENEFITS

Problems remain. The properties that motivate and sustain Platonic love are repeatable properties, which give us equal reason to love others than our current beloveds. This lack of focus on the particularity of the object of love explains, in part, why *philia* can play a broader role for Plato in binding citizens together within a community (e.g. *Rep.* 424A, 449C, 464AC with 424A; *Pol.* 311B9-C1; *Laws* 697C, 698C, 699C, 743C, 759C). The notion that it is constitutive of friends to share a common good, and to act in agreement with a shared goal, is used in political contexts, where concord between different elements in the state "constitutes a form of friendship" for Plato (*Gorg.* 508A; *Rep.* 443CD, 424A; *Pol.* 311B9–C1; *Laws* 689AE).[27] This indicates something about the range of *philia*, which, for the Greeks (Plato among them), was not conceived as narrowly as our modern notion of friendship.[28] It is broad enough to capture the scope of ethical and political concerns, though it fails to capture the intimacy we require of friendship.

This might lead one to think that we stray too far here from a recognizable notion of "friendship"; perhaps Plato operates on a less specific level of conceptual analysis in these contexts, and *philia* is treated as almost equivalent to agreement (*homonoia*).[29] This need not be the case. The *Laws* emphatically stresses the value of *philia* for the legislator (639B3–5, 701D7–9, 743C5–6 with Schofield (2013) and provides an account strikingly reminiscent of the *Phaedrus*. Three kinds are distinguished (836E5–837D8), and the privileged kind, which holds between "those who are like each other in respect of virtue" (837A6–7) and "aims to make a young man perfect," is the one encouraged by law (837D6–8).[30] Some of the hallmarks of the best kind of *philia* can be seen in relations between the citizens. They are brought together in a variety of communal contexts to increase their familiarity and awareness of each other.[31] A shared striving for virtue is developed from early education (643E4–5), and they are alike and equal in this respect (837A). They cultivate virtue in common by cooperative participation in a wide range of religious festivals and athletic contests.[32] This strengthens "affective bonds and their shared perception of life."[33] They contend in virtue "without envy" (731A2–3), and actively promote the good of each other, seen not only in their co-operative participation in communal practices, but in the investment of each in the common meals (955E3–4, 847E2–848B6). Their ability to appreciate the good nature of each other is fostered by an education in which they learn to value what is fine, good, and just, and "how they should be reflected in our conduct if we aim to be happy" (858D–859A with Bobonich (1991) 383); this ethical grasp informs their ability to value the good nature of others in the proper way.[34]

Appreciating the value of this kind of friendship highlights significant features of the political community.[35] What constitutes the city as a community is not just that it is something shared by the citizens, who aim at some good together and who choose to live together in agreement with that aim, but, insofar as they are bound together in friendship, the good of each is an end in view for all, and all act in a way that promotes those interests. We can appreciate, then, why friendship is paired with other legislative goals: freedom (693B3–5, 701D7–9), reason (*ibid.*), and happiness (743C5–6).[36] For friendship (of the best kind) supports and expresses those ideals; it manifests the proper relationship between free and equal parties, where neither is subject to the instrumental concern of another, but each is free to pursue their own good and happiness in voluntary partnership with others, seen as capable of so doing, and supported in that enterprise.[37]

The fact that fostering such bonds of connectedness is of concern to the legislator indicates the importance, for Plato, of other-regarding concerns in anything worthy of the name "community." A community is a shared, mutually supportive, common way of living, which aims at the flourishing of each member. The fact that the members of the state are bound together in friendship is a way in which Plato recognizes the moral claims of others, who deserve to be treated as ends of care and concern, and whose agreement is secured because they recognize that they can each flourish and develop virtue to the extent to which they are capable. And yet, given the grounds of *philia* – a shared striving for virtue – and what it requires for Plato – promoting the good of another in a shared life – this other-regarding concern will be restricted to those virtuous others with whom one shares that communal life; those outside of that community will have no moral claim on us (Irwin (1995) 316).[38] *Philia* only takes us so far morally speaking, then, but politically it underpins the pursuit of freedom, equality, and happiness.

NOTES

1. Kahn (1996), ch. 1.
2. Aeschines, *Alcibiades: SSR*, frag. VI A53, with Kahn (1996) 21.
3. Belfiore (2012) 10, 22–5.
4. Barney (2010) and Kosman (2010).
5. Lear (2006) 112.
6. References from Pappas (2016).
7. The work as a whole consists in a series of speeches in praise of *eros*, each of which makes a contribution to the whole account, which, arguably, emerges explicitly in Socrates' speech, hence my focus here. See Sheffield (2006).
8. As Long (2004) 126 has argued, "In order to understand ancient philosophical usage of *eudaimonia* we need to attend to the word's etymology and its implicit reference to goodness conjoined with divinity or *daimon*."

9. It is not clear whether Socrates is committed here to the claim that *all* desire (*epithumia*) is for good things and happiness, or the more restricted claim that all *eros* is so directed. For the former view see Irwin (1995) 303, Price (1997) 254–55, and Rowe (2006); for the latter view see Sheffield (2006) 214–15.

10. Halperin (1985) 182: *eros* is "the desire to realize an objective potential in the self."

11. It is not clear whether understanding beauty is a necessary condition for producing true virtue (212A5–6), or whether contemplation is itself an expression of intellectual virtue (211D1). See Price (1989), White (2004), Sheffield (2006), Obdrzalek (2010).

12. Obdrzalek (2013).

13. Sheffield (2012).

14. Cf. *Phaedrus*, where the lover: "forgets completely about mother, brothers and companions, and isn't concerned in the slightest if it loses its property through neglect. As for social norms, and seemly behavior, in which it used to take pride, now it despises them all" (252A).

15. Ludwig (2002) 13.

16. Lane (2007) 55.

17. For similar attempts to reconcile interpersonal love with eudaimonism compare Kraut (1973) 330–44; Price (1989) chs 2 and 3; Brink (1999) 258–59.

18. Price (1989) 52; Irwin (1991) 243–45.

19. There is no mention of any other person or thing in which the philosopher embodies virtue at the top of the *Symposium's* ascent, for example.

20. Another neglected resource is *Laws* VIII (836E5–837D8), which coheres well with the account in the *Phaedrus*. See Sheffield (2011); El Murr (2014).

21. Though Penner and Rowe (2005) argue for a positive account.

22. Compare Penner and Rowe (2005) 8, n.22; cf. 190–1, who argue with reference to the *Lysis* that the discussion of *philia* is grounded in a broader account of desire.

23. It is not always clear what is involved in this notion, but (since Aristotle) it has involved a contrast with "instrumental" or "utility" love where one uses a person for the sake of some further end. "End love" as it is sometimes now called, includes the notion that persons are to be valued as ends in themselves, and is taken to involve an active desire to promote that person's good for their sake, not for ours.

24. Loving the goodness of the other is to love them for their true nature (252D). See Whiting (1991) who emphasizes the way in which an "impersonal" account of friendship (based on goodness) grounds concern in the friend's virtuous character.

25. Vlastos searched for evidence of "love for another for their own sake, and *not* one's own" in Plato (1981a) 143, esp. n.24. But Gill (1998) argues that notions of reciprocity and shared life replace notions of altruism in much of Greek ethics. Annas (1999) avoids all talk of egoism and altruism for similar reason and talks instead of self-concern and other-concern.

26. "Kantian" concerns with ancient eudaimonism are addressed by Irwin (1998).
27. Schofield (2013) 297.
28. Adkins (1963) 36 perhaps goes too far when he says that "*philein* is an act which creates or maintains a co-operative relationship, and it need not be accompanied by any friendly feeling at all." The range of the term in Plato can be seen in those places where *philia* is a cosmological principle of attraction, in continuity with Pre-Socratic thinkers (e.g. *Gorgias* 507E9–508A, *Tim.* 32BC, 88E–89A). Konstan (1997) 55–56 argues that the verb *philein* also refers to a variety of loving and affectionate feelings, but this is compatible with a broader sense.
29. *Homonoia* is a defining characteristic of *philia* in the *Clitophon* (409C3–8) and *Alcibiades* 1 (126B8–C5); cf. *Politicus* (311BC), *Rep.* (351D).
30. Bobonich (2002) 428 and El Murr (2014).
31. The citizens recognize each other "in mutual friendship" and must know each other's characters (738D6–E1 with 771D5–E1) with Prauscello (2014) 130–31, 137.
32. Bobonich (2002) 409.
33. Prauscello (2014: 137) on the rhythmic bodily agreement fostered in choral participation. The city is modeled on a living organism in which those elements that are proper to the individual – eyes, ears, hands – become "common to all" as the citizens come to rejoice and feel pain at the same things (739C8–D3 with Prauscello (2014) 105 and compare *Republic* on the community of pleasure and pain (464C5–D4)).
34. Given how much virtue friendship requires it is hardly surprising that it is questionable how far *philia* extends in the more restricted regime of the *Republic*, though see El Murr (2014) and Prauscello (2014) 56.
35. Vlastos (1981a) 145, by contrast, uses an interpretation of "utility love" from the *Lysis* to see whether it "fits" political contexts. This supports the most objectionable readings of Plato's politics.
36. It is also associated with equality, community, and rule "for the sake of the ruled" in the analysis of the Persian constitution in Book III (697C8–D3).
37. Important here are the Athenian's remarks about current legislation (857C2–E5) which now proceeds as if "for slaves being doctored by slaves" and which is contrasted to a free doctor who proceeds by means of dialogue, using arguments that 'come close to philosophizing.'" Being treated as "free" involves recognizing that each is capable of grasping the reasons for the action under consideration. This is respected by the lawgiver in the "preludes," designed to explain the laws governing the citizens. See Bobonich (1991).
38. Compare Aristotle *NE* VIII, 9 on the congruence of the demands of justice with the circle of friendship.

III Aristotle

6 Aristotle on Virtue and Happiness

David Charles

I INTRODUCTION

Aristotle's discussion of *eudaimonia* (happiness) in the *Nicomachean Ethics* takes as its starting point some generally agreed claims about the highest (human) good. The resulting suggestion, in *N.E.*I.7, is that it is the activity, whichever it is, which is (i) always chosen (by humans) for its own sake and never for the sake of anything else (1097a30ff) and (ii) makes (human) life worth living and lacking in nothing (1097b5ff). Aristotle identifies this activity with (human) *eudaimonia* on the basis of popular views (1095a18ff) and because it meets the two conditions set out in I.7 (1097a34; 1097b15–16). On this basis, he concludes that human *eudaimonia* is the activity, whichever it is, which is (i) always chosen (by humans) for its own sake and never for the sake of anything else and (ii) makes human life worth living and lacking in nothing.[1]

Many issues remain. Aristotle has not yet addressed the question: Which activity is the highest human good (or human) *eudaimonia*? Nor has he said, even in general terms, what it is about the relevant activity which makes it always chosen for its own sake, never for the sake of anything else and renders human life worth living and lacking in nothing. This is why he remarks: "while it may be generally agreed that the highest good is *eudaimonia*, a clearer account is still needed of what the highest good is" (1097b22–4). To gain such an account, he introduces talk of the function (*ergon*) of man, suggesting "Perhaps it may emerge if we grasp the function of man" (1097b22–24).

What role does discussion of the human function play in Aristotle's account of the highest good, concluding in his famous remark: "the human good turns out to be an activity of the soul in accordance with virtue, and if there are many virtues, activity in accordance with the best and most goal-like (*teleiotatên*) virtue" (1098a16ff)? It is important properly to understand the link he proposes between the human good and activity in accordance with virtue, specifically ethically virtuous activity. Since his strategy in the *Ethics* depends, in large measure, on establishing this connection, the "function" argument and central aspects of his discussion of ethical virtue are best studied together. Discussion of each is seriously impoverished when treated in isolation as a separate topic. This chapter is designed to clarify certain features which both share by seeing them as parts of one continuous ethical argument.

2   A POPULAR VIEW OF THE "FUNCTION ARGUMENT": 1097B25–1098A18

The "function argument" (as it is often called) is standardly understood as proceeding by (i) defining the human function in terms solely of what is unique to our species, (ii) isolating an activity that meets this condition, (iii) claiming that to be a good man is to perform that unique activity excellently, and finally concluding (iv) that to perform that unique activity excellently is to achieve what is good for a man to achieve.[2] The argument can be set out as follows:

[A] The human function is to perform that activity which is unique to humans [Definition of Function]. ("Uniqueness" is understood as something that all and only humans possess.)

[B] The activity which is unique to humans is the activity of reason [Identification of human function].

[C] To be a good human is to perform the human function well [The good carrying out of the human function is what distinguishes someone as a good human] (from [A] and [B]).

[D] If one carries out well the activity which is unique to humans, one therein achieves the good for humans [the highest good/*eudaimonia*] (from [C]).

Several pieces of text are taken to support this interpretation:

[Support for A] The function of man "is an activity" (1098a7) "unique to man" (1097b35), "what is sought is what is unique."

[Support for B] The activity in question is that of a being with reason (1098a4–6).

Aristotle qualifies this by adding "in this case, something has reason in so far as it is obedient to reason, something else in so far as it has reason and thinks."

[Support for C] To be a good human is to perform the Human Function [*ergon*] well (1097b25–27, 1098a14–16).

Given [B], it follows that to be a good human is to perform well the activity of reason.

[Support for D] The good for a human is an activity in accordance with his excellence (1098a15–16).

3   INITIAL PROBLEMS WITH THE FUNCTION ARGUMENT

The argument (so understood) is flawed. Two problems arise concerning [A] and [B]:

(1) Other beings beside us share in the activity of reason. Indeed, in Aristotle's view, the gods are better at it than we are.
(2) There are too many activities which are unique to man. All and only humans walk upright on two feet, speak a language, play games, smile, laugh, or get angry.

While there have been several attempts to overcome these difficulties, each faces severe problems. One is to limit the relevant activity of reason to that of practical reason, excluding theoretical reason (which we share with the gods) from the human function. There is, however, no indication of this strategy in the text. Moreover, the conclusion of the argument ("if there are many virtues, the activity in accordance with the best and most goal-like of these") seems to leave space for subsequent discussion of the activity of theoretical intellect (as our best virtue). Another suggestion is to understand the relevant activity as the unique combination of theoretical and practical intellect which all and only humans are said to enjoy. However, if perceptual activity is excluded from the relevant composite because it is shared with other animals, how can it include theoretical activity, which we share with the gods? Only the activity of practical wisdom remains. But that faces the difficulties already mentioned.

Although there are serious problems with this version of the function argument, there are also some signs that Aristotle is not arguing in the way suggested. The first concerns his use of the term "activity," the second his idea of function. Aristotle, from 1097b33 to 1098a5, talks not of activity (in general) but of living (zên): 1097b33, zôê 1098a1, assumed subject of aesthêtikê (1098a2), assumed subject of praktikê (1098a3). He reverts to this terminology in 1098a13, noting that the function of man is a way of life, a special case of an activity. Ways of living, in this passage, are distinguished by what guides or controls the activities engaged in. A horse may eat but still lead a perceptual life, since its nutrition (unlike that of a plant) is guided by perception. Humans see but our perception is guided by our capacity for reason.

Lives, so understood, are individuated by (i) the activity which guides or controls the other activities and (ii) the activities so controlled. They are different if either the activities controlled or their controller (or both) are distinct. Human lives will differ from those of other animals because they contain different activities and a different controlling activity. They differ from that of the gods, even if the controller is the same in the two cases, because humans engage in activities which the gods eschew. Unlike them, we act on emotions and sensual desire, perceive, and have a nutritive faculty. Even if theoretical reasoning guides both our choices (see 1147a9) and theirs, our way of life is unique because, in our case, this type of reason controls (in some measure) a range of activities which we do and the gods do not.[3]

While proper attention to the meaning of "life" reveals something unique to humans, it does not capture all of Aristotle's thought about the function of man. He adds:

> we say that the function of a kind of thing is the same in type (*genus*) as that of an excellent individual of that kind.   *(1098a8–9)*

The function of a kind of thing is the activity which an excellent (*spoudaios*) individual of that kind does well. Nor is the connection accidental: The function is the type of activity which excellent individuals of a kind have to do well if they are to be excellent members of that kind. In the human case, it is doing this activity well that marks some out as excellent humans. This claim puts an additional constraint on what it is to be the function of a kind. The function of an A is not simply:

(i) The life-activity which all and only A's do,

but also

(ii) That life-activity whose doing well distinguishes an excellent A.

The addition is important: even if all and only humans learn language, tell jokes, get angry, and walk upright on two legs, engaging in these activities is not part of our function since doing them well is not what makes someone an excellent human. Indeed, nearly all of us do some of them (such as walking upright on two feet or learning a language) equally well. Others, such as smiling or playing games, are not, in Aristotle's account, ones which if done well make us excellent human beings. Less than excellent human beings can excel at these. Even if all (and only) excellent people were excellent at smiling or playing games, it would not be these abilities which marked them out as excellent people.

The addition of (ii) circumscribes the activities which constitute the human function. They are just those, which – if done well – distinguish an excellent human being. Human excellence (or virtue: *aretê*) is excellence in that activity, the doing well of which marks out a good human.[4] A good human performs the distinctively human function in accordance with human excellence. In (ii) Aristotle uses the idea of doing well and what it is to be a good (or excellent) human to determine what is to count as the human function. He does not (as in the popular version) define the human function in terms of what all and only we do and then infer that one who does that activity well is a good human.

Aristotle's approach suggests a solution to our second problem. Many things that all and only humans do are unconnected with being a good human because they are not ones whose doing well marks out an excellent human being. Provided that one already has a grasp on what counts as an excellent A (or the characteristic excellences of an A), one can discount some activities which all and only As do and explain why it is only their success in other activities which constitutes being a good A. The very idea of a function, so understood, selects just that type of activity whose excellent performance distinguishes excellent As.

4   A FURTHER PROBLEM: THE STEP FROM [C] TO [D]

The next problem is easily stated: Aristotle, guided by the thought that humans have a function, seems to conclude from

[C] To be a good human is to perform the Human Function [ergon] excellently (1097b25–27, 1098a14–16)

that

[D] The good for a human is to perform the human function excellently (1098a16–17).

But why accept this inference? Why believe that there is any connection between being a good human (reasoning excellently) and achieving what is good for a human? One could, of course, make the step valid by adding a premise:

[P] To be a good human is to achieve what is good for humans to achieve.

But why accept [P]? It is not universally true that if S is a good A, S achieves what is good for As to achieve. Consider skillful self-harmers, martyrs, suicide bombers, or liars. There is, no doubt, an activity which each group alone performs, the doing well of which marks out a good liar or self-harmer. But there need be no good for them achieved by their actions. What is achieved is, we generally suppose, bad for the self-harmer. When liars achieve their goal, it is not obvious that it is good for them to do so. In neither case, is there a straightforward step from being an excellent A to achieving anything good, still less something that it is good for As to achieve.

Aristotle, however, has the resources in his conceptual "tool kit" to address this problem. In *Metaphysics Theta* 8 he comments on a range of activities:

> The function (*ergon*) is (in the case of action) a goal, the actuality (*energeia*) is a function, and this is why the term 'actuality' is predicated on the basis of what is the function (in the case of action) and extends to the perfected state (*entelecheia*).[5]   *(1050a21–3)*

The function (*ergon*) in cases of action can be the finished product (e.g. an enformed statue) or the activity itself (such as flute playing). In the latter case, the activity itself is the function (the characteristic functioning of the flute player). The activity, understood in terms of function, is, as he notes, the goal (1050a23–5, 34-b1): The function is the goal *(telos)* for one engaging in the relevant activity. However, if this is the goal, it will be (in Aristotle's account) something which it is good for the agent to achieve *(Physics* 198b8ff). The function is, as a consequence, something which it is good for the agent to achieve. If it is an activity, it is one which it is good for the agent to do.

The connection between goals and what is good for the agent is clear in Aristotle's discussion of teleological causation. Actions, such as walking for health, and natural processes such as a plant's roots pushing down for nutrition *(Physics* 199a 29) are ways of achieving a goal which it is good for the agent, animal, or plant to achieve. These activities contribute to the goal of living or living well *(De Anima* 415b14, 435b21f.). The agents' lives go better if the goal is achieved. Another set of examples includes artifacts (such as medical instruments or axes: *Physics* 200b5) and parts of animals (such as teeth (198b29) or the organs of the body).[6] Artifacts are required to achieve the goals of the designer or user of the object (such as cutting in the case of the axe). Parts of the body, analogously, are required for the goals of the animal whose parts they are (as the eye is required for seeing, essential to the animal in question living well). Artifacts and parts of organisms are present because they contribute towards some relevant goal, whose achievement is good for the agent, animal, or plant involved.[7]

These remarks indicate that there is a third condition implicit in Aristotle's account of a function (*ergon*): The relevant activity is one which if an A performs it well, A will (in performing it) achieve what is good for an A to achieve. This is because A's function (F) is the life-activity which meets the following conditions: (1097a21ff):

(1) it is distinctive of As (as defined above);
(2) S (an A) is a good A if and only if S performs F well; and
(3) S achieves what is good for A's to achieve if and only if S performs F well.

The notion of a function, so understood, ties together two ideas that are, at first sight, independent of each other: doing an activity well and the good for a human. In this account of what it is to be a function, humans will have a function if and only if there is a type of activity which a good human performs well and therein achieves what is good for a human to achieve.

From this perspective, the basic question is not "is the function argument valid?" but "does man have a function?" The conclusion of the function argument will follow if (and only if) the latter question is answered in the affirmative. Aristotle, to secure his conclusion, needs to establish that man has a function. How does he do so?

5   HOW DOES ARISTOTLE ATTEMPT TO ESTABLISH THAT HUMANS HAVE A FUNCTION?

I shall consider three answers to this question:

[*Suggestion 1*] Aristotle aims to establish that man has a function by means of a few, unanswered, rhetorical questions in *N.E.* I.7:

> Does a carpenter and the leatherworker have their functions and characteristic actions, but a human being lack one? Is he by nature functionless? Or just as an eye, hand and foot, and in general every bodily part has a function, may we in similar fashion ascribe to a human being some function apart from these?   *(1097b30–5)*

However, these considerations are, as often noted, strikingly weak. Carpenters and leather workers have functions associated with their allotted roles in production. They accept these roles when they become carpenters or leather workers. But there is no similar mechanism for accepting one's role, or function, as a human. Aristotle's question, "how can man be functionless if carpenters have a function?" is easily answered. Similarly, there is no obvious reason to generalize to the case of a human being (as a whole) from consideration of our parts. While the latter contribute to the well-being of the whole organism, it need not be the case (for all Aristotle says here) that humans have a similar function, contributing to some greater whole of which they are a part. Even if Aristotle thought that these rhetorical questions might encourage us to think that man has a function, it would be surprising, and disappointing, if the argument of the *Ethics* rested on such weak foundations. The type of conviction sought should be based, as he remarks later, on deeds and resulting lives (1179a19 f).

[*Suggestion 2*] Aristotle relies on a background metaphysical account of human nature: It is because our nature is as it is that a good human achieves what is good for a human to achieve. The function argument, so understood, rests on a prior conviction that human nature has as its goal the attainment of certain natural goods which are achieved if and only we act excellently (or virtuously). The form of kinds is defined in terms of teleological goals in the *Metaphysics* and *De Partibus Animalium*. If Aristotle believed that we fully realize our form if and only if we are (ethically) virtuous, he could reasonably conclude that it is through (and only through) being ethically virtuous that we achieve our teleological goals.[8]

This suggestion requires scrutiny. Aristotle, no doubt, believed that given our nature we achieve what is good for us if and only if we act virtuously. However, it does not follow that he took this claim to be true *because* our nature has certain natural goals, ones which can be achieved if and only if we act virtuously. Other explanations are available. Perhaps virtuous activity is intrinsically valuable and, as such (given our natures), good for us to do. On this view, the role of our nature is to enable us to experience, when we act virtuously, the intrinsic value of virtuous action. The connection between virtuous activity and what is good for us to achieve would rest on the value of virtuous activity (which our nature allows us to appreciate), not on our having natural goals which we can achieve if and only if we act virtuously. The metaphysical account is only one of several possible explanations of the contention that, given our natures, we achieve what is good for us to achieve if and only if we act virtuously.

There are two issues to consider: (i) Did Aristotle think that the metaphysical, human nature-based explanation offered the basic ground for his central claim that we achieve what is good for us to achieve if and only if we act virtuously? (ii) Did that background belief play a significant role in his argument in the *Ethics*? These questions are distinct: He could have accepted the nature-based explanation but not relied on it in the *Ethics*.

There are grounds for a negative answer to (ii). As the *Ethics* develops, there is no further sign of a metaphysical argument designed to prove that it is *because our nature is a given way* that we have certain natural goals which can only be achieved if we act virtuously.[9] Aristotle generally takes as his starting point the idea of a good human performing ethically and intellectually excellent activities and attempts to show that, in doing these, he (or she) achieves what is good for a human to achieve. The latter notion is understood in terms of the conditions specified in *N.E.* I 1–7 (what makes life worth living and lacking in nothing, etc.), not in terms of our natural goals (as members of the human species). Aristotle does not argue that the reason why in acting virtuously we achieve what is good for humans to achieve is *because* our nature has certain natural goals which can be achieved only by virtuous agents.

Had Aristotle, in fact, attempted to develop a metaphysical argument of this type in the *Ethics*, his first step would have been to specify a number of natural goods whose achievement constitutes human flourishing, the next to show that ethically virtuous activity (and only such activity) leads to, or constitutes, the achievement of these goods. But this is not how he proceeds. Sometimes, he identifies natural goods as those which are good for the good person (1170a14–15: "what is by nature good is said to be what is good and pleasant in itself to the good man"). He does not offer a more basic account of what is good by nature to support this claim. When he does talk of what is good and fine by nature, he focuses not on our achievement of such goods but on the manner in which we do so (1148a27ff: "some things are in their nature choiceworthy for themselves, but excess in them is to be avoided"). The correct goal for humans is to gain these natural goods in an ethically appropriate way. Aristotle, far from following the metaphysical route in these sections, takes ethically virtuous engagement with the natural goods (not those goods themselves) as the relevant goal for humans.[10]

Did Aristotle, outside the *Ethics*, establish that our natural goal consists in performing ethically virtuous activity? In *De Anima*, he suggests that animals possess certain forms of perception in order to live well (435b20ff) but does not generalize these claims to the capacities for the passions and actions essential for ethically virtuous activity. Since these claims concern capacities shared by humans and animals alike, the relevant notion of living well is "biological" rather than "ethical." Equally, while in *De Anima* the object of desire is the good or the apparent good (433a28ff), no attempt is made to connect what is good (for humans) with ethically virtuous activity. Nor does he seek to establish this connection in his discussion of thought or imagination. Neither in *De Anima* nor the central books of the *Metaphysics* does he explicitly connect the human form with ethically virtuous activity. Nor does he attempt to show that the human form grounds a connection between ethically virtuous activity and human flourishing. Even if he believed this, he did not argue for it outside the *Ethics* itself. But, as we have seen, his argument there did not follow the suggested metaphysical pattern.

There is, indeed, some indication that Aristotle did not think the metaphysical style of argument appropriate in the *Ethics*. Its crucial claim is that those ethical goods which it is good for us to achieve are so *because* they are the goals of our distinctively human nature. However, immediately after the "function argument," he comments that one should not search for further justification in some areas, as this will involve a degree of "precision" beyond that required for the relevant subject matter (1098a26–31). In the present case, it is enough to show the relevant starting points by induction or perception. Through these, or perhaps by habituation (1098a33–b4), we grasp that humans in acting virtuously achieve what is good for humans to achieve. It appears to be a mistake to look for further explanation of why all and only those who engage in excellent activity achieve what is good for humans. Aristotle's immediate project is to establish the latter claim, not to ground it in an argument based on a more basic, metaphysically inspired view of human nature.

[*Suggestion 3*] Aristotle aims to establish that humans have a function by showing that there is one type of activity which (1) an excellent (virtuous) human does and (2) therein he/she achieves what is good for a human to achieve. To do this, he needs to secure two sub-goals:

> Sub-goal (1): case by case strategy – to show that there are, in each relevant area, activities involving reason which (1) a good/excellent human does well and (2) in doing, he/she achieves what is good for a human to achieve (Test by actions and lives: 1179a18–20)

Sub-goal (2): to show that there is one type of activity of which all these differing activities are instances.

Aristotle could move towards the first sub-goal by establishing that, in the case of an ethically virtuous activity, one who acts excellently finds so acting enjoyable and worthwhile – an instance of doing (or living) well. This would be a step towards establishing both that the good for a man consists in doing excellent activity and that humans have a function. To complete the argument, he would need to show that there is a similar connection between excellent activity and living well in the whole range of relevant cases, including pleasures and the activities characteristic of friendship and intellectual excellence. His goal in the *Ethics* would be to establish (by induction and perception) that in all relevant cases there is a general, non-accidental, connection between engaging in excellent activity and living well, achieving what is good for humans to achieve.

This is, in my view, Aristotle's basic project throughout the *Ethics*. In the case of ethically virtuous activity, he seeks to secure the relevant connection between doing this type of activity and achieving what is good for a human by establishing two further claims: (i) ethically virtuous activity is fine (*kalon*) activity and (ii) as fine activity, it is activity which it is good for a person to do. It is the fineness of ethically virtuous activity which is the basis for the connection between the type of activity a good human does and what it is good for a human to do. (i) is considered in Section 5, (ii) in Section 6.

Many writers take Aristotle's account of ethically virtuous activity to rest solely on one or more of the following claims, understood as definitive of the "theory of the mean":

[1] The ethically virtuous person is disposed to do the action one should, when one should, to the people one should, as one should for the reasons on which one should act and to act with the emotional attitude to so acting that one should have.

[2] One can go wrong, with respect to ethical virtue either by doing too much or too little of some relevant type of action or by doing it with too much or too little of the relevant type of emotion (or both).[11]

Aristotle's own comment on this approach is revealing. It is, he says "true but not clear" (1138b25–26). A clearer account, he suggests, is required of what one should do and how one should emotionally react (or, equivalently, of what correct reason prescribes). Further, for his overall project in the *Ethics*, he needs to secure a connection between acting virtuously and achieving what is good for humans to achieve. There has to be more to his account of ethically virtuous activity than [1] and [2].

6   THE FINENESS OF VIRTUOUS ACTIVITY

There is evidence that, in Aristotle's view, ethically virtuous activity is fine (*kalon*) activity.

(i) In 1120a23–4, he says as much. While focusing on ethical virtue, he asserts that "activities in accordance with virtue are fine and done for the sake of the fine." Nor is this his only general statement to this effect. In 1176b7–8, virtuous activities are identified as actions which are fine and excellent (*spoudaios*).[12] Both are choiceworthy for their own sake. Excellent (*spoudaios*) people choose what is fine above everything else (1169a31–2) and are good judges of what is fine and pleasant (1113a31–33), not misled by pleasure. As such, they direct their actions in the light of what they see as fine.

(ii) Aristotle's discussions of particular virtues exemplify the same connection. Here are some of his claims:
   (a) courageous people act for the sake of the fine (1115b12–13, 21–4) and their actions are themselves fine (1169a24–5);
   (b) generous people give money to their friends but gain what is fine for themselves (1169a27–8), acting for the sake of the fine (1120a24–5) and doing fine actions (1169a23–5, 1120a23);
   (c) "magnificent" people act for the sake of the fine, "a feature common to all virtue," (1122b6–7) and do fine actions (1169a22ff);
   (d) the temperate, like the generous, are constrained by the fine (1119a22, 1121a1–2). Further, the pleasures which the temperate enjoy are directed to the finest of objects for each sense (1174b15ff). It is because they are derived from fine sources that these pleasures are choiceworthy. Indeed, their being derived from such sources is what makes them the pleasures they are (1173b28–30).[13]

Nor is it, in Aristotle's view, an accidental fact that ethically virtuous activity is fine activity. The connection is stronger: being fine is taken to be constitutive of ethically virtuous activity. Its fineness is a central aspect of what makes it such activity. Here is some evidence for this further claim.

(iii) Virtuous activity is introduced (in part) as action chosen for its own sake (1105a32). In discussing specific virtues, Aristotle clarifies this remark: courageous activity is chosen because it is fine (1116a15) and for the sake of the fine (1115b12). The action in question, we may suppose, is chosen under the description under which it is a fine activity to do: standing in line with the aim of defending one's city and securing the well-being of one's fellow citizens (to use Aristotle's preferred example: 1178a13–15). This action is chosen because, so described, it is a fine action. Aristotle, however, goes further: Virtuous activity is defined (or marked out) as the activity it is because its goal, the end for which it is chosen, is fine (1115b22–4). Being chosen for the sake of the fine is what makes ethically virtuous activity the activity it is.

(iv) In 1120a22ff Aristotle argues as follows:

(a) Virtuous actions are fine and for the sake of the fine, so

(b) Generous people give correctly and for the sake of the fine.

He clarifies (b) in the next line:

(c) their giving correctly is "giving to whom one should, how much one should, and when one should" (the features used to distinguish the mean in action: 1107a21ff).

The order of explanation is significant: It is because the action is fine and for the sake of the fine that the generous give as they should, when they should, to whom they should. What makes their giving correct is that it is a fine giving: a giving when it is fine to do so, to whom it is fine to do so, how much it is fine to do so. It is because it is fine to give to certain people that one should do so. The standard of correctness rests on the notion of fineness. It is not simply that one ought to give to certain people in certain conditions (although, of course, it is true that one should).[14] Instead, one ought to give to those to whom it is fine to give in conditions when it is fine to do so. Nor is this a one-off remark: when Aristotle subsequently censures those who spend more than they should, he immediately clarifies the latter notion in terms of the fine (1121a1–2). Here, too, the notion of what one ought to do rests on what it is fine to do.

This connection should not surprise us: When Aristotle introduced the idea of the mean in terms of what we ought to do, when we ought to do it, to whom and the rest (1106b21–2), he associated what is medial with what is best (see also 1109b26). The reason why, in craft, one aims at the mean is that this is the route to the good (1106b8–9). What makes something medial in the case of craft is that nothing can be added or taken away (1106b11ff). The product is as good as it gets. By analogy, what makes an action medial will be that nothing can be added or taken away to make it better. Although Aristotle's initial discussion emphasizes the role of the mean (between extremes), this notion is introduced in terms of the goodness of the action performed. There are, for Aristotle, three good-making factors: the fine, the useful, and the pleasant (1104b30–2). Since the good-making feature of virtuous action is fineness (not pleasure or utility), Aristotle specifies the relevant type of goodness in terms of fineness. Its fineness makes an action medial.

(v) The centrality of fineness is evident in Aristotle's discussion of practical wisdom. The goal of the practically wise is what is fine (1144a27). They know what is fine and just (1144a12). Aristotle's aim in this book, as we have noted, is to give a better characterization of the type of reason that distinguishes acting virtuously than is offered by the unclear invocation of what is the mean between excess and deficiency (NE VI. 1138b20ff). In NE V, he had achieved only very limited success in applying the mean to the case of justice, describing it as a mean between acting justly and being unjustly treated (1133b31–2). As NE VI develops, Aristotle specifies the correct account (or reason) using the idea of a fine goal (1144a26f), the goal which appears to the virtuous person. Elsewhere he had used fineness to constrain the means to be used to achieve such a goal. The wise deliberate well by finding the easiest or finest means (1112b17, see 1142b24) to achieve a fine goal. Fineness is the basic ideal governing both goals and the means to achieve them. So far from defining fineness in terms of the mean or what the correct account says, Aristotle specifies the mean and the correct account in terms of fineness. What marks out the practically wise is that they grasp the fineness of virtuous action and act accordingly.

7   FINENESS AND WHAT IS GOOD FOR HUMANS TO DO

Is fine activity, as such, activity which it is good for a human to do? Does fineness provide the link, hypothesized in the function argument, between what a good human does and what it is good for a human to do?

Several considerations support an affirmative answer to this question:

(i) Near the beginning of his investigation (and shortly after the function argument), Aristotle suggests that for those who love the fine, virtuous activity is pleasant (1099a18ff). He adds a further point: It is not simply that such actions are pleasant and seem so to the lovers of the fine. Rather, one cannot separate what is best, finest, and most pleasant (1099a24–27): all such features are present in the best activities. Indeed, fineness is itself pleasure-involving: As Aristotle remarks in *Rhetoric* 1366a33–4, the fine is what is "what in being good is pleasant in that it is good." One cannot define the kind of goodness involved (in fineness) without reference to pleasure. The type of goodness involved will be, in its nature, pleasure-involving. In acting finely, we gain pleasure or enjoyment. Since pleasure is a human good, we gain in acting finely something which it is good for us to have.

(ii) Given this connection between acting finely and enjoyment, we can understand why, in Aristotle's account, it is characteristic of the virtuous to enjoy acting virtuously (1104b5–7, 1117a35-b2, 15ff, 1120a26 "with enjoyment or without pain"). This is an important thesis which Aristotle strives to maintain even in difficult cases, such as those involving courage. The virtuous are guided in their emotional reaction to situations by their awareness of what it is fine to do. In the case of the temperate, their sensual desire is directed towards what is fine (1119b15–17). On this basis they will desire as they should, when they should, what they should, etc. Similarly, the courageous person will not (in Aristotle's account) be moved by fear when confronted with the prospect (however imminent) of a fine death (1115a33–4). In both cases their passions are regulated by their perception of what is fine. Indeed, it is because this is the case that they are able to act virtuously with pleasure or without pain. They are emotionally influenced by the fineness of virtuous activity. Fineness underlies both aspects of the theory of the mean, constraining both what ought to be done and how one ought to emotionally react to doing it. Against this background, it is no surprise to find that, in the human case, acting finely is doing what is good for a human to do.

(iii) One further aspect of Aristotle's account can be clarified by considering the fineness of acting virtuously: his claim in 1144a35ff that the "goal only appears to the virtuous person." This remark initially seems surprising: One might have thought that the relevant goal would also appear to the self-controlled (and perhaps the akratic). However, it can be explained as follows: While the self-controlled may have been taught that acting virtuously is a good (or

even a fine) thing to do, the fineness of so acting does not appear to
them. They do not experience for themselves the fineness of acting
virtuously. Had they done so, they would enjoy acting virtuously
and be disgusted with themselves if they were to act differently
(1151b34–1152a2). However, lacking the experience of the fineness
of virtuous activity, the self-controlled do not see such activity as
enjoyable (or part of living well). The virtuous, by contrast, take so
acting as an aspect of the human good because they experience for
themselves the fineness of so acting.

8   CONCLUSIONS AND GAPS

Aristotle's project in the *Ethics*, I have suggested, is to confirm his initial
claim about the human good (in 1098a16–17) by showing that by doing
(and only by doing) excellent activities (including ethically virtuous
activity) we achieve what is good for a human.[15] He aims to give an
inductive argument in support of his initial hypothesis: The human good
consists in doing excellent human activity. This will also be his route to
establish that man has a function. The grounds which Aristotle offers for
the conclusion of the function argument are to be found in the argument
of the *Ethics* itself.

In the case of ethically virtuous activity, fineness, I have argued,
plays a central role.[16] Such actions are chosen and done with pleasure by
the virtuous because they are fine. The latter know what to do and why.
What makes their claims true is the fact that the actions they do are fine
actions. Since knowledge presupposes truth, the actions in question will
not be fine simply because they are chosen by the virtuous. On the contrary, it is because such actions are fine that they are chosen by the
virtuous. Although virtue of character is important in Aristotle's account,
it is not the prime bearer, or source, of ethical value. What is good about
ethical virtue is that it enables us to grasp what is fine to do and why it is
fine to do it and, so grasping, act accordingly. It is fineness which, as we
have seen, makes it the case that virtuous actions are the ones they ought
to do. The reasoning of the virtuous is correct when, and only when, it is
guided by fineness of this type. In this respect, his ethical theory differs
from that proposed by contemporary virtue theorists who define what is
good in terms of what the virtuous person would choose.[17] For Aristotle,
the virtuous choose to do certain actions because they are fine (and known
to be such). His account differs, for similar reasons, from theories which
define fineness in terms of correct reasoning or correct situational

appreciation. In his view, one's reasoning and situational appreciation will only be correct if one responds to, and grasps, what it is fine to do.[18]

What does the virtuous' grasp on fineness consist in? There is no reason to assimilate Aristotle's ethical theory to those in which the fineness of actions resides solely in their beneficial consequences. The just are, in his account, guided by what is just to do (e.g. repaying a debt) not by the general beneficial consequences of so acting. The value of friendship appears to lie in shared perception and joint activity (1170b10–12). The courageous may choose *in extremis* to die "with their boots on," fighting bravely like the Spartans at Thermopylae in a hopeless cause (even one which they know will not be remembered). In such a situation, acting courageously (1115b20–23) or "laying down one's life for one's friends" (1169a25f) may itself be the goal. The last but one Spartan may do the latter, even knowing that his surviving friend will suffer the same fate. The last Spartan may do the former, preferring to die fighting those who would enslave his country rather than beg their mercy. There is, it seems, value in virtuous activity itself even when no beneficial consequences actually follow (or are thought to be likely).

That said, a more positive characterization of Aristotelian fineness is still required, one which ties it (at least in part) to activity. Acting well (*eupraxia*) is, after all, the basic value in Aristotle's ethical theory (1139a34). It is not enough to note that his account differs from those offered by contemporary virtue theorists, neo-Kantians and classical consequentialists, all of whom claim (erroneously, as I have suggested) to capture Aristotle's insight. What is needed is an account of (i) the nature of fineness in activity and (ii) how the practically wise acquire and grasp it. In conclusion, I shall note three issues where further investigation is required.

(i) What is the nature of the relevant activities? Aristotle seems to regard these as actions which (like processes) continue through time. They have intrinsic value and (as such) are desirable in themselves. One can engage in activities such as discussion, campaigning for justice, and thinking philosophically, finding them pleasant and worthwhile as one does so. How are they individuated? They clearly differ from actions, understood as bodily movements whose value lies only in the consequences they produce or the reasons which generate them. How are they to be understood?

(ii) In the *Ethics*, although fineness like pleasantness is a way of being good, it is not, it appears, analyzed there as a combination of goodness and a further factor (such as pleasantness). It may be a distinctive, irreducible, way of being good – as being red is a distinctive, and irreducible, way of being colored (not analyzable in terms of being colored plus some further factor). Indeed, like other basic features in Aristotle's thought (such as capacity and actuality: 1048b1–4), fineness may resist definition. If so, while fine activities are, no doubt, ones which are well ordered for the human good in an intelligible and pleasant way, the presence of the latter features (in an organized unity) will be a consequence of their fineness, not its definitional basis.[19] Indeed, it is doubtful that one can, in Aristotle's account, define the relevant type of pleasure involved in fineness without reference to goodness (or excellence) or the relevant type of goodness without reference to pleasure. Further, if these are inextricable in this way, fineness will not be a purely "moral" notion since it will be definitionally connected with pleasure (and further aesthetic and prudential considerations) as well as with what one ought to do. Indeed, fineness may be what defines both what one ought to do and the type of pleasure one should experience in doing it.

(iii) The practically wise know which actions are to be done and why (because they are fine). What does their knowledge of the "why?" require? While this goes beyond knowledge of which particular actions are to be done, it need not require that they have a complete grasp of fineness, encapsulated in exceptionless general principles or a grand aim (or life plan). Perhaps they have only a grasp of the point of such activity which can be progressively developed as they encounter the diverse and complex situations of ordinary life. Particularism and grand aim theory may not exhaust the relevant epistemological options.

In each of these areas, Aristotle's ethical theory does not fit easily into the pigeonholes with which contemporary ethics is most familiar. The next step is to test how far, when properly spelled out, it withstands sustained critical scrutiny.

NOTES

1. For differing views on these remarks, see Ackrill (1974), Irwin (2012), and Charles (2015).
2. See, for example, the essays by Glassen (1957), Nagel (1972), Whiting (1988), and Everson (1988).

3. For recent discussion of the role of "life" in Aristotle's biology, see Lennox (2010).

4. I shall use "excellence" and "virtue" interchangeably in this essay (as translations for the Greek term *aretē*). Virtue is to be distinguished from ethical virtue.

5. For discussion of this passage, see Charles (2010).

6. See *P.A.* 645b14: "every part of the body, like every other instrument, is for the sake of a goal." For further discussion, see Lennox (1997).

7. For discussion of these cases, see Charles (2012).

8. For this line of thought, see Irwin (1980) and Whiting (1988).

9. For critical discussion of this strategy, see Williams (1985).

10. If natural human goods are defined as those goods whose virtuous use constitutes human *eudaimonia*, they will not be prior in definition to human *eudaimonia* or human virtue.

11. See recent essays by Rapp (2006), Crisp (2014), and Brown (2014).

12. There is, it seems, one class of actions which are simultaneously fine and excellent.

13. Aristotle does, it should be noted, subsequently talk of the "strongest" rather than the "finest" objects of sense (1174b19, 29), possibly reflecting some reluctance to characterize the objects of (e.g.) touch as fine.

14. For a contrasting view, see Crisp (2014). He takes as basic the idea of acting appropriately in the circumstances, suggesting that (for Aristotle) if humans act in this way, they will (as a matter of empirical fact) gain what is good for them.

15. He will need to achieve a similar result in his remarks on, for example, friendship, pleasures, and intellectual activity also.

16. This should not surprise us. Returning to the function argument, we can see – as for the first time – the importance of Aristotle's talk of "acting finely" (1098a15), apparently to explicate acting well. The key notion was there, unnoticed, from the very beginning!

17. See, for example, Hursthouse (1999) and Annas (2011).

18. Contrast Korsgaard (2008).

19. Compare Lear (2006).

7   Aristotle's Ethical Psychology

Jessica Moss

> Since happiness is an activity of the soul expressing complete virtue,
> we must examine virtue ... But by human virtue we mean not the
> virtue of the body but that of the soul ... The student of politics
> therefore must study the soul, but for the sake of these things and to
> the extent that is sufficient for the things sought.   (NE 1102a5–25)[1]

The study of the human good requires the study of the human soul;
Aristotelian ethics requires Aristotelian psychology. Not too much psychology, Aristotle warns us here, but enough for the purpose at hand –
the *Ethics'* purpose of defining the human good and explaining how it is
achieved. Thus as ethicists we can for instance ignore questions about
the ontological status of soul-parts. What can't we ignore?

Aristotle's answer comes from the function argument (*NE*
1097b21–98a20), whose conclusion he restates in our opening quotation.
The human good consists in the excellent performance of the human
function; the human function consists in distinctively human activity,
i.e. a distinctively human life; this can only be the activity of the distinctive parts of the human soul.[2] The ethicist must thus study these
parts enough to understand what they do – their functions – and what
makes them do that excellently – their virtues.

Aristotle assumes without argument that these parts are distinguished by a crucial feature: they are those that have *logos* – reason.[3] He
states this already in the function argument (*NE* 1098a3–5); later discussions give us more detail.

Two parts of the soul have *logos* in themselves (*NE* VI.1–2). One
is the theoretical part (*epistêmonikon*), the other the calculative
(*logistikon*). The former contemplates necessary, eternal truths; the
latter deliberates about how to achieve goals. Each has various virtues
enabling it to perform its function well in various domains, supreme
among them *sophia* (theoretical wisdom) for the contemplative part,
and *phronêsis* (practical wisdom) for the deliberative. A third part of

Many thanks to audiences at NYU, Yale, and Hopkins for comments on versions of this
chapter; I also benefited greatly from discussion with Elena Cagnoli Fiecconi.

the soul shares in *logos* "in a way," not by possessing *logos* in itself, but by being able to listen to, agree with it, or fight against it (I.13). This part Aristotle first identifies as the appetitive or desiderative part, and later as the seat of all the non-rational passions, emotions, as well as appetites; I will follow his own practice in the *Politics* of calling it the passionate part (*pathêtikon morion, Pol.* 1254b9; cf. *NE* 1168b20–21). Its function is evidently to feel passions, although we will want to refine this slightly below; the virtue that enables it to do this excellently is what Aristotle calls character-virtue, a genus that includes courage, temperance, justice, and others.

This effectively exhausts Aristotle's explicit statements about the soul in the *Ethics*. His main concern there is of course with the virtues of the soul and, ultimately, the activity they enable – happiness (*eudaimonia*); he offers no further direct characterizations of the soul-parts that underlie them. The explicit statements of *Ethics*, however, leave open some very important ethical questions about the soul, because they fail to explain the nature of reason (*logos*).

It is clear that this notion is central to Aristotle's ethical psychology: It is because each soul-part shares in reason to the extent that it does that it has its particular role in virtue and happiness. Yet the *Ethics* say almost nothing by way of definition or explanation. (Contrast, for example, the detailed accounts of decision or the voluntary.) What is reason, what does it mean for a part of the soul to have a share in it, and why does this make the ethical difference that it does?

More specifically: First, in what sense is the passionate part rational at all – why do emotions and desires count as rational enough and hence distinctively human enough to play a role in virtue and happiness? Second, what do the strictly rational parts have in virtue of being strictly rational, and why does this make them so ethically important? As we will see below, Aristotle relegates a good deal of what we might consider crucial for virtue to the passionate part; he nonetheless insists that one cannot have full ethical virtue – and hence cannot achieve happiness – without the excellent condition of the practical rational part. Non-rational virtue and non-rational activity are ethically deficient, and must be under the command of reason. To understand why, we need a better account of what it is for this superior part of the soul to have reason. This should also illuminate what it is for the theoretical part to have reason, and thus why its exercise is the most fully human thing we can do.

My aim in what follows is to look beyond Aristotle's *Ethics* to get a fuller picture of the distinctively human parts of the soul, with an eye to understanding what it means for each of them to partake in reason. What I offer will be an overview, brief and sometimes dogmatic; I will, however, note controversies as I go along, and refer to fuller defenses of my interpretations elsewhere.

The picture I develop is one on which Aristotelian reason is above all an ability to grasp causes or explanations, along with the phenomena they explain: reason is what lets us grasp what Aristotle calls the *why* (*dioti*) in addition to the *that* (*hoti*). In the theoretical realm, the relevant causes will be those that ultimately explain why things are as they are; in the practical realm, they will be the final causes that explain why we should act in the ways that we should – goals that give our actions their value.

Thus what reason adds to a life lived on the basis of good non-rational parts is a better grasp of phenomena, but also and most distinctively a grasp of the explanations that underlie them. A flourishing, virtuous human life is not merely one of doing and believing the right things, but of understanding the causes that explain our world and our own actions.

I PARTS OF THE SOUL

Just after our opening quotation Aristotle refers us to "the exoteric discourses" for a fuller picture of the parts of the soul (1102b26–7). He may have in mind some now lost texts, but modern readers must look among his surviving works.[4] The most obvious place to turn is to his treatise on the soul, the *de Anima*, and in particular to its discussion of the parts of the human soul.

The *de Anima* distinguishes between various psychic faculties or, equivalently for our purposes, parts of soul:[5] the nutritive, the perceptive, the desiderative, and the intellectual.

Most primitive is the nutritive or plant-like part, found in all living things; its activities are nutrition, growth, and reproduction. It makes a brief cameo in the *Ethics*, where it is dismissed as irrelevant to human virtue and happiness and so not a subject of study for the ethical psychologist (I.13). In what follows we will thus mostly ignore it, but it will prove useful as a contrast: Whatever it is that *logos* bestows on a soul-part must be something this part lacks, so by considering its deficiencies we can hope to illuminate the higher parts' distinctive abilities.

At the other end of the scale is a part the *de Anima* identifies as distinctively human: the thinking part (*dianoêtikon* or *noêtikon*). These seem obviously equivalent to the *Ethics*' strictly rational parts (called the *noêtika* in *EN* VI.2), and although the *de Anima* makes very little of the

Ethics' distinction between practical and theoretical rational parts it does acknowledge that distinction at least in passing (*de An.* 433a14–16).

What remains on the *de Anima's* scheme are the in-between parts that we share with animals but not with plants: the perceptive and the desiderative. The *de Anima* eventually declares that there is in fact just one part here: the perceptive and desiderative parts are "the same, although different in being" (431a13–14). This seems to mean at a minimum that while *what it is to be* perceptive differs from *what it is to be* desiderative, the two capacities and their activities are necessarily found together. (Compare another pair that stands in this relation: the road from Athens to Thebes and the road from Thebes to Athens.)[6] Since the *Ethics* too identifies in the human soul a plant-like part, an intellectual part, and one in between, an obvious hypothesis is that the *de Anima's* perceptive-cum-desiderative part is identical with the in-between part in the *Ethics*, and indeed we have seen that the *Ethics* introduces this as the desiderative part (*EN* 1102b30, cf. *EE* 1219b23).

Moreover, we find abundant evidence for a close link between perception and non-rational desire (and other passions) in Aristotle's most extensive treatment of the passions, in the *Rhetoric*. Here Aristotle argues that passions are caused or perhaps even partly constituted by an offshoot and close cousin of perception: *phantasia*, "imagination" or "appearance."[7] Fear is "a pain or disturbance arising from the *phantasia* of a destructive or painful future evil" (1382a21–23); shame is "a *phantasia* of a loss of reputation," (1383b13); appetites involve pleasurably remembering a past experience or expecting a future one (1370b15–17), where memory and expectation are both functions of *phantasia* (1370a28–35), and the other passions too involve *phantasia* in one way or another. *Phantasia* is defined in the *de Anima* as caused by and sharing its objects with perception (428b12–13, 429a1–2), and in the *Rhetoric* as "a kind of weak perception" (1370a28–9): it thus seems to be an activity of the perceptive part of the soul, and indeed Aristotle elsewhere says that the perceptive and phantastic parts too are "the same but different in being" (*de Insomniis* 459a16–17).

For present purposes, we need not distinguish between perception and *phantasia* as causes of passions. The main point is that the *Rhetoric* characterizes passions as underwritten by cognitions belonging to the perceptive part of the soul; this confirms that the part of the soul that feels passions is identical to the part of the soul that perceives, thus completing the parallels between the *de Anima's* psychology and the *Ethics'*.

There is, however, one *prima facie* argument against this identification: The *Ethics'* passionate part seems to play its special ethical role
precisely because it is uniquely human, while the *de Anima's* perceptive-cum-desiderative is explicitly identified as present in animals too.[8]
On the other hand, there is some sign in the *de Anima* that the perceptive
part in humans differs significantly from what is found in animals.
Animals have perception while lacking *logos* (e.g. 427b13–14), and yet
Aristotle says that it is "not easy to classify perception as *logos*-having or
logos-lacking" (432a30–1). We can reconcile the two claims if we take
him to hold that in animals the perceptive part has no share in *logos*
while in humans it does; this would render the human version of this
part different enough from the animal version to justify the *Ethics'*
treating our perceptive part as distinctively human. In the next section
we will see confirmation of this reading.

We have seen strong evidence that the *de Anima's* soul-parts line
up with the *Ethics'*, and thus we should be optimistic that we can use
Aristotle's overall psychology to illuminate his ethical psychology, and
in particular to answer our questions about reason. We can hope that
Aristotle's discussion of thought in the *de Anima* and in other works will
illuminate the nature of the strictly rational parts of the soul, that his
detailed account of perception will illuminate the passionate part, and
that his account of the differences between thought and perception will
illuminate the superiority of the rational parts.

2   THE PASSIONATE PART

The *Ethics* does not say as much as we would like about what this part
does, although Aristotle's names for it – "appetitive" or "desiderative,"
or "passionate" in the *Politics* – imply that its main function is to feel
appetites and other passions. The *Ethics* does, however, have a great deal
to say about the virtues of this part, the character-virtues. Given that
Aristotle follows Plato in defining the virtue of a thing as what enables it
to perform its function well (*EN* 1106a15–18), we can use his discussion
of character-virtue to infer a fuller account of this part's function.

Character-virtue is a disposition to act and feel passions in ways
that hit the mean, that is, in accordance with right reason (II.6). This
implies that the function of this part of the soul is not simply to feel
passions (and so contribute to action), but rather to do so *in relation to*
reason, and Aristotle's discussion of this part in I.13 confirms this. When
the passionate part has its proper virtue and so functions well, it feels

passions in agreement with reason; when it lacks this virtue and so functions poorly, it feels passions against reason, or in reluctant obedience to it (1102b13–28). This connection with reason is what gives the passionate part of the soul a role in human virtue and hence in human happiness.

We now see an answer to the worry noted above about how the passionate part can be distinctively human while in some sense shared with animals: The human version of this part is different from the animal, for it has an importantly different function. As Aspasius puts it, in the oldest extant commentary on the *Ethics*, the animal and human versions of this part are the same insofar as they "partake of spirit and appetite and in general of pleasure and pain," but differ insofar as the animal version "is not obedient to reason" (comment *ad NE* 1102b13).[9]

But this may seem to raise more questions than it answers. What does it mean for a passionate part to agree with or listen to or resist reason? If it means simply that our passions can push us either in the same or the opposite direction as our reasoning, how does this make for any intrinsic difference between this part and its animal counterpart – or, for that matter, between this part and our nutritive part? After all, a dog can be fearful in accord with or against its master's commands, and we can digest or grow in accord with or against our own reasoned wishes. Hence the first of the specific questions about reason we raised above: In what sense can the passionate part of our soul really be said to partake of reason, even "in a way"?

Here we can hope for significant help from the connections we have seen between passions and perception (or *phantasia*). Aristotelian passions are not brute reactions to stimuli, but instead underwritten by rich, complex, value-laden perceptions, e.g. the perception of something as painful evil or a shameful insult. This suggests an answer to the question of how passions can be genuinely subject to rational influence. There is strong evidence that Aristotle thinks reason can influence perception; if passions are grounded in perception, reason can thereby influence passions too.

Aristotle seems to allow for two sorts of rational influence on perception.

First, on a compelling interpretation of Aristotle's view, reason can expand the range of what we can perceive, through what is nowadays called "cognitive penetration": If you have the concept of triangle, or of injustice, you can perceive things as triangular or unjust, while an animal cannot.[10] Thus a perceptive part housed in a human soul can come to share the rational part's vocabulary in a way that allows for real agreement and disagreement. If you have the concept of the shameful, for example, you have the capacity to *perceive* an insult as shameful, and your perceptive part thereby has the capacity to harmonize or conflict with your reasoned judgment of the insult. Therefore the passion your perception generates – anger or shame, in this case – will genuinely agree or disagree with *logos*, rather than merely falling into or out of line with it.

Second, reason can "persuade" the perceptive part by exploiting its capacity for quasi-perceptual imagination or appearance, *phantasia*. Unlike animals we can consider different possible courses of action, using our powers of deliberation, and along with that ability comes the ability to imagine those courses and their consequences. Given the connection between *phantasia* and passions, this means that deliberation can generate new passions by generating new *phantasiai*.[11]

Here is an example to illustrate both forms of rational influence. If a dog has not eaten for some time and is presented with a juicy steak, it will perceive the steak as pleasant and want it, even if its master commands it to hold back.[12] A human, by contrast – one with well-habituated, virtuous passions – has the capacity to reason herself out of desiring the steak if there is some reason not to have it: she can (a) perceive the steak as unhealthy or intemperate, perceptions arguably informed by her conceptual repertoire, and/or (b) deliberate about the consequences of eating it and as a result imagine it causing pain. Her passions will follow suit, and so will agree with *logos*. (Recall that her nutritive part is completely *logos*-lacking, and hence on this score no different from the dog's: Her stomach will still rumble and she will still drool. This highlights the difference between the nutritive and passionate parts, and the sense in which the latter alone partakes of reason.)

Thus a deeper picture of the *Ethics'* passionate part of the soul illuminates its function and, crucially, the sense in which it is rational. We have an answer to the first specific question about rationality that we raised above.

On the other hand, the second question has become more pressing. Now that we recognize the cognitive richness of the passionate part we may wonder why Aristotle thinks it ethically deficient, and thinks the rational part so central to our virtue and flourishing.

Consider a life guided mostly by a well-habituated passionate part, with some rational supplementation. The agent perceives the morally relevant features of situations, feels desire, pity, anger, aversion, and other passions in response to these perceptions, and acts on them. Reason may have supplied the conceptual material for these perceptions, if the cognitive penetration interpretation is right. Reason may also intervene on occasion to guide the perceptive part towards the right objects through deliberation, but good habituation has ensured that this part's own immediate responses will be for the most part correct; furthermore, even when reason does intervene it is the resulting *phantasiai* and passions that are decisive for action.

This is a life that Aristotle would deride as lived "according to passion rather than reason." And yet it looks like a very human life, and a morally worthy one at that. Why insist on any larger role for reason? Why insist that action in the strict sense, and fully virtuous action, must be done on the basis of decision rather than passion (VI.2, II.4), and so must be based on rational deliberation rather than perceptual evaluation?

There is a quick answer to this question, formally correct but very unsatisfying: reason is ethically crucial regardless of any issues about practical guidance or moral worth, because *given that humans are distinctive in virtue of having reason, our flourishing must consist in the exercise of reason*. This is the main idea of the function argument. Even if a life largely guided by the non-rational part of the soul could consist in correct actions accompanied by correct feelings, it would not be a fully human life, and hence not a happy life.

Does this resolve the worry? Surely not, unless Aristotle can show us that what he calls reason is something we can recognize and value in ourselves. If the function argument is to be more than stipulative – if it is to have a chance of persuading us that reason plays the chief role in our flourishing – Aristotle needs to give us an account of reason which shows it worthy of that role. And to repeat the worry, it may seem that he cannot: if the non-rational perceptive-cum-passionate part is capable of complex evaluations and emotions, perhaps a mostly non-rational life is good enough not only morally but also prudentially – satisfying enough, fulfilling enough, human enough for us.

To make headway here we clearly need a better grip on what precisely Aristotle means by reason – the very general question with which we began. What is this essentially human quality that is so crucial to our virtue and to our flourishing, but absent even in the most admirable perceptions and passions? Let us turn then to consider the strictly rational parts of the soul, to see what Aristotle thinks reason amounts to, and thus to see why it plays its crucial ethical role.

3   THE DELIBERATIVE PART[13]

We can begin with the practical rational part, the one that oversees the passionate part and produces action. Aristotle calls this the calculative part (*logistikon*) and explains the name by saying that "to deliberate and to calculate are the same thing" (*EN* 1139a11–13): its essential function is thus deliberation. Deliberation is a form of reasoning that begins with a goal for which one has a wish (*boulêsis*), consists in reasoning out the means or best means to achieve this goal, and results in a decision (*prohairesis*) to perform the action identified as the proximate means (*EN* III.2–3), which decision in turn causes action (VI.2). Evidently all this has a very special ethical status. If we do not go through the process of deliberation but act instead on the promptings of passion alone, our behavior does not count as action (*praxis*) in the strict sense (VI.2), and does not count as done virtuously (II.4): We are merely doing what animals can do. Our rational nature is expressed only when we act on the basis of deliberation, and we act virtuously in the strict sense only when we act on the basis of excellent deliberation.

Our task is to try to determine what gives deliberation this special ethical status by determining what makes it specially rational.

One might think the answer obvious: Deliberation is important because it is often hard to hit on the right thing to do, and it counts as rational because reason is what makes us able to figure things out. This might also seem a natural fit with Aristotle's characterization of thought as one faculty of *krisis*, discrimination. Perception allows us to discriminate hot from cold or red from green, but thought – an activity of the rational part – is needed to discriminate imperceptible properties, and among these are the properties most important to action: the just and unjust, fine and shameful, beneficial and harmful, and so on. Without reason, then, we cannot identify the right things to do. Let us call this the Information view of reason.

Is this in fact Aristotle's view? He clearly thinks that we sometimes need to exercise reason in order to hit on the right thing to do: "naturally virtuous" passions without the guidance of reason can cause harm (VI.13); *phronêsis*, the virtue of practical reason, "makes right the things toward the goal," i.e. tells us which particular actions to perform (VI.12–13). But his account of reason's practical role cannot be quite as simple as this.

First, we have already seen evidence that Aristotle's view of perception is more generous than the Information view of reason implies; in the *Politics* he says explicitly that humans can *perceive* "the good and bad and just and unjust and the others like these" (*Pol.* 1253a17–18). Second, and crucially, we will now see that when Aristotle directly addresses the question of what deliberators can do that non-deliberators cannot, he does not emphasize the ability to discriminate further properties at all. Instead, he emphasizes something very different: reason is superior to perception not by virtue of grasping a special range of phenomena, but rather in grasping the *causes* or *explanations* that underlie these. To anticipate Aristotle's language in a passage we will consider below, reason is needed in addition to perception not because it gives us more *thats*, but because it alone gives us *whys*. Let us call this the Explanation view of reason.

Aristotle explicitly addresses this question of what makes deliberation rational in a passage from the *Eudemian Ethics*, and while what he says here goes beyond what he says in the *Nicomachean Ethics* it looks like an elaboration of the same account of deliberation:

> (a) [D]ecision (*prohairesis*) is not present in the other animals nor in people of every age nor of every condition. For neither is deliberation [present], nor grasp of the that-on-account-of-which, but nothing prevents many from being able to opine whether something is to be done or not to be done, while not yet doing this through reasoning (*dia logismou*). (b) *For the deliberative capacity of the soul is the capacity contemplative of a certain cause (to theôrêtikon aitias tinos).* For the that-for-the-sake-of which is one of the causes, because the that-on-account-of-which is a cause ... Wherefore those for whom no goal is laid down are not deliberative.
>
> *(EE 1226b20–30, emphasis mine)*

Part (a) singles out deliberation (and hence decision) as uniquely rational: It is only found in well-developed humans,[14] and it is a form of *logismos*, reasoning (cf. *NE* 1139a11–13, *de An.* 434a7–11). Part (b) explains this fact (note the "for" (*gar*) at 1226b25) by characterizing deliberation as contemplation of one kind of cause or explanation (*aitia*), the final cause or "that-for-the-sake-of-which" (*hou heneka*). Forming goals, deliberating, and forming decisions all involve final-causal thinking: In adopting *x* as one's goal, and in deciding on *y* as a means to it, one is taking *x* to explain why *y* is-to-be-done – one is choosing *y because of x*. Aristotle's "for" at the start of (b) implies that it is this essential connection with explanation that marks these activities as rational.[15]

If this is right, then a life ruled by decent passions is deficient because the agent has no thoughts about *why* she acts as she does, and natural virtue is deficient because it includes no understanding of *why* the actions done are the right ones. What practical rationality adds to perception and passion is the dimension of explanation.

We find strong confirmation that Aristotle holds this Explanation view of reason when we turn to the texts that most promise to reveal the ethical value of rationality: texts that contrast strict character-virtue, the kind that requires *phronêsis* (see especially *EN* VI.13), with mere "natural" virtue, a disposition of the passionate part which is found also in children and beasts.

> The courage on account of spirited passion seems most natural, and when *decision* and *the that-for-the-sake-of-which* are added, [seems really] to be courage. People too [like animals] feel pain when they are angry, and pleasure when they get revenge; those who fight on account of these things are warlike, however, but not courageous. For they do not [act] *on account of the fine*, nor *as the logos* [says], but on account of passion.   *(EN 1117a4–9, emphases mine)*

The problem with the naturally courageous person is not that she tends to do or feel the wrong things, but that she is not acting for the sake of any goal, let alone the correct goal.[16] To become strictly virtuous she must recognize the fine as the "that-for-the-sake-of-which" of her actions – that which explains why they are valuable, to-be-done – and thereby acquire the ability to deliberate with a view to that goal and decide on actions as means to it. The naturally virtuous person lacks an explanatory account of why she should act as she does, which is another way to say that she acts without *logos*: she does not act "as the *logos* [says]" (a9); compare the parallel discussion in the *EE*, where strict courage, by contrast with natural and other deficient types of courage, is called "a following of the *logos*" (*EE* 1229a1–2). She needs reason to give her a *why*, and the correct *why* at that.

This passage on natural courage may seem to imply that non-rational perception and passion suffice for right action and right feeling while reason adds only the element of explanation, but as we saw briefly above, Aristotle elsewhere makes clear that practical reason also identifies the actions that lead to the goal.[17] Indeed, coming up with the right *that* – telling us what to do – cannot be the exclusive province of the passionate part of the soul, for that would give this part a leading rather than following role in action. Deliberation tells us *what* to do, and this function is crucial, for when we φ virtuously we are φ-ing *because* we have decided to φ on the basis of deliberation. The virtuous passionate part of the soul follows and agrees with reason and so generates a passion to φ in harmony with the decision, but it is the decision that plays the lead role in causing action.[18] Thus while the Information view of reason does not give the whole story, it does give part.

Nonetheless, when Aristotle discusses reason's contribution to virtue and action he tends to emphasize the less practical, more purely intellectual function of providing explanations – he writes as if he subscribed to the Explanation view alone. Perhaps he thinks that the information-providing function is often redundant: There is no having *phronêsis* without also having a well-habituated, strictly virtuous passionate part, and such a part, unlike a merely naturally virtuous one, is sufficient in most cases to generate right action and right feeling on its own.[19] But the main idea may be that reason makes us better at figuring out *what* we should do precisely by giving us a grasp of *why* we should do it: "Just like archers who have a target," those who understand the goal are better at achieving it (*EN* I.2 1094a22–4).

I have argued that the practical rational part is rational because it can grasp explanations as well as the phenomena they explain, and that this also explains – as the function argument demands that an account of rationality should – why this part is necessary for virtue and happiness. The deliberative part exercises reason when it grasps *whys* along with *thats*. The passionate part of the soul shares in reason insofar as it can be influenced by reason's deliverances, harmonizing with the *thats* (i.e. wanting to do what reason prescribes), but it is not strictly rational because it has no grasp of the *whys*.

Is this account correct? To answer that question we need to complete our account of Aristotle's ethical psychology by looking at the remaining rational part of the soul, the theoretical part. In the final section I return to consider the ethical consequences of this picture of reason.

4 THE THEORETICAL RATIONAL PART

In Book VI of the *Ethics*, in the *de Anima*, in the *Posterior Analytics*, in the *Metaphysics*, and in scattered discussions throughout the corpus, Aristotle discusses theoretical intellect and its activities and virtues: thought (*dianoia, noêsis*), calculation (*logismos*),[20] intellectual intuition or understanding (*nous*), scientific knowledge (*epistêmê*), and wisdom (*sophia*). When we look at these discussions do we find an account of what marks all these as rational, setting them apart from and above perception?

This is an enormous question: Aristotle has a lot to say on the subject, but it is not at all obvious how to unify his various remarks, and I will not attempt to give an exhaustive or decisive answer here.[21] I want merely to point out that when Aristotle directly addresses the question of what makes perception inferior to reason, as well as when he discusses the *telos* of reason – the activity in which its distinctive features are fully expressed – what he says provides striking support for an Explanation view.

The *telos* of theoretical reason is excellent contemplation (*theôria*), contemplation on the basis of scientific knowledge (*epistêmê*) and wisdom (*sophia*). Aristotle makes very clear that such contemplation consists in the grasping of the ultimate causes of things: see especially *Metaphysics* I.1–2 on *sophia*, and the *Posterior Analytics* on *epistêmê* (e.g. 71b9–12, 74b27–8, 90a5–7). Reason is valuable because it allows us to grasp causes; that is what it does when it functions at its best.

Moreover, there is good evidence that this ability to grasp causes is what distinguishes reason from perception.

The most obvious evidence comes from the *Metaphysics'* account of perception's limitations. Perception does not count as wisdom because it does not grasp causes:

> The senses do not tell us the *why* (*to dia ti*) of anything, e.g. why fire is hot; they only say *that* it is hot.   *(Met. 981b12)*

This account of the crucial difference between perception and reason gains much more support from other sources than has been recognized. In the *de Anima*, Aristotle distinguishes the two as follows:

> One discerns what-it-is-to-be-flesh [i.e. flesh's essence], and flesh, either with something different or with something in a different condition. For flesh is not without matter [while its essence is] ... With the perceptive faculty one discerns the hot and the cold, and the things of which flesh is a *logos*, but with something else [i.e. *nous*] ... one discerns what-it-is-to-be flesh.   (de An. 429b12–16)

Reason is superior to perception in that it can grasp essences. But the essence of *F*ness is on Aristotle's account a kind of *cause*: The formal cause of *F* things being *F* – what explains their being what they are, and also explains most of their qualities.

Moreover, this turns out also to be the main point underlying one of Aristotle's clearest and most frequent contrasts between perception and reason, his claim that perception cannot grasp universals (see for example *de An.* 417b23–4, *APo.* I.31). This might seem a different contrast from what we have just seen, but Aristotle holds that universals *are* causes: formal causes, i.e. essences. Significantly, moreover, Aristotle makes clear that perception's inability to grasp universals is a deficiency precisely because in failing to grasp universals it fails to grasp causes. Perception cannot yield knowledge because it cannot grasp universals, but universals yield knowledge just insofar as they are causes:

> One necessarily perceives the particular, but *epistêmê* (scientific knowledge) is knowing the universal ... [Even if we saw an eclipse up close] we would perceive *that* [the moon] is now eclipsed but not at all *why*; for there is no perception of universals ... *The universal is valuable (timion) because it reveals the cause (aition).*
>
> *(APo. 87b37- 88a6, emphases mine)*

Perception is deficient precisely because it cannot grasp causes. Reason is valuable precisely because it can: What distinguishes it from lower forms of cognition is its ability to grasp causes, and it achieves its *telos* when it actualizes this very ability through excellent contemplation.

Moreover, just as in the practical case, Aristotle's view is that reason is exercised to its fullest when it not only grasps causes but also thereby enhances its grasp of the phenomena they explain. Someone who has *nous* of the ultimate causes in a domain can use these as first principles in a demonstration of the phenomena in the domain, thereby coming to have *epistêmê*, scientific knowledge, of these phenomena. Perception is limited to *thats*; reason gives us an enhanced grasp of *thats* by deriving them from *whys*.

This has been a very brief argument: I have not attempted anything like an overview of all Aristotle's characterizations of theoretical reason nor of its differences from perception. I have, however, focused on what he himself presents as reason's most valuable features and perception's most important limitations. I hope therefore to have shown that what Aristotle says about theoretical reason provides support for the Explanation account of rationality implied by what he says about practical reason. What makes us rational is our ability to grasp explanations; we reach our *telos* when we exercise this ability well, in the practical domain and in the theoretical.

5   CONCLUSIONS

A fuller picture of Aristotelian psychology yields a fuller picture of Aristotelian virtue and Aristotelian happiness. We understand the human good and human virtue when we understand the distinctively human function, and we understand this when we understand the distinctively human parts of the soul. In particular, since what makes these parts distinctively human is their rationality, we illuminate Aristotle's picture of virtue and happiness when we see what it means for each of these soul-parts to be rational.

The theoretical and practical rational parts are strictly rational because they can grasp explanations along with the phenomena that they explain. The former can grasp the eternal truths that explain why all phenomena are as they are, and the latter can grasp the goals that explain, as final causes, why we should act the way we should. The passionate part has some share in reason insofar as it can be influenced by these practical explanations: being non-rational it can have no grasp of the *whys*, but it can be influenced by reason's enhanced *thats*.

The implications for the very best life are clear, and fit well with a received view of Aristotle's ethics. We fulfill our function (we reason) most completely when we contemplate the very highest causes – ultimately God (*Met.* I.2) – and since these are unchanging things which cannot be the object of practical reasoning (*EN* VI.1), the best life is a life of theoretical contemplation.

The implications for the life of ethically virtuous activity are more surprising, and reveal afresh what is by modern standards somewhat alien in Aristotle's ethics. For Aristotle's view that strict virtue and excellent ethical action require the active exercise of reason turns out to be a very demanding one.

The thought is not simply that reason is necessary for doing and feeling the right things (as on the Information view): A well-habituated passionate part of the soul is often enough for this, and even when reason does identify the right passions and actions this does not exhaust its role.

Is the idea then that reason is necessary for doing and feeling the right things *for the right reasons*? Yes and no.

We might mean "for the right reasons" in the familiar sense on which it simply rules out actions that are done for bad motive, like helping a friend in order to get a reward. But this doesn't require reason on Aristotle's picture. Good passions will suffice: The naturally virtuous person does not act for ulterior motives; she helps her friend out of pity, fights injustice out of anger, and so on. Or we might mean "for the right reasons" in what is probably the dominant sense in modern ethics, to pick out motivations that respond to ethically relevant features of a situation: "because he is in pain," "because she is my friend," even "because doing so would be fine, and failing to do so would be shameful." But here, too, well-habituated or naturally good passions will often suffice.[22]

What our account of Aristotle's ethical psychology has shown is that Aristotelian virtue and flourishing requires acting for the right reasons in a much more demanding sense. Excellent ethical activity requires grasping the correct goal, deliberating about how to achieve it, and deciding on one's actions as the means to that goal. When we act in this way we do not merely do the right things, nor do we merely do them in response to the right considerations: We do them on the basis of a full understanding of why they are to-be-done. (Note that this condition will be more or less difficult to meet depending on how general or abstract the relevant goals are. On a persuasive although contested reading of Aristotle's *Ethics*, the virtuous deliberator's explicit ultimate goal is a worked-out conception of happiness: The deliberative path from this to a specific decision will be very complex indeed. Aristotle also routinely describes virtue as aiming at the fine (*to kalon*) or at the mean; the deliberative path from such abstract goals will also be complex and difficult. If he thinks virtuous deliberation never needs goals more general than "Distribute these goods" or "Save the city," the path will be simpler.)

We might well think this an excessively intellectual account of virtue and virtuous action. If someone reliably does what is right on the basis of the right considerations and with the right feelings, why refuse her full praise simply because she does not have an explicit account of how her actions contribute to her goals?[23]

But here we must remember that Aristotle's way in to questions about virtue and virtuous action is through the function argument – through questions about the flourishing human life. Aristotle's psychology teaches that we are essentially rational creatures – that is, I have argued, creatures who can give and grasp explanations. Thus his ethics teaches that we are only excellent humans, and only live excellent human lives, when we exercise that ability, in the practical sphere as well as the theoretical. Virtue is what allows us to do this well. Thus the point of being ethically virtuous and acting virtuously is not – or at least not only – to do and feel what is right. It is also, and above all, to exercise our distinctive human capacity for reason to its best and fullest.

NOTES

1. Translations are mine throughout.
2. Aristotle here assumes the theory of soul he expounds in the *de Anima*: the soul of an *x* (human, mushroom) is what makes an *x* a living thing, for it is the set of capacities for all the activities that constitute an *x*-type life (*de Anima* II.1).
3. In Moss (2014) I argue that the primary or focal sense of *logos* in this context is "account," and show how the word comes to play the role it does in Aristotle's ethics and psychology; there is no harm for present purposes, however, in sticking with the traditional translation.
4. Some think he means instead the theory of Plato's Academy; even if this is so we need to understand what Aristotle takes the right version of Plato's rational/ non-rational distinction to be.
5. Aristotle says in *NE* I.13 that we do not need to ask, for ethical and political purposes, if the parts are separate or in what way; this seems to license us in using "part" as a functional synonym for faculty. For discussion see Johansen (2012).
6. See *Physics* III.3; for discussion see Whiting (2002) 156–60.
7. Some argue that Aristotle's talk of *phantasia* in the *Rhetoric* should not be taken in the technical sense of the *de Anima*; his real view is that passions are underwritten by intellectual cognitions (e.g. beliefs), and he uses *phantasia* and cognates – words connoting appearance – to highlight the subjective nature of these beliefs, or their vividness, rather than to connect them with perception. There is, however, overwhelming evidence that he means *phantasia* and cognates precisely in their technical psychological sense (see Moss (2012) ch. 4).
   The connections between passion and belief are complex, but the directive cognitive basis for passions is non-rational perception or *phantasia*.
8. The *Nicomachean Ethics* argues that the human function must be something distinctive (*idion*) to us, and thus must be the activity of the parts of the soul that have *logos* rather than a life of nutrition or perception (1097b33–98a5).
   The *Eudemian Ethics'* version of the argument states outright what this seems to imply: the passionate part, as well as the part that has *logos* more strictly, is distinctive (*idion*) of humans (*EE* 1219b37–8).
9. For fuller arguments see Moss (2012) ch. 4.
10. See e.g. Whiting (2002) 188.
11. For fuller argument see Moss (2012) ch. 6.
12. Fears caused by memory of past pains following on disobedience might overwhelm the power of appetite, and so the dog might hold back, but this cannot be the kind

of rational persuasion Aristotle has in mind, precisely because it is available to animals too.

13. I provide much fuller arguments for the main claims of this section in Moss (2014).

14. Presumably the qualifications are meant to exclude children and "natural slaves," who according to the *Politics* both lack the power to deliberate.

15. But don't animals act for the sake of goals too, for example stalking their prey for the sake of getting food? Aquinas considers this objection in his discussion of the Aristotelian thesis that animals have no share in decision (*electio*), and offers a promising solution: Animals can act on account of a goal (*propter finem*), but do not grasp the notion of a goal (*non apprehendunt rationem finis*) and so do not grasp goals as goals (*Summa Theologica*, First Part of the Second Part, Question I article 2). For a somewhat different resolution see Lorenz (2006) ch. 12.

16. Those who do courageous actions on account of the wrong goal exhibit some other form of pseudo-courage: For example, those who act for the sake of honor have civic courage (1116a28–9).

17. See the passages cited above on *phronêsis* making right the things towards the goal, and on natural virtue without *phronêsis* leading us to act wrongly; moreover, and most obviously, Aristotle characterizes deliberation as the process of figuring out what to do, e.g. whether to do one thing or another.

18. When we act without deliberation – in emergencies, for instance, where there is no time for deliberation – the passionate part must take the lead, directly causing action, but this does not seem to be virtuous action *par excellence* (*NE* III.8 1117a18–22).

19. Towards the end of his discussion of *phronêsis* Aristotle considers the objection that it is practically redundant because anyone who has it will also have character-virtue, and this alone is sufficient for right action: "For what is [*phronêsis*] needed? For if *phronêsis* is the [virtue] concerned with the just and fine and good for man, but these are the things which it belongs to the good man to do, we are *no more practical* about these things by virtue of knowing" (*NE* VI.12 1143b21–4, emphasis mine). Although he does go on to say that *natural* virtue without reason is dangerous, he never makes the same claim about habituated virtue. Indeed, his immediate response to the practical redundancy objection is to accept it while insisting that *phronêsis* is nonetheless valuable: "But about being no more practical concerning fine and just things on account of *phronêsis*, we must begin a bit farther back, taking this as our starting-point: Just as we say that some do just actions without yet being just ... so, it seems, it is possible to do each of these things in such a condition as to be really good – that is to say, *on account of decision and for the sake of the things done themselves*" (*NE* VI.12 1144a11–20, emphasis mine). Even if *phronêsis* made no difference in *what* we do it would still make the crucial difference in our understanding of *why* we do it, and that is enough to render *phronêsis* ethically necessary.

20. Thought and calculation can be practical as well as theoretical (see especially *de Anima* III.7–11), but I mean here to be asking about Aristotle's characterizations of theoretical intellectual activity, or his characterizations of intellectual activity that are not limited to its practical aspects.

21. For compelling treatments of the question see Modrak (1987) ch. 5, arguing that thought is distinguished by being more abstract and universal than perception, Irwin (1988) ch. 14, arguing that thought essentially involves inference, and Johansen (2012) ch. 11, arguing that thought essentially involves being responsive to *logos*.

22. Well-habituated people who are not yet fully virtuous, and need the help of *logos* to become so, nonetheless already love and live oriented towards the fine (*kalon*) (1179b30, 1180a10).

23. For compelling arguments to this effect see Arpaly (2003), especially ch. 3. Note, however, that if I am right Aristotle's account is even more demanding than the one she argues against: The virtuous agent does not merely grasp ethically relevant considerations (like "because it is fine") as reasons, but has a worked out understanding of how her actions serve her goals.

8 Aristotle on Love and Friendship

Corinne A. Gartner

Friendship (*philia*) is a central topic in Aristotle's ethical treatises. This may strike modern readers as strange, since, to the extent that we think of it as an ethical topic at all, we tend to regard friendship as a problem case for normative ethical theories that demand impartiality. But Aristotle's ethics is far from impartial, and he takes it as obvious that we should prioritize the interests of our friends. That said, the ancient Greek conception of *philia* is considerably broader than our contemporary notion of friendship; it comprises not only the voluntary personal associations that most closely resemble our friendships, but relationships among family members, business partners, erotic lovers, and even unmet fellow citizens of the *polis*. And it is primarily within his lengthy discussions of *philia* that Aristotle addresses what we take to be a central aspect of the project of moral philosophy, for only in explaining the attitudes of friends does Aristotle explicitly countenance wishing and acting for the sake of another and not for the sake of oneself. Indeed, this is a core characteristic of *philia*.

I

Aristotle argues that friendship is mutually reciprocated liking on account of (*dia*) goodness of character, pleasure, or utility.[1] The three grounds of friendship give rise to three basic forms of friendship. In *Nicomachean Ethics* VIII 2, when distinguishing love for inanimate objects from love for people, Aristotle indicates that friends wish good things to one another for the friend's sake,[2] and he identifies this mutual well-wishing with reciprocal goodwill (*eunoia*). His initial characterization of friendship thus suggests that, regardless of which lovable feature (*philêton*) provides a basis for the friendship, a friend has disinterested concern for the good of her friend. However, Aristotle qualifies this initial claim less than twenty lines later in a way that seems to undermine it: Friends wish good to one another insofar as they are friends, so

I am indebted to Emily Austin, Chris Bobonich, Rachel Parsons, Ravi Sharma, and Claudia Yau for their helpful suggestions and criticisms.

friends on account of pleasure or utility wish goods to one another insofar as the other is pleasant or useful to oneself. We are thus led to wonder whether there is genuine other-regarding or disinterested concern only within the complete friendships of virtuous agents. If so, this would saddle Aristotle with a strikingly pessimistic view of most of our relationships, since complete friendships are rare.[3]

Several recent interpretations have put forward different ways of resolving this tension. Some scholars embrace the pessimistic view that only in the complete friendships between virtuous agents is there genuine disinterested concern for the friend.[4] Others, however, including John Cooper,[5] Alexander Nehamas,[6] and Jennifer Whiting,[7] argue that all three kinds of friendship involve non-egoistic wishing well, though they diverge with respect to what, exactly, such well-wishing comes to, and whether it aligns with our contemporary notion of wishing a friend well for his sake. Cooper has influentially argued, preserving Aristotle's initial identification of wishing goods to the friend for his sake and goodwill (*eunoia*), that a friend on account of pleasure or utility wishes goods to her friend for his sake, though the agent's attachment to her own pleasure and utility conditions her well-wishing. That is, "one's first commitment is to [the friend's] retention of the property of pleasantness or advantageousness, and any good one wishes him to have, for his own sake, must be compatible with the retention of that special property under which, as his friend, one wishes him well in the first place."[8] We might worry that this self-interested commitment is at odds with what it is to have disinterested concern for another: To what extent is the agent wishing her friend well for *his* sake when her well-wishing is both informed and constrained by her own interests?

Nehamas shares this worry and supplies a criterion, based on our contemporary conception of wishing and acting for the friend's sake, for assessing the extent of an agent's genuine regard for her friend: The real test of whether an agent wishes her friend goods for his own sake and not merely *not* for the sake of herself is whether she would be willing to sacrifice one of her own interests for his.[9] Nehamas differentiates lacking a self-interested reason for action from being moved to act for the friend's *own* sake. Acting for the friend's *own* sake, as opposed to acting for the *pleasant* friend's sake or the *useful* friend's sake, means acting for the sake of the friend's essence – her virtue. So even though all three forms of *philia* contain wishing and acting for the sake of the friend under some description, only the complete kind between virtuous agents involves doing so for the friend's *own* sake.

The result of Nehamas's proposal is not what we might hope. Instead of concluding that all three forms of friendship contain robust regard for the friend, Nehamas argues that none of them satisfy the self-sacrifice criterion: Not even the virtuous agents in a complete friendship would sacrifice any interests of their own for the sake of the virtuous friend – indeed, in their case, self-sacrifice is impossible. As Aristotle explains at the end of *NE* IX 8, in sacrificing her life for friends or country, the virtuous agent achieves what is fine (*kalon*) for herself.[10] While his reading avoids the unpalatable consequence that all three forms of friendship are wholly self-serving, as all three contain non-egoistic well-wishing, Nehamas maintains: "In no case ... could the interests of another party take precedence over one's own welfare."[11]

Whiting agrees with Cooper that there is genuine other-concern in all three kinds, but, like Nehamas, she distinguishes between the well-wishing found in the complete friendships of virtuous agents and that found in pleasure and utility friendships.[12] In the former case, virtuous agents wish goods to one another for the friend's sake on account of virtue, and thus, as we have seen, on account of who the other essentially is. Whiting argues, *pace* Cooper, that Aristotle's initial use of goodwill (*eunoia*) in *NE* VIII 2 reports a common opinion, and that his revised account of *eunoia* in *NE* IX 5 presents his official view. According to the considered account, Aristotle identifies *eunoia* with this more restricted well-wishing – well-wishing for the sake of who the friend essentially is – found only in character friendships, and, more generally, in the other-regarding attitudes of virtuous agents. In the two latter cases, pleasure and utility friends may wish each other well in particular instances without looking to their own pleasure or gain, but, Whiting claims, the fact that these friendships would come to an end if the friends did not expect to receive pleasure or benefit from the friend suggests that the primary concern remains the agent's own pleasure or benefit.[13] We might worry, however, that this concession supports the conclusion that all Aristotelian friendships are essentially self-interested, for Aristotle also recommends that a virtuous agent should dissolve her character friendship with another agent if he becomes vicious, or failed to advance in virtue in the first place, and his character cannot be improved.[14] Of course, virtue is stable and enduring, and so friendships based on virtue share these properties;[15] it is thus unlikely that dissolution would occur. Nonetheless, if we take contingency and the possibility of dissolution in the absence of the agent's own pleasure, benefit, or good to be the way in which pleasure, utility, and even genuine goodness of character condition friendships, we might find it hard to resist attributing a generally self-interested account of *philia* to Aristotle.

2

I argue that even these defenses of Aristotle's view are too pessimistic. Cooper is right that all three forms of friendship contain at least *some* genuine well-wishing and well-doing for the sake of the friend. Yet that wishing need not entail, *pace* both Cooper and Nehamas, that an agent's first commitment is to her own pleasure or utility. Even if we accept Nehamas's self-sacrifice criterion as a way of assessing the depth of other-regarding concern for our friends, Aristotle's account can satisfy it. This is so despite the fact that, as Whiting argues, *eunoia* is only found in the other-regarding wishes of virtuous agents.

Three distinctions will help to clarify these issues. The first and most important is the commonplace distinction, which Aristotle adopts but modifies, between self-interest and disinterested regard for another;[16] the second is a distinction between a pre-theoretic and a metaphysically informed notion of the self (i.e., the target of well-wishing when an agent wishes another well); the third is Aristotle's distinction between genuine and apparent value.[17] Wishing and acting for the sake of the friend's virtue – for the sake of the friend's genuine, if not self-acknowledged, interests – is the exclusive purview of virtuous agents, for only virtuous agents have the right conception of value; only virtuous agents are capable of fully appreciating and responding to the value of a virtuous friend in the right way. But acting for the sake of the friend's *apparent* interests, and not the agent's own apparent self-interest, remains possible for all agents. Recognizing this will allow us to see how Aristotle's pleasure and utility friendships, which are open to individuals with all sorts of characters, still, to the extent that they count as friendships at all, contain disinterested well-wishing, though they do not contain *eunoia*.

First, Aristotle's initial claim at *NE* VIII 2 1155b31 is, "To a friend, however, *it is said (phasi)*, you must wish goods for his sake." Whiting duly emphasizes the fact that the next statement, in which Aristotle seems to equate *eunoia* and wishing goods to the friend for the friend's sake, is attributed to others, but it is important that this initial claim about wishing goods is also attributed to others. This is not a reason to discount it or to doubt that Aristotle endorses it in some sense, but it is a reason to avoid treating the sketch in VIII 2 as an official definition into which all subsequent claims must be neatly fitted.[18] Similarly, when

Aristotle makes this claim in other contexts, he presents it as a common belief. At the start of *NE* IX 4, for instance, Aristotle enumerates five features that people take to define friendship, the first among which is wishing the friend goods or apparent goods for the friend's sake:

> The defining features of friendship that are found in friendships to one's neighbors would seem to come from (*eleluthenai*) features of friendship toward oneself. For a friend is taken to be (1) someone who wishes and does goods or apparent goods to his friend for the friend's sake; or (2) one who wishes the friend to be and to live for the friend's sake – this is how mothers feel toward their children, and how friends who have been in conflict feel. Others take a friend to be (3) one who spends his time with his friend, and (4) makes the same choices; or (5) one who shares his friend's distress and enjoyment – and this also is especially true of mothers. And people define friend by one of these features.[19]

The first two features make clear that the wishing at issue is for the sake of the friend. I return to this passage in Section 4, but for now it is enough to notice that Aristotle is reporting common beliefs that, I argue, he endorses with technical refinement.

In several other places Aristotle mentions this first characteristic feature as a widely accepted marker of *philia* by drawing a contrast between wishing the friend goods for his sake and self-interested well-wishing. In *Rhetoric* II 4, Aristotle says that liking (*to philein*) is, "wanting for someone what one thinks good, for his sake *and not one's own*, and being inclined, so far as one can, to do such things for him." In *Eudemian Ethics* VII 6, at 1240a23-b11, Aristotle similarly details the defining features of friendship. As in the *Rhetoric*, he likewise sharply distinguishes attitudes and actions that are for the sake of the friend and self-interest:

> For we believe that a friend is someone who wishes good things (or the sort of things he thinks are good) for someone, *not for his own sake but for that person's sake*. In another way, one would most be thought to love a person if one wishes that he should exist, *for his sake and not one's own*, even if one doesn't confer goods on him, let alone existence. In another way, it is the person with whom one chooses to live, *just for the sake of their company and not for any other reason*.[20]

Aristotle's repetition of the self- versus other-regarding contrast in each of the features is striking. The passage culminates by showing how all of these features apply to the virtuous agent's relation to herself, but this application sheds light on the distinction: The virtuous agent wishes goods to her friend with no other motivation, not looking to any return, not even acknowledgment, for that is how an individual wishes goods to herself. Paradigmatic liking or loving consists in other-regarding attitudes and responses, even though, Aristotle argues, it is grounded by the agent's own attraction to and appreciation for some perceived value in the friend.

Aristotle confirms the commonplace conception of liking at the start of *NE* IX 8, where he constructs a puzzle about whether the virtuous person should like herself or someone else most of all, but one might worry that he also undermines it. He explains, establishing the first prong of the dilemma, that the base person seems entirely self-interested, while the decent person acts on account of (*dia*) the fine, and for the sake of (*heneka*) the friend, setting aside her own interests.[21] The second prong of the dilemma invokes Aristotle's earlier claims from *NE* IX 4, which show how the virtuous agent best satisfies the five characteristic features of liking in relation to herself; she, e.g., wishes goods to herself most of all, in the sense that her well-wishing in relation to herself is never due to some ulterior motive, for she does not care whether anyone else knows about her self-regarding wishes.[22] Aristotle's ultimate resolution at the end of the chapter suggests that he rejects the contrast on which it is built: He denies that acting on account of the fine, and for the sake of the friend, could ever require the agent to set aside her own best interests. As we saw, this is precisely Nehamas' worry for the case of virtue friendship. And, indeed, once we accept Aristotle's technical and narrowed conception of selfhood according to which the agent is essentially her virtue, it may be impossible to generate a case of virtue-friendship that would satisfy his self-sacrifice criterion, since Aristotle might deny the existence of genuine conflicts of interest between virtuous agents.

This brings me to the second distinction. In *NE* VIII 2–3, IX 4, and IX 8 – the three places where Aristotle discusses wishing goods for the sake of the friend – he not only identifies it as a common belief, but justifies its status as the central characteristic of liking by appeal to his own substantive metaphysical views. As I discussed, Whiting and Nehamas also notice that Aristotle relies on the technical distinction between essence and accident in VIII 3, arguing that only virtuous agents wish a friend well for the friend's *own* sake, where that means for the sake of who he essentially is – his virtue. Friends in pleasure and utility friendships are friends merely incidentally (*kata sumbebêkos*), for they do not like the friend, and do not wish the friend well, on account of his virtue. And in IX 4 and IX 8 the conception of selfhood or the proper target of well-wishing with which Aristotle operates grows increasingly narrow: He identifies the target of correct well-wishing as the virtuous agent's *nous*.[23] Aristotle's strategy has the effect of introducing a success condition on wishing goods: In order to count as wishing well to the friend for the friend's *own* sake, the well-wishing must be aimed at the friend's virtue.

The third distinction is between genuine goodness and merely apparent goodness. Aristotle's Eudemian argument for the three kinds of friendship in *EE* VII 2 turns on this distinction, and Aristotle introduces the same distinction in our original passage from *NE* VIII 2: "In fact, each one loves not what *is* good for him, but what *appears* good for him." Aristotle claims that the pleasant appears good,[24] but of course, as he explains in *EE* VII 2, what an agent finds pleasant can come apart from what is truly good for her. In the case of the virtuous agent, what appears good and what is genuinely so do not, for the most part, come apart, for she perceives value correctly, and "what is good by nature is good and pleasant in itself for a virtuous person."[25] Virtuous agents alone have the right conception of value, and so virtuous agents alone will share Aristotle's understanding of both the correct, refined target of well-wishing and the sorts of goods that promote the good of that correct target (e.g., encouraging the friend to act virtuously, preventing her from acting viciously).[26] Virtuous agents wish to the friend things that are good for the sake of the friend's virtue.

Aristotle's narrowing of the strictly appropriate target of the virtuous agent's disinterested concern should not, however, cast doubt on his commitment to thinking that a version of the original commonplace distinction between self- and other-regarding concern is present in all friendships. The virtuous agent wishes goods to the friend for the sake of the friend, where that means her wishing looks to the friend's interests and not her own (the commonplace distinction), and her well-wishing is for the sake of the friend's virtue, since that is what her friend's interests, properly understood, consist in. Indeed, in *NE* IX 4 and *EE* VII 6, Aristotle appropriates the common conception of disinterested well-wishing: The features of liking, at least at their best, lack any ulterior motive, and Aristotle's arguments that these features apply most of all to the virtuous agent's attitudes towards herself necessitate taking seriously the claim that they lack any secondary or external consideration.

Furthermore, in *NE* IX 8, in sketching the second horn of the puzzle about whether the virtuous agent should love herself or someone else most of all, Aristotle points out that the virtuous agent wishes goods to herself *even if no one will know about it*. We would expect that here, if anywhere, Aristotle would appeal to his technical account of wishing goods to set up the dilemma, since he needs a contrast with the common view. And he does. But he does not thereby undermine the notion that loving looks to the good of the beloved (even when, as it happens, the loving is also in the interests of the lover, as in the case of proper self-love). The common view is faulty because it does not rest on the correct conception of the self or of value, but it contains an important kernel of truth in the contrast between self-interest and regard for the friend: Aristotle thinks that it is possible and in some cases desirable to wish and act in a way that looks solely to the good of a friend. There is no reason to doubt that the absence of any ulterior, self-interested motive for wishing and acting towards the friend is one aspect of the way that a virtuous agent responds to her virtuous friend. This does not entail that the virtuous agent fails to attend to her own good in general; rather, when she acts in a way that expresses the settled state (*hexis*) of friendship with her virtuous friend, in relation to the friend (as opposed to, say, in a joint virtuous endeavor that aims at the common good), the virtuous agent is moved by her perception of the friend's good to promote and preserve that good.

3

I have been arguing that Aristotle endorses a rarefied version of the commonplace conception of *philia*, according to which friends are those who wish goods to one another for the sake of the friend and not for the sake of themselves. Aristotle supplements the common conception of friendship with his own account of value while preserving the core other-regarding aspect of the commonplace view. If Aristotle's view of *philia* were such that, when conflicts arise, friends always act for the sake of their own apparent ends instead of what they see as the friend's ends, this would represent a stark break with the commonplace view; we would then be left to account for the emphasis that Aristotle seems to place on the other-regarding aspect of friendship. In this section I explain how Aristotle's picture of friendship accommodates cases in which an agent sacrifices, for the sake of her friend, something that she takes to be good for herself.

Recall Nehamas' distinction between not being moved out of self-interest, on the one hand, and being moved out of concern for the friend, on the other. He claims that the former is not sufficient for the latter: The kind of regard that we care about when we talk about loving a friend for her sake requires, according to Nehamas, that a true friend be willing to sacrifice one of her interests to the friend. However, contra the distinction, Aristotle repeatedly treats not being moved out of self-interest as evidence of being moved for the sake of the friend. In *NE* IX 8, the fact that the virtuous agent does not care whether anyone knows of her well-wishing in relation to herself provides a reason for thinking that she best instantiates wishing goods to the beloved for the beloved's own sake. At *NE* VIII 8 1159a34–5 Aristotle deems the activity of loving the virtue of friends, and in arguing for the superiority of loving to being loved, he relies on a favorite case, that of a mother who gave away her child for his sake, even though, as a result, he would never know her.[27] The mother who gives her child away is an exemplar of loving because she loves open-handedly, looking to promote and preserve the beloved's good with no ulterior motive, even at apparent cost to herself.

To be clear, according to Aristotle's technical conception of what it is to wish goods to the friend for the friend's own sake, not being moved out of self-interest can and does come apart from wishing and acting for the sake of the friend himself; the latter requires a correct conception of the self and of value. But this should not trouble us, since the commonplace version of regard for a friend that Aristotle endorses broadly captures what we care about. The mother who gives away her child to save him is sacrificing a deep interest in being a part of his life, in raising him and interacting with him, in being loved in return. She need not act or see herself as acting for the sake of the child's future self, where that means his future virtue. And yet Aristotle thinks she is moved by her love for the child, for, in acting, she is not attending to her interests.

Perhaps one could point out that the mother is still acting in service of her own all-things-considered good in the sense that she is doing what she takes to be best, even though she is not doing what she takes to be best *for herself*. But, read in this way, the self-sacrifice criterion is unsatisfiable: Anytime an agent is rationally acting as she thinks best, all things considered, even if her action is moved wholly by love for another and psychologically aims at the other's good, it will vacuously qualify as in her own interests. While acting solely with an eye to another's good may also contribute to an agent's own good when the agent acts virtuously, this contribution is not sufficient to show that the agent's loving action is perniciously self-serving.[28] Aristotle treats the case of the mother who gives away her child as a stock case of loving precisely because it embodies the other-regarding element of loving.

Aristotle considers in *NE* IX 11 how the presence of a friend lightens the agent's pain when she suffers ill fortune.[29] Because friends are pained by one another's pain, and a decent person wants to avoid causing pain to her friend, she will not be quick to share her sorrows with her friend.[30] She will, on the other hand, go eagerly to see her friend when he is struggling with misfortune, for she aims to mollify his pain.[31] In the Eudemian version of the argument, at *EE* 1245b37–8, Aristotle relies explicitly on the premise that a friend, it is thought, should not choose what is in her own interests. The friend errs on the side of suffering pain herself so that her friend will suffer less. Of course, in so doing she may be acting virtuously, so, once we import Aristotle's technical conception of the self and revised conception of value, her action may not be at odds with her genuine interests, but it nevertheless comes with a cost to herself.

It is difficult to see how an agent might satisfy the self-sacrifice criterion if we examine only virtuous agents or actions that might plausibly be taken to exemplify virtue, for it is not clear whether genuine conflicts of interest are possible between virtuous agents, and so it is not clear that an agent acting virtuously would ever be capable of sacrificing her own genuine interests.[32] Even if conflicts between genuine interests are not possible, conflicts between apparent interests are ubiquitous, and they are sufficient for satisfying the self-sacrifice criterion; it is, after all, a criterion that relies on what *we* mean in wishing the friend well for her sake, and so we need not import Aristotle's refined conceptions of selfhood and genuine goodness. Furthermore, on Aristotle's revised conception of self-love, though the virtuous agent will not see herself as making a sacrifice when she acts for the sake of the fine, this is no reason to doubt that her motivational structure retains the same other-regarding aspect of liking. From the first-person perspective, the virtuous agent is attending to the friend's good and not her own when she acts out of liking.

To be sure, Aristotle seems to think that most people tend, as a matter of fact, to assess their own value charitably and treat their own interests as paramount.[33] We might compare the common human tendency to go to excess when it comes to bodily pleasures (the opposite vice of asceticism is vanishingly rare). Yet Aristotle does not think that people are by nature lascivious gluttons. More troubling, perhaps, is his apparent concession to the normativity of this common phenomenon:

The virtuous agent, as we have seen, wishes goods to herself *most of all*. But, in the conclusion of the *NE* IX 8's puzzle about whether an agent should love herself or someone else most of all, we do not find Aristotle repeating this superlative claim. What we find, rather, is Aristotle confirming an earlier statement from *NE* VIII 5: In loving the friend, the agent loves what is good for herself.[34] In acting for the sake of the fine, for the sake of the friend's good, the virtuous agent realizes her own.[35]

Examining the friendships of vicious agents affords a further consideration in favor of the view I have been sketching. Base people, explains Aristotle, can only be friends to a slight degree,[36] for they associate for their own benefit,[37] or to escape the pain of being with themselves and their own memories and regrets.[38] They cannot be properly like-minded with others, since, as Aristotle says at *NE* IX 6 1167b9–16, they look to their own profit and not to the good of others, and, at *EE* VII 7 1241a27–30, they fight when they cannot both get what they want. And vicious agents like inanimate objects more than people.[39] In all of these explanations of their inferiority as friends, what bad agents are lacking is sufficient regard for others.

Aristotle's comments about the friendships of the bad support a spectrum of disinterested well-wishing. The extent to which an agent wishes goods or apparent goods to her friend with the friend's good or apparent good in mind, and not her own, is one factor that determines the extent to which she genuinely likes, and is a friend to, her friend. It is telling, moreover, that these are Aristotle's criticisms of *bad* people. But this implies that the friendships of non-vicious agents are *not* self-serving to this degree: Most people do not love inanimate objects more than people, and most friends do not fight when they cannot both get what they want. Friendships of all kinds may contain apparent conflicts of interests that vary in magnitude, but people who are not bad compromise, sometimes sacrificing an (apparent) interest for the friend, other times, if the (apparent) interest at stake is too big, sacrificing the friendship.

I have argued that a non-virtuous agent can wish apparent goods to her friend out of loving regard, even if, lacking the correct conception of value, she is unable to wish genuine goods to the friend for his own sake strictly speaking. The commonplace notion of love as concern to promote the good of the friend supplies a crucial aspect of friendship of all kinds. If even non-virtuous – though not thoroughly bad – agents regard their friends in this way to some extent, then virtuous agents, too, will regard their friends in this way to an even higher degree, for virtuous agents more fully exemplify all of the characteristic features of loving. There is a necessary connection between being virtuous and responding to a friend with loving concern for the friend's own sake; there is no necessary connection, however, between lacking virtue and lacking other-regarding concern for the friend. There are, Aristotle explains, many ways to be in error, but only one way to be correct.[40]

Another reason for thinking that pleasure and utility friendships will not be devoid of well-wishing and well-doing for the sake of the friend is that virtuous agents, too, participate in them.[41] A virtuous agent may, for instance, like and form a pleasure friendship with a witty person.[42] Though it is pleasure that grounds her attachment to her witty friend and shapes the way that she expresses liking, the virtuous agent's virtue also invariably shapes her interactions. When the non-virtuous witty friend tells a crass and hurtful joke, the virtuous agent will not find it funny. What she finds funny, and takes pleasure in, are *good* jokes. Not laughing at her friend's joke is not in his apparent interests, but it is in his genuine interests, for though he wanted his pleasure-friend to laugh at his joke, to share pleasure with her, she resisted, and in so doing promoted his good by preventing him from taking further pleasure in the vicious joke.

So too, in the utility case, Aristotle explains at *EE* VII 2 1238b1–9 that a virtuous friend will wish her non-virtuous friend whatever is in fact good for him, given the condition of his soul. That is, Aristotle endorses a version of the dependency thesis,[43] according to which the value of external goods like wealth depends on virtue. Wealth is only genuinely good for the virtuous agent, since only virtuous agents are in a position to use it well, though it appears good to most people. The virtuous agent may, then, wish poverty to her non-virtuous friend, as that might be what is genuinely good for him, for it would prevent him from committing vicious actions with the money and so promote his virtue. Of course, he will likely think his friend is thwarting his interests, and it is true that she is thwarting his apparent interests, but her wish is in his genuine interests. In both of these cases, there are apparent conflicts of interest, and these friendships may dissolve as a result. But they need not. Regardless of the outcome, the virtuous agent's first commitment is always to virtue, both her own and that of her friends, even within pleasure and utility cases, though pleasure or utility explain why, in these cases, she likes the friend.

We are now in a position to see how the fact that all friendships are subject to dissolution when their grounds – whether pleasure, utility, or genuine goodness – fail to obtain is not objectionably self-serving. All three kinds of friendships contain, to differing degrees, wishing and acting for the friend's sake without an eye to one's own interests. And all three kinds of friendship are also such that the agents within them take one another to be in some way good; apparent value of the friend sustains all friendships. But that is as it should be. Within the context of a friendship, the agent might well give up her afternoon plans to rock climb in order to help a friend in need without a second thought. But if it turned out that she was regularly going to the aid of a friend who she ceased to find likable, she would be well advised to examine the relationship: Why should an agent stay in a relationship with a person she does not find good solely for the other's benefit? That is not friendship; that is servitude. Friendship is equality and reciprocity.[44] We should hope that people leave relationships when they cease to find those relationships valuable.

4

I have been defending an interpretation of Aristotelian *philia* according to which all friendships contain well-wishing for the sake of the friend. But we might wonder about Aristotle's use of the claim, in the context of *NE* IX 4, that the virtuous agent's virtuous friend is "another self."[45] One might construe this claim as a reason for thinking that Aristotle accords primacy to self-interest. According to a prominent vein of interpretation, when Aristotle claims that a friend is another self, he means not only that the agent adopts the same set of attitudes towards her friend that she has towards herself, but, moreover, that the adoption of these attitudes is justified precisely because and insofar as she sees the friend *as herself*. Because she sees the friend's rational activities as expressions of her own rational agency, his virtuous activities are, along with the virtuous agent's own, constitutive of her *eudaimonia*.[46] I call these views self-extension views. There are several difficulties with these views; I briefly mention three of them.

First, as Whiting convincingly argues,[47] this justification strategy subsumes the friend's interests – indeed, it subsumes the friend. In making the friend a part of the self, self-extension views are at odds with Aristotle's insistence that the virtuous friend wishes and does well for her virtuous friend for the friend's own sake, as opposed to her own; the opposition is lost. Second, although *NE* IX 4 does rely on the claim that the friend is a second self, it does so in an argument that draws a parallel between the good person's loving attitudes towards herself and her loving attitudes towards her virtuous close friend. What justifies these attitudes in both cases is the beloved's genuine goodness, and not the beloved's status as a self. Indeed, these attitudes are only found in agents who suppose themselves decent.[48] Third, any attempt to justify or even explain, on the basis of IX 4, how an agent comes to develop appropriate other-regarding concern for others in the first place must confront the fact that the starting point of Aristotle's argument is the decent agent. Aristotle's decent person is concessive and accommodating, sometimes taking less than she justly could in order to benefit another.[49] The first half of NE IX 4 cannot, then, be an argument that accounts for how the already decent person extends proper regard to others in general.

I claimed earlier that Aristotle supposes it is possible to have concern for the friend's good for his sake. But he does not *argue* for it. He *assumes* that other-regarding concern is possible when he reports and continues to endorse this aspect of the common view of what it is to love someone. Julia Annas[50] and Richard Kraut[51] also maintain that Aristotle neither conceives of self-love as explanatorily basic nor reduces regard for others to self-love. Returning again to the opening of NE IX 4, we see that Aristotle's first task in the chapter is reconciling the set of features that characterize liking. Recall that when Aristotle lists the five markers of friendship, he is reporting the views of others. These others do not all share the same views about who counts as a friend. Some people, but presumably not others, believe, e.g., that a friend is one who spends time with his friend. In the Eudemian analogue of this argument, Aristotle makes the disagreement explicit.[52] Directly following the list of characteristic features, at EE VII 6 1240a30–3, he explains, "All of these views clash with each other. Some people think that they are not loved if the other party doesn't wish good things for them, others if the other party does not wish that they should exist, others if the other party does not wish to live with them." The people who falsely believe that they are not loved if a particular one of these characteristic features is missing are mistaken, thinks Aristotle, since each of these features can constitute an expression of liking.

The conclusion of the first half of NE IX 4 confirms that what Aristotle is explaining is why we are entitled to count as a friend someone who exhibits one of these features with our awareness and reciprocity: "Hence friendship seems to be one of these features, and people with these features seem to be friends."[53] All of these features are in fact genuine manifestations of liking, and what legitimizes all of these competing markers of friendship is the case of the individual virtuous agent, for she is, as Aristotle points out, a normative standard.[54] The way that Aristotle defends these features as expressions of loving is by reference to the virtuous agent, but it is not in relation to herself as such that the virtuous agent possesses these features; it is, rather, in relation to herself *as good*. For it is only insofar as and to the extent that an agent takes herself to be decent that she possesses these features.[55]

If we think back to the initial argument for three kinds of friendship that Aristotle presented in *NE* VIII 2, the conclusion of *NE* IX 4 comes as no surprise: Perceiving value in an object or person is precisely what gives rise to and sustains liking. Liking is a psychological response to perceived value. So when Aristotle claims that the decent person is related to her friend as she is related to herself, since the friend is another self, he is not claiming that what *justifies* the presence of these attitudes towards the friend is the fact that the friend is another *self*; it is, instead, the fact that the friend is good, which is also, in the case of the decent person, a way of being relevantly similar to oneself. Now, to be sure, Aristotle grants that most people *suppose* themselves to be decent, but this is because, by nature, each thing is pleasant to itself.[56] An individual does not have to be genuinely good in order to like herself, but she needs to find herself pleasant – i.e. apparently good. The fact, then, that an agent's friend is another self does help to *explain*, psychologically, why she likes him, since it indicates that she finds him pleasant. But unless her pleasure is the pleasure of the virtuous agent, rooted in his genuine goodness, it is not justified.

We are now in a position to make sense of Aristotle's claim at the start of *NE* IX 4 that the features of friendship "come from" (*eleluthenai*) the attitudes that the decent person possesses towards herself. Aristotle does not mean that the good person is justified in extending self-love to her virtuous friend by seeing the friend *qua* self; we should reject self-extension views. Kraut succinctly sums it up: "Friendship towards others 'comes from' self-love in the sense that the latter provides the paradigm case of the attitudes characteristic of the former."[57] If we want to get a grip on the features that express genuine and optimally instantiated loving – loving to the fullest extent – we should look to the virtuous agent's attitudes towards herself.

Good people are friends most of all,[58] but it does not follow that all of our friendships should aspire to complete friendship. For one thing, we are psychologically limited in the number of intimate friendships that we can have, since we cannot live with (*suzên*) many people at once, nor can we share joys and sorrows with many people at the same time.[59]

For another, we ought to regard friends of different kinds in different ways; not every feature of liking should be expressed towards every person the agent likes. This set of characteristics of friends crosscuts the threefold distinction in types of friendship, but they are not unrelated. In finding the friend good in some way, an individual expresses her perception of the friend's value through one or more of these features. Friends who take pleasure in one another, for example, wish to spend time together and live together (suzên), and this is most characteristic of friends.[60] The way that we find someone good, and thus the basis on account of which we like him – pleasure, utility, or virtue – shapes the way we respond to him, the way we love him, and so the wishes and desires we have in relation to him. But in no case does the well-wishing of a *friend* collapse into self-interested well-wishing.

NOTES

1. I use both "liking" and "loving" to translate to philein. I do not intend "loving" to have erotic connotations, but instead to indicate something the same in kind as, but stronger than, liking. Aristotle, in contrast with Plato, devotes very little attention to erotic love (eros). Where eros does occur, Aristotle tends to denigrate it, tacitly comparing erotic relationships, which are based on pleasure, unfavorably with character friendship (see, e.g., NE VIII 4 1157a6–10). I also use "like" and "love" interchangeably with "be a friend to" when the liking or loving occurs within the context of a friendship, since my focus is the voluntary friendships of equal mature agents. At NE VIII 2 1155b27–1156a5 and EE VII 2 1236a7–15, Aristotle explains philia in terms of mutually aware and reciprocated liking on one of these three grounds (pleasure, utility, and goodness), but only in the NE version does he present the first characteristic feature of liking – wishing goods to the friend for his sake – as part of the initial account. The EE version does not confront the tension in the NE version.

2. NE VIII 2 1155b31.

3. NE VIII 3 1156b25, NE VIII 6 1158a10–11, EE VII 2 1237b34–5.

4. Irwin, e.g., in the notes to his Nicomachean Ethics translation, endorses the view that unqualified eunoia and wishing goods to the friend for the friend's sake are found only in complete friendships.

5. Cooper (1999a).

6. Nehamas (2010).

7. Whiting (2006).

8. Cooper (1999a) 326.

9. Nehamas (2010) 224.

10. *NE* IX 8 1169a18–34.

11. Nehamas (2010) 236.

12. Whiting (2006) 281–7.

13. Whiting (2006) 287.

14. *NE* IX 3 1165b13–31.

15. *NE* VIII 3 1156b11–12, 17–19; *NE* VIII 8 1159b4–5; *NE* IX 1 1164a11–13.

16. I avoid referring to the common view as an *endoxon*, since Aristotle himself does not label it as such. Recent work on Aristotle's methodology casts doubt on equating commonly accepted beliefs and *endoxa*. See Frede (2012).

17. On the role of merely apparent value in Aristotle's psychology, see Moss (2012).

18. Aristotle does not think that friendship admits of a single definition (*EE* VII 2 1236a16–18, b23). In the Eudemian analysis, he explains at 1236a17–18, b26 that the three kinds of friendship are focally related (*pros hen*). The primary kind of friendship is between virtuous agents who are drawn to one another on the basis of virtue. The accounts of pleasure and utility friendships make reference to the primary kind of friendship, but not vice versa (1236a20–2). In the *NE* Aristotle says that the kinds of friendship relate by resemblance (VIII 4 1157a1, a31–2, 1157b5, VIII 6 1158b6).

19. *NE* IX 4 1166a1–10.

20. *EE* VII 6 1240a23–9.

21. *NE* IX 8 1168a33–5.

22. *NE* IX 8 1168b3–4.

23. At *NE* IX 4 1166a16–17 and a26–27, Aristotle refers to the thinking part of the soul (*dianoêtikon*) and the decent person's thought (*dianoia*), respectively; at IX 8 1168b34–1169a3, a17–18 he uses understanding (*nous*). I do not take a stand on exactly how Aristotle conceives the self in this context. For my argument, what matters is that his conception of the self is narrower than the common Greek conception and requires the cultivation of our natural capacities for virtue, or some subset of the virtues. See Kahn (1981) and Stern-Gillet (1995) for views that treat the identification of the agent with her *nous* in the *NE* account of friendship as essential for grasping how friends contribute to the value of our lives. See Kraut (1989) for a less narrow conception of the agent.

24. *EE* VII 2 1235b26–29; cf. *EE* II 10 1227a39, *NE* III 4 1113a33-b2.

25. *NE* IX 9 1170a14–16; cf. *EE* VII 2 1237a3–9, *NE* X 5 1176a15–29.

26. *NE* VIII 8 1159b5–7.

27. *NE* VIII 8 1159a27–33. On mothers as exemplars of loving, see *NE* VIII 12 1161b26, *NE* IX 4 1166a5, a8–9, *NE* IX 7 1168a24–6, *EE* VII 6 1240a35–6, *EE* VII 8 1241b7–9. At *EE* VII 4 1239a35-b2, Aristotle explains how the desire to *be* loved is

self-serving, and he provides the reference for the example to which he alludes at *NE* VIII 8 1159a27–33: Andromache in Antiphon's tragedy gave up her son. Similarly, he reports at *EE* VII 12 1245b29–31, "Heracles' mother chose for him to be a god rather than to stay with her and be a slave to Eurystheus."

28. I remain neutral about whether Aristotle is committed to rational eudaimonism. Whether or not there is some sense in which all of the agent's actions aim at her own *eudaimonia*, Aristotle's accounts of *philia* indicate that a friend, *qua* friend, does not attend to her own good while acting for the sake of her friend.

29. *NE* IX 11 1171a27–34.

30. *NE* IX 11 1171b5–10, b16–17; cf. *EE* VII 12 1245b33–1246a2.

31. *NE* IX 11 1171b20–1.

32. Kraut (1989) argues that genuine conflicts of interest are possible and that virtuous agents compete for the fine (see ch. 2, esp. 125–8). I am hesitant about the possibility of genuine conflicts where virtue is concerned, given that ceding an opportunity for virtuous action to a friend is itself virtuous (*NE* IX 8 1169a32–4). But if Kraut is right, then Aristotle's view even more readily satisfies the self-sacrifice criterion.

33. *EE* VII 4 1239a15–17.

34. *NE* VIII 5 1157b33.

35. Whiting (2006) 302 puts the point well.

36. *NE* IX 6 1167b9–16.

37. *NE* VIII 4 1157a19–20; cf. Aristotle's remarks about "the many" at *NE* VIII 14 1163b25–8, *NE* IX 7 1167b27–8.

38. *NE* IX 4 1166b13–17.

39. *EE* VII 2 1237b30–2.

40. *NE* II 6 1106b30–2, *NE* VIII 8 1159b7–9, *EE* VII 5 1239b11–12. Vice is multiform; some vices are excessively rather than deficiently other-regarding. The obsequious agent desires to produce pleasure in others with no ulterior motive (*NE* IV 6 1127a8).

41. At *NE* IX 10 1170b23–9, Aristotle grants that an agent should only have a few friends for utility and for pleasure, but, in context, the agent is clearly someone who is serving as a normative standard.

42. *NE* VIII 3 1156a13, *NE* VIII 6 1158a31.

43. I here adopt the terminology that Bobonich (2002) 131–53, 179–85, applies to Plato.

44. *NE* VIII 2 1155b27–31, VIII 3 1156b7–17, VIII 4 1156b34–5, VIII 5 1157b33–1158a1, VIII 6 1158b1–3. Aristotle also addresses unequal friendships, but even in these cases there must be a return to equalize the relationship. The friend who has less worth in one respect must compensate in another respect. For example, if the agent receives money or virtue as a benefit from her friend, she owes him honor in return (*NE* VIII 14 1163b13–14).

45. *NE* IX 4 1166a31–2.

46. Terence Irwin (1988) 393 offers this formulation of self-extension. Whiting (1991) dubs views of this kind "colonizing ego" views.

47. See both Whiting (1991) and (2006). I am deeply indebted to Whiting's work on this topic.

48. *NE* IX 4 1166b2–6.

49. *NE* V 10 (=*EE* IV 10) 1237b34–1238a1.

50. Annas (1988) and (1993) 249–62.

51. Kraut (1989) 131–34.

52. Aristotle's discussion of self-love in *EE* VII 6 is admittedly very different from *NE* IX 4. I cannot discuss these differences here. It suffices for our purposes that in both texts different people have different views about what counts as liking.

53. *NE* IX 4 1166a32–3.

54. *NE* IX 4 1166a10–13.

55. *NE* IX 4 1166a11, 1166b2–6.

56. *EE* VII 5 1239b18; cf. *EE* VII 2 1237a26–9, *NE* VIII 3 1156b15–16.

57. Kraut (1989) 132.

58. *NE* VIII 3 1156b10, b23–4, *NE* VIII 5 1157b25.

59. *NE* IX 10 1171a3–20; cf. *NE* VIII 6 1158a10–13, *EE* VII 2 1238a8–10, *EE* VII 12 1245b23–5.

60. *NE* VIII 3 1156b4–6, *NE* VIII 5 1157b17–24, *NE* VIII 6 1158a8–10, a23–25, *NE* IX 12 1172a3–8, *EE* VII 12 1245a18–22, a37-b7.

IV   The Hellenistics and Beyond

9 Epicurus and the Epicureans on Ethics

Raphael Woolf

I

In English the term "epicurean" suggests a devotee of fine dining or, more generally, a dedicated pursuer of sensual pleasure. Yet Epicurus himself (341–270 BC), founder of the ethical tradition considered in this chapter, and from whose name the term is derived, would not, it seems, have approved. The following is an excerpt from the main surviving text on ethics by Epicurus, the *Letter to Menoeceus*:[1]

> [W]hat produces the pleasant life is not continuous drinking and parties ... or the enjoyment of fish and the other dishes of an expensive table, but sober reasoning which tracks down the causes of every choice and avoidance, and which drives out the opinions that beset souls with the greatest confusion. *(LM 132)*

Our modern epicurean would, perhaps, be disappointed. But while the historical question of how "epicurean" acquired its meaning is not one I shall pursue here, from a philosophical point of view, the connection between the actual tenets of ancient Epicurean ethics and the sort of life suggested by the modern term is a little less distant than the above citation might suggest.

2

Fundamentally, Epicureanism is a hedonistic philosophy, one which holds that pleasure is the ultimate source of value. While Epicurus deems things other than pleasure to be of value, for example, wisdom (*LM* 132) and self-sufficiency (*LM* 130), it is clear that these are adjudged so because they assist in the maximization of pleasure. As Epicurus puts it, "pleasure is the beginning and end of the blessed life" (*LM* 128). It is the "end" in that it is the goal whose attainment, correctly understood (a point I shall return to below), will give us a happy life. It is the "beginning" in the sense that, according to Epicurus, we treat pleasure from our earliest days as our principal goal.[2]

Cicero elaborates on the latter point in his ethical work *De Finibus* (*On Ends*), via his Epicurean spokesman Torquatus:

> Every animal, as soon as it is born, seeks pleasure and rejoices in it as the greatest good, while shunning pain as the greatest evil and avoiding it as much as possible. This is behavior that has not yet been corrupted, when nature's judgment is pure and whole.   (On Ends *1.30*)

This text is an example of what is sometimes known as a "cradle argument."[3] Epicureans take the natural, instinctual behavior of animals and infant humans as normative – that is, they regard what we do in a state unencumbered by (later) conventions and beliefs as the best guide to what we *ought* to do to live a happy life. Correspondingly, Epicurus holds that in the ethical context feeling (*pathos*) is the ethical "criterion" or "measure" (*kanôn, LM* 129) – that is, the means by which we determine things as good or bad. The notion of a criterion is an important part of Epicurean methodology, which regards sensation generally (including sense-perception and feeling) as a foundational source of truth about the world.[4]

3

This is, however, in the ethical domain, indeed only the beginning. As our opening quotation from *LM* 132 shows (Section 1 above), Epicurus allots to reason an important role in the figuring out of which pleasures and pains should be chosen and avoided. He says that while all pleasure is good and all pain bad, not every pleasure is chosen nor every pain avoided (*LM* 129): Sometimes avoiding certain pleasures prevents greater pains – consider, for example, the adoption of a diet low in sugar in order to avoid tooth decay and other painful conditions. Likewise, he says, certain pains bring greater pleasures in their wake – one might think of the health benefits, and corresponding increase in the pleasantness of one's life, of strenuous exercise, for example.

The role of reason brings into focus two related features of Epicurean theory. Firstly, it is eudaimonistic: It takes the primary goal of ethical theory to be the specification of happiness (*eudaimonia*). As we shall see, some important aspects of Epicurean ethical theory can be explained with reference to this eudaimonistic constraint. Secondly, it takes itself to be laying out the contours of a happy *life*. In particular, it assumes that human existence is characterized by a certain structure, rather than consisting of an unconnected series of momentary events. In the hedonistic context, that means we need to reflect on the consequences of our selection of individual pleasures and pains so as to determine what maximizes the pleasantness of our lives overall.[5]

Reason, then, does not supplant feeling as the criterion, but it does enable us to bring about a life for ourselves that is as pleasurable as possible. Epicurus thinks that many of the beliefs that humans find themselves with as they grow up in their societies are ones that militate against the living of a maximally pleasant life. Most humans do not live their lives in full accord with their nature, pursuing such false idols as wealth and fame, when these sorts of objectives will, in Epicurus' view, fail to produce the desired end of a maximally pleasant life. Reason is needed to correct such wrongheadedness.

4

This brings us to one of the most distinctive and controversial components of Epicurean hedonism. It turns out to be a very specific form of pleasure that constitutes the goal of our lives:

> When we say that pleasure is the goal we do not mean the pleasures of the dissolute and those that consist in enjoyment ... but freedom from pain in the body and from disturbance in the soul. *(LM 131)*

Epicurean hedonism thus lays down as its goal the attainment of a physically pain-free and mentally untroubled existence. Two questions present themselves at this point: (1) why does Epicurus think that just this is the form of pleasure we should aspire to; and (2) why does he think that freedom from pain and distress is a form of pleasure at all?[6] The answer to (1) is, it seems to me, given by the general structure of eudaimonistic theories that Epicurus aligns himself with. To do justice to our intuitions about its value and importance, we must regard happiness as something that is within our power to acquire and retain. It represents, after all, the fulfillment of our human nature, and should not therefore be something that is overly dependent on contingencies outside our control. Epicurus declares:

> What frees us from mental disturbance and produces significant joy is not possession of huge wealth, nor the respect and admiration of the multitude, nor anything else that depends on indeterminate causes.
>
> *(SV 81)*

Why is freedom from pain and distress regarded as most secure against contingency? The answer for Epicurus is a point about what accords with our nature. "Everything natural is easy to procure, but what is empty is hard to procure" (*LM* 130). Our genuine needs, according to Epicurus, are few and easily met. Satisfaction of our physical wants, both present and future, is within our power. And if that is so, then there is no reason for us to have troubled minds. By contrast, the main sources of physical and mental discomfort are our own misguided efforts to seek far more than we actually need.

5

This view is underpinned by the Epicurean categorization of desires. Epicurus divides desires, first, into those that are natural and those that are empty; and then subdivides natural desires into necessary and non-necessary (*LM* 127). Empty desires, which he refers to as being due to "empty opinion," are neither natural nor necessary (*PD* 29). Necessary desires in turn consist in those that are necessary for life, for lack of bodily discomfort, and for happiness (*LM* 127). One can clearly be alive without being free from bodily discomfort; and one can be free from bodily discomfort without being happy. One might then speak of the desires to eat and drink as necessary if we are to be alive; the desires for, say, certain amounts or kinds of food and drink as being necessary for lack of bodily discomfort; desires necessary for happiness are perhaps those concerned with the way one wants one's life to be. At *LM* 126, Epicurus characterizes the good Epicurean as being one who seeks to enjoy the most pleasant, not the longest, time, just as people choose the most pleasant food rather than the largest portion. Desires necessary for happiness, then, might be for those general features, such as simple living and lack of toil, that character-ize an Epicurean good life.

Working back up the division of desires, Epicurus tells us that unnecessary desires are those that do not bring on pain when unsatisfied (*PD* 26). What this must mean, I think, in contrast with the idea of a necessary desire, is that any form of desire which does not have pain as an intrinsic consequence, should the desire be unsatisfied, is to be classified as non-necessary. Epicurus does not mean that if I have, say, a desire for caviar, then I might not feel pain – or at least pained – if the desire is unsatisfied. Rather, there is nothing in the nature of such a desire that entails pain pursuant to its being unsatisfied. Contrast this with basic desires, such as hunger or thirst, which inevitably cause pain if left unheeded.

The wise person, then, is the one who sees that only necessary desires need be pursued and who is thereby able to restrict his desires accordingly. Desire for luxuries, or for fame and wealth, are not only unnecessary but often enough militate against happiness in virtue of the toil, physical and mental, that those driven to satisfy them undergo. It is, nonetheless, significant that Epicurus' fundamental distinction is between what is natural and what is (as he calls it) empty, rather than between the necessary and unnecessary. All that we *need* to survive and thrive are things easy to procure: bread and water rather than cake and wine (cf. *LM* 131). But since one can satisfy natural desires such as hunger and thirst with cake and wine, as well as with bread and water, a desire for cake and wine can be regarded as natural, albeit non-necessary; such desires should be pursued if (but only if) they cause no harm (*SV* 21). If pursued with intensity, they too are due to empty opinion (*PD* 30).

An ancient "scholion," or note, on *PD* 29 suggests that natural but non-necessary desires are for such things as luxurious food, whereas empty (that is, neither natural nor necessary) desires are for such things as fame. That may not quite be right, since intensity of pursuit of the object makes a difference, as we saw, to how a given desire should be classified. That desires hard to satisfy are said by Epicurus to be due to empty *opinion* suggests, in any case, a broadly rationalistic outlook: It is the (false) opinions we have about the value of things that cause us to desire or (as the case may be) to fear them disproportionately. And as we saw in Section 1 above, reason drives out false opinion. We can, by rational reflection, come to reject our opinions as false, and by so doing shed the fears and desires we were subject to by holding them.

6

Indeed, the tackling of people's false outlooks is integral to the Epicurean approach. Epicurus uses medical terminology to express the idea: Philosophy, he is reported as saying, is of no use if it fails to expel suffering from the soul as medicine provides therapy for illnesses of the body;[7] and he bids us "heal ourselves" rather than worry about the esteem of others (*SV* 64): Genuine philosophizing brings genuine health (*SV* 54).

I shall not discuss in detail the workings of Epicurean psychotherapy,[8] but will emphasize here its rationalistic elements in keeping with the notion that misguided beliefs often lie at the root of human unhappiness, such that removing these will rid us of needless fear and desire, and dispel our unhappiness, commensurately. If it is our fears that Epicurus seems chiefly to focus on in the therapeutic context – though desires are certainly included as one of the main items the control of which is said to be the point of studying natural science (PD 11) – that is perhaps because he sees our vain pursuit of supposedly desirable goods, such as wealth, fame, and power, as deriving ultimately from our insecurities (see e.g. PD 7).

There is, I think, a stronger and a weaker rationalism at play in therapeutic mode. The stronger version sees the curing of our psychological ills as a matter of providing arguments and explanations concerning, for example, the true nature of death and the gods, such that, in coming to be rationally persuaded of their harmlessness, we cease to regard them as objects of dread. The weaker version advises us to get the appropriate Epicurean doctrines ingrained in our psyche, whether or not we have fully grasped the arguments for them. Sometimes, then, Epicurus speaks of his work providing reasoning and explanation that will enable his followers to remember what conduces to a happy life (LH 82, LP 84–5). Sometimes he simply speaks of one needing to remember "the most important matters" or "a basic outline" (LH 35), where the memorizing seems to carry more weight than the following of argument. An example of this would be the famous "four-fold remedy" (tetrapharmakos), preserved in a papyrus fragment of the Epicurean philosopher Philodemus: "God presents no fears, death no worries; what is good is easily obtained, what is bad is easily endured." Even where Epicurus describes our anxieties about god and death as based not on beliefs but on what he calls "some crazed irrationality," the cure seems to be the continuous remembrance of the most important points of Epicurean doctrine (LH 81–2). While our terrors might not always be the consequence of anything as clear and articulable as a set of beliefs, it is the acquisition of the right set of beliefs that will chase the terrors away.

It seems likely that both elements – the understanding of argument, and the memorizing of doctrine – have a role to play in Epicurean therapy, perhaps partly depending on the state of progress of the individual: Epicurus speaks of those "not fully initiated" silently running through the principal points (LH 83). And it may be that the two elements are not entirely separable. Epicurus famously enjoins us to accustom ourselves to believing that death is nothing to us (LM 124), where "accustoming" may suggest a process of rote repetition of a slogan, but what follows in the text is actually a miniature argument: All good and evil lies in sensation, and death is the absence of sensation; so death is nothing to us. Both of the premises are based on more detailed Epicurean physics and epistemology, which one would need to master to have a fully rational underpinning for one's belief in the conclusion. Meanwhile, though, it seems that habitually going through the miniature argument is one route to our becoming committed to its conclusion. Conversely, Epicurus holds that the inability to offer a concise summary of the main points of his system may itself indicate a failure to have genuinely comprehended it (LH 36).

7

Let us, then, recap its basic ethical tenets. The goal of our lives is the attainment of freedom from physical pain and mental distress. This is a state achieved through the fulfilling of our natural needs – which are few and easy to satisfy – and by a corresponding confidence that those needs will be satisfied in future too. Desires for anything beyond that being illusory, and treatable by our coming to adopt correct beliefs, tranquility is at hand.

We can see, in the light of this, that Epicurus need not – and does not – have a problem with luxury per se. It is the over-valuation of luxury, in particular the belief that we need it for a happy life, that he targets. He advocates self-sufficiency, but not, he says, so that we use few resources come what may, but to enable us to be satisfied with few if we don't have many and to realize that the ones who enjoy luxury most are those who need it least (LM 130).[9] Our modern epicurean, then, can find some connection with authentic Epicurean doctrine. At any rate, one who enjoys whatever luxuries life may bring, without either expending great trouble on getting them, or minding greatly if one lacks them, would be close to leading a properly Epicurean life.

But this only highlights the second of the two questions that I raised, in Section 4 above, about Epicurean hedonism: Even if we regard freedom from pain and distress as the right ethical goal, why should that state be considered a form of *pleasure*? Epicurus takes sides here in a debate that was already established in his day, about whether or not absence of pain constitutes a neutral state between pain and pleasure. He is clear that it does not (LM 128), and that absence of the pain of want in fact marks the maximum physical pleasure, while reflection on what causes the greatest fear – Epicurus means chiefly pain, death, and the gods (PD 10) – secures the maximum pleasure of the mind (PD 18). In short, freedom from pain and distress constitutes maximal pleasure.

Is he right? One needs to distinguish two theses here, both of which Epicurus holds: Firstly, freedom from pain and distress is a form of pleasure; secondly, and more strongly, pleasure is at its height when we are in the condition of freedom from pain and distress. One plausible way of defending the first thesis is to distinguish various senses in which we might call something a pleasure. For example, we might think of a pleasure as a certain sort of feeling; but we might also think of a pleasure as something that we take pleasure in, or enjoy, where this need not imply the presence of any particular sort of felt sensation. Thus stepping when cold into a warm bath will give me a distinctive sort of sensation; enjoying the gleam of my freshly cleaned bath may not, but the gleam is still something I can be said to take pleasure in.

Perhaps, then, Epicurus means that freedom from pain and distress is a pleasure of this sort: something we enjoy but which is not necessarily characterized by a pleasant feeling. Thus we might on Epicurus' behalf retain the idea that (mere) absence of pain and distress is, in terms of feeling, neutral, while admitting that it is certainly a state that I can enjoy being in.[10] However, the problems of reading Epicurus this way seem to me to outweigh the benefits. For if one drops the connection of pleasure with feeling, then we seem to have abandoned what Epicurus himself tells us is the criterion of value.[11] Now it is true that the Greek term *pathos* that Epicurus uses to pick out the criterion can mean, more broadly, "affection" – that is, any way of being affected or acted upon.[12] But his proposal is that pleasure is the good on the grounds (*hôs*) that we judge good by the criterion of affection (*LM* 129); and what marks off pleasure, as a way of being affected, from other candidates for goods is precisely its felt character. If so, then it seems hard to make sense of Epicurus' position if it posits as the goal of our lives something he insists is pleasure but does not essentially have that character.

Why, though, does Epicurus affirm not just that freedom from pain and distress is a form of pleasure, but that maximal pleasure is reached once one is in that state? Here, I think, the eudaimonistic framework is important, in particular the idea that happiness, once attained, must be something permanent and secure, free to the greatest possible extent from contingencies. At this point we need to note an Epicurean distinction between two forms of pleasure – "kinetic" and "katastematic." What the distinction amounts to is a matter of controversy that I shall not pursue here.[13] For present purposes one may take it as referring to a distinction between pleasure as a standing state and pleasure as episodic. The paradigmatic katastematic pleasures would thus be the states of freedom from pain and distress that represent the Epicurean goal. Examples of kinetic pleasures might be watching a sunset, sipping a fine wine or perhaps (though this again is a matter of controversy) a pleasure of replenishment such as drinking when thirsty.

With this in hand, we can see how freedom from pain and distress, given Epicurus' view that it is a pleasant state minimally dependent on external contingencies, can meet the formal criteria for happiness. Happiness being something stable and persisting, it makes sense to deny that it can be significantly increased or decreased by reference to external circumstance. Thus Epicurus insists that once one has reached a state of freedom from pain, one's pleasure cannot be increased, but is only "embellished" or "varied" (*poikilletai*, PD 18). That seems on the face of it implausible: Surely being in that state and enjoying, in addition, a sunset is more pleasant than being in it without the sunset to enjoy? But perhaps if we regard freedom from pain and distress as a state of joyous and abiding tranquility, which enables one to enjoy to the full whatever other pleasures may come one's way, there is an important truth captured in the claim that the addition of other pleasures will merely vary or embellish the pleasantness of one's life. To talk of increase would be to misrepresent the role of freedom from pain and distress as one substitutable pleasure among others, rather than as the core component of the pleasant life, whose character is not fundamentally altered by the presence or absence of episodic pleasures.

8

Reaching the state of freedom from pain and distress requires, as we have seen, that we avoid or rid ourselves of a number of fears that could plausibly upset our peace of mind, chief among them the fear of pain, of death and of the gods. The cure for such fears is Epicurean natural science (PD 11 and 12); and having briefly discussed, in Section 6 above, the method of applying the cure, let us also touch briefly on some salient aspects of its content. The world is made up of atoms moving in the void (LH 39–41); and though there are gods, they do not interfere in human affairs, which would require toil and trouble incompatible with their blessed existence (LH 76–7). Correspondingly, various celestial and meteorological phenomena can be explained not as signs of divine wrath but in naturalistic terms (see e.g. LP 100–6); humans themselves are atomic compounds which dissipate upon death (PD 2).

The consequence of this last point is that we do not survive death as sentient beings; and since without sentience there is no pain (or anything else) that one can experience, death should hold no terrors for a rational person.[14] One might reply that it is precisely the extinction brought on by death that we fear, a point Epicurus is well aware of (LH 81). The Roman poet and Epicurean follower Lucretius, in his famous Latin poem on Epicurean philosophy De Rerum Natura (On the Nature of Things), presents in Book 3 a series of arguments in favor of the view that, given that death means we no longer exist, it ought not to be feared. One of the most influential of these arguments is the so-called Symmetry Argument, which states in a nutshell that since we do not bemoan our past non-existence prior to our birth, it is inconsistent to mind about our future non-existence after our death.[15]

This sort of argument seems to overlook a rather significant asymmetry. When we die, we stand to lose, especially if we have been good Epicureans, the wonderful life that we have been enjoying. When we did not yet exist, we had nothing to lose. Dying deprives us of goods that we have by being alive. It is the loss (rather than mere lack) of goods that creates the asymmetry and makes it reasonable to adopt a distinctively negative attitude towards death.

Epicurus himself has resources to respond to this objection. In particular, he claims that once one has attained the state of freedom from pain and distress, the pleasantness of one's life is not increased by indefinite prolongation of one's existence (PD 19, 20). Thus the coming of death means we will not be losing an extra amount of good that would have been ours had death not intervened.

What underlies this response is the non-episodic view of pleasure that characterizes the Epicurean conception of the good life. If one thinks of pleasure as consisting in a series of episodes of a certain kind, then it seems hard to deny that the more episodes one accumulates, the more pleasant one's life is, and indeed that there is no upper limit to this. Epicurus, however, conceives of the pleasantness of one's life in terms of the maintenance of a state of freedom from pain and distress. Once this state is achieved, one's life cannot become pleasanter, any more than, say, a beautiful statue becomes more beautiful by lasting longer. We should, then, while not craving death (LM 126), not be anxious, either, about how long our life will continue once we have obtained the Epicurean goal.

Could not an objector respond that such a life is evidently still better than death, the former being maximally pleasant, the latter not pleasant at all? But that is to imply that the two states are commensurable in terms of value. Recall, however, that on the assumption that death is a state of non-existence without any form of sentience, it is not subject to value assessment, since the measure of good and bad for the Epicurean is feeling, and being dead entails the absence of feeling. It is not, then, that death is worse than a pleasant life; to suppose that death can be an element of such a value judgment is to make a category error.

9

The case of pain, as an object of fear, seems in some ways harder to dismiss, since despite the Epicurean view that our needs are easily satisfied, pain being to that extent avoidable (*PD* 21), it seems optimistic to maintain that a life without pain can be guaranteed; and pain, unlike death, is admitted to be a bad thing. Epicurus does indeed concede that pain is likely to befall us and responds by claiming that severe pain is brief in duration, while long-lasting pain will be outweighed by pleasure (*PD* 4, cf. *LM* 133). One aim of this maxim is to teach us not to worry about pain. Epicurus is reported to have said that mental pains – worry, distress, and the like – are worse than physical, since while physical pain concerns only the present, mental pain can relate to the past and future too; and that mental pleasures by the same token are greater than physical ones (DL X. 137). If we are confident that severe pain will not be threatening because it is of short duration, and that more enduring pain will be outweighed by pleasure, we can lessen or extinguish our fear of pain and thereby make our lives more tranquil.

The emphasis here on pain being outweighed by pleasure is noteworthy; and although *PD* 4 implicitly restricts the point to pain that is not severe, it also claims that any pain that outweighs one's pleasure will be short. Moreover, in a striking letter that Epicurus is said to have written on his deathbed (DL X.22), he assures his correspondent that although he is suffering agonizing physical pain, this is counterbalanced by the joy he feels at the memory of their past conversations.

Epicurus thus seems to recognize that the mere thought that severe pain will be short-lived may not be sufficient to prevent one from being anxious about it. Instead, he exploits his point about the temporal range of the mental to suggest that even in the case of the greatest physical pain there are pleasures that can be set against it. Why, though, should that be a source of comfort? Part of Epicurus' idea may be that of focusing on something pleasant – here the memory of past conversations – as a way to mitigate physical pain. We have probably all experienced the phenomenon of becoming less aware of some painful condition such as toothache when pleasurably absorbed in some other activity. If even severe pain is amenable to this treatment, we can have confidence that pain is manageable and thus not to be feared. But part of the point may lie in the power of example. Epicurus calls his last day a "blessed" one. If it is possible to regard even such a day as blessed, we are encouraged to suppose that we too have nothing to fear. The explanation of why, for a hedonist, that might be the case is perhaps here subordinate to the exemplary demonstration that it can be the case.

10

Epicurus seems to have died an honorable death; and this raises the question of what the relation is between a life lived in accordance with Epicurean hedonistic principles and a life lived virtuously. There is no question that a good Epicurean aims to maximize the pleasantness of his or her own life (LM 126). Is one who lives in such a fashion also to be accounted a good person? Epicurus holds that it is impossible to live pleasantly without living wisely, honorably, and justly, or vice versa (LM 132, PD 5). Wisdom he connects with making the right choices to attain a pleasant life and avoid distress (LM 132), so it is fairly obvious how that might be regarded as inseparable from the attainment of the Epicurean goal. The case of justice seems to present more of a challenge.[16] Epicurus views justice as a contract between human beings for the prevention of mutual harm (PD 33). Laws in turn are just only insofar as they conduce to expediency in mutual transactions (PD 37, 38).[17]

How does this view of justice square with Epicurus' claim that living pleasantly is inseparable from living justly? It might be objected that if the maximization of pleasure is my aim, then surely there may be occasions when I should be unjust – that is, breach an agreement for mutual benefit in such a way that I will gain more pleasure than if I had not done so. Say, for example, there is a law against theft such that the parties to it have determined that everyone is better off if no one steals from anyone else. It may well be that I am indeed better off given the existence of this law – it protects me from having my property taken, and so on. But it may also be that if the opportunity presents itself for me to steal from another and get away with it, then I will be able to maximize my pleasure by acquiring the use of those extra resources without the prospect of a counterbalancing painful punishment. Should I not be unjust in those circumstances?

One Epicurean response is that I can never in fact be sure that I have acted with impunity: Fear of discovery and subsequent punishment will haunt the wrongdoer in such cases (PD 34, 35). There is something unsatisfactory about this. Surely there are occasions when either it is pretty clear that I can get away with some wrongdoing undiscovered, or that the chance of discovery is such that it is not reasonable that it be an object of dread. Moreover, Epicurus' emphasis on the covert commission of injustice seems to leave a rather important type of case out of account: that of an agent who is sufficiently powerful to commit injustice overtly with impunity.

Now Epicurus might respond that such a figure could not be regarded as part of the contracting community to which the notions of justice and injustice would be applicable in the first place. He does at any rate make it clear that neither notion applies beyond communities who have made a contract for mutual expediency (PD 32). Nonetheless, that would hardly suggest that for a powerful predator who seizes the resources of others openly and with impunity, living pleasantly is inseparable from living justly. It may, then, be that the Epicureans' defense of justice rests on their particular conception of the pleasantness of a life. Recall that this is one free from pain and anxiety. As we have seen, a major part of what constitutes this state is that none of one's desires are for the sorts of things that are likely to cause one toil and trouble in acquiring them. If that is the case, then the pleasant life and the just life may yet go hand in hand, since the agent living a maximally pleasant Epicurean life will not have the motivation to engage in the kind of large-scale predations that characterize the powerful interloper – indeed, they will be strongly motivated to avoid them and live a quiet and peaceful life.

But there is a danger of circularity here. After all, what is it about the pursuit of desires beyond basic needs that might involve one in toil and anxiety? Surely it is, to a significant degree, the difficulty of satisfying them and the risk of punishment. Yet by hypothesis the agent in question is one with sufficient power to be able to take from others with impunity – without, it may be, much toil and trouble at all. So I want to return to the question of covert acts of injustice and suggest that, while fear of the punishment contingent upon discovery is unquestionably part of what, for Epicurus, should deter an agent from committing injustice, it may be that we are supposed to see the need to live covertly as itself unpleasant; and this indeed may explain why it is covert, rather than overt, practices that he focuses on. Epicurus says that one should do nothing in life that would bring one fear if it became known to one's neighbor (SV 70). The "if" seems important here, since by implication one should refrain from doing things that require covert behavior whether or not one is actually found out. Conversely, what is implicitly recommended is that one live one's life such that one has nothing to hide.[18]

It may then be that the inability to live openly within one's community is itself regarded by Epicurus as a miserable thing, and to that extent a powerful deterrent to injustice. Living openly will, in this sense, be a problem even for the overt wrongdoer, since that person must of necessity be either outside a community or set against it. In PD 39 Epicurus recommends that where possible one deal with things that threaten from without by treating them as kin, and where not possible at least not treat them as alien, with separation seen as a last resort. The maxim would have no force were it not taken to be in the true interest of the threatening party to be cooperative. And while it is clear that the model of an Epicurean community is one that is relatively small and self-contained (PD 14), participation in community is clearly deemed an essential ingredient, for any rational agent, of the pleasant life (PD 40).

I I

Epicurus is indeed reported to have said that to dine without a friend was to live the life of a lion or a wolf[19] – one of isolation. And friendship, unsurprisingly, is a central component of the Epicurean good life. Epicurus calls friendship the possession that most conduces to a blessed life (PD 27). How so? If one bears in mind the Epicurean goal of freedom from pain and distress, then one of the most important aspects of friendship is that it provides a kind of support network: Friendship does more than anything to enhance our security (PD 28). And in line with the Epicurean emphasis on the importance of our mental attitudes, it is the confidence that friendship gives of help being at hand that is said to be more important than the help itself (SV 34).

Friendship evidently enhances the pleasantness of our lives in some obvious ways. Yet we also think of genuine friendship as being more than about how much our friends can contribute to our own pleasure. Friendship must be reciprocal, and there is plenty of evidence that the Epicureans recognize this. Epicurus is reported, for example, to have said that one must not betray a friend, and that one will even on occasion die for a friend (DL X.120). Noble sentiments though these may be, they raise some questions about how well the relation of friendship fits the core tenets of Epicurean hedonism.[20]

Let us distinguish between what one might call the "soft" and the "hard" problem of Epicurean friendship. The "soft" problem is how looking out for a friend is compatible with seeking to maximize the pleasantness of one's own life. And here a ready answer presents itself: One will only have the confidence of a friend's support if one is ready in turn to support a friend, perhaps even to die for a friend if the alternative is the loss of trust that one's unwillingness to do the right thing by a friend might engender. Nor indeed does Epicurus hold that the value of friendship lies merely in its extrinsic benefits such as a sense of security or material aid. When he says that friendship "dances around the world" (SV 52), this is surely supposed to indicate that friendship is an intrinsically joyous thing as well.

The "hard" problem is whether Epicurus can consistently recognize an attitude towards one's friends that is based on more than what one can get out of them – be that joy, security, or any other kind of benefit. We think of the true friend as one who will look out for a friend regardless of what the latter can provide. Does Epicurus acknowledge this? There is an intriguing maxim (SV 23) in which he asserts that all friendship is a virtue in itself, or possibly (the text is doubtful) choiceworthy in itself, though it begins from benefit.[21] Now to call friendship a virtue in itself need not mean, given the general Epicurean view of the virtues as based on expediency, that its grounds are anything other than the benefits that accrue from it. Yet the contrast with benefit must mean something, and it is hard to see what this might be if not that friendship develops into a state whose maintenance is not justified solely by reference to benefit.

On the other hand, if we read "choiceworthy" here, then to call friendship choiceworthy in itself though beginning from benefit might simply mean that we come to appreciate our friends in their own right, rather than simply for the benefits they give us, where appreciating a friend in his or her own right would refer to the intrinsic joyousness of the relationship, based upon the friend's character,[22] rather than its extrinsic benefit in terms of security or aid. In this case, Epicurus has not contravened the dictates of his hedonism. And it seems possible, in the light of this, to read the "virtue" alternative in that way too.

Has he, though, contravened the norms of friendship if he only allows that friendship can be justified as a source of pleasure, one way or another, for the agent? Intriguingly, Cicero reports certain Epicureans as holding that while friendship in its initial stages is undertaken on account of pleasure, as the bond deepens friends love each other for their own sake regardless of utility (*On Ends* 1.69). With its highlighting of a beginning stage from which things then develop, this is reminiscent of the Epicurean maxim we have just been discussing, with a similar potential ambiguity, revolving around the meaning of "for their own sake." Does this mean one loves one's friends for their own intrinsic qualities, by contrast with any extrinsic benefits one may gain, or does it mean regardless of any pleasure we get from the friendship at all? If the former, then the position remains compatibly hedonist but would thereby offer an apparently cold view of friendship as based only on what pleasure the agent derives from it. If the latter, then it is unclear what has become of Epicurean hedonism.

It seems to me that both interpretatively and philosophically the dilemma is to be resolved in favor of the first option. We should allow that, given their hedonism, Epicurus and his followers ought to be read as justifying friendship by reference to the agent's pleasure, but as appreciating the value of one's friend's joyous qualities rather than simply the help and security friendship provides. What, then, of the worry that pleasure as the sole ground of friendship offers a cold and callous view of what friendship is? Should we not still care for our friends even if we do not get pleasure out of them?

The worry is, I think, over-played. If a friend's character changes, or if we realize their character was not what we thought it was, then there seems in principle nothing objectionable about withdrawing from the friendship. Of course, circumstances play a role. If a friend ceases to give pleasure because of certain problems in their life, we might still expect their friends to be supportive. Epicurus is in fact credited with the view that it is more pleasurable to confer a benefit than to receive one,[23] and there is psychological truth in that. But it does not seem, either, disreputable to support a suffering friend for the sake of bringing back the pleasures one had before. It is, perhaps, the mark of a friend to wish to restore one's friend to (as one says) their old self; and we do not, I think, require that a friend be so selfless (as one, significantly, also says) that it should not be a proper part of their motivation in such cases to seek to benefit themselves in terms of pleasures renewed.

There will evidently be cases where the change in one's friend is, or is likely to be, permanent: Mental decline would be one example, an issue perhaps more pressing in our own time than it was in the ancient world.[24] Here it would seem callous to abandon one's friend, though also legitimate to wonder whether, depending on how much of the friend's self had been lost, we could still correctly refer to a friendship at all. We have perhaps reached a position that does more than, or other than, expose the limits of the Epicurean approach. Yet Epicurean ethics is hardly squeamish about human vulnerability. It is because of, not in spite of, our human condition, that it urges us to celebrate what we have rather than lament what we do not. If, but only if, we do this, with those of like mind, shall we live like a god (*LM* 135). I append (and commend) by way of conclusion Epicurus' *Vatican Saying* 14:

> We are born once and cannot be born a second time, but must for eternity exist no more. You don't control tomorrow, yet you defer joy. Life is wasted in delay and each one of us dies without having had time to live.

NOTES

1. Surviving texts by Epicurus himself are few: three Letters (to Herodotus [*LH*], Pythocles [*LP*], and Menoeceus [*LM*]) containing summaries of various aspects of his thought; some collections of maxims (the *Principal Doctrines* [*PD*] and the *Vatican Sayings* [*SV*]); and some scattered fragments of his voluminous treatises.
   The Letters and the *Principal Doctrines* are preserved, together with material on Epicurus' life and thought, in Diogenes Laertius [DL], *Lives of Eminent Philosophers*, Book X. I shall draw where possible on Epicurus' own writings, supplementing on occasion with later Epicurean authors or reports of Epicurean doctrine. I shall by and large ignore issues of doctrinal difference between Epicurus and his followers, though a possible debate within the School about the grounds of friendship will be noted in Section 11 below.
2. There is debate about whether, in addition to being an ethical hedonist (one who thinks that pleasure is the goal we ought to pursue), Epicurus is also a psychological hedonist (one who thinks we all do pursue pleasure as our ultimate goal). In my view he thinks we all do pursue pleasure but that most of us go about it in the wrong way. See further Woolf (2004), responding to Cooper (1999b).
3. See here Brunschwig (1986); Sedley (1998) 136–39.
4. On the role of sensation and its relation to truth in Epicureanism, see e.g. Taylor (1980); Everson (1990); Striker (1996b).
5. On the eudaimonistic structure of Epicurean ethics see e.g. Mitsis (1988) 11–58; Annas (1993) 334–50.

6. After discussion of (1) and its corollaries in this and the next two sections, I return to (2) in Section 7 below.

7. Porphyry, *Letter to Marcella* 31.

8. See further Tsouna (2009) with references.

9. On this passage, see Irwin (1986) 103–4; Cooper (1999b) 507–8.

10. For elaboration and defense of a reading along these lines, see Purinton (1993).

11. See here further Woolf (2009) 173–75.

12. It is also the term he uses to describe the "suffering" of the soul in the passage from Porphyry quoted in Section 6 above.

13. For further discussion see e.g. Gosling and Taylor (1982) 365–96; Stokes (1995); Striker (1996a); Nikolsky (2001); Wolfsdorf (2013a) 144–81.

14. On the Epicurean approach to death and its relation to contemporary views, see Warren (2004).

15. Whether Lucretius' text can sustain this reading is debated, but it is perhaps the most philosophically interesting version of the argument.

16. For discussion see e.g. Vander Waerdt (1987); Armstrong (1997); O'Keefe (2001b).

17. On the relation between law and justice in Epicureanism see Alberti (1995).

18. Epicurus' famous exhortation to "live unnoticed" can be read in this light, as encouraging us to not to act in a way liable to draw the hostility of the community against us.

19. Seneca, *Letters* 19.10.

20. For discussion see e.g. O'Keefe (2001a); Evans (2004).

21. On this text see Brown (2002).

22. Epicurus tells us (*SV* 15) that we should value the characters of those who are near to us, so long as they are decent.

23. Plutarch, *Against Epicurean Happiness* 1097A.

24. But see Lucretius, *On the Nature of Things* 3.445–58.

10 The Stoics on Virtue and Happiness

Katja Maria Vogt

The Stoics hold that virtue is knowledge, and that knowledge is one: the good state of the rational soul. Unlike the rest of us, a person who is in this state of mind is happy. Today and throughout much of antiquity, Stoic ethics is compared to Platonic and Aristotelian views. The Stoics' immediate interlocutors, however, are skeptics.[1] With them the Stoics discuss how hard it is to think straight, to arrive at carefully considered views and stable insights. The skeptics regularly suspend judgment, assessing disputes as unresolved. The questions of what is good and bad and how to live appear to them difficult and deserving of extensive study.[2] The Stoics largely agree with the skeptics: These questions appear to them to be in need of further investigation. The Stoic approach is to ask what a person would be like who has the answers: how she would think, feel, and act.

A brief disclaimer. "The Stoics" as I speak of them never existed. Instead, there were individual philosophers. Stoic philosophy begins with Zeno (334/3–262/1 BCE), who spent more than twenty years in Plato's Academy, developing his views in conversation with the then emerging Academic skepticism (Zeno was roughly twenty–thirty years older than Arcesilaus, the first major Academic skeptic). Cleanthes (331/0–230/29 BCE), Zeno's successor, is best known for ideas in theology and physics. Chrysippus (c. 281–c. 208 BCE), the third head of the school, is as far-ranging as Zeno. Though he develops further Zeno's premises, he is an innovator, creating much of Stoic logic. Fast forward to the so-called Middle Stoa, whose main figures are Panaetius (c. 185–c. 110 BCE) and Poseidonius (c. 135–c. 50 BCE). And finally there is the Late Stoicism of Roman and Imperial times, with Seneca and Epictetus as the most influential figures.

The Stoics I refer to are the early Stoics, namely Zeno, Cleanthes, and Chrysippus. Their views are considered as orthodoxy. Dissenters or inventors depart from theories formulated by them. It is, admittedly, somewhat disturbing to suggest that the Stoics are cousins of the

I am grateful to Jens Haas for input on several drafts and to Sam McVane and Nandi Theunissen for comments.

skeptics, and yet to ascribe to them an "orthodoxy." Are the Stoics, after all, the dogmatists that the skeptics take them to be? Compared to the skeptics they are, simply on account of putting forward theories. And yet, theirs is a movement where each philosopher aims to get clear(er) about questions that were previously addressed, and which prolific authors like Chrysippus discuss over and over again. None of the Stoics thinks that he is an example of the elusive figure that is theorized, the sage. That is, none of them thinks they have formulated a complete system of knowledge in logic, physics, and ethics. Further questions can be raised, theories can be refined, and so on. Hence the position I shall sketch has at times a skeptical feel. It sometimes involves several ways in which a given problem might be solved, indicative of a lively philosophical debate.

I begin with a sketch of a puzzle, the so-called Unity of Virtue, that is at the heart of Stoic views on virtue (Section 1). Outlining the Stoic response, I turn to virtue as a unified state of mind (Section 2); then the three Stoic virtues of logic, physics, and ethics (Section 3); as well as the conventional virtues and their place in Stoic ethics (Section 4). I argue that the Stoics hold a distinctive view about the relation between happiness and virtue (Section 5), and end with some remarks about the nature of happiness and misery as the Stoics conceive of them (Section 6).

I   THE UNITY OF VIRTUE

The Unity of Virtue is one of the best-known ideas in ancient ethics.[3] A minimal version can be called Interentailment. It says that whoever has one of the virtues must have all of them. The Stoics accept this claim, and so does Aristotle.[4] Though Interentailment is discussed as an extreme position in today's ethics, it is a fairly uncontroversial and modest claim within ancient ethics. A stronger claim, cited alongside Interentailment in a report on the Stoics, is that whoever performs an action in accordance with one virtue, performs it in accordance with all virtues.[5] This claim is distinctively Stoic insofar as it presupposes a monistic psychology. For the Stoics, the soul is *one* faculty, rather than dividing up in parts or powers such as reason and desire, as the Platonic-Aristotelian tradition has it. Agents set themselves in motion by assenting to impressions like "I'll walk now."[6] No matter whether the agent wisely decides to get some exercise or leaves a room in anger, this motivation originates in her rational soul. Call this Motivational Monism. It supplies the Stoics with a strict version of another widespread view in antiquity, which I call the Knowledge Premise: Virtue is knowledge. For the Stoics, virtue is knowledge in a straightforward sense, not knowledge of some distinctively practical kind as the Aristotelian tradition has it.

Interentailment, Motivational Monism, and the Knowledge Premise are the building blocks of the Stoic account of virtue. A yet stronger version of the Unity of Virtue says that conventional virtue terms are misleading. This can be called an "error theory:" We speak of different virtues, but we are consistently mistaken. We should speak, at every instance, of virtue in the singular. This error theory can be attributed to Aristo, a student of Zeno who turned into a "fallen" disciple. The Stoics think he is pushing things too far.

To see why, turn for a moment to the most famous ancient discussion of the Unity of Virtue, in Plato's *Protagoras* (328E–334C).[7] The dialogue addresses a question set in everyday life, a question that parents consider as well as young people who seek an education. What kind of environment, training, and so on, make one a better person? This question supplies the first leg of a puzzle. It implies that there is such a thing as being a good person. The puzzle's second leg is that we also refer to different virtues, such as justice, courage, wisdom, and moderation. Moreover, it seems that some virtues rarely occur with others, to the extent that one wonders – given different dispositions and the limits of molding one's psychology – whether they *can* occur together.[8] This is how the Unity of Virtue becomes a problem and a puzzle.

Ethicists today often proceed as if one set of phenomena, namely the existence of several distinct virtues, was rooted in everyday practices. To them the Unity of Virtue appears to be a puzzling claim, grounded in abstract concerns that come into view only through theorizing.[9] Arguably, ethicists here miss out on an important set of phenomena. Plato's *Protagoras* is rather true to life. By starting from the question of how one becomes a better person the dialogue also explores another set of phenomena, namely that we care a lot about a person's goodness. Parents typically do not just want their children to acquire specific traits. They hope to raise good people. Indeed, parents may think that, whatever specific traits their child has, if only she is a good person things will be fine. That is, the Unity of Virtue is not an abstract philosophical concern. It is as deeply rooted in everyday practices as the multiplicity of virtue. Philosophers face two puzzles, not one: how to make sense of the notion of a good person, and how to account for particular good features of persons.

The Stoics take on both challenges. Hence they cannot endorse Aristo's error theory of Virtue. And their position is neither well described as virtue monism (that there is strictly one virtue) nor as virtue pluralism (that a given set of virtues is fundamental to ethics). According to the Stoics, the state of mind that is called virtue is unified: It is a state of mind where everything one holds to be true fits together as a systematic body of knowledge.[10] This is the core of virtue's unity. It is, however, a far cry from virtue monism. A body of knowledge can plausibly be divided up into subfields. Moreover, it may be carved up into subfields in more ways than one. For example, today students in medicine take courses in microbiology, clinical chemistry, pathology, and so on. They also take courses devoted to individual organs or parts of the body, like the heart, eyes, brain, and so on. Both are compatible ways of approaching the field, and yet they carve it up differently.

Similarly, the Stoics divide up virtue, understood as a unified state of mind, in multiple ways. Hence the label "pluralism" is as misleading as the label "monism." It suggests that a given set of virtues is basic, as, say, talk about "cardinal virtues" implies. But the Stoics consider physics, ethics, and logic – the three philosophical disciplines – as generic virtues, *and* they describe the traditional virtues wisdom, moderation, courage, and justice as generic. These are not competing classifications. And the fact that the Stoics put forward these distinctions does not mean that, fundamentally, there are three – or four – kinds of virtue. "Generic" here means that more fine-grained distinctions between virtues classify them as falling into these kinds.[11] Physics, ethics, and logic are generic insofar as they each have subfields. Similarly wisdom, justice, moderation, and courage are, for the Stoics, fields with subfields. Each of these virtues "studies" this or that.[12] And they have subfields insofar as, say, quick-wittedness is subsidiary to wisdom, endurance to courage, and so on.[13]

2   VIRTUE IN THE SINGULAR

The unified state of mind of the virtuous person takes center stage in Stoic ethics. The Stoics define virtue as benefit. It is the state of mind that is also called wisdom or knowledge.[14] What does this mean? The Stoics distinguish between the kind of value one should ascribe to matters that are conducive to a life that is suitable for the kind of being one is – say, the value of intact limbs – on the one hand, and goodness on the other hand.[15] According to the Stoics, having one's limbs intact is "to be preferred" and "to be taken."[16] One should aim to keep one's limbs intact, seek treatment if one's arm or leg hurts, and so on, thereby responding to the value of intact limbs. Still, and this is a point to which I return in Section 5, it is not true that a human being cannot be happy if, say, she loses one of her arms.[17] Put more generally, a human being can be happy when losing something of value, even though she has reason to prefer what has value. A human being cannot, however, be happy without that which is good. What is good? Virtue, wisdom, knowledge: the state of mind that one needs to figure out correctly what to do. This state of mind is the only thing that genuinely benefits us.[18] It is thereby also the state of mind that permits one to lead a good human life when things of value are lost.[19]

Virtue, hence, is the state of mind that enables one to act as one should. In order to act as one should, one needs knowledge. This knowledge includes knowledge of what is valuable and disvaluable for human beings, such that we can lead lives that are suitable for the kind of being we are. But "getting it right" in a way that is still subject to change – say, thinking today that whether one catches a cold is merely a question of value, and forgetting this insight tomorrow, despairing at the first symptoms of what might be a cold – does not suffice. It would be, in Stoic terms, mere belief, *doxa*, which is weak and changeable.[20] To lead a good life, one needs to integrate those views in such a way that gradually they become a system. The interrelations between one's views stabilize them.[21] This means, *inter alia*, that one acts reliably on one's insights.[22] This is why virtue is knowledge: a state of mind in which one knows what to do and actually does it. The motivational side of knowledge means that a widespread way of talking about knowledge today – in terms of what "we" know, where some know A and others know B – does not make sense for the Stoics. For one's affective and reactive attitudes to be reflective of knowledge, the knowledge must be one's own.

3 THREE GENERIC VIRTUES: PHYSICS, ETHICS, AND LOGIC

The Stoics are literalists about the Knowledge Premise. When they say that virtue is knowledge, they do not have some special kind of knowledge in mind – moral intuition, moral sensibilities, or anything of that sort.[23] Instead they propose that, in order to live well, one needs knowledge in an ordinary way: knowledge of the world. Hence one of their divisions between generic virtues is threefold. It is the Stoics' most basic way of dividing up knowledge into physics, ethics, and logic.[24] This is more pedestrian than, say, explaining the knowledge needed for virtue as moral intuition. It is also more laborious. The knowledge of virtue involves, in effect, knowing everything, or rather, everything that pertains to leading a good life.[25] Moreover, it involves that one counteracts tendencies that the Stoics consider widespread. The Stoics think that we are prone to sloppy thinking, rash acceptance of impressions where careful consideration is needed, and so on.[26] That is, virtue is hard because of the sheer difficulty and scope of what needs to be known *and* because of the extensive training that is needed if one wants to consistently adhere to epistemic norms.

Consider first logic, the discipline that is perhaps least expected in this context.[27] Stoic logic comprises what today falls into several disciplines, including logic, philosophy of language, philosophy of mind, and normative epistemology.[28] The Stoics' extensive interest in logic is an implication of the Knowledge Premise: For the acquisition of knowledge, one needs well-trained thinking abilities. In the eyes of their critics, the Stoics are obsessed with the study of fallacies.[29] And yet this is a straightforward interest for anyone who assumes that flawed thinking translates into mere belief, emotional uproar, bad decisions, and rash action. The Stoics observe that there are patterns, typical ways in which cognizers "jump to conclusions." In part, a study of these patterns is motivated by an interest in the workings of our minds. But one may also study these patterns because one wants to avoid them.

Vagueness is a prominent example. The Stoic position differs from today's epistemicism by taking, from the get-go, a normative perspective.[30] The Stoics envisage teachers who play "sorites games" with their students, asking, say, "is two few?", "is three few?" and so on. The novice at this game will say "yes," "yes," "yes," until it is too late: She realizes that she should have stopped answering at some point, when her impressions were no longer (what the Stoics call) cognitive.[31] This is what the virtuous person does: She shuts up when impressions are non-cognitive, not assenting to, say, "eight is few."[32] Why did the novice assent? Perhaps he felt pressured when called upon and could not think clearly. Perhaps he made some irrelevant connection, say, thinking of a situation like having only eight minutes left until a store closes, which makes "eight" sound like an awfully low number. And so on. The presumption is that practicing sorites games will help one become a more careful assenter in any number of contexts in life.[33]

Consider next physics.[34] Physics, according to the Stoics, covers bodies, principles, elements, gods, and limits/place/void. According to an alternative Stoic division into subfields, physics studies the world, the elements, and causality.[35] Stoic physics describes the world as a living being. The world is held together by the active principle (reason, god). The active principle acts on the passive principle, matter, such that they blend entirely. The active principle is strictly speaking the only cause. But it divides up into portions that – *qua* portions of the only cause – also are causes. In this sense, human beings, animals, plants, stones, and so on are causes. They differ by their principle of movement: Stones and logs can only be moved from the outside; plants move through the movement of growth; animals through their cognitive faculties; and human beings through reason.[36] This sketch, though minimal, helps see how the study of physics pertains to leading a good life: It supplies, among other things, a self-conception of us as parts of a whole; a perspective on other human beings as components of the same sort that we are; an analysis of the "whole" as a living being with which we are, through our relations with many of its components, intricately interrelated; and an understanding of the causality of agency.

What, then, is left for Stoic ethics, other than to fill out this picture – a picture that leads to the Stoics' distinctive kind of cosmopolitanism? Major topics in Stoic ethics are impulse, appropriate action, the good and bad, value and disvalue, the emotions, virtue, and the end.[37] The Stoics propose that human beings are born with a "first impulse," that is, an initial motivation for actions. These early motivations are directed at that which immediately "belongs" to the human being. A newborn child experiences its own arms, legs, vision, and so on as hers. She is attached to being able to move around, see, hear, and so on. The child's so-called affiliation, however, is not only with her own body and faculties. It extends to those closest to her, her immediate family. They are felt to be "hers," and motivations for things of value extend accordingly. One wants food, shelter, health, and so on, not just for oneself but also for those with whom one belongs together. This is the beginning of the so-called *oikeiôsis* theory.[38] *Oikeiôsis* means, roughly, integration of X into the scope of what belongs to oneself, where belonging is an affective and motivational relation.

The first impulse is merely a starting point. This starting point is not itself considered ethically good. It provides the agent with an initial familiarity with, and a psychological root of, the attitudes that are essential for ethical behavior. For there to be virtue, the scope of what is affiliated must grow. As the Stoics see it, it grows once a human being gains insights about the natural world and its components. Eventually, and this is the motivational disposition required by cosmopolitanism, one relates to everyone in the world as a fellow inhabitant of the same "home."[39] This relation involves an ability to figure out which actions are appropriate (*kathêkonta*). In these actions, matters of value and disvalue as they pertain to oneself and to everyone else are "selected" and "deselected" in the way in which perfect reason – the mind of the person with knowledge – selects them. This is how the theory of appropriation leads to the theories of what is to be done; of value and disvalue; of the right affective attitudes, namely "rational feelings" instead of emotions; of the goodness of virtue, which consists in selecting rightly; and of happiness or the end (to which I turn in Sections 5 and 6).

What, then, does it mean to call logic, physics, and ethics virtues? The claim here is not merely that the study of logic, physics, and ethics is conducive to becoming virtuous. It means that mastering these fields immediately translates into virtuous action. A person who, for example, has mastered epistemic norms is not going to act rashly or in emotional uproar; a person who understands that she is a part of a whole acts differently from someone who conceives of herself as a self-standing individual; a person who sees others as parts of the same sort that she is relates to them with concern for value and disvalue in *their* lives; and so on.

4 FOUR GENERIC VIRTUES: WISDOM, MODERATION, JUSTICE, AND COURAGE

How then do the conventional virtues fit into the picture? The Stoics distinguish between *phronêsis, sôphrosunê, dikaiosunê,* and *andreia,* each identified with a particular body of knowledge. Wisdom, here, is the science of what should and should not be done and which actions are neutral; moderation the science of what should be chosen and avoided and what is neutral; justice is the science concerned with distribution; courage the science of things that are fearful and not fearful and neither of these.[40] In a similar vein, Chrysippus defines courage as knowledge of matters requiring persistence. A variant of this definition captures the idea that knowledge is a stable way of holding true: Courage is "the maintenance of stable judgment in undergoing and warding off those things which seem fearsome."[41] This formulation highlights how the distinction between mere belief (*doxa*) and knowledge matters to ethics.

In the face of danger, it is easy to forget earlier insights. Occurrent impressions – the approaching tiger! – are vivid. If one's insights are not *firm* judgments, and that is knowledge, one is not virtuous. This idea has also a physiological side. In the language of physics, virtue is a matter of the overall tension that controls and unifies an agent's soul. According to Cleanthes, the soul of the virtuous agent has the right kind of tension, namely "strength." Applied to matters that demand persistence, this strength is called wisdom; to matters requiring endurance, courage; to questions of desert, justice; and to choice/avoidance, moderation.[42]

These definitions raise two puzzles, which I shall take in turn. One puzzle concerns the status of wisdom. Wisdom is, like virtue and knowledge, a name for the overall condition of the good agent's soul. Hence it can hardly be one of the virtues. Instead the virtues should be subfields of wisdom, as they are subfields of knowledge. This view is reported on behalf of Zeno, who defines the virtues as subfields of wisdom: Justice is wisdom in matters requiring distribution, moderation is wisdom in matters requiring choice, and courage is wisdom in matters requiring endurance.[43] Here wisdom is the master-virtue, and does not show up alongside justice, moderation, and courage. Presumably, the definition of wisdom cited earlier (and ascribed to the Stoics in general) is an outlier. It pretends to delineate a specific domain for wisdom ("what should be done"), while actually ascribing the whole sphere of action to it.

The other puzzle concerns the nature of subfields. If knowledge is a system, as the Stoics think it is, what are subfields? This puzzle relates to the Stoics' dispute with Aristo and Aristo's claim that conventional virtue terms are misleading. Virtue should only be spoken of in the singular. That captures how things really are, namely that the so-called virtues are nothing but virtue relative to a given context. To posit several virtues, in Aristo's view, is as if one posited "white-seeing" and "black-seeing" as different faculties of vision.[44] This comparison makes fun of an idea that is by no means far-fetched. Namely, virtue, understood as the state of mind of the wise person, may be brought to bear on different spheres of action; it may be adequately referred to as justice, moderation, and courage depending on the sphere in which the wise person acts.

Why is this a view that the Stoics reject?[45] A further report on Stoic doctrine may help. All virtues, it says, share their theorems; and yet they differ by the topics they put first and that are specifically theirs.[46] Courage, for example, primarily studies the theory of everything that should be endured; and secondarily that with which the other virtues are concerned. This proposal implies a way in which one may conceive of subfields: as having some subject matter of their own, and yet being tied to a body of knowledge by sharing theorems with the system as a whole. That is, the Stoics' disagreement with Aristo seems genuine. They do not propose that one system of knowledge is brought to bear on different circumstances, such that the differences between the virtues lie, as it were, entirely outside of the agent's mind and in the spheres of action she encounters. Instead, they seem to take seriously the idea of subfields in a system: subfields with specific content of their own, and yet integrated into the body of knowledge.

5   THE POSSIBILITY OF HAPPINESS

Alexander asks a desperate question on behalf of the Stoics: "How could man not be the most miserable of all creatures in having vice and madness ingrown in him and allotted?"[47] This question picks up from the Stoic view that people are prone to ignorance and vice – sloppy thinking, rash actions, irrationality, and so on. That is, Stoic views about virtue translate into pervasive ascriptions of misery. And yet, happiness is possible, in the very way in which it is possible to attain virtue. Moreover, in spite of pervasive ascriptions of misery, human beings can be happy under rather diverse, sometimes challenging, circumstances.

Scholars tend to distinguish between three ways in which ancient ethicists think of the relationship between virtue and happiness:

Necessity: Virtue is necessary for happiness.
Sufficiency: Virtue is sufficient for happiness.
Identity: Virtue is identical with happiness.

Necessity is inadequate for the Stoic position. It means that, though virtue is necessary for happiness, other goods too affect happiness and misery. Sufficiency and Identity are more plausible candidates.[48] In a sense, the Stoics think that if an agent is virtuous, this suffices for her happiness. And they identify living virtuously with living happily.[49] Nevertheless, neither Sufficiency nor Identity addresses the relationship between virtue and happiness on Stoic terms. All three options – Sufficiency, Necessity, and Identity – are conceived in a tradition that thinks about "goods" in Platonic-Aristotelian terms. But the Stoics do not distinguish between different kinds of goods, asking how goods other than virtue affect one's happiness. Instead, they propose a distinction between two kinds of valence: goodness (*agathon*) and value (*axia*).

The goodness of good deliberation is not one "kind of good" next to other kinds of goods. Its valence is of a different nature than the valence of what is considered in deliberation.[50] Why? One reason is that goodness relates differently to happiness than value. It is impossible to be happy without the good; it is possible to be happy when things of value are lost.

"Indifferent" is used in two senses. First, it is used unconditionally, of things which contribute neither to happiness nor unhappiness, as is the case with wealth, reputation, health, strength, and the like. For it is possible to be happy without these, though the manner of using them is constitutive of happiness or unhappiness. In another sense those things are called indifferent which activate neither impulse nor repulsion, as is the case with having an odd or even number of hairs on one's head, or stretching or contracting one's finger. But the previous indifferents are not spoken of in this sense. For they are capable of activating impulse and repulsion. Hence some of them are selected and others deselected, but the second type is entirely equal with respect to choice and avoidance. (DL 7.104–5 = LS 58B, tr. LS).

The formulation employed here – it is possible to be happy without X – deserves close attention. It names a fourth option:

Possibility: Virtue is that without which it is not possible to be happy.

Consider an example. Someone climbs in the mountains. His arm gets stuck between a dislodged boulder and a canyon wall. He cannot extricate it in more than five days of trying. After careful consideration, he cuts off the arm, walks down and checks into a hospital. A year later, he is back climbing in the mountains. With some caveats (perhaps a wise person would not climb in remote areas alone and without informing others in advance – but for the purposes of the example, I set this aside), this person acts precisely as the Stoics say a virtuous person would. He considers having his limbs intact as valuable. Nevertheless, he judges that it is possible to live well without one of his limbs. Hence he cuts off his arm, and yet, responding to the value of health, seeks the best treatment he can. He continues to lead a good life, albeit a different one, namely a life that can be lived with only one arm.[51]

How does the example depart from Necessity, Sufficiency, and Identity? Virtue, here, is more than just a necessary ingredient of happiness. Nevertheless, to say it is sufficient for happiness is to make a nonsensical claim, given that virtue precisely consists in dealing well with matters of value/disvalue. Similarly, and to use a related locution, to say that virtue guarantees happiness loses sight of the role and value of indifferents such as health. Further, the claim that virtue is identical with happiness neglects that the Stoics take seriously the question how value/disvalue affect one's life. As long as limbs can't be restored biologically to the effect that they are fully like "natural" limbs, it seems ridiculous and perhaps even offensive to claim that losing a limb does not affect how the life of the agent goes. Indeed, one needs to adjust a lot in one's life if one loses an arm. Nevertheless, this does not affect whether one *can* be happy. The agent can build a life after the accident in which he lives well – as many indeed do after life-changing accidents. Matters of value/disvalue affect one's life. And yet they do not affect whether it is possible to be happy.

6   HAPPINESS, THE GOOD, AND THE END

What, then, is happiness for the Stoics? According to a formal notion, happiness is the life that is all things considered best for a human being.[52] Like a number of ancient ethicists, the Stoics endorse this notion. Further, and again like other ancient ethicists, the Stoics offer a philosophical version of traditional notions of happiness that have religious overtones. *Eudaimonia*, here, is a life that goes well because divinity is present in it. *Eu-* means well, and a *daimon* is a god or demi-god. Intuitively speaking, a person who is *eudaimôn* is someone for whom "the stars align": Things go well for her because a god is at her side. According to the Stoics, the wise person's mind is perfectly in tune with the world's reason; that is, with god's reason.[53] This semblance is so strong, and taken so literally, that the sage's life in no way falls short of the life of a god.[54] Her actions are consistently appropriate. Happiness, according to Chrysippus, supervenes on these actions if they are done with the kind of firmness and stability that characterizes the mind of the wise person.[55]

The Stoics' substantive account of happiness, or the end, is expressed in well-known formulae. Zeno describes the end as "a good flow of life" and as "living in agreement (*homologoumenôs*)." The Stoics elaborate on these proposals in various ways, describing the end as life in agreement with nature, with virtue, with reason, with experience of what happens by nature, and so on.[56] But Zeno's initial formulation may capture, concisely, a complex idea. The virtuous agent's life is "in agreement" in multiple ways: insofar as her own reason is in a consistent state; insofar as being guided by perfect reason is to live in agreement with the world's reason; and insofar as doing so means that one's actions reflect knowledge of one's own nature, human nature in general, and nature as a whole.[57]

Vice is the opposite. It is the misery of flawed thinking, emotional uproar, being torn between different views, and so on – in short, the absence of the stability of knowledge. Psychological dissonance and cognitive chaos are disturbances which, the Stoics think, are perceived as agitation. They come with fear and feelings of powerlessness, with excessive longing and turmoil.[58] Of course, someone who is not wise might at times feel elated and say that she is happy. But she would make a mistake, and soon enough, or so the Stoics think, the agonies of being less-than-virtuous would again make themselves felt.

These proposals seem comprehensible, at least in outline. What is harder to understand is the way in which happiness, for the Stoics, is the end. In calling something the end, one assigns to it a crucial role in motivation. And yet, it is not a straightforward matter in which sense happiness, according to the Stoics, motivates. The Aristotelian tradition assumes, roughly, the following.

(1) Human beings desire happiness.[59]
(2) Particular actions are performed for the sake of some end; agents are motivated by seeing the action or its outcome as good.
(3) Other things are pursued for the sake of happiness, but happiness is not pursued for the sake of anything else; it is the final end.

The Stoics must share (1), otherwise their discussion of how it is possible to be happy when something of value is lost is incomprehensible. (3) is, at least according to Stobaeus, a claim the Stoics endorse.[60] And yet the Stoics do not endorse (2). Namely, they do not analyze particular actions as motivated by the pursuit of ends. This makes Stobaeus' ascription of (3) puzzling. If at all, the Stoics must hold (3) in a sense that does not imply a hierarchy of ends. They think of agents as selecting and deselecting matters of value, not as acting for the sake of ends or as pursuing goods. Action is set off by assent to an impression to the effect that a certain action is "to be done," not to the effect that such-and-such is good. For example, the thought "I'll have a cup of tea" occurs as the conclusion of a thought process about what to drink at a given occasion. Assent to "I'll have a cup of tea" sets off an impulse for the action of drinking the tea. The considerations that lead up to this thought are concerned with value, as well as perceptual and descriptive matters. "I need something to drink," "it is too early in the day for wine," "I've had too much coffee lately," "I'm cold," "there's tea in the kitchen," etc.

are such considerations. All things considered, it seems to the agent that she should have a cup of tea, and that is the thought she assents to.[61] The Stoic account of what goes on in the agent's mind, thus, does not involve reference to particular ends of particular actions, or to a relation between immediate ends and higher-order ends. Their proposal is so deeply at variance with standard approaches that it even affects the textual evidence. The authors on whose reports scholars draw offer unsympathetic sketches. Indeed, one ancient critic finds the Stoic proposal absurd, another idiotic.[62]

What can be said on behalf of the Stoics?[63] One premise is well attested: Only the good – virtue – qualifies as desirable.[64] Valuable things are reasonably preferred and selected, but only virtue is desirable. The Stoics argue that in growing up, a person learns to select things of value. She becomes acquainted with selection and deselection that is according to nature. And she observes instances of virtue. Even if these instances are far from perfect, agents can extrapolate. They form a conception of virtue; that is, of the good, in the Stoic sense. This glimpse of the good provides a motivation that is of a different nature than motivation that responds to value and disvalue. It is a motivation for becoming, as one might put it, a good deliberator. Agents acquire this motivation if and when they progress towards virtue. But it is not easy to sustain. As a non-wise agent, one easily falls back into seeing – mistakenly – matters of value as good. That is, the good is not simply, as a matter of course, desired. It is the only thing that *should* be desired. On the Stoic construal, (3) thus amounts to the following: In any given situation where an agent decides what to do, what should ultimately motivate her is the end of becoming a good deliberator. This end is not pursued for the sake of anything else, but for its own sake.

NOTES

1. On the closeness of skeptic and Stoic philosophy, cf. Frede (1983).
2. On the Socratic heritage in Hellenistic philosophy, cf. Long (1988) and (2011).
3. On the Stoic version, cf. Schofield (2013) and (1984). Much of my analysis is in agreement with Schofield, though I focus on knowledge while he starts out from the discussion of wisdom.
4. The principal point of reference in Aristotle is *Nicomachean Ethics* VI. Discussions of the Unity of Virtue in today's ethics mostly address Aristotle's view, a trend that was initiated by McDowell (1979).

5. Plutarch, *On Stoic self-contradictions* 1046E-F = LS 61F. Throughout this paper, LS refers to Long and Sedley (1987). Many, though not all, texts I cite are included in LS.

6. Stobaeus 2.88,2–6; Seneca, *Letter* 133.18.

7. A classic contribution is Vlastos (1981c).

8. *Protagoras* 349A-350E.

9. Wolf (2007).

10. *Epistêmê* is sometimes translated as "scientific knowledge." I refrain from doing so because it misleadingly implies that, for the Stoics, there is also some other, non-systematic or non-scientific knowledge. Cf. Vogt (2012) ch. 7.

11. Plutarch, in whose eyes Stoic philosophy is full of flaws, observes that Chrysippus recognizes too many virtues. *On moral virtue*, 440E-441D = LS 61B.

12. Stobaeus 2.63,6–24 = LS 61D.

13. Stobaeus 2.59,4–60,2; 60,9–24 = LS 61H.

14. Aetius I, *Preface* 2 = LS 26A

15. On virtue as good, cf. S.E. *M* 11.22 = LS 60G; Stobaeus 2.58,5–15 = LS 60K; 2.71, 15–72,6 = LS 60M; on value/disvalue, cf. D.L. 7.101–2 = LS 58A and Stobaeus LS 58C-E; on value/disvalue as not benefitting/harming, cf. D.L. 7.101–3; on appropriate action and value, see all the fragments in LS chapter 59.

16. The opposites are "to be dispreferred" and "not to be taken." Stobaeus 2.79,18–80; 2.84,18–85,11 = LS 58C.

17. On the good and the valuable, cf. Vogt (2014).

18. Cf. Cicero, *On Ends* 3.50 = LS 58I and 3.17,20–1 = LS 59D.

19. Vogt (2008b).

20. On the translation of *doxa* as "belief" rather than "opinion" and on the Stoic notion of *doxa*, cf. Vogt (2012) ch. 7.

21. Cf. Sextus Empiricus, *M* 7.151: "Knowledge is a cognitive grasp that is secure and firm and unchangeable by reason."

22. Both wise and non-wise cognizers have so-called cognition, *katalêpsis*, which I here refer to as "getting it right" or "insight": a cognizer grasps something that is the case precisely as it is. Still, this grasping can be mere *doxa*, a changeable doxastic attitude.

23. Contrary to, say, McDowell (1979).

24. Aetius I, *Preface* 2 = LS 26A.

25. Frede (1996) and (1999); Vogt (2008a) 118–26.

26. Ranocchia (2012).

27. In agreement with other scholars, I call "logic" what the Stoics call "dialectic" and what is only part of Stoic logic (the other part being rhetoric).

28. On the subfields of logic, see D.L. 7.41–4 = LS31A.

29. Long (1996) ch. 4.

30. Timothy Williamson (1994) calls his position on vagueness epistemicism.
31. D.L. 7.46 = LS 40C; Cicero *Academica* 2.77–8 = LS 40D.
32. SE *M* 7.416 = LS 37F.
33. One topic where philosophical contributions today display a similar mix of technicality and normative injunctions is the study of generics. The truth-conditions of generics can be approached as a topic in philosophy of language; and yet they matter to understanding and counteracting prejudice, stereotyping, etc. Cf. Leslie (forthcoming).
34. Menn (1995). An influential contribution that aims to pull apart Stoic ethics and physics is Annas (1993) ch. 5.
35. D.L. VII 132. On both lists, cf. Brunschwig (2003) 206–7.
36. Origen, *On principles* 3.1.2–3 = LS 53A.
37. D.L. 7.84 = LS 56A.
38. Brunschwig (1986).
39. Vogt (2008a) ch. 2.
40. Stobaeus 2.59,4–60,2; 60,9–24 = LS 61H.
41. Cicero, *Tusculan Disputations* 4.53 = LS 32H.
42. Plutarch, *On Stoic self-contradictions* 1034C-E = LS 61C.
43. Plutarch, *On moral virtue* 440E-441D = LS 61B; Plutarch, *On Stoic self-contradictions* 1034C-E = LS 61C.
44. Plutarch, *On moral virtue* 440E-441D. Cf. Schofield (1984) on Zeno's and Cleanthes' rejection of Aristo's views.
45. This question is especially urgent in the light of Stoic claims to the effect that the sage does everything – or rather, everything that she does – well. Stobaeus 2.66, 14–67,4 = LS 61G.
46. Stobaeus 2.63,6–24 = LS 61D.
47. Alexander of Aphrodisias, a Peripatetic philosopher and commentator on Aristotle, *On fate* 199.14–22 = LS 61N.
48. Cf. Bobonich (2010b) on Identity esp. 314–16.
49. Plutarch reports the reverse identification, of living viciously and living unhappily. *On Stoic self-contradictions* 1042A = SVF 3.55 = LS 63H.
50. Deliberation is *not* concerned with virtue/vice. In Chrysippus' terms, "virtue quite on its own has no relevance for our living." Plutarch, *On Stoic self-contradictions* 1039E = SVF 3.761 = LS 61Q.
51. The Stoics use "mutilating oneself" as an example; cf. DL 7.108–9 = SVF 3.495, 496 = LS 59E. Cf. Vogt (2008a) 212–13, where I also use the example of the mountain climber.
52. Cf. Bobonich (2010b).
53. Cf. D.L. 7.87–9 = LS 63C. This aspect of Stoic ethics is fore-fronted in Cooper (2012) 150–8.

54. Plutarch, *On common conceptions* 1076A = LS 61J.

55. Stobaeus 5.906,18–907,5 = LS 59I.

56. Stobaeus 2.77,16–27 = LS 63A; Stobaeus 2.75,11–76,8 = LS 63B; Striker (1991).

57. These are ideas captured by the various Stoic formulae; cf. D.L. 7.87–9 = LS 63C.

58. Cf. for example Cicero, *Tusculan Disputations* 4.29, 34–5 = LS 61O.

59. Any more precise formulation, in particular one that would take a stance on whether this is a descriptive or a normative claim, would be contentious. For present purposes, I'm setting these questions aside.

60. Stobaeus 2.77,16–27 = LS 63A.

61. Vogt (2015); Inwood (1985).

62. Alexander, *On soul* II 164,4–9 = LS 64B; Plutarch, *On common conceptions* 1070F-1071E = LS 64C.

63. Scholars have recognized this question as tantalizingly difficult. Frede (2001); Inwood (2005) 271–301. My sketch draws on two sources, interpretation of which is contentious: Seneca, *Letter* 120; Cicero, *De finibus* 3.20–2.

64. Only the good is, according to the Stoics, *haireton*. Stobaeus 2.78,7–12.

11 The Stoics' Ethical Psychology

Margaret Graver

The best entry point for the ethical psychology of the Hellenistic Stoics is to be found not in the surviving utterances of those philosophers, numerous though they are, but in the works of Plato, and above all in the function argument of *Republic* Book I, 352D-54A. In brief, Plato had reasoned that since the human being's most distinctive attribute is the activity of judging and reasoning, the best and most complete rational activity must constitute the good specific to humans, and that if that is our good, we should seek to achieve it. This strategy for grounding the norms of ethics in descriptive claims about the human mind is deeply significant not only for Plato's ethical thought but also for Aristotle, who reworks and extends it in *Nicomachean Ethics* 1.7.[1] It was the Stoics, however, who pressed the argument to its logical conclusion. In their system, the human good consists in perfected rationality *alone* – an uncompromising axiology that differs markedly from that of Aristotle's Peripatetic successors. At the same time, it was the Stoics who took most seriously Socrates' claim that human action, though not always *properly* rational, is nonetheless *essentially* rational in the sense of being determined solely by the judgments of the reasoning faculty. It follows for Stoics that virtue, i.e. the disposition to act correctly, consists entirely in the knowledge of what actions are correct; and further that virtue in this sense is the sole good of human existence.

Adherence to this principle gives rise to a series of systematically interrelated views within the realm of action, emotion, character, and moral development. These require some effort to understand, for the chief tenets of the system are stated with disconcerting boldness, and the argumentation that initially supported those claims is imperfectly preserved at best. With close study, however, it is possible to discern the motivations of many of the Stoics' positions and to refute some of the charges leveled against them by rival ancient schools. Such is my aim in this overview account. After a basic explanation of Stoic notions concerning the rational psyche, I treat first the determinants of action generally, then the special case of action that constitutes emotional response, and finally the individual varieties of character and moral progress. I endeavor to show, concerning the theory of action, that

Stoic philosophy did not preclude engagement with the objects of common pursuit; concerning emotion, that Stoics did not wildly misdescribe
emotional response nor urge a life devoid of feeling; and concerning
character, that their system did not lack resources for describing varieties of character and stages of moral progress.

Evidence on these points is, in general, abundant, but somewhat
difficult to manage. Extensive texts survive only for the Stoics of the
Roman Empire, notably Seneca and Epictetus; but the core principles of
Stoic thought were established much earlier, by Zeno of Citium, teaching in Athens at the beginning of the third century, and by his immediate
successors, Cleanthes of Assos and especially Chrysippus of Soli. For
these original doctrines we rely on fragments and doxographical reports
preserved by later authors, so that assembly is required and, at some
points, reconstruction to fill gaps in the record. Because of space constraints, I present here only the results of this process, citing just the
most crucial bits of evidence. For further information about the sources
and for alternative interpretations, readers are encouraged to consult the
works cited in the bibliography to this volume.[2]

I   THE RATIONAL PSYCHE

For the ancient Stoics, as for most present-day philosophers, it is axiomatic that the mind is material in nature. As a matter of principle, the
founders of the school took the view that mind-body interactions occur
because the mind is itself a body.[3] Mental activity as such is always
related to some propositional content, to "sayables" (lekta) or propositions; at the same time, though, mental events are always also changes in
the physical substrate. At the material level, that substrate is described,
in continuity with larger presuppositions of Stoic physics, as a blend of
air and fire called pneuma or "breath." This is the same material that
operates throughout the Stoic universe as a vehicle for what Zeno called
the "designing fire" or the "active principle," or simply "god."[4]
The respiration that sustains life in human beings is thus also our
physical connection with the surrounding cosmos and with the divine
element in the cosmos.

Pneuma confers on all things whatever structural and functional
properties they have, from the hardness of stones and whiteness of silver
to the complex life-functions of plants and animals. The variety among
these properties is explained by differences in the "tension" that bal-
ances the airy and fiery components of that material: The more complex

and intelligent something is, the more tension there is in its *pneuma*. Unlike the *pneuma* in a plant or an inanimate object, human and animal breath possesses a basic property of sensitivity and is designated *psuchê*, which may be translated as "soul" or "psyche." Centralized in the upper torso, where respiration takes place, the psyche of a human being accounts for such high-level capacities as reasoning skills and the ability to use language, but also for such basic life-functions as digestion and reproduction and even for our bodily configuration.[5]

Ultimately, however, the material account of psychic function plays only a minor role in Stoic thought. The point of interest for these thinkers was the functioning of the soul's central directive faculty or *hêgemonikon* – roughly equivalent to our "mind" – and in particular the mind-functions that have some claim to be distinctively human.[6] These are two in number: rational impression (*phantasia logikê*) and assent (*sugkatathesis*). Together, these two functions constitute our mental life, in which we receive and process information about our environment, formulate the thoughts we express in language, and make decisions. They are also the basis of the Stoic understanding of moral responsibility, for in certain cases an assent initiates some sort of action. In these cases it is termed "impulse" *(hormê)*.

Impression, in the form characteristic of rational beings, is an alteration of the mind through which it becomes aware of something; that is, of a state of affairs, past, present, or future, actual or possible. In physical terms, the mind-material takes on a new configuration, comparable to an imprint in wax, that corresponds in some way to the incorporeal proposition one has in mind. That proposition might simply link something perceived by the senses to some concept ("that is a horse") or it might arise "by inference and combination," as must be the case with more complicated sorts of thinking and reasoning.[7] Either way, merely having an impression does not yet amount to an opinion that something is present or is the case. We entertain many ideas without actually believing them. A belief, as opposed to a passing thought, is the product of a further alteration of mind, termed assent or judgment. In assent, we assign a truth-value to an impression: We accept the corresponding proposition as true or reject it as false.

Non-rational animals must have their own versions of impression and assent, since their behavior shows recognition of things in their environment. The Stoics remark also that many animals give evidence of inferential reasoning: The horse trembles at the sight of the whip.[8] What is it, then, that sets the rational animal apart from the non-rational? Here we can take a clue from Sextus Empiricus, who points out that for philosophers like the Stoics, the rational creature's ability to produce impressions by inference and combination depends on its possessing a concept of "following"; that is, of logical inference itself.[9] While many animals can link one idea to another and react accordingly, only a rational creature recognizes and evaluates the inference as such, comparing it with a prior notion of what it is for one proposition to follow from another. Even with simple impressions, our characteristically rational form of assent would seem to be a matter of perceiving a relation between the occurrent impression and one or more prior beliefs, and then deciding whether those beliefs do or do not support the new belief. We may not always do this correctly, but that we do it at all makes our mental life quite different from that of animals or very young children.

This rational nature brings upon adult humans the full weight of moral responsibility. What determines assent, and thus action, is the agent's own mental character. One who held many beliefs of a certain kind, or who was antecedently committed to some general principle, would assent accordingly to further impressions, while another person who had different prior commitments would not find those same impressions plausible at all. Stoic texts emphasize that minds that are subject to error typically give their assent in a "weak" or "precipitate" manner: One gives in too easily to a false impression because of weakness in the mind's existing structure.[10] Chrysippus uses the analogy of a cylindrical object that rolls when pushed. The push, he argues, is only a proximate cause of the rolling; the principal cause is the object's own roundness. In just the same way, the impression to which a rational agent responds is merely a proximate cause of the response: The principal cause lies in the mind itself; that is, in the beliefs one already holds and the relations one recognizes among those beliefs.[11] Yet there is also an important difference between the human being and the cylindrical object, in that the rational psyche also bears primary responsibility for its own mental character. As we have just seen, rationality includes a capacity for self-correction. It is my own prior errors that cause me to assent wrongly on this particular occasion, but I could have eliminated those errors before now, by self-examination and reflection. Thus I am responsible for my present mistake in a much more robust sense than a log is responsible for its own rolling.

By the same token, the rational nature of the human mind also endows our species with an exciting opportunity. Since we have the capacity to evaluate our own judgments, we can also improve our own mental contents over time, eliminating false beliefs and tightening our criteria for what impressions we admit as true. In theory at least, a person might even perfect this rational mind, establishing a belief-set containing only true beliefs that relate to one another in some logical way.[12] One would then be in a state of wisdom, and since assent is regulated by the character of the belief-set, wisdom also implies infallibility. One who had wisdom would assent only in what Stoics call a "strong" manner, meaning not that the assent is especially forceful but that it comes of a well-structured mind.[13] What this person believes and does constitutes perfected rational activity: knowledge and specific instances of knowledge, virtue and virtuous actions. Inasmuch as rational activity is the single most characteristic function of the human being, it is this perfected rational activity that for Stoics constitutes the human good. Hence the person of perfect wisdom, or sage, figures in this philosophy as the standard of happiness as well as that of knowledge and of conduct – a theoretical construct to be sure, but still an ideal against which ordinary persons can measure themselves. Understanding that good and finding ways to approximate it will be the central task of ethical inquiry.

2   ACTION AND THE OBJECTS OF COMMON PURSUIT

Stoic philosophers insisted firmly that only the psychological dimension of action is of concern in ethics. This is to say that for the purposes of moral philosophy, action can be defined strictly as an event within the psyche. That event, termed "impulse" (hormê), is defined as "a motion of the psyche toward something," where "something" is to be filled out by a verb phrase of some kind, something like *acquiring money* or *eating some meat*.[14] Other reports make it clear that in every case of impulse, the agent forms a thought expressible in language as, "It is appropriate for me, here and now, to do such and such."[15] In assenting to a proposition of this general form, one is also performing the relevant action; and conversely, the performance of an action implies that such an assent has been given, whether or not the thought was ever consciously articulated.[16] That is, anything one does on purpose, meaning to act thus, is *in effect* also a judgment with the specified content. We may not be aware of it at the time, but if asked afterwards, we can invariably state what it was we had in mind, even for our most trivial acts. Only with responses of a different order, like blinking or sweating, are we unable to say anything on that score; but such things do not have to be counted as actions.

Because the expression "what is appropriate" (*to kathêkon*) is quite central to Stoic ethics, it is well to ponder what can possibly be meant by it within the theory of action. The Greek word normally expresses fitness or suitability; to Cicero and other Romans, it made sense to render it in Latin as *officium*, which in English is often translated as "duty" or "responsibility." It would hardly make sense, however, to interpret the Stoics as stating that the mental event that initiates action always concerns one's duty as that word is usually understood in English. Since the doctrine is meant to apply uncontroversially to all instances of human action, we should understand "it is appropriate" in a weaker sense, more like "it is fitting" or "this is what suits me."[17] The view then is that if one means to be performing an action, one is at least committed to that being the action that suits oneself under the circumstances.

In all ordinary cases, an action consists also in some observable behavior. Barring external hindrance, my assent to the proposition *it is appropriate for me to walk now* does bring about various movements of my feet and legs. Unlike some other philosophers, however, Chrysippus was prepared to leave the feet out of the definition, defining walking solely in terms of the directive faculty.[18] To the objection that certain things outside the directive faculty are at least necessary conditions for walking to occur (some sort of body, a surface to walk on), he says in effect that even so, what matters about walking is only what is in mind when one chooses to walk. His interest, then, is in the ethical meaning of any given action; that is, in what it says about one's character. Two people who decide on the same set of foot and leg movements, but for different reasons or out of a different overall mental disposition, might turn out to have performed quite different actions. One might walk intelligently or foolishly, by reason of good character or bad, and any particular instance of walking would need to be evaluated accordingly.

With this point in mind, let's consider the class of action the Stoics called "selection" (*eklogê*). These are impulses in which the implied process of practical reasoning makes reference to the "selective value" of some object.[19] Objects with selective value are those that accord with our nature broadly understood, so that when circumstances permit we prefer to have them rather than their opposites: health and strength of body, wealth adequate to one's needs, a favorable reputation among other people, and so on. But we need not think of these objects as goods – that is, as things constitutive of our ultimate well-being in life. In many everyday instances of choosing, it is enough for us that they are the sorts of object creatures of our kind tend naturally to prefer. When we act on this basis, we act in keeping with the Stoic system of value. For it is a central postulate of Stoic ethics that objects of this kind are *not* important for our overall happiness: It is not health, reputation and so on that differentiate the truly good and desirable human life from a less-than-optimal life, but the possession and exercise of good qualities like wisdom, justice, and courage. Objects of the former type are thus termed "preferred indifferents" rather than goods.[20] Even the person of perfect wisdom favors such things, and ordinary people can do so without necessarily being in error. For any given agent and situation, there is a correct choice to be made among all the available preferred and dis-preferred indifferents, balancing one against another. The wise person will make that choice, but even the non-wise person may hit upon it, by chance or by careful deliberation. His or her actions are then indeed "appropriate actions" (*kathêkonta*), overlapping with the "right actions" (*katorthômata*) of the wise.[21]

The Stoics' contemporary opponents sometimes accused them of mere name-switching, inventing a fancy term without changing the associated concept.[22] But these critics failed to grasp what the doctrine actually was. The concept of preferred and dispreferred indifferents enabled the Stoics to distinguish between two ways of valuing things. When something is good for us, they argued, it benefits us every time it is present and thus merits our unconditional allegiance.[23] The preferred indifferents are not like this: They benefit us in many situations, but not in all, and it will sometimes be to our advantage to give up one of them in order to gain another. One way to explain the relation between goods and preferred indifferents is to say that goodness inheres in our *manner of pursuing* the preferred indifferents – in the adverbial term.[24] An objective like personal safety or victory in war can be pursued in more than one way: It is when one pursues it justly or courageously that one behaves as a human being should. Still, one cannot act justly or courageously without some kind of object in prospect. For this reason, the preferred and dispreferred indifferents are sometimes referred to as "the material of virtue."[25]

The notion of preferability also plays an important role in the Stoic account of moral development. Infants are born without any innate stock of concepts and at first behave pre-rationally, like animals. However, they do have certain innate tendencies to prefer those objects that accord with our nature, broadly understood: a healthy bodily condition, human contact, proper functioning of the sense organs and of the faculty of reason. Tending to choose these, they begin to develop certain regularities in conduct, which they themselves eventually come to recognize. At this point, the mind starts to favor what is beginning to be a systematic pattern of conduct, even above the objects towards which its individual actions are directed. There is a transfer of allegiance, from the preferred indifferents to the good proper to a human being – for the completion of that pattern is, once again, the perfected rational activity that is both virtue and wisdom.[26] There will be mistakes along the way; indeed, it is inevitable that we will sometimes mislabel indifferents as goods and evils, in a way detrimental to our real happiness.[27] But if ever the process of moral development does come to fruition, it will owe its beginnings to what some authors call the "starting points" or "seeds" of the virtues; namely to our innate preference for some indifferents over their opposites.[28]

3 EMOTIONAL RESPONSE

Actions on the basis of selective value stand in contrast to another broad class of impulses that are again shared between wise and non-wise agents: in ordinary persons, the impulses called *pathê* or "emotions"; in the wise, those termed *eupatheiai* or "proper feelings." All of these have in common that they involve a movement of the psyche of a specific kind. Our source texts speak of "contracting" the psyche in distress, "elevating" it in either joy or delight, "withdrawing" it in fear or in the *eupatheia* called caution, and "reaching out" in desire or in the *eupatheia* called wishing. Additional terms that are used in a similar way include "lowering," "biting," "shrinking," and "outpouring."[29] It is an inference, but I think a safe one, that this language of physical movements is the ancient Stoics' way of accounting for the characteristic feel of different emotions, by mentioning the underlying change in the psychic material. Since the psyche is sensitive by definition, it is perhaps not surprising that it should be able to sense its own movements.[30] Anger, for instance, produces an internal sensation of "something evaporating from the heart and blowing outwards toward the hands and face."[31] In addition, these same alterations may be expressed in observable behavior: changes in facial expression, crying, blushing or trembling, but also extending a hand to grab something or running away from an object of fear.

These sensed and in some cases observed alterations in the psyche are attributable to the type of judgment that is involved. Unlike other sorts of impulse, the emotions and related affective responses are always directed at some object understood by the agent as a genuine good or evil; that is, as something that makes a difference in his or her overall happiness. That attribution of value could be made in accordance with the Stoic system of value, keeping in view only the objects those philosophers consider to be good or bad. The person of perfect wisdom does experience affective responses on that basis, as will be seen shortly. In ordinary people, however, the typical case is one in which some preferred or dispreferred indifferent is misconstrued as being genuinely good or bad. We desire money, or are upset about losing it, because we believe that money is good for us; we fear death because we believe that death is bad. The strength of the feeling relates directly to this evaluative element of the response, even though in these cases the evaluation is a philosophical error.

With closer study one can discern a more precise account of the judgment made in any given emotion. Some evidence can be drawn from the definitions that are reported in several sources for the principal emotion in each of the four genera defined by the parameters good/bad and present/prospective: fear, with its various species, being concerned with objects viewed as bad and as impending; the various forms of desire with objects viewed as good and in prospect; distress with objects viewed as bad and immediately present; delight with goods immediately present. When defining these generic emotions, the Stoics typically provide a fairly full statement of the proposition endorsed by the agent, as for instance in the following definition of distress:

> Distress is a contraction of psyche which is disobedient to reason, and
> its cause is a fresh believing that an evil is present toward which it is
> appropriate to be contracted.[32]

The definition spells out a complex belief. The agent must believe that an object is present which is of a kind he or she recognizes as bad, and further, that it is appropriate for him or her to contract the psyche when such an evil is present. The evaluative component and the appropriateness component may well be of long standing; what is new in the moment is just the information that the election has been lost or the illness diagnosed. Recognizing this as belonging to a type previously conceived as bad, and adding the belief that present evils merit psychic contraction, the rational mind generates the impulsory impression *it is appropriate for me now to contract my spirit*, and it is to this that assent is given. The contraction itself supervenes on that assent.

In his treatise *On the Emotions*, Chrysippus made efforts to clarify the definition left by his predecessor Zeno. While both philosophers held that emotion involves a psychic movement supervening on an assent of the kind just described, Chrysippus took care to specify that the essential element – what the emotion "is" – is the assent. Chrysippus also spelled out what it is for the psychic movement to be "disobedient to reason." Of course, he might have said, and certainly held, that the emotion is irrational in the sense of being a mistake in judgment. But his particular concern was to explain the phenomenon virtually everyone has experienced, of being involuntarily carried away by one's emotion. Here he speaks of a particular force or "excessiveness" (*pleonasmos*) that some emotions have. To make his point clear, he brings in an analogy. When a person runs, especially if he runs downhill, he cannot immediately stop even if he chooses to do so; the momentum of his running will carry him forward for a moment. Yet no one would say that running is not a voluntary action; instead, we say that the kind of movement running is prevents a subsequent decision from taking effect. Emotion is like this: the decision to elevate or lower or extend the psyche is fully voluntary, but that psychic movement has such vigor that it carries us forward in spite of any subsequent decision *not* to experience that emotion. We are helpless to stop the impulse that we ourselves have initiated.[33]

The ethical implications of this point become clearer when we reflect that emotion in this account is not solely a matter of feeling. Especially in those cases where the event one is concerned about has not yet occurred, the movement of psyche may well be expressed in some observable behavior. "Withdrawing the psyche" might include backing away from the poisonous snake; "reaching" might include reaching out a hand to strike an offender. Stoic texts do not treat such actions as separate events from what one feels in emotion; rather, the behavior is considered to be part of the relevant emotion, equivalent to jumping for joy or wailing in distress. Thus in the Stoic system of thought there are two ways one can back away from a snake. Someone who assumes that being bitten by a snake is bad for his overall happiness will back away fearfully, in an instance of emotional response; one who considers it merely a dispreferred indifferent will do so calmly, in an instance of selection. The two actions may appear just the same to an observer, but they come of different judgments and are evaluated differently. They are also experienced differently by the agent, since in the emotion case the movement of the body corresponds to an inner sensation of shrinking back, perhaps coupled with a sense of helplessness as the emotion takes control.

The consequence of this line of thinking is that the emotions of familiar experience need to be eliminated from human life. In that they arise from mistaken evaluation of their objects, there is no way to defend them, no argument for keeping even a limited version of them. Besides, allowing one's actions to be driven by emotion can be dangerous, since on this account there is no guarantee that one will be able to reverse a decision made on an emotional basis. We may wonder, though, whether the emotion really can be eliminated. Aren't such responses part of human nature? The Stoic answer to this is that false beliefs are *not* part of human nature: As rational beings, we prefer not to be deceived and will reject a view when we realize it is false. What seems more like part of human nature are the psychic movements themselves, with the inner sensations that are how emotions feel to us. But these movements do not have to come about through false belief. For the wise, too, judge some objects to be good or bad for themselves and experience psychic movements, the so-called *eupatheiai*, towards those objects. And psychic movements may also occur without any judgment having been made at all, as in the instantaneous startle response and similar involuntary reactions. As long as the movement is not occasioned by any false judgment and does not rise to the level of action, the Stoics were perfectly willing to concede that it might be ineliminable.[34]

What then are the affective responses that belong to the person of perfect wisdom? Like the *pathê*, the *eupatheiai* are classified into genera according to their content as judgments. Just as the ordinary person experiences an "irrational elevation" which is delight in present goods, so the sage who is aware of present goods experiences a "rational elevation" which is the *eupatheia* of joy.[35] Similarly, the sage experiences a "rational reaching" directed at prospective goods, which is the *eupatheia* called "wishing," and a "rational withdrawing" from prospective evils which is the *eupatheia* called "caution." But we can hardly think that the Stoic sage is assigning the terms "good" and "bad" to the objects Stoics count as indifferents. The objects of the *eupatheiai* can only be genuine goods and evils, which is to say that they must be features of the wise person's own character or conduct. We may think of the virtues, but perhaps more likely are specific virtuous activities. The wise person who finds himself performing a generous action might feel joy in the goodness of that action; one who considers the possibility of performing some unkind deed should feel a strong repugnance.

Logically, no act of vice could ever be performed by the perfect agent, and hence there is no need for a eupathic response towards present evils. Consequently, there is no time when the wise person experiences the full force of psychic contraction or any of the other movements associated with distress or grief. It is a life filled with joy in deeds well done and with eagerness to perform yet more excellent deeds. Significantly, it is also a life filled with affection. Under each of the three genera of eupathic response, our sources list further, more specific *eupatheiai*, and among these, in the genus of "wishing," we find some affective responses that are directed towards other people: "good intent," which is said to consist in "a wish for good things for another for that person's own sake," and similarly "goodwill," "welcoming," and "cherishing."[36] The context for these impulses is the domain of friendship, which in Stoic ethics exists in its truest form only among the wise.[37] Even erotic love is part of the wise person's experience, when its object is not sexual intercourse but the creation of a friendship.[38]

This distinction between the ordinary person's emotions and the wise person's *eupatheiai* raises a further question: Surely non-wise persons are also capable of recognizing features of their own character or conduct, and surely they too will sometimes conceive of these features as either good or bad? It seems, then, that they too might respond emotionally to such objects in keeping with their moral status. Not possessing the human good, they could not experience wise joy, but they might at least be distressed by their lack of wisdom, or long to improve it or shrink back from egregiously vicious behavior. These kinds of reactions might even be conducive to moral progress, directing us away from the activities of vice and towards the attainment of virtue. But the Hellenistic Stoics do not seem to have explored this possibility; at most, they merely recognized the theoretical opening.[39] It was left for the Stoics of the early Roman Empire to develop the thought. Seneca, for instance, makes much of the ordinary person's longing to attain wisdom, and Epictetus explores the advantages of moral shame.

4 CHARACTER AND CHARACTER DEVELOPMENT

The fundamental distinction that structures Stoic discussions of character is that between the wise and virtuous person, or sage, and the ordinary, non-wise person. As we have seen, virtuous wisdom is a condition of a mind in its entirety. In theory – though hardly ever in practice – a person might bring his or her set of beliefs into such good order that all of them are true and all in harmony with one another and with the rational principle that governs the cosmos. Since action is determined by belief, perfect wisdom is also perfect virtue, an overall disposition to behave well that manifests in different realms of action as prudence, courage, justice, self-control, and a host of more specific virtues. Courage, for instance, is defined as "intelligence in matters requiring endurance"; justice as "intelligence in matters requiring distribution."[40] Consequently, the virtues interentail: Although they are not merely the same thing, still the possession of any one of them guarantees that one possesses them all.[41] It follows that all wise agents possess exactly the same set of virtues, and are ready to exercise any of them when the relevant circumstances arise. Likewise, all non-wise agents are characterized by the same set of vices, for each of the vices is nothing other than the lack of the corresponding virtue. Moreover, anyone who possesses either a virtue or a vice must possess it absolutely. These are the kinds of properties that by definition do not vary in degree, just as in geometry a straight line cannot be any more or less straight.[42] Where virtuous wisdom is concerned, it is all or nothing.

But if this were all one could say about the Stoic understanding of moral character, the system could never supply a nuanced description of any one person's moral character. There seem to be only two kinds of person in the world: one endowed with all the good qualities there are, and the other with all the bad ones. Such lack of variety would surely be problematic for the Stoic position on moral responsibility, in which each of us bears responsibility for our own actions just because those actions were determined by our own moral character. If there were no important differences between one person's character and the next, there would be little to say about individual responsibility except that one is, in general, virtuous or not virtuous. Nor would there be much for a Stoic to say about moral progress. Given that the virtues necessarily interentail and each is necessarily possessed in its entirety, moral progress could not be a matter of taking on more and more virtues, and neither could it consist in developing or increasing the virtues one has. The transition from vice to virtue has to occur instantaneously and, from what we have seen thus far, inexplicably.[43]

It is of significance, then, that some of our more detailed sources mention traits of character that yield at least some of the needed flexibility. In addition to the invariable characteristics (*diatheseis*) that are the virtues and vices, there are also mere conditions (*hexeis*) that do not interentail and may be exhibited in greater or lesser degree.[44] In the wise, these traits include what are called "habitudes" (*epitêdeumata*), consisting apparently in various non-moral skills. In the non-wise, the variable traits sound more like faults. They include the so-called "sicknesses" (*nosêmata*), i.e. unjustified cravings, as well as aversions towards certain objects and proclivities towards particular emotions. Varying constellations of traits at this level constitute the different personalities we observe and explain why individuals respond differently in the same situation.

Most carefully explained in the sources are the *nosêmata*, or "sicknesses." The definition makes a *nosêma* "a desirous opinion which has hardened into a condition and become entrenched, according to which people suppose that things which are not choiceworthy are extremely choiceworthy."[45] The examples given include fondness for women (*philogunia*), fondness for wine (*philoinia*), fondness for money (*philarguria*), and the like, individuating the condition by the class of objects favored. From this it is clear that the *nosêma* consists in a single controlling belief. The person who has such a trait believes something like *money is extremely choiceworthy* and is "entrenched" in that belief; that is, assigns it a great deal of salience in determining his or her actions. Aversions are described similarly, as beliefs that incline one to avoid certain types of objects; misogyny is a standard example. The proclivities seem to be different in that they are individuated not by their objects but by the kind of response to which one is disposed. Examples include irascibility, enviousness, timidity, and tendencies towards certain kinds of action, like stealing or violent acts. Although evidence on this point is lacking, one can guess that these too consist in single beliefs, e.g. a deeply entrenched version of the belief that it is appropriate to become angry when slighted. For the habitudes of the wise, we have only a rather obscure definition and a few examples, among which are "fondness for literature" and "fondness for hunting with dogs."[46] By inference, since the wise are not given to mistakes in evaluation, we can assume that these fondnesses must consist in *ceteris paribus* preferences for activities that accord with an individual's physical abilities, situation, or experience.

The realm of Stoic character theory may seem to be a philosophical backwater. It is, however, quite important for us to recognize that the attainment of wisdom is not conceived by Stoics as flattening out all individualities of taste and personality. Still more crucial is the role played by the sicknesses and proclivities in accounts of moral responsibility and moral progress. In order to establish a meaningful account of moral responsibility, one needs to show that the good or bad actions of agents are attributable to traits they possess as individuals, and moreover to traits for which they themselves are to some extent responsible. With their remarks on the *nosêmata*, the Stoics make a start on the necessary reasoning. Multiple sources indicate how Chrysippus explained the formation of such traits. Someone who desires money on some single occasion may not yet have the *nosêma* of greed, and if there is "an immediate application of reason," the full-blown characteristic of greed may never develop.[47] It is when one neglects to reason oneself out of the desire that the mind begins to develop a lasting disposition, yielding more and more easily to stimuli of that kind until eventually the fault becomes entrenched. According to this causal story, our essentially rational nature is implicated in the formation of the trait, even though environmental influences and the like may also be involved. The *nosêmata* also feature prominently in Stoic efforts to mark out differing levels of moral progress. Because the non-wise agent can exhibit these traits singly, in various groupings, or not at all, it is possible to supply formulas for more and less promising moral states even among those who do not yet possess the virtues. The person who has one or more *nosêmata* is morally distinct from one who has eliminated them all, even where the latter is still susceptible to error and to the emotions.[48] One is not beyond the possibility of relapse until wisdom takes on the security of perfection; yet even so, the sustained exercise of the rational capacities we have will make a difference.

In Book 4 of his treatise *On Ends*, Cicero criticizes Stoic ethical psychology on behalf of the skeptical Academy. His complaint is that Stoics define the human good in relation to rational activity alone, not giving consideration to health, freedom from pain, and all the other conditions human beings need in order to thrive both in body and in mind. Chrysippus speaks of the supreme good "not as if the mind were predominant in us, but as if there were nothing in us *except* mind."[49] This is meant to be a devastating remark, and yet it is one that Chrysippus need not have disallowed. The simpler aspects of our nature – those in which we resemble other animals, or living things generally – he could acknowledge, as indeed he does, and yet maintain that the good of the human species has to be defined in terms of human excellence. Putting it another way: The reasoning abilities that characterize the human species actually define what it is for a human being to have an excellent life. What this line of thought produced is exactly what was intended: a rather cerebral but not unappealing system of ethics that develops Greek rationalism to its furthest extent.

NOTES

1. Ar. *NE* 1.7, 1097b24–1098a18. For Stoic versions see D.L. 7.86 [LS (= Long and Sedley (1987)) 57A]; also Cicero's criticism of Chrysippus at *Fin.* 4.28 (on which see below); and especially Seneca, *Ep.* 76.12–16.

2. The evidence is collected in Long and Sedley (1987), in Inwood and Gerson (2008), and in von Arnim (1921–24) (= *SVF*). For interpretation see especially Inwood (1985), Long and Sedley (1987), Annas (1992), Long (1996), Striker (1996c) 221–80, Brennan (2005), Graver (2002) and (2007).

3. See the report of Cicero in *Acad.* 1.39 [LS 45A]; also the arguments reported in Nemesius 2.78–79, 81 [LS 45C-D].

4. For these basics of Stoic physics see Long and Sedley (1987) chs 45–47. A helpful overview is White (2003).

5. For the *scala naturae* and for the capacities conferred by *psuchê* see especially Origen, *Princ.* 3.1 [LS 53A] and Calcidius 220 [LS 53G]; for the basic property of sensitivity D.L. 7.156 [*SVF* 2.774]; Eusebius, *Evangelical Preparation* 15.20.2 [*SVF* 1.141].

6. For the *hêgemonikon* and its distinctively mental functions see S.E., *AM* 7.234 [LS 53F], Aetius 4.21 [LS 53H], Philo Alex. *Leg. Alleg.* 1.30 [LS 53P]; for the term "rational impression," D.L. 7.51 [LS 39A].

7. Cic. *Pr. Acad.* 2.21 [LS 39C]; S.E. *AM* 8.275 [LS 53T].

8. S.E. *AM* 8.270 [*SVF* 2.727]; a yet more impressive inference is reported by the same author in *Pyrrh. Hyp.* 1.69 [LS 36E]. Inwood (1985, 72–91) argues, convincingly, that while animals certainly react to impressions of their environments, they cannot properly be said to assent. What is assigned to them in some sources must in fact be quasi-assent, perhaps originally termed *eixis* or "yielding."

9. S.E. *AM* 8.275 [LS 53T].

10. Cic. *Acad.* 1.41 [LS 41B], Gel. 7.2.6–13 [LS 62D].

11. Cic. *Fato* 39–43 [LS 62C]. Beliefs can be specified as causes because a belief in Stoicism is a body, a corporeal mind in a state of believing some incorporeal proposition.

12. My reading of the underlying epistemology is that Stoic wisdom could in fact be adequately described *either* as the condition in which all propositions believed correspond to objective features of the world *or* as that in which all propositions believed cohere logically with another. Two doctrines are relevant here. First, Stoic cosmology does not have room for unrelated facts: Any set of propositions that corresponds to the world as it is must be interconnected via the seminal principles that structure the cosmos. Second, Stoics are inclined to assume that every human mind (excluding those of young children) contains a core of true beliefs. These develop in all persons in consequence of our providential

orientation towards our own constitution (D.L. 7.85 [LS 57A]) and cannot be eliminated. In all ordinary cases, errors and inconcinnities develop as well (see note 27), but the establishment of full coherence would necessarily discard the false rather than the true.

13. *PHerc.* 1020 [LS 41D], Stob. 2.7.11m, 111–12 W, [LS 41G]. Compare note 10 above.

14. The Greek word also means "inception." For the definition see Stob. 2.7.9, 86W [LS 53Q]. Impulses are "toward the predicates contained in the propositions," Stob. 2.7.9b, 88W [LS 33I]; compare Cic. *Tusc.* 4.21.

15. The key witness is Arius, in Stob. 2.7.9, 86–87W [LS 53Q]: "What sets impulse in motion is nothing other than an impulsory impression of what is then and there appropriate."

16. Thus impulses are one category of assent, Plut., *St. Rep.* 1057A [LS 53S]; Stob. 2.7.9b, 88W [LS 33I].

17. For this reason I stand clear of the interpretation of Cooper (2012), 203, that the *kathêkon* is "moral duty" performed "for duty's sake."

18. Sen. *Ep.* 113.23 [LS 53L].

19. Cic. *Fin.* 3.20; Stob. 2.7.7 [SVF 3.118], 7f–g [LS 58D-E].

20. See for instance D.L. 7.101–3 [LS 58A], but the terminology is widespread.

21. Cic. *Fin.* 3.58–59 [LS 59F; note that LS uses the translation "proper functions"]; S.E. *AM* 11.200 [LS 59G].

22. This line of attack was favored by Antiochus of Ascalon; it goes back to the Academic philosopher Carneades (Cic., *Tusc.* 5.120).

23. D.L. 7.101–3 [LS 58A]; Cic. *Fin.* 3.33–34.

24. Adverbial formulations are ubiquitous in Stoic ethics: see for example D.L. 7.103 [LS 58A]; Sen. *Ep.* 118.11; S.E. *AM* 11.200–201 [LS 59G].

25. Chrysippus in Plut. *Comm. Not.* 1069c [LS 59A]; Sen., *Ep.* 71.21, 86.39.

26. Cic. *Fin.* 3.16–22 [LS 59D].

27. D.L. 7.89 [*SVF* 3.228]; Galen *PHP* 5.5.14–21; Calcidius *In Tim. Plato.* 165–66 [*SVF* 3.229].

28. Cleanthes in Stob. 2.7.5b8 [LS 61L]; Cic. *Tusc.* 3.2; Sen. *Ep.* 120.4.

29. Galen *PHP* 4.2.1–6 [LS 65D]; D.L. 7.116 [LS 65F].

30. See above, note 6, with Hierocles *Elements of Ethics*, col. 4.38–53 [LS 53B].

31. Chrysippus *apud* Galen *PHP* 3.1.25 [*SVF* 2.886].

32. Stob. 2.7.10b, 90W [*SVF* 3.394]; cf. Cic. *Tusc.* 3.25, 4.14; ps.-Andr. *On Emotions* 1 [LS 65B].

33. Galen *PHP* 4.2.10–18 [LS 65J].

34. See for instance Cic. *Tusc.* 3.83, Epict. frag. 9 [LS 65Y]; Origen fr. 19.68–75; this last uses the term "pre-emotion" *(propatheia).*

35. Cic. *Tusc.* 4.12–15, D.L. 7.116 [LS 65F].

36. D.L. 7.116 [LS 65F]; ps-Andron. 6 [*SVF* 3.432].

37. D.L. 7.124; Stob. 2.7.11m, 108W.

38. D.L. 7.129–30; Stob. 2.7.5b9, 65–66W, 2.7.11s (115W).

39. Had Chrysippus discussed the point, Posidonius could not have made the objection offered in Galen *PHP* 4.5.26–28 (= fr. 164 Edelstein and Kidd, lines 12–25). See also Cic. *Tusc.* 3.77.

40. Plut. *Virt. Mor.* 441ab [LS 61B]; Stob. 2.7.5b2, 60W [*SVF* 3.254].

41. Plut. *St. Rep.* 1034c-e [LS 61C]; Stob. 2.7.5b5, 63W [LS 61D].

42. Simplicius *On Aristotle's Categories* 237.25–238.20 [LS 47S].

43. Chrysippus *apud* Plut. *Comm. Not.* 1063ab [LS 61T]; Cic. *Fin.* 3.48.

44. Stob. 2.7.5f, 70–71W [*SVF* 3.104].

45. Stob. 2.7.10e, 93W [LS 65S].

46. Stob. 2.7.5b11, 67W [*SVF* 3.294].

47. Cic. *Tusc.* 4.24–25, citing Chrysippus. Compare Epictetus *Diss.* 2.18.8–10; Seneca *Ep.* 75.12.

48. The clearest account is in Sen. *Ep.* 75.8–14, where a mention of alternative views (*quidam*, 75.10) suggests that Seneca is drawing on older Stoic texts. Compare note 47.

49. Cic. *Fin.* 4.28.

12 Skeptical Ethics

Luca Castagnoli

In contemporary meta-ethics, the term "skepticism" is often used (and sometimes abused) for a wide variety of stances. These include

- a cluster of *epistemological* positions; for example, various forms of denial of, or doubt about, the existence or very possibility of *moral knowledge* or *justified belief*; and
- a range of *metaphysical* positions; for example, the rejection of, or suspicion about, the existence of *moral properties* or *facts*.

These forms of skepticism have complex interconnections, and are intertwined with theories of

- the *semantics* of moral language, according to which moral statements either are meant to be truth-apt and assertoric or function as different speech acts, having expressive or prescriptive force.

Moral skepticism can be a fragment of global skepticism, or a distinctive approach within an otherwise non-skeptical world view (for example, scientific naturalism); and it can be exceptionless, or directed only at some moral concepts, properties, views, and arguments.

The picture is complicated by the fact that moral properties or truths have been targeted differently by different forms of "skepticism." Whereas "moral nihilism" or "error theory" deny their existence tout court, other positions reject the idea that moral properties or truths can be absolute, universal, or independent of the beliefs, attitudes, or conventions of particular communities or individuals. These attacks on ethical objectivism are best described not as "skepticism," but as varieties of ethical *relativism* or *subjectivism*.

In light of this breadth of uses, "skeptical" ethical attitudes could be traced back to the birth of philosophical inquiry in Greece, and to pre-philosophical and non-philosophical approaches to morality as well. Just consider the sophistic opposition of *phusis* ("nature") and *nomos* ("law" or "convention"), the rejection of "natural" morality, and the emergence of Protagorean relativism and Thrasymachean "immoralism" in the fifth century BC. This chapter will focus on the two main ancient skeptical traditions, the Academic and the Pyrrhonian.

Plato's dialogues often end in *aporia*, with no positive conclusion concerning the subject matter examined, and are peppered with disavowals of knowledge by their main character, Socrates. Some aspects of the Socratic method were revived and radicalized within Plato's Academy by the two most influential heads of the school in the Hellenistic period, Arcesilaus (c. 316–241 BC) and Carneades (214–128 BC). Many ancient interpreters – including later Academics – understood Arcesilaus and Carneades, who wrote nothing, to be committed to the denial of the possibility of knowledge and to universal "suspension of judgment" (*epochē*). Later in the first century BC, Philo of Larissa relaxed this skeptical tendency, by allowing fallible assent in the absence of certain knowledge, and Antiochus of Ascalon led Platonism towards full-blown dogmatism.

As for the Pyrrhonian tradition, since antiquity Pyrrho of Elis (c. 360–270 BC) has been identified as the ideal representative of a life without beliefs. He too did not write anything, nor did he found a school, and after his death his contribution was overlooked, until in the first century BC Aenesidemus introduced a new brand of skepticism, which he baptized "Pyrrhonism," in reaction to what he took to be contemporary forms of positive and negative (Academic) dogmatism. Sextus Empiricus (second century AD), the last important Pyrrhonist known to us, is the most valuable source on the Pyrrhonian outlook and arguments; his work testifies to the level of sophistication that Pyrrhonian skepticism reached.

Both Academic and Pyrrhonian skepticism systematically targeted ethical concepts, beliefs, and theories just as they targeted concepts, beliefs, and theories in the other areas of the Hellenistic tripartition of philosophy (logic, physics, ethics). Section 1 will examine some argumentative strategies marshaled by the ancient skeptics in ethics, and the status of their conclusions.

Unlike modern forms of "insulated" epistemological skepticism, ancient skeptics aimed to show that a life without beliefs (including, crucially, ethical beliefs) is practically possible, adopting models of human agency which do not presuppose assent and belief. Section 2 will sketch the Academic and Pyrrhonian responses to the charges of "inactivity" (*apraxia*).

Skepticism was presented by the Pyrrhonists as driven by an ethical goal: happiness understood as psychological "tranquility" (*ataraxia*), to be reached through complete detachment from beliefs about values. Section 3 will examine how the Pyrrhonian therapy is supposed to lead to *ataraxia*, and whether the proposed route is viable and worth pursuing.

I   THE SKEPTICS' ARGUMENTS IN ETHICS

Arcesilaus and Carneades

While our sources provide enough information to reconstruct the general motivations, methods, and goals of Arcesilaus' skepticism, we know very little of the specific arguments he marshaled, especially in the sphere of ethics. Arcesilaus' universal *epochē*, described as the withholding of assent from any claim, whether positive or negative, is linked to his relentless practice of arguing against *any* claim put forward by his interlocutors.[1] Any ethical concept, view, or theory must have been, in principle, the target of Arcesilaus' arguments. But what were these arguments meant to conclude? Imagine Arcesilaus debating with a Stoic, who proclaims that virtue is the only good. He would have attacked this doctrine, producing arguments concluding that virtue is not the only good, for example on the grounds that there are also other goods (e.g. pleasure, health, or tranquility), or that virtue, as such, is not good at all. Does this mean that Arcesilaus believed that virtue is not the only good? This would be inconsistent with universal *epochē* and with the practice of refuting any claim, *whether positive or negative*. When facing an Epicurean, then, Arcesilaus would have attacked his hedonism too, for example by arguing for the (Stoic) conclusion that virtue is the only good.

According to this picture, Arcesilaus' dialectical practice[2] did not commit him to any ethical position. Did it commit him, however, to a meta-ethical stance? In their accounts of Arcesilaus' argument against Zeno's Stoicism, our sources connect *epochê* with *akatalēpsia*, "inapprehensibility": since (1) "apprehension" or "cognition" (*katalēpsis*), understood as an infallible grasp of its object, is impossible, and since (2) we ought to assent only to what we have apprehended, (3) we should suspend judgment about everything.[3] Whether Arcesilaus was committed to *akatalēpsia*, to the connection between *akatalēpsia* and *epochê*, and to the conclusion that we ought to suspend judgment is debated. On the plausible interpretation according to which, in some sense, he was "committed" at least to *akatalēpsia*, Arcesilaus' position would be a form of skepticism that excludes the possibility of moral knowledge, while making no positive or negative claim about the nature and very existence of moral facts, properties, or truths. Arcesilaus' moral skepticism did not attest, however, to distinctive ethical concerns, and did not result from a context-dependent skeptical methodology.

If Arcesilaus could oppose any party to the philosophical debate, he must have been ready to argue *contra* and *pro* any position. Several sources speak of Arcesilaus and Carneades in the same breath when they report on the Academic argumentative practices:

> In arguments he [Carneades] adopted the same approach as Arcesilaus; for he too practiced arguing on both sides, and used to refute everything said by the others. [4]
>
> *(Eusebius of Caesarea,* Preparation for the Gospel *[PE] 14.7.15)*

The most notorious illustration of Carneades' taste for arguing on both sides belongs to the ethical/political sphere: the two opposed public speeches he made for and against traditional conceptions of justice on consecutive days during an Athenian embassy at Rome in 155 BC.[5]

Moral disagreement has been traditionally invoked to support a range of meta-ethical positions, including relativism and several forms of anti-realism. The Academics frequently set up philosophical disagreements (*diaphôniai*), pitting conflicting views one against the other. Cicero's survey of the three parts of philosophy in the *Lucullus* (2.116–147) is an excellent illustration of this. The payoff is, again, epistemological: the realization that we lack any firm grasp of the disputed issue, and thus assent to any of the conflicting views would be rash. Suspension of judgment is not the result of the realization of the "equipollence" or equal strength (*isostheneia*) of the conflicting positions: *Epochê* is arrived at *via akatalêpsia*, and the assumption that without infallible cognition assent is unwarranted. The Academics were ready to concede that some views appear, at least provisionally, more persuasive than others (cf. e.g. *Luc.* 124). With his opposed speeches about justice, for example, Carneades aimed "to show that its defenders had no certain or firm arguments about justice" (Lactantius, *Divine Institutions* 5.14.5), and not the absolute equipollence of the reasons on both sides.

The collection of *diaphôniai* also provided the Academics with ammunition for their attacks. Consider the so-called *Carneadea divisio* of ethical "ends" or "goals":[6] "Carneades surveyed all the philosophical theories that had been propounded to date concerning the supreme good, and all those that could possibly be propounded as well" (Cicero, *On Ends* 5.16). Within his attack on the Stoics' view on the *summum bonum*, for example, Carneades would adopt a conflicting position "not because he approved it, but to oppose the Stoics" (*Luc.* 131). An additional function of the Academic classification of conflicting views was to *deconstruct* their conflict, revealing the lack of substance of their proponents' claims to originality.[7]

The Pyrrhonists

The systematic collection of *diaphôniai* is prominent also in Sextus Empiricus. The key texts for Sextus' ethical arguments are his discussion of the tenth mode of *epochê* in the first book of the *Outlines of Pyrrhonism* (*PH* 1.145–163), the second half of the third book (3. 168–279), and *Against the Ethicists* (*M* 11).

The tenth of the modes of suspension that Sextus attributes to the "older skeptics" (*PH* 1.36) and other sources credit to Aenesidemus is presented as "mainly concerned with ethical matters" (1.145).[8] The section, like the parallel one in *PH* 3.198–234, lists conflicting ways in which a certain action, behavior, or ethical position is assessed from the perspective of different "ways of life" (*agôgai*), customs (*ethê*), laws (*nomoi*), mythical beliefs (*muthikai pisteis*), and philosophical dogmatic theories (*dogmatikai hypolêpseis*). For example, having sex in public is regarded as appropriate in Indian custom, but considered shameful among most peoples; adultery appears acceptable if we stand by the countless mythical stories about the gods' love affairs, but is prohibited by law in some places; stealing is deemed wrong and illegal in most societies, but clearly not by those who call Hermes "a most stealing god" (for how could a god do something wrong?). One might object that most of these examples do not even qualify as illustrations of *moral* disagreement by the standards of modern ethics; but this could be construed as a higher-order ethical disagreement which Sextus would have welcomed.

What conclusions should we draw from the observation of endemic disagreement? The tenth mode follows the same pattern as the previous nine:

> Since so much contradiction (*anômalia*) has been shown in objects by
> this mode too, we will not be able to say what each existing thing is
> (*esti*) like in its nature (*kata tên phusin*), but only how it appears
> (*phainetai*) relative to (*pros*) a given way of life, or a given law or a given
> custom and so on. Because of this mode too, therefore, it is necessary
> for us to suspend judgment on the nature of external existing objects.[9]
>
> (*Sextus Empiricus*, Outlines of Pyrrhonism *1.163*)

In the presence of disagreement on whether *x* (e.g. stealing) is F (e.g. wrong) or F* (e.g. right, or at least acceptable), we will be able to record how *x appears* differently, F and F*, relative to different "contexts" R and S (e.g. particular laws, customs, or mythical beliefs); but we will have to suspend judgment on whether *x is really*, in its own "nature" or essence, F or F*. For the Pyrrhonist, the observation of the variability and relativity of moral attitudes and judgments does not lead to moral relativism (*x is both* F, relative to R, and *is* F*, relative to S) or nihilism (*x is neither* F nor F*). We are not told *why* suspension of judgment should follow; but the context suggests that the disagreement is undecidable (or has not been satisfactorily decided so far), since the reasons and arguments for the opposite sides appear equally strong (or weak):

(1) *x* appears F relative to S.
(2) *x* appears F* relative to R.
(3) We are unable to prefer S and F to R and F*, or vice versa, because of equipollence.
(4) We can neither affirm nor deny, neither believe nor disbelieve, that *x* is F, or that *x* is F* (or that it is both, or neither), i.e. we suspend judgment.[10]

Consider also Sextus' presentation of the first mode of Agrippa,[11] which generalizes over some of the material of the ten modes:

> According to the mode deriving from disagreement, we find that undecidable conflict about the matter proposed has come about both in ordinary life (*para tôi biôi*) and among philosophers. Because of this we are not able either to choose or to reject anything, and we end up with suspension of judgment. (PH 1.165)

The evidence surveyed so far suggests that Pyrrhonian skepticism in ethics was epistemological, and not some form of ontological anti-realism. It has been suggested that Sextus' arguments in all areas of philosophy rely on tacit realist presuppositions.[12] This goes too far, however: Since the disagreeing parties will include anti-realist ethical attitudes and theories, one issue on which the Pyrrhonist ought to suspend judgment is the very existence of moral properties or facts. What is clear is that, unlike the Academics, Sextus does not exclude the possibility of moral knowledge.

The picture is complicated by some conflicting evidence suggesting that Pyrrhonian ethical skepticism was actually a peculiar mix of moral nihilism and relativism. Here is an argument pattern frequent in *PH* 3 and *M* 11:

If, then, things which affect us by nature (*phusei*) affect everyone in the same way, while we are not all affected in the same way in the case of the so-called goods, then nothing is by nature good. *(PH 3.182)*

The argument does not aim to induce *epochê* through the equipollence of the conflicting views about the good surveyed immediately before (3.180–181). It purports to establish the negative conclusion that nothing is "by nature" good, on the basis of what we can label the "invariability condition":

For an object to be F "by nature," it should be and appear F *invariably* and *without qualifications*.[13]

Something that manifests itself as F only to some people, or only in some circumstances, or only in certain respects, cannot be F "by nature." The conclusion seems to be associated, at times, with a form of relativism. For example, because of the disagreement among ordinary people, poets, and philosophers, Sextus concludes that

not even death can be deemed something by nature dreadful, just as life cannot be deemed something by nature fine. None of these things is so and so by nature; all are matters of convention (*nomista*) and relative (*pros ti*). *(3.232)*

This use of disagreement is incompatible with the general thrust of the Pyrrhonian strategy depicted in *PH* 1, and exemplified in *PH* 2 and 3. It has been suggested that the invariability condition represents a distinctive trait of Aenesidemus' Pyrrhonism, influenced by Heraclitean, Eleatic, or Platonic views, possibly already present in Pyrrho,[14] and sporadically emerging, as a relic, in some Sextan texts.[15] The suggestion was prompted by the observation that in several reports of views and arguments which either are attributed to Aenesidemus or could have an Aenesideman pedigree (including, notably, the bulk of Sextus' *Against the Ethicists*),[16] we find negative claims and conclusions, e.g. the goals of life celebrated by dogmatic philosophers do not exist [Phot. *Bibl.* 212.170b12–14], nothing is good or bad by nature (e.g. S.E. *M* 11.71, 130) and formulations and uses of the invariability condition (e.g. *M* 8.8; 11.69–71).

These occurrences appear insufficient, however, to establish the existence of an earlier Pyrrhonism essentially different from Sextus'. Frequently in his writings the context unequivocally shows that *epochê* is the goal, but Sextus only makes a case for the negative conclusion that something is not true or does not exist, since the positive arguments require no rehearsing, as they represent the "default" com-monsense or philosophical position. Some ancient sources could have misunderstood or misrepresented this strategy. As for the invariability condition itself, both Aenesidemus and Sextus might have used it dialectically, to reach anti-dogmatic conclusions from a dogmatic prin-ciple to which they had no commitment, following an argumentative trope pervasive in Pyrrhonism.[17] Finally, some apparent relativistic conclusions could be read as shorthand claims about the *relativity of appearances*:

> The eighth mode is the one deriving from relativity (*pros ti*), by which we conclude that, since everything is relative, we will suspend judgment as to how things are absolutely and in their nature. It should be recognized that here, as elsewhere, we use "is" (*esti*) loosely instead of "appears" (*phainetai*), implicitly meaning "everything appears relative."
>
> (PH 1.135)

2 IS A SKEPTICAL LIFE POSSIBLE?

Since antiquity, two stock objections have been that skepticism is incoherent and self-refuting and that the skeptics cannot "live" their skepticism. According to the first charge, the skeptic incurs "reversal" (*peritropê*) whenever he claims or argues that knowledge is impossible or that we ought to suspend judgment about everything.[18] According to the second, skepticism should lead to *apraxia* or *anenergêsia* ("inaction" or "inactivity").[19] Since philosophical argumentation was the skeptics' most distinctive activity, it is not surprising that their defenses against the two charges were often couched in similar terms.

Arcesilaus and Carneades: Eulogon *and* Pithanon

Our sources attribute to Arcesilaus two answers to the *apraxia* charge.[20] How exactly to interpret them, the distinct versions of the charge they address, and their mutual relationship, is debated. Within his criticism of the Epicurean attacks on Arcesilaus, in *Against Colotes* Plutarch reports that it was the Stoics who first used the *apraxia* charge to show that whoever suspends judgment about everything is condemned to paralysis (1122A–B). The charge is later reformulated as a challenge to the possi-bility of rational skeptical agency:

> But how is it that someone who suspends judgment does not rush away
> to a mountain instead of to the baths, or stands up and walks to the door
> rather than the wall when he wants to go out to the market-place?[21]
>
> (1122E)

Arcesilaus replied that impulse (*hormê*) and action can spring directly
and naturally from our impressions (*phantasiai*), in particular those
derived from sense perception (*aisthêsis*), without the medium of assent
(*sunkatathesis*) and belief (*doxa*). The skeptic will walk to the door, and
not to the wall, simply because the door appears to him to be a door, and
not a wall, and not because he assents to the proposition "there is a door
over there" (1122B-F). This reply adopts Stoic concepts and terminology
to tackle the Stoic charge. Whether this use is purely dialectical, or
commits Arcesilaus to a particular theory of action, cannot be addressed
here, but it is clear that the suggestion that impressions are sufficient for
action makes the account analogous to what the Stoics would have
recognized as the mechanism of *animal* behavior. Moreover, with its
focus on perceptual appearances, Arcesilaus' solution, as reported by
Plutarch, does not explain why, in the absence of any belief, one should
want to go to the baths or to the market in the first place (an explanation
might need to refer to moral motivations and beliefs).

It was perhaps against the rejoinder that activity without belief is
not *human* rational agency that Arcesilaus introduced the "reasonable"
(*eulogon*):

> Arcesilaus says that one who suspends judgment about everything will
> regulate his choices and avoidances and actions in general by the
> reasonable; and that by proceeding in accordance with this criterion he
> will act rightly (*katorthôsei*).
>
> (S.E. M 7.158)

Since the term *eulogon* has a Stoic pedigree, it is a question whether
Arcesilaus' use should be understood as merely dialectical.[22] The details
of that use are controversial, partly because the Stoics themselves appear
to have adopted the term in different contexts. On the one hand, they
defined a "reasonable proposition" as one that "has more tendencies to
be true, like 'I will be alive tomorrow'" (D.L. 7.76), but can turn out to be
false (D.L. 7.177); on the other hand, they described an "appropriate
action" (*kathêkon*) as one which falls short of the sage's "right action"
(*katorthôma*) but, once done, has a "reasonable justification" (*eulogos
apologia*) (S.E. M 7.158; Stob. 2.85).[23] Arcesilaus' identification of the
eulogon itself with right action might then be a misrepresentation or

parody of the Stoic position. However that may be, in order to vindicate the possibility of a skeptical human life the *eulogon* should have functioned as a practical "criterion of action," and not as a criterion for justified belief: Although we can act in accordance with what appears "reasonable," we should not assent to it as something true, or to the truth of the second-order proposition that it is (or was) reasonable to act as we do (or did).

According to Clitomachus, Carneades tackled the self-refutation charge by claiming that *akatalêpsia*, like all the other Academic "doctrines," was "approved" as "persuasive" or "convincing" (*pithanon*, Latin *probabile*) but not assented to and believed (Cic. *Luc.* 109–110). The *pithanon* was also Carneades' answer to the *apraxia* charge:

> Since he himself [Carneades] too has some criterion demanded of him
> for the conduct of life and attainment of happiness, he is virtually
> compelled, as far as he himself is concerned, to adopt a position on this
> by taking as his criterion both the persuasive impression and the one
> which is simultaneously persuasive, undiverted (*aperispaston*) and
> thoroughly examined (*diexôdeumenên*).　　　　　　　(S.E. M 7.166)

Persuasive impressions had been defined by the Stoics as "those that produce a smooth movement in the soul, for example now that it is day, and that I am conversing, and everything having a similar perspicuity" (S.E. *M* 7.242). They strongly pull us towards assent, but can be false, and fall short of the Stoic demanding standards of assent. They must be sufficient, however, to guide our actions:

> After all, the wise person you [Stoics] promote also follows persuasive
> impressions in many cases ... Indeed, if he didn't approve them, his
> whole life would be undermined. Here's one case: when he steps into
> a boat, does the sage apprehend in his mind that he is definitely going
> to arrive? How could he? Still, should he set out from here to Puteoli,
> thirty stades away, in a tested vessel, with a good helmsman, and in
> calm weather like this, he would have the persuasive impression that
> he will arrive there safely.　　　　　　　　　　(Cic. Luc. 100–101)

As this scenario exemplifies, the prima facie persuasiveness of a certain impression should undergo more and more stringent tests depending on the importance of the choice we face. Persuasive impressions warrant additional confidence when they are consistent with other relevant contextual impressions (they are "undiverted"); and even more when they and their context are "thoroughly examined" (*M* 7.176–184).

On Clitomachus' interpretation, these tests are still insufficient to war-rant assent; nonetheless, following the *pithanon* can be recognized as rational, responsible, purposive, human agency.[24] Carneades is credited with the view that it is "in matters which contribute to happiness (*eudaimonia*)" that thorough examination is in order (*M* 7.184), but our sources focus on sense impressions, and fail to address the question of the degree of confidence we can have in our ethical impressions, including our views about value. In Cicero's passage, for example, the issue decided via the *pithanon* is not whether we should want to go to Puteoli, whether this choice might be right or good, or whether a shipwreck would be bad for us. We can imagine, however, that some of the Academic critical examinations in ethics, including the *Carneadea divisio* (cf. Section 1), aimed not only to undermine dogmatic positions, but also to assess their relative persuasiveness.[25]

One enduring debate is whether Carneades adopted the *pithanon in propria persona*. I can only mention two relevant considerations here. Against the contention that Carneades' adoption must have been purely dialectical, because it would have been inconsistent for him to commit to a particular criterion, it should be noted that the view that the *pithanon* is an appropriate guide for action and thought could itself have been approved by Carneades as *pithanon*.[26] Moreover, if Carneades only meant to illustrate, dialectically, the unwelcome theoretical and practical consequences of Stoic epistemological rigorism, why on earth should he have also offered to the Stoics a way out with the *pithanon*? And why should so many opponents of the Academics, including the Stoics, have kept using the *apraxia* charge *against them*?[27]

The Pyrrhonists: Following Phainomena

That ancient Pyrrhonists advocated *epochê in propria persona* is beyond doubt. Unlike modern forms of skepticism, Pyrrhonism was not an "insulated" theoretical stance: it proposed itself as a philosophical ther-apy meant to have a deep, positive, and lasting impact on how we live (see Section 3). Unsurprisingly, then, the *apraxia* charge was a weapon of choice against the Pyrrhonists, and they endeavored to develop appro-priate defense strategies.

Later Pyrrhonists identified Pyrrho of Elis as their noble father, a skeptic who embraced a life without beliefs as the recipe for mental tranquility (*ataraxia*). It is debated whether his reasons to conclude that things are "equally undifferentiated, undetermined, and undecided," as reported by his pupil Timon according to our key source, Aristocles of Messene (Euseb. *PE* 14.18.2–5), were epistemological (the impossibility of deciding between the conflicting reports of our senses and intellect)[28] or metaphysical (the indeterminacy of reality itself).[29] It is also debated whether the scope of the "things" (*pragmata*) on which Pyrrho suspended judgment was universal, or his interest was narrowly ethical, and his suspension involved only value and moral notions such as good and bad, just and unjust.[30]

Pyrrho's practical attitude emerges from a number of colorful anecdotes. Some of them illustrate his utter "indifference" (*adiaphoria*) in all situations: For example, he would keep speaking after his interlocutor had left, and once he did not stop when he saw his friend Anaxarchus in a ditch (D.L. 9.63). Others portray Pyrrho's disregard for social conventions: He would leave his family without warning, wandering around like a vagrant (9.63), or would engage in housework which would have appeared inappropriate for a man of his social standing, including washing pigs or taking poultry to the market (9.66). Other anecdotes stress Pyrrho's lack of susceptibility to emotional reactions: He remained calm on a ship during a storm, pointing at a piglet peacefully eating its food as a positive model of *ataraxia* (D.L. 9.68; Plut. *De prof. virt.* 82E-F). Not even in the face of extreme physical pain did he frown (9.67), displaying an impassibility (*apatheia*) which goes beyond the tranquility and "moderation of affection" supposedly secured by *epochē* (see Section 3). When he failed to live by his own standards, he would acknowledge this as a weakness: "when he was once scared by a dog that set on him, he responded to criticism by saying that it was difficult to strip oneself completely of being human" (D.L. 9.68; cf. Eus. *PE* 14.18.26).

All in all, this picture is consistent with the "theory" outlined in Aristocles: Someone with no opinions on how things are, and especially on what is good or bad, right or wrong, fine or shameful, will not be concerned about what is socially sanctioned, and will not fear pain, injury, or even death. Whether such an outlook is psychologically possible is debated. But it is its "livability" that was especially scrutinized in antiquity. According to Antigonus of Carystus, Pyrrho would take no precaution against dangers, such as precipices, oncoming carts, and rabid dogs, and thus constantly needed to be rescued by his friends (D.L. 9.62). The story has been discarded as a hostile fabrication, foisting upon Pyrrho the random, self-destructing behavior which someone who held his position would have to display, *according to his critics*, to be consistent.

Later Pyrrhonists made "appearances" (*phainomena*) their "criterion of action": while suspending judgment on whether things are as they appear, they "went along with" *phainomena* in their day-to-day life, conducting an outwardly ordinary existence. Timon claimed that Pyrrho "did not depart from normal practice" (D.L. 9.105);[31] Aenesidemus maintained that Pyrrho "did not act carelessly in the details of daily life" (9.62) because he "followed appearances" (9.106). But the hypothesis that Pyrrho might already have adopted appearances as a practical criterion need not force us to dismiss Antigonus' stories completely. Pyrrho could have made a display of his daredevil attitude only occasionally (he lived to be nearly ninety), as memorable "trials of strength" against those critics who protested that his adoption of *phainomena* betrayed attachment to his own welfare, and some trust in the *phainomena* themselves.

Unless the anecdotes on Pyrrho's eccentric behavior are pure fabrications, social norms and conventions were not included among the appearances he followed. It is probable that with Aenesidemus the scope of appearances became broader (cf. the discussion of the tenth mode of *epochē* in Section 1, and possibly D.L. 9.107–108). It is in Sextus Empiricus, however, that we find a full articulation of *phainomena* as practical criteria:

> "Criterion" has two senses: there are criteria adopted to provide conviction about the reality or unreality of something ... and there are criteria of action, attending to which in everyday life (*kata ton bion*) we perform some actions and not others ... the criterion of the skeptical way is what is apparent (*to phainomenon*), implicitly meaning by this the appearance (*phantasia*) of it; for it depends on passive and unwilled feelings and is not an object of investigation ... Thus, attending to appearances, we live in accordance with everyday observance, without beliefs (*adoxastôs*) – for we cannot be inactive. This everyday observance (*biôtikê têrêsis*) seems to be fourfold, and to consist in guidance of nature, necessitation of feelings, handing down of laws and customs, and teaching of skills ... By the handing down of customs and laws, we accept, in everyday life (*biôtikôs*), that piety is good and impiety is bad. (PH 1.21–24)[32]

If the Pyrrhonist feels cold, he will put on his coat; but "acquiescing" (*eudokein*: 1.13) in his present affection and acting accordingly is not believing that it is in fact cold, for he recognizes the existence of equipollent appearances and reasons for the opposite conclusion (for example, someone else's feeling that it is pleasantly warm, or the atomistic arguments for the "conventionality" of secondary qualities). Similarly, if the Pyrrhonist craves for something sweet, and samples some honey which tastes sweet, he will not deny or doubt his present experience, and will keep eating, but with no belief that the honey he is eating, or honey in general, is sweet.

Phainomena are also part of Sextus' complex answer to the self-refutation charge: A Pyrrhonist does not assent to anything he says or argues for, but only expresses what appears to him at any given time (cf. *PH* 1.4), and dialectically retorts dogmatic reasoning against itself, while suspending judgment on whether knowledge is possible, whether the arguments he uses are conclusive, and whether we must (and will) suspend judgment.

Whether this is consistent with *epochê*, and sufficient to account for the complexity of human thought and agency, are questions often raised by critics. As for the former, some of the Pyrrhonist's appearances, unlike feeling cold or tasting something sweet, can hardly be construed in purely phenomenological and non-doxastic terms (for example, can the appearance that two arguments are equipollent really differ from the belief, however weak, that the arguments have equal strength?).[33] The second objection is more directly relevant to ethics. According to Sextus, the Pyrrhonist, "following ordinary life," will not refrain from saying that gods exist and are provident, and making a display of piety, in accordance with the customs of his community, but "without holding opinions" (*adoxastôs*) (*PH* 3.2). But *why* will he act this way? Will his behavior resemble the instinctive urge driving us to food whenever we are hungry, or the involuntary reaction making us withdraw our hand from a flame? Or is it more like a deeply ingrained habit, which perpetuates itself even when we have no motivation for or attachment to it? If these answers appear unsatisfactory, can the Pyrrhonist offer any reason why he goes along with the customs of his community, rather than some others? Does he take this adherence to be something good, or at least better than the alternative? If so, why, and is this not incompatible with his proclaimed *epochê* on what is good, bad, and indifferent? If, on the other hand, no such reason can be offered, we are left with a behavior which appears mysterious or random: "since we cannot be completely inactive" (1.23), we must do *something*, so why not *this*?

It is with morally salient choices, and moral dilemmas as limiting cases, that the problem becomes especially acute:

Hence one also needs to look down on those who think that he [the Pyrrhonist] is reduced to inactivity (*anenergêsian*) or inconsistency (*apemphasin*). To inactivity, because ... the person who neither chooses nor avoids anything in effect renounces life and stays fixed like some vegetable, and to inconsistency, because if he comes under the power of a tyrant and is compelled to do some unspeakable deed, either he will not endure what has been commanded, but will choose a voluntary death, or to avoid torture he will do what has been ordered, and thus no longer "will be without avoidance and choice" ... They do not understand that the skeptic ... in accordance with non-philosophical observance is able to choose some things and avoid others. And if compelled by a tyrant to perform some forbidden act, he will choose one thing, perhaps, and avoid the other by the preconception which accords with the ancestral laws and customs.[34]   (M 11.162–166)

The tyrant scenario focuses our attention on the second charge, inconsistency: Sometimes even inaction can only be understood as a voluntary, belief-based choice. Let us accept that the Pyrrhonist can "perhaps" make a choice, whatever it is, "by the preconception which accords with ancestral laws and customs,"[35] but without opinions. Sextus' critics have objected to his reticence, and possibly indifference, as to the course of action the Pyrrhonist will adopt, and suspected he will have no qualms about acting immorally to save his skin. It is difficult, however, to imagine any laws or customs *prescribing* committing a crime to avoid torture. If Sextus' point is rather that some laws and customs *condone* a crime in such circumstances, and following them the Pyrrhonist will choose to do the unspeakable deed, then this choice must be motivated by something else, presumably the desire to avoid painful torture. Does this mean that the Pyrrhonist believes that pain, as such, is bad? Not necessarily, since the avoidance of pain, even future pain, can probably be subsumed under the observance of the "necessity of affections," which is consistent with *epochê*. If anything, it is the possibility that a Pyrrhonist might ever choose to submit to torture that appears puzzling. Pain is presented by Sextus as something that as human beings we naturally avoid, and as a limitation to the happiness secured by the skeptical therapy (cf. Section 3). But then how could "ancestral laws and customs" to which the Pyrrhonist has supposedly no doxastic attachment trump a fundamental instinct? If those laws and customs have become so deep-rooted that the Pyrrhonist no longer chooses to conform to them, but follows them involuntarily and instinctively, avoiding the unspeakable deed as he would avoid a flame, then the question of whether the fourfold observance of *phainomena* leaves us with a *human* moral psychology raises its head again.

3 SKEPTICAL HAPPINESS?

As we have seen in Section 1, the Academic skeptics engaged critically with dogmatic theories about the supreme good and the goal of human life. There is no evidence, however, that their activity was meant to promote some goal distinct from the activity itself, and from the "intellectual hygiene" of Socratic self-knowledge.[36] Sextus attributes to Arcesilaus the view that the goal (*telos*) is *epochê* itself, and that particular acts of suspension are good, while particular acts of assent are bad (*PH* 1.232–233). He criticizes Arcesilaus on the grounds that he dogmatically took these views to hold true "by nature," whereas a Pyrrhonist would simply express the same feelings in accordance with what appears to him.[37]

What is missing in the Academics, and is distinctive of the Pyrrhonian tradition, is the connection between *epochê* and *ataraxia*, and the identification of the latter as the *telos* of skepticism.[38] According to Timon, Pyrrho's inquiry was motivated by practical concerns:

> whoever wants to be happy must consider these three questions: first, how are things by nature? Secondly, what attitude should we adopt towards them? Thirdly, what will be the outcome for those who have this attitude? ... The outcome for those who actually adopt this attitude [sc. a life without inclinations and beliefs], says Timon, will be first non-assertion, and then tranquility.   (*Eus.* PE *14.18.2–5*)

The idea that *ataraxia* is constitutive of human happiness (*eudaimonia*) was not new: The Democritean influence is evident.[39] What is groundbreaking is the suggestion that *ataraxia* will not result from understanding reality, and abandoning false beliefs, but from living without beliefs altogether. Aristocles' summary does not explain *how* tranquility is supposed to result. Timon portrays Pyrrho as an extraordinary creature, who discovered how "to escape the servitude from opinions (*doxai*) and the empty theorizing of the sophists" and how to "unloose the shackles of every deception and persuasion" (D.L. 9.65); he "acted most easily with calm, always heedless and uniformly undisturbed, paying no attention to the whirls of sweet-voiced wisdom" (S.E. *M* 11.1; cf. also Eus. *PE* 14.18.17).

Later Pyrrhonists spelled out the rationale for connecting belief with unhappiness, *epochê* with mental health. Aenesidemus' claim that "he who philosophizes after Pyrrho is happy not only in general but also, and especially, in the wisdom of knowing that he has no firm cognition of anything" (Phot. *Bibl.* 212.169b28–29) has a quasi-Socratic flavor (cf. Plato, *Apology* 21B4–5), probably inspired by his anti-Academic polemic.[40] Sextus depicts the would-be Pyrrhonist as someone particularly sensitive to the pervasive discrepancy and contradiction (*anômalia*) of his experiences, who embarks on philosophical inquiry to resolve his distress (*tarachê*) and puzzlement (*aporia*) by discovering the truth (*PH* 1.12, 26). Suspending judgment on what is true and false, good and bad, cures at the same time this condition and the distress caused by intense desires, expectations, fears, and frustrations:

> For those who hold the belief that things are good or bad by nature are perpetually troubled. When they lack what they believe to be good, they take themselves to be persecuted by natural evils and they pursue what (so they think) is good. And when they have acquired these things, they experience more troubles; for they are elated beyond reason and measure, and in fear of change they do anything so as not to lose what they believe to be good. But those who make no determination about what is good and bad by nature neither avoid nor pursue anything intensely (*suntonôs*); and hence they are tranquil.[41]   (PH *1.27–28*)

It is not just the conflict of appearances and opinions that creates psychological turmoil. Belief itself is the disease. This is why *ataraxia* follows *epochê*, although not in the way the would-be skeptic had envisaged:

> A story told of the painter Apelles applies to the skeptic. They say that he was painting a horse and wanted to represent in his picture the lather on the horse's mouth; but he was so unsuccessful that he gave up, took the sponge on which he had been wiping off the colors from his brush, and flung it at the picture. And when it hit the picture, it produced a representation of the horse's lather. Now the Skeptics were hoping to acquire tranquility by deciding the contradiction in what appears and is thought of, and being unable

to do this they suspended judgment. But when they suspended judgment, tranquility followed as it were fortuitously, as a shadow follows a body.   (PH *1.28–29*)

Sextus acknowledges that the skeptical therapy will be ineffective against "passive," "natural," "necessary," "involuntary," "non-rational," and "sensory" affections such as being hungry or thirsty, feeling cold or pain; but the skeptic will bear such affections more easily, because unlike both ordinary people and philosophers he will not add the upsetting belief that these conditions are bad, a belief often more troubling than the condition itself. While *ataraxia* is the goal in matters of opinion, then, *metriopatheia* ("moderation of affection") will suffice in matters beyond our control (*PH* 1.30, 3.235–236; *M* 11.141–161).

Sustained philosophical engagement with Pyrrhonian ethics is beyond the scope of this chapter. I will instead list some of the problems that a defense of the Pyrrhonian proposal should address.

- Can the Pyrrhonist identify, state, and pursue the goal of *ataraxia* in a way consistent with universal *epochê*, and robust enough to make of *ataraxia* something more than the object of a subjective preference?
- Is the very pursuit of *ataraxia* self-effacing, since striving to attain and preserve it engenders anxiety? If, on the other hand, the Pyrrhonists ask us not to attach too much value to *ataraxia*, why should we be interested in the therapy they offer?
- Why should suspension of judgment about values lead to *ataraxia*, rather than heightened anxiety and moral vertigo? The admission that there might well be something really good or bad, right or wrong, to be done or to be avoided, which we have been unable to identify yet, should be deeply worrying. A form of moral nihilism, according to which nothing is in fact good or bad, or a strong denial of the possibility of moral knowledge, appear more effective than *epochê* in rescuing us from the poisonous effects of ethical belief.
- Even granting that the extreme detachment produced by universal *epochê* is psychologically possible, and that we could live without beliefs (cf. Section 2), why should we consider this an attractive prospect, a *good* life? Is the Pyrrhonian life without "intensity" an impoverished existence? Should we take very seriously Pyrrho's invitation to strip ourselves of our humanity, and be deeply worried by it?
- Can a Pyrrhonist be considered a robust moral agent if all he can do is (re-)act in accordance with *phainomena*, with no rational conviction

or emotional investment? Is he condemned to mindless passivity and ethical conformism?[42] Can we make sense of his therapeutic philanthropy (*PH* 3.280) within this framework, and explain its consistency with the agent-centered goal of *ataraxia*?

- How can the condition of *aporia* which produced *tarachê* before the skeptic's inquiry started accompany *ataraxia* when the inquiry ends in *epochê*? If anything, inquiry-resistant *aporia* should reinforce the distress, and *epochê*, if it corresponds to Apelles' throw of the sponge, could be seen as a manifestation of the highest degree of frustration.

- How is the goal of *ataraxia* compatible with Sextus' constant emphasis that the skeptic is a life-long inquirer (cf. e.g. *PH* 1.4, 7)? If, like Apelles, he attains his goal when he throws in the sponge, why does he keep inquiring? Further inquiry should be not only unnecessary, but potentially damaging and perverse, in light of the argument that having beliefs is, in and of itself, harmful.

Answers can be and have been offered on behalf of the Pyrrhonists to these and analogous objections.[43] How convincing they appear should not be prejudged here either way. But it is worth stressing that these answers, and our assessment of them, often intersect with broader exegetical questions at the heart of our reconstruction of Pyrrhonian skepticism. For example, the suggestion that moral nihilism might be better suited than *epochê* to the Pyrrhonists' practical goals could shed some light on the possible traces of such a negative meta-ethical stance in Pyrrho, Timon, and Aenesidemus (cf. Section 1). But the proposal that it was associated with a form of relativism faces, in turn, the objection that this seems difficult to reconcile with the therapeutic vocation of Pyrrhonism. If Pyrrhonian arguments conclude that nothing is good or bad in its own nature, while admitting that things should be judged good or bad in relation to certain individuals, times, and circumstances, then the disturbing effects of the dogmatic belief will be replaced by the equally disturbing effects of the belief that certain things are good or bad *for me, at this time* and *in my present circumstances*. The objection of therapeutic futility can be leveled, *mutatis mutandis*, at several versions of the "urbane" interpretation of the Pyrrhonian outlook, according to which a Pyrrhonist only refrains from assenting to high-powered tenets concerning the nature of things, grounded in controversial philosophic-scientific theory, but happily retains all kinds of ordinary beliefs.[44] Non-philosophical, or even irrational attachment to our values, projects, and goals can be as intense and "dogmatic" as the prescriptions of philosophical reason.

Not only is Pyrrhonian skepticism far from being "insulated" then; its essentially practical concerns,[45] and the skeptical life and morality it advertises, can and should be used to unlock the interpretation of other central aspects of skeptical theory.

NOTES

1. Cf. e.g. Cic. *Fin.* 2.2, *De or.* 3.67–68.
2. On dialectic in the Hellenistic Academy, cf. Castagnoli (forthcoming)b.
3. Cf. e.g. Cic. *Luc.* 66–67, 77 and 83; S.E. *M* 7.154–157.
4. Cf. also Cic. *De or.* 3.80, D.L. 4.28, Eus. *PE* 14.6.1–3.
5. Cf. Lact. *Div. Inst.* 5.14.4. For the embassy, cf. Wilkerson 1988.
6. Cf. e.g. Lévy (1992), Algra (1997), Annas (2007).
7. Cf. Schofield (2012b).
8. For this mode, cf. also D.L. 9.79 and Philo *De ebr.* 193–202. For the ten modes, cf. Annas and Barnes (1985).
9. Translations of *PH* are based on Annas and Barnes (2000); of *M* 7 on Bett (1997); of *M* 11 on Bett (1997); of Cic. *Luc.* on Brittain (2006). The other translations are mine.
10. For a different reconstruction of the logic of the modes of Aenesidemus, cf. Morison (2011).
11. For the modes of Agrippa, cf. Barnes (1990).
12. Cf. e.g. Burnyeat (1991); *contra* Fine (2003).
13. For other occurrences of the principle in *PH*, cf. 1.177, 3.179, 190, 196, 220, 222, 226.
14. According to D.L. 9.61 Pyrrho "used to claim that nothing is fine or shameful, or just or unjust ... but men do all things by custom and habit." The same idea is attributed to his pupil Timon in relation to good and bad (S.E. *M* 11.40).
15. Cf. especially Woodruff (1988) and Bett (2000) 189–222.
16. Cf. Bett (1994) and (1997).
17. Cf. e.g. Thorsrud (2009) 102–22, Hankinson (1994) and (2010). Polito (2004) 40–101 attributes to Aenesidemus some commitment to a version of the condition relativized to ordinary experience. For analysis of all our evidence on Aenesidemus, cf. Polito (2014).
18. Cf. Castagnoli (2010).
19. Cf. Vogt (2010).
20. On the *apraxia* charge and Arcesilaus' and Carneades' responses, cf. e.g. Striker (1980), Couissin (1983), Ioppolo (1986), Vander Waerdt (1989), Bett (1989), Allen (1994), Burnyeat (1997), Schofield (1999), Vogt (2010).

21. For an antecedent to both versions of the charge, cf. Arist. *Metaph*. 4.4, 1008b7–31.

22. Cf. e.g. Striker (1980), Couissin (1983), and Brittain (2005).

23. Cf. Striker (1980) and Brennan (1996).

24. Two later Academics, Philo of Larissa and Metrodorus of Stratonicea, interpreted Carneades' adoption of the *pithanon* as a form of "probabilism" or "fallibilism." On this reading, he acknowledged that, since assent is necessary for action, one should assent to persuasive impressions, but with the awareness that one is only opining (cf. e.g. Cic. *Luc*. 148).

25. Cf. Cic. *Luc*. 139 for Carneades' apparent approval of Callipho's view, according to which the highest good consists of a combination of pleasure and the honorable (2.131).

26. For critical assessment of this possibility, cf. Bett (1989).

27. For some attempts to solve the problem, cf. e.g. Couissin (1983) 40–41; Snyder (2014) 358–61.

28. Cf. e.g. Stopper (1983), Brennan (1998), and Thorsrud (2009).

29. Cf. e.g. Long-Sedley (1987), Hankinson (1995), and especially Bett (2000).

30. Cf. e.g. Ausland (1989), Brunschwig (1994) and (1999), Warren (2002) 86–97, and Beckwith (2011).

31. Timon's references to the strength of appearances (9.105) have been used as evidence that he and Pyrrho adopted *phainomena* as a practical criterion.

32. Cf. also *PH* 1.17. For discussion of the passage, cf. Barnes (1982).

33. Cf. e.g. Burnyeat (1980).

34. For analysis of the passage and its context, cf. Bett (1997).

35. *His* ancestral laws and customs, as suggested by several translators, or the laws and customs of the community in which he happens to live?

36. On Arcesilaus' Socratic leanings, cf. e.g. Cooper (2004).

37. This strategy could defuse the problematic implications of Sextus' argument at *PH* 3.238: "Hence we deduce that, if what produces bad is bad and to be avoided, and if confidence that these things are by nature good and those bad produces troubles, then to hypothesize and be convinced that anything is bad or good by nature is a bad thing and to be avoided."

38. Cf. D.L. 9.107 for Timon's and Aenesidemus' claim that *epochê* is the *telos*; S.E. *PH* 1.30 for the attribution of the claim to "some notable skeptics."

39. Cf. Warren (2002).

40. According to Aristocles (*PE* 14.18.4), Aenesidemus identified the state of tranquility with "pleasure" (*hêdonê*), but this need not mean that he espoused a form of hedonism over and above the pursuit of *ataraxia* itself.

41. Cf. *PH* 3.237.

42. According to Sextus, Pyrrhonism is "a way of life which follows some account in accordance with appearance (*tên logôi tini kata ton phainomenon akolouthousan*

agôgên), that account which shows how it is possible to live rightly (*orthôs*) [where "rightly" is taken *not only* with reference to virtue, but more loosely] and extends to the ability to suspend judgment" (*PH* 1.17).

43. For some of these objections, cf. e.g. Burnyeat (1980), Hiley (1987), Striker (1990), Nussbaum (1991), Annas (1998), Moller (2004), Irwin (2007), Perin (2010), Bett (2011) and (2012). For some answers, cf. e.g. McPherran (1989) and (1990), Johnsen (2001), Thorsrud (2003), Laursen (2004), Grgić (2006), Taylor (2014), Castagnoli (forthcoming)a.

44. For an influential statement of this interpretation, cf. Frede (1987); for the debate on the scope of *epochê* in Sextus, cf. Burnyeat and Frede (1997).

45. *Contra* Machuca (2006). For the differences between ancient and modern moral skepticism, cf. Annas (1998).

13   Ethics in Plotinus and His Successors

Dominic J. O'Meara

The subject of this chapter has typically been ignored in English-language handbooks covering ancient ethics. The reason for this seems to be the supposition that the Platonist philosophers of Late Antiquity had no ethical theory, no interest in ethics comparable to what we can find in Plato, Aristotle, Epicurus, and the Stoics. This supposition derives from various caricatural conceptions of the Platonists of Late Antiquity: They are thought to be mystical ascetics entirely concerned with removing themselves from bodily existence and reaching union with a transcendent god. Such mystics, it is assumed, can have no interest in the sorts of ethical issues discussed, for example, by Aristotle. They will be concerned only with themselves, with the ascent of their soul to the transcendent, not with others. They are otherworldly, detached from the affairs of this world. Consequently their philosophy will be heavily metaphysical and will have no place for ethics. However, in the last twenty years, these views have been increasingly challenged and a new field of research has opened up. In this chapter, I would like to give some idea of these recent developments.[1]

The difficulty with speaking about ethical issues in the Platonism of Late Antiquity derives, in part, from poor knowledge and understanding of the writings of these Platonists. However, there are difficulties which are also of a theoretical nature. If the philosopher, in Late Antiquity, is concerned with reaching an otherworldly existence, how might this self-concern relate to a concern for others? Is it the case that this sort of self-concern necessarily excludes concern for others, or might it be the case, on the contrary, that this self-concern *also* entails concern for others? And on what grounds? If the philosopher is concentrated entirely on reaching union with a transcendent principle, the absolute One (or Good), does it follow that this leaves no room for ethics? Is ethics entirely absorbed by metaphysics, the human good fused with the absolute transcendent Good? Can there be an ethics which is so dependent on metaphysical principles? How is morally good action, in this world, to be related to a transcendent Good?

The chapter is divided into the following sections based on questions which traditionally feature in ancient philosophical ethics: (1) What is it that constitutes the human good, the best life for humans, *eudaimonia* ("happiness")? What place has pleasure in this life? (2) What is virtue (*aretê*) and its relation to the good life? I will then discuss (3) the question of the relation between concern for oneself and concern for others; and (4) the relation between theoretical (metaphysical) knowledge, practical knowledge, and action. A portrait of the sage (5) will then serve to show how these themes come together, as instantiated in the biography of Plotinus. These sections will be almost entirely concerned with Plotinus, probably the most interesting and important (and today most read) of the Platonists of Late Antiquity.[2] However, in a final section (6), I will mention briefly the domain of ethics, as it was discussed by Plotinus' philosophical successors, from the third to the sixth centuries CE. Of course, this last section can do no more than provide some signposts to a largely unexplored field.

I   HAPPINESS

The principal text in which Plotinus discusses the question as to what would constitute the best life for humans, happiness (*eudaimonia*), *Ennead* I 4, begins with a difficulty Plotinus finds in the approach of his philosophical predecessors.[3] If they identify happiness with living well (*eu zên*) – understood in various ways, as unhindered natural living, as having good experience (*eupatheia*), as accomplishing one's natural function (*ergon*) – then they must assign happiness, not only to humans, but also to animals and plants, which are also capable of living well. However, these predecessors do not accept this and restrict happiness to *rational* beings. But then happiness would seem to be some property additional to life (rationality), and not to belong primarily to life itself (see 3, 9–14). Plotinus explores the difficulties and dilemmas he finds in the positions of his predecessors in chapters 1–2, and then comes, in chapter 3, to his proposed solution. The difficulty, he suggests, comes from treating "life" as if it were a synonymous term, as if it means the same thing for the different sorts of living beings (3, 3–4). However, he claims that the word "life" is "said in many ways"(3, 18). The term is homonymous (3, 20), it has different meanings, not in the sense that the meanings are unrelated, but in the sense that they are structured in terms of a primary sense and derivative senses, a series of prior and posterior terms, corresponding, in the different forms of life, to a structured series of primary and secondary derivative forms of life (3, 18–22). The term "good" (eu) manifests the same structure,[4] such that the best life would correspond to the highest form of life. Thus happiness (eudaimonia) is not a property added (epakton, 3, 28) to life, but belongs essentially to life as being identical with the highest form of life, life at the highest degree: rationality as a living activity, the life of intellect (nous). This life fulfills the conditions which Aristotle had already stipulated[5] as determining what would qualify as happiness: it is lacking in nothing, it is the best (ariston), and complete in itself (teleion) (3, 25–29).

The implications of Plotinus' position will become clearer if we place it in the context of his theory of human nature. Humans are primarily rational souls which exist in themselves, independently of the body, and illuminate and take care of the body. Rational souls are linked through their intellect to a transcendent Intellect (nous) which itself derives from an absolute first cause, the "One," or the "Good," which, as first cause, is prior to all determinate being and knowledge.[6] So, the highest level of life, that of Intellect, can be lived by human soul and this life is what Plotinus identifies as happiness. But this claim seems far too ambitious to be plausible: It seems to restrict happiness to a god-like life and to have little to do with human life. Aristotle had accepted this consequence when he identified primary happiness as the life of theoretical intellect, i.e. a life such as we might reasonably ascribe to the gods: this happiness we should live, as humans, as far as possible, since it corresponds to what, in our human nature, is divine (i.e. intellect).[7]

Plotinus is also concerned with happiness for humans (4, 1–5) and with the human good, the good immanent in human life, which he distinguishes from the absolute Good, the One (3, 32–33). Since Plotinus maintains that the highest aspect of soul, intellect, remains in communion with transcendent divine Intellect, despite soul's turning to affairs arising from her relation to the body,[8] and since our intellect remains active (it is activity), then it would seem to follow that we – all humans (not just adult, free, well-off males, as in Aristotelian ethics) – are happy, always, even if, inasmuch as our attention is directed to, and we are busy with, corporeal matters, we are not aware of this. A part of us, one might infer, would then be already and always happy, other parts of us often not. However, Plotinus does not seem to mean this when he speaks of part of us as having happiness (4, 13): Humans are happy, in part, in the sense of being *potentially* happy – we become actually happy when we become identical with the life of intellect, when we *are* happiness (see 4, 14–15). Plotinus' original doctrine of the "self"[9] seems to be involved here. Our self ("we") is mobile, as the focus of our awareness and activity: It can move across the range of soul's operations, and can associate itself with bodily matters, or turn itself to living fully on the level of intellect. We cannot be happy in part: This is ruled out by the conditions of completion and of lacking in nothing. But we are all potentially happy and become happy in actuality when we live fully the life of intellect.

Plotinus establishes in this way an essential link between life and happiness: Happiness is, and is only, the highest level of life. This means that the lower levels at which we live, in particular aspects of our life in relation to the body, are no part of our happiness. If we still seek other things, then it is not because they might constitute our good (which we already have, if we are happy), but because they are necessitated by the body:

> The good person (*spoudeios*) has all that is needed for happiness and the acquisition of the good, for there is no good he[10] has not got. What he seeks [in addition to this], he seeks as a necessity, not for himself but for something that belongs to him; that is, he seeks it for the body which is joined to him ... it lives its own life and not the life which is that of the good man. He knows its needs, and gives it what he gives it without taking away anything from his own life. His happiness will not be reduced even when fortune goes against him.[11]

As the following lines make clear, this position is quite radical: The blows of fortune can include the death of relations and friends. Such losses will not affect the happiness of the good person, who will understand death, sickness, poverty, and suchlike as concerning life with the body, and not the independent life of intellect.[12] Health and freedom from pain (6, 25) have to do with the existence of the body, not with the happiness of the good person (7, 2–4). The good person will seek them as required by the body:

> Some of his activities will tend towards happiness; others will not be directed to the goal (*telos*), and will really not belong to him but to that which is joined to him, which he will care for (*phrontiei*) and bear with as long as he can, like a musician with his lyre, as long as he can use it; if he cannot use it he will change to another, or give up using the lyre and abandon the activities directed to it. Then he will have something else to do which does not need the lyre, and will let it lie unregarded beside him while he sings without an instrument. Yet the instrument

was not given him at the beginning in vain (*ou matên*). He has used it often up till now.[13]

The treatise ends with these words. Bodily affairs matter to the good person: This person will care for the body and seek what it needs, since soul has care of the body for a good reason (*ou matên*; I come back to this point in Section 3). However, these affairs play no part in the happiness of the good person which, as the life of intellect independent of the body, is complete and self-sufficient. The independence in relation to poverty, sickness, pain, loss of family and friends, and death reminds us of the impassibility of the Stoic sage, who is immune to such things. However, the independence of Plotinus' good person rests on the independence of soul in relation to the body.

If all humans are potentially happy, it would seem that the conditions which must be satisfied for a life to be considered happy are so demanding that few can actually reach such a life. The same is true, we might say, of primary happiness in Aristotle and, even more so, of the happiness of the Stoic sage. However, since Plotinus believes that every human being is linked by nature to divine Intellect, which is therefore always present and available to us, even if we do not turn our attention to it, then the goal of happiness does not seem to be impossible or even distant. This happiness, which might seem at first sight so abstract and austere, is neither: It is a full life lived in pleasure, just as is Aristotle's life of theoretical wisdom. Plotinus characterizes the life of intellect as a life which includes pleasure, not bodily pleasure, which involves changes (violent or otherwise), but a joyful (*hileôs*), peaceful state (*katastasis*) (12, 2–10). The last term reminds us of Epicurean "katastematic" pleasure, pleasure as a state free of pain and anxiety.[14] In Plotinus, as in Aristotle, a certain kind of pleasure goes with living the life of intellect.

2   VIRTUE

In ancient ethics, the question of happiness is linked with the theme of virtue. Very schematically, we could say that virtue was thought to relate to happiness in the sense that virtue *is* happiness (a Stoic position), or that virtue (especially virtuous activity) is a central part of the happy life (an Aristotelian position), or that virtue is a necessary means for attaining the goal of happiness (an Epicurean position). In a passage of Plato's *Theaetetus* (176AB), which Platonists of the Roman imperial period took as defining the goal (*telos*) of human life, Socrates says:

> We should make all speed to take flight (*phugê*) from this world to the other, and that means assimilation to the divine (*homoiôsis theôi*) as far as possible, and that again is to become just and pious with wisdom.

Quoting this passage at the beginning of *Ennead* I 2, Plotinus takes Plato to mean that it is *by means* of virtues (justice, piety, wisdom) that we assimilate ourselves to the divine.[15] Assimilation to the divine, as the human goal, can be identified with happiness, as the life of divine intellect. It would seem, then, that virtues have an instrumental role in realizing the goal, the life of happiness, but that they are not part of this life. This implication emerges in the puzzle which Plotinus formulates as the subject of this treatise: How can we become like the divine, by means of virtues, if the divine itself does not have these virtues? This question had been debated by Platonists before,[16] and is inspired ultimately by Aristotle's refusal to attribute moral virtues (such as justice, courage) to the gods (*Nicomachean Ethics* X, 8). How then can we become *like* something else, by means of having that (virtues) which it does not have? Likeness seems to imply, on the contrary, that the divine has the virtues by means of which we become like it.

Plotinus distinguishes between two sorts of virtue: "political" virtues and "higher" virtues (1, 21–22; 2, 13; 3, 1–2). "Political" virtues are those defined by Plato in *Republic* Book IV. Plotinus quotes Plato's definitions of these virtues (wisdom, courage, moderation, and justice) (1, 16–21): Wisdom (*phronêsis*) is the virtue of the rational part of the soul, courage the virtue of the spirited part, moderation (*sôphrosunê*) is the harmony of (bodily) desires with reason, and justice is each part of the soul fulfilling its appropriate function with regard to the part which rules (reason) and the parts which are ruled. Plotinus describes these virtues a little later (2, 13–19) as giving limit and measure to our desires and affects. The "higher" virtues are those which Plotinus finds in Plato's *Phaedo* (69BC), where virtues are described as purifications of the soul from the body. These virtues include the four cardinal virtues of the *Republic*, but redefined now (3, 12–23) as what separates soul from the life of the body (which includes the desiring and the spirited aspects of the soul arising in the context of soul's relation to the body).[17] The question of assimilation to the divine then becomes the question of the role which each of these two sorts of virtue might have in bringing us to being like transcendent Intellect.

A further move Plotinus makes is to distinguish between two kinds of "becoming like," or "assimilation" (2, 4–10): (1) that which involves what I would call reciprocal likeness, and (2) that which involves non-reciprocal likeness. (1) A reciprocal likeness obtains when two things (A, B) share in the same property (C): A and B are "like" each other, in that they both have the same property (C). (2) Non-reciprocal likeness would occur when A shares in C, due to the causality exerted by D, and thus in a certain sense is like D, but the reverse does not obtain, and so D is not like A in sense (1). As examples of this we can make use of the cases introduced by Plotinus in chapter 1 (1, 29–35 and 42–45). If two things (A, B) are warmed by the presence of fire, then they are like each other (1) in virtue of being warmed (C); fire itself (D), however, is not warmed in the way that A and B are; its intrinsic (fiery) activity is different from that of being warmed.[18] Plotinus also compares a house (which is visible) with the (intelligible) plan which determines the structure of the house: The visible house is like the plan, because it is structured in accordance with the plan, but the plan is not itself something structured, and thus is not like the visible house, in sense (1). Thus, the idea of non-reciprocal likeness means that we can say that soul can *become* like the divine by being virtuous, without our having to say also that the divine itself is virtuous. It remains then to see how this works out in the case of each of the two sorts of virtue.

"Political" virtues make soul like the divine in that they give measure and order to the soul: Soul is, so to speak, the "matter" (2, 19) to which form is given by the political virtues. Plotinus is thinking of the irrational aspects (spirit and desires) which arise in soul due to its relation to the body; what gives these aspects measure must be the rational part of soul, which, in having wisdom (*phronêsis*), derives the measure which it gives from a higher, theoretical wisdom (*sophia*), as we will see below, this wisdom being inspired in turn by divine Intellect. Thus the measure brought to the irrational aspects of soul by "political" virtue derives from divine measure: By being measured, as souls living in bodies, we become *like*, we bear a trace of the divine measure, which itself, however, is not measured (2, 14–26).[19] However, a greater degree of assimilation to the divine is achieved by the "higher" virtues which purify the soul of its occupation with the body and turn it towards itself and to its original orientation towards divine Intellect (ch. 3). This is the "flight" of which Plato speaks in the *Theaetetus* passage; this is the "assimilation" which is this flight (3, 5–10). While being much nearer, and more like, the divine Intellect, the soul, as having the higher virtues, is still not this Intellect. Virtue is a disposition (*diathesis*) of soul; divine

Intellect, as prior to soul, has no virtue. Plotinus is quite clear about this.[20] Virtue remains a means for reaching the perfectly felicitous life of Intellect, not a characteristic of this life.

In our seeking assimilation to the divine, it seems that a first stage is reached by means of the "political" virtues, which bring divine measure, order, to our lives in relation to the body. The higher virtues bring us much nearer the divine in turning soul away from the body and towards divine Intellect. In chapter 7, Plotinus maintains that having the higher virtues necessarily involves having (potentially) the lower ("political") virtues, but that the possession of the lower virtues does not necessarily imply having the higher virtues (7, 10–12). So it seems that we can have the "political" virtues, without reaching the higher virtues, but that if we have reached the higher virtues, we must already have the "political" virtues, at least "potentially." What this means is that the good person (*spoudeios*), who already has the higher virtues, will act on the level of the lower, "political" virtues "according to the circumstances" (*peristatikôs*) (7, 21). What this seems to mean is that the good person, while living in relation to the body, will still need to deal with the circumstances that this relation brings and will exercise the appropriate "political" virtues on this level.[21]

However, we probably should not understand this scale of virtues as if it means that we might first acquire the "political" virtues, acquiring them completely, and then move on, once this job is done (so to speak!), in order to acquire the higher virtues. *Ennead* I 3, a treatise written in the same period as *Ennead* I 2,[22] suggests a more dynamic process, in which the various levels of virtue grow together and enrich each other such that the higher virtues perfect the lower.[23] Consequently, "political" virtues, if not enriched by the higher virtues, remain imperfect, deficient (6, 15). This follows also if we consider (see Section 4) the relation between theoretical and practical wisdom (*sophia* and *phronêsis*). So it seems that a soul, on the way to assimilation to the divine, acquires the "political" virtues as a first stage in this assimilation, but does not possess these virtues in the same way that a good person, who has reached the higher virtues, possesses them: The good person will have the "political" virtues completely, while the person who has not (yet) reached the higher virtues, will possess them incompletely.

3   CONCERN FOR OTHERS

So far, we have been considering the attainment of the best life for humans. This has involved the individual soul and the virtues it must develop so as to reach this goal. The attention seems to be entirely self-centered, concentrated on the individual soul's care for itself. Does this imply that concern for others has no place in Plotinus' philosophy? In the following I would like to pursue two lines of reflection which show how care for others is also part of Plotinus' philosophy.[24]

In *Ennead* IV 4, 43 Plotinus speaks again of the good person (*spoudeios*) not being affected in the rational part of his soul by sickness, passions, or death, things which occur in his bodily existence and which affect the irrational parts of the soul. Plotinus then distinguishes between self-directedness (*pros hauto*) and being directed to another (*pros allo*): What is directed to itself (the life of intellect, *theôria*) cannot be affected, does not come under the "spell," of another,[25] whereas practical life (*praktikos bios*), being directed outwards, to another, can be affected and come under its spell (43, 16–21 and 44,1). The practical life takes place in corporeal existence, in the world of nature. We are affected, in our relation to bodily affairs, by passions and desires, and can come under their spell:

> For the care of children and concern for marriage have a manifest drawing power, and so do all the things which entice humans since they give pleasure to their carnal desires (*epithumiai*). And the practical actions (*praxeis*) which are caused by our spirited part (*thumos*) are the result of an irrational impulse, as are in the same way those caused by our carnal desires; political activity and the pursuit of office have the desire for power in us provoking them. And the activities which are undertaken to avoid suffering have fear as their origin, those for the sake of getting more, carnal desire. But those actions which are undertaken because of what is needed, since they seek to satisfy a need of nature, clearly have the force of nature behind them, which appropriates us (*oikeiôsasan*) to living.   (44, 6–17)

Plotinus distinguishes between acting under the power of irrational impulses which come to us in our corporeal existence, and acting in response to necessities derived from nature, needs requiring to be met and which correspond to our natural appropriation (*oikeiôsis*) to living in the world. In a sense, since the latter way of acting is called for by what is outside us, the other, we are under its spell:

> One has come under the spell by the force of human nature and by appropriation (*oikeiôsei*) to the life of others, or indeed of oneself, for it seems, perhaps, reasonable not to take one's own life on account of this appropriation (*oikeiôsin*).   (44, 22–24)

But we are not under a spell if we distinguish between the *necessity* to act, due to our nature and the nature of the universe, and the morally fine and good (*to kalon, to agathon*), which is another life, that of intellect.[26] Traces of the good can be found in practical action, but these should not be taken for the good itself, which, for humans, is lived in the independent life of intellect (44, 25–37).

The distinction we found above (see Section 1), between the good life, as the life of intellect, and the necessities linked to the need to take care of the lower parts of our lives, as involved in our relation to the body, is developed here in an interesting way. It looks as if Plotinus has taken the Stoic theme of "appropriation" (*oikeiôsis*)[27] to describe a natural need, in our nature (as humans, as souls living in bodies) and in the nature of the universe, to care for our lives and the lives of others, a care such that suicide, for example, is in general not reasonable. This care is natural and good, as a trace of the good. But it is not to be confused with the good which we, as souls, seek and which is to be found at a higher level of life. Nor is a life responding to natural and necessary needs to be confused with a life driven by irrational impulses. The good person will take care of the material well-being of those around him and of himself (his body), as we will see (see Section 5). His actions in this regard will be reasonable, natural, and good, very different from the actions of someone else who acts under the pressure of irrational drives, such as lust, fear, or desire for power, all of which are wrongly taken to yield the good life.

The care for others and for oneself which has been described so far has to do with humans as souls living in bodies, involved in the natural universe. But we might also wonder about souls taken in themselves, independently of bodily concerns: Is there room, here also, not only for self-care, but also care for others? Souls, taken in themselves, do not live in isolation, each in its own world. Rather, since they are incorporeal intellects, there are no spatio temporal distances separating them from each other, no materialistic drives which alienate them from each. Rather they are present to each other, united with each other, without loss of their individuality. They constitute, so to speak, a metaphysical family,[28] a family of intellect, not of the body, a community of knowledge comparable to an ideal city,[29] united in a friendship in which all knowledge is shared.[30] Such souls, so united with each other, hardly need to *care* for each other: they already enjoy and share all that they need, the life of intellect. It is rather souls which, in their relation to bodily existence, have become alienated (*allotriôtheisai*) from each other by bodily desires and passions, exiled from their metaphysical homeland and from the good,[31] which would require care. And we can imagine that it is souls which, while living in the body, have not alienated themselves, maintaining their life of intellect, which will exercise this care. But why?

It may be helpful here to introduce Plotinus' metaphysical principle that what is good will do good, will communicate its goodness.[32] This principle serves to show that the first cause of everything, the One, or the absolute Good, will produce things, giving of its goodness. But the principle also applies to what comes from the absolute Good and is itself good. Thus Intellect, which comes from the Good, produces soul. And soul as good will give of its goodness in producing and structuring the material world. The world-soul animates and directs the world, gives it rational order on the basis of the knowledge which it has from Intellect. This rational order which world-soul provides to the world Plotinus describes as providence.[33] Individual souls also have a function in bringing rational order, beauty, and goodness when they relate to individual bodies: This is the "good reason" (ou matên) why individual soul is present in body.[34] But individual souls can become obsessed with bodily passions and be ruled by these passions. Souls who live in the world, but who have not deviated in this way, will seek to express the good in their lives and this will include care for the immaterial good of others, bringing them back to knowledge, to their metaphysical homeland. Thus certain individual souls, acting like the world-soul, will be in a position to exercise a providential function with respect to other, alienated souls. But this care will concern, not material welfare (as in the case of natural appropriation described above), but the true good of souls in themselves, helping them to reach the life of intellect. This, for Plotinus, is precisely the function of philosophy.[35]

4 KNOWLEDGE AND ACTION

So far we have followed a distinction separating the practical life, as soul's dealing with the necessities arising from its life with the body, from the theoretical life, the life of knowledge, of intellect, as constituting the best life for soul. But these two lives are related: "Traces" of the good can feature, as we have seen, in the practical life, while measured lives in the body can become "like" the life of intellect. In what follows, I would like to consider the relation between the theoretical and practical life in more detail, beginning with the general relation between theôria, the activity of knowing, and praxis, acting, discussing then the relation between theoretical wisdom (*sophia*), practical wisdom (*phronêsis*), and action.

Ennead III 8 proposes a playful and daring extension of the relation of *theôria* and *praxis* to the description of reality as a whole.[36] Plotinus' purpose is to argue against certain religious groups of his time, Gnostics, who believed that the universe was produced by an ignorant and malevolent god. He wishes to show, on the contrary, that the universe is the expression of knowledge and the good. Taking the concepts of *theôria*, *praxis*, and *poiêsis*, which, in Aristotle, serve to distinguish between the activity of pure knowledge (theoretical knowledge), a knowledge aimed at realizing actions (practical knowledge), and one aimed at producing things (productive skills and crafts), Plotinus tries to show that all things in nature, not just humans, desire by nature to reach knowledge (1, 1–10), and that action and production arise secondarily as a result of this desire. And so the universe is a product, a result, of knowledge. Action and production correspond to and depend on a rational plan (*logos*), which they are not, and this plan is an expression of knowledge. So everything in reality, it turns out, is both knowledge (*theôria*) and the result of knowledge (*poiêsis* and *praxis*): knowledge, as the cause of lower effects; the result of knowledge, as the effect of higher causes.[37] I would like here, however, to leave aside this large metaphysical thesis and examine how it works in particular in the case of humans.

In chapter 4, Plotinus claims that humans act for two reasons. (1) They act out of weakness (*astheneia*) in knowledge: they wish to attain knowledge, but failing in this, act as a way of externalizing what they have difficulty in grasping by thought. They externalize what they cannot adequately grasp in thinking so that both they and others can better see it, as far as possible. Or (2) action can accompany (*parakolouthêma*) knowledge which has been attained. In the latter case, action is not a substitute for inadequate knowledge, but a result of fulfilled knowledge.[38] The example of geometrical diagrams might be used to illustrate these two cases: One might make a diagram in order better to grasp the geometrical concept (e.g., that of a circle) one is trying to understand, or one might make a diagram when one already knows what a circle is and wants to help others come to grasp it. So, humans act, in practical life, either as a way of projecting outwards, in their weakness, the knowledge that they seek to attain in the theoretical life of intellect, or because they already possess this theoretical life and give expression to it in actions, communicating their knowledge in this way to others.[39]

It has been plausibly suggested[40] that the relation between knowledge and action fits into Plotinus' more general metaphysical theory of double activity, according to which every nature has a primary intrinsic activity, that which it is, which is accompanied by a secondary, extrinsic activity, which images the primary activity.[41] Thus fire, for example, is an activity which gives heat, as a secondary activity, to others. The principle applies throughout reality. Thus Intellect is the secondary activity of the One, and soul the secondary activity of Intellect. Action would then be related to knowledge as the secondary activity of knowledge. But how does this work precisely in the case of human action? Does action "automatically" flow from knowledge, in the way, for example, that Intellect derives from the One?[42] Does it suffice to have theoretical knowledge, and correct action will then automatically follow? The situation is not quite this simple in Plotinus, as can be seen by attending to the distinction he makes between theoretical and practical wisdom.

The distinction between theoretical and practical wisdom (*sophia* and *phronêsis*) is introduced by Aristotle in order to differentiate between the kind of intellectual virtue reached in scientific knowledge of universal and necessary truths and the virtue involved in thinking well about what is good for us, as humans, and what to do in specific circumstances, which may vary (*Nicomachean Ethics* VI, 7). Plotinus identifies theoretical wisdom with the highest knowledge, which Plato calls dialectic in the *Republic* (511BC), and distinguishes it from practical wisdom:

> The [science] about ethical dispositions (*êthê*) also derives knowledge from [dialectic], but adds virtuous states (*hexeis*) and the practices (*askêseis*) which produce them. The rational states (*logikai hexeis*) have what they receive from there [i.e. from dialectic] almost as if it is already proper to them, for indeed most of this comes with their subject matter. And the other virtues apply reasoning to particular passions and actions, whereas practical wisdom (*phronêsis*) is a comparative reasoning (*epilogismos*)[43] concerned more with the universal, with questions of mutual implication [of the virtues], and whether to refrain from action, now or later, and whether an entirely different course would be better. Dialectic and theoretical wisdom (*sophia*) furthermore provide practical wisdom, in a universal and immaterial way, with everything for its use.[44]

Plotinus appears to be following here, to some extent, the Aristotelian distinction between moral virtues, which are acquired by practice, by habituation, and intellectual virtues, acquired by teaching, which include theoretical and practical wisdom.[45] Practical wisdom derives knowledge from theoretical wisdom, presides over the other (moral virtues), and is concerned with their coordination, thinking about different courses of action, in varying circumstances. The knowledge practical wisdom derives from theoretical wisdom seems to take the form of premises (*protaseis*) on the basis of which practical wisdom, considering the circumstances, may decide to act.[46] These premises, coming from above, can be compared with the premises which derive from below, from irrational impulses,[47] which can also orientate action, in the false direction. Practical wisdom seems to involve knowledge of the particulars and circumstances of the world of practical life, the material world. It involves choices and decisions on what to do. These decisions are guided by norms of action derived from theoretical wisdom, which itself is uniquely concerned with another life, that of intellect.[48] It thus seems that theoretical wisdom does not simply and automatically issue in action. Practical wisdom is required for action, a wisdom which is different from theoretical wisdom, which includes theoretical principles of action and also knowledge of the particulars, the circumstances of a situation in practical life and which can then decide to act and how to act. We can see from this that the virtues of practical life, the "political" virtues, which include practical wisdom as the ruling virtue, require the inspiration of a higher virtue, theoretical wisdom, as the source of the premises of action. They would otherwise be incomplete. The good person will have this higher source of knowledge, which he will be able to use, as contributing to practical wisdom, when he is called to act in life associated with the body. A person without these virtues may be motivated by irrational impulses to actions which lead the soul to a life opposed to the good life.

One might note, finally, that if reason and virtue in the soul are not under the "spell" of another power, if, therefore, they are autonomous and free, yet the actions they initiate are necessitated by external circumstances and take place in a context, the material world, where they come under the influence of a nexus of other causes. Thus our actions are autonomous, free, and morally good, to the extent they derive from our reason and from virtue.[49] But their autonomy is mixed in with heteronomy to the extent that they are conditioned by the external circumstances which require them and which can modify them: We are not in control of the outcomes of our actions.[50]

5 A PORTRAIT OF THE SAGE

In *Ennead* I 2, Plotinus speaks of the soul which has the higher virtues, in which the irrational impulses are calmed by the presence and proximity of reason. It is as if we were to live near a wise man (*sophos*), who would inspire emulation in us, our refraining from that which the good person would not want (5, 25–31). A portrait of the wise man is sketched by one of Plotinus' closest pupils, Porphyry (234 – c. 305), in the *Life of Plotinus*, which he composed as a frontispiece to the edition of Plotinus' works (the *Enneads*) that he published at the beginning of the fourth century, some thirty years after Plotinus' death.[51] The *Life of Plotinus* is full of fascinating information about the practice of philosophy in the late third century, but it also presents the ideal to which the reader of the *Enneads* might aspire, the ideal life that philosophy can bring, as exemplified by Plotinus. The ideal is to some extent an expression of Porphyry's own views. For example, the *Life* begins with suggestions of a contempt and neglect of the body in Plotinus matching Porphyry's own ethics better than Plotinus', who advocates care of the body.[52] Porphyry also collects anecdotes (some fabricated on the basis of passages in Plotinus) and testimonies (some of dubious value) in order to magnify the aura of his model sage. But other passages seem to come nearer to Plotinus himself and to what he held. I give some examples.

In chapter 8 Porphyry describes how Plotinus seemed to have been able to live on two levels, in himself, in his life of thought, and in relation to others, directed outwards, the latter activity flowing from or accompanying simultaneously the former.[53] Thus, concentrated on intellect, he would write continuously, "as if copying from a book," his writing flowing from his thought. He could take part in discussions with someone else, while keeping his thought fixed without interruption on its object. Thus, "he was present at once to himself and to others" (8, 19), living the life of intellect within and living in relation to the outside, in relation to others. Concern for others is exemplified in chapter 9, where Plotinus is described as acting as the conscientious guardian of orphans left in his trust, administering their financial affairs and supervising their education. "Yet, though he shielded so many from worries and cares of ordinary life, he never, while awake, relaxed his intent concentration upon the intellect" (9, 16–18). This care for others included his close friends and pupils. When Porphyry was thinking of "removing" himself from life (11, 11–15), Plotinus intervened, saying that this thought stemmed, not from a rational state, but from sickness, and advised going away (Porphyry went to Sicily). This concern for the material welfare of others, for one's own life and the lives of others, had been described by Plotinus in *Ennead* IV 4, 44.[54]

Plotinus' concern for others extended to a concern for the well-being of their soul: This is surely the motivation for his philosophical teaching and writing. As a teacher Plotinus was not dogmatic, domineering, or arrogant, but kind, gentle, sociable,[55] patient, taking the time to explore the philosophical questions of a hearer to the point of exasperating some of his less patient pupils (ch. 13). The concern for others seems to have extended at one point beyond domestic life and the life of his philosophical school. Plotinus, who had the friendship of the Emperor Gallienus and his wife, undertook to re-found an abandoned city of philosophers in Campania, to be called Platonopolis, in which he and his companions would live, using "Plato's laws" (ch. 12). However, resistance in the imperial court meant that the financial support for this project was not provided. In *Ennead* VI 9, 7, Plotinus speaks of how knowledge of the absolute Good can inspire a soul to wish to legislate, in the image of the Good, as the mythical legislator of Crete, Minos, was said to have been instructed by his father Zeus (7, 21–26). The knowledge of the Good and its communication might then extend beyond a providential care for those around us and take political form as legislation.[56]

6   SIGNPOSTS TO THE FIELD OF PLATONIST ETHICS AFTER PLOTINUS

Platonist schools, deeply influenced by Plotinus' interpretation of Plato, developed in Syria, Asia Minor, Athens, and Alexandria from the fourth to the sixth centuries. They are characterized by a strong scholastic structure: Platonic philosophy was systematized as a hierarchy of sciences and a curriculum was developed in the teaching of these sciences. The hierarchy of sciences began with practical philosophy (ethics, "economics" (i.e. household ethics), politics) and rose to theoretical philosophy (physics, mathematics, metaphysics), the summit and goal of philosophy being metaphysics, understood as the knowledge of transcendent causes. Plotinus had spoken of the benefits brought by metaphysics ("dialectic") to ethics and physics (natural philosophy),[57] but the division of sciences does not have an important place in his philosophy. In editing the *Enneads*, Porphyry arranged Plotinus' treatises in groups corresponding (in ascending order) to ethics (*Enn.* I), physics

(*Enn.* II-III), and metaphysics (*Enn.* IV-VI). The division of sciences became fundamental in the school of Iamblichus (c. 245–325) in Syria and in the schools of Athens and Alexandria in the fifth and sixth centuries. This meant that ethics was seen as a distinct philosophical discipline, having its proper domain and place in the scale of sciences.

A curriculum was prescribed for the teaching of the philosophical sciences on the basis of authoritative texts. Plato's *Alcibiades* and *Gorgias* were chosen for the teaching of practical philosophy, in particular the "political" virtues, the *Phaedo* dealing with the higher, purificatory virtues. (Diligent students like Proclus, who would become head of the school in Athens in 437–85, would also read the *Republic* and perhaps the *Laws*). The teaching of Plato would be prefaced by a reading of Aristotle, whose ethical treatises (principally, it seems, the *Nicomachean Ethics*) were designated for the teaching of practical philosophy. As a pre-scientific initiation to ethics, beginning students would first read, however, the edificatory sayings of the (pseudo-Pythagorean) *Golden Verses* or the *Handbook* of Epictetus. We still have some texts relating to this teaching of ethics, the commentaries by Hierocles on the *Golden Verses* and of Simplicius on Epictetus' *Handbook*. Unfortunately, only a few fragments survive (in Arabic) of Porphyry's commentary on Aristotle's ethics. For Plato's *Alcibiades*, *Gorgias*, *Republic*, and *Phaedo* we can still read commentaries by Proclus, Damascius, and Olympiodorus. To these sources of information on ethics we can add Porphyry's *Letter to Marcella*, his *On Abstinence*, and the fragments remaining of Iamblichus' correspondence.

The ascending scale of sciences was seen as corresponding to the ascending scale of types of virtues, going from the practical to the theoretical virtues. Plotinus' distinction between "political" virtues and the higher virtues of purification was extended by Porphyry, in an influential chapter (ch. 32) of his *Sentences*, to four levels: the "political" virtues (which Porphyry saw as concerning not only the inner life of the soul, but also social relationships), the purificatory, the theoretical, and the paradigmatic. With Iamblichus, it seems, the scale of virtues becomes even more extensive, starting from natural virtues (i.e. good qualities of soul and body with which we are born), the "ethical" virtues (i.e. good habits, without rationality, such as are acquired by animals and children),[58] and the "political" virtues (where practical wisdom is required), then ascending to the purificatory, theoretical, paradigmatic, and "theurgic" virtues.[59]

The scale of types of virtue was exemplified in biographies which, like Porphyry's *Life of Plotinus*, presented model philosophical lives.

Iamblichus' *Pythagorean Life* concerns principally the "ethical" and "political" virtues, whereas Marinus, in his *Life of Proclus*, seeks to show that his teacher Proclus manifested *all* of the levels of the virtues in his life. The work is also entitled *On Happiness* and, at the beginning (ch. 2) claims that Proclus (he had died the year before) was the happiest of men: He had attained not only the (theoretical) happiness of the sage, but also that of a virtuous (i.e. practical) life, and was not lacking in the external goods praised by the many. Thus he lacked nothing and enjoyed a happiness composed of theoretical and practical perfection. The passage is reminiscent of Aristotle's *Nicomachean Ethics*,[60] which is quoted (I, 11, 1101a14–16), to the same effect, at the end of the text (ch. 34, 24–27). In speaking of Proclus' ascent from the "political" to the "purificatory" virtues, Marinus makes much use of Plotinus' *Ennead* I 2 and suggests that "political" and "purificatory" virtues, as assimilation to the divine, represent different degrees in the separation of the soul from bodily affairs (ch. 18). Composed by Damascius, last head of the Athenian school when it was closed due to the Emperor Justinian's anti-pagan measures of 529, the *Life of Isidore* illustrates, in stories about a wide range of different lives, how people could succeed (and fail) in reaching various degrees in the scale of virtues: Few, it seems went beyond the "political" virtues and reached the highest perfection.[61] These biographies (and there are others) are a rich source of information on the ethical ideas of the Platonists of Late Antiquity.

The interested reader will find in this corpus of texts discussions which both continued in the wake of what Plotinus had written, and which also reflected the evolution of Platonist philosophy and the changing social circumstances in which the philosophers lived. Platonism after Plotinus tends to go in the direction of an increasingly elaborate metaphysical theory, adding many intermediary levels to Plotinus' relatively simple scheme of reality (the One – Intellect – Soul – the corporeal world). In particular, the idea of the transcendence of the ultimate first cause of everything was driven to the negation of any coordination of it with what it produces. The effect of this, together with the intervention of many intermediate levels, is to make the One, as the absolute Good, much more remote. These later Platonists also laid greater stress than did Plotinus on the importance of life in the body for the soul: Soul was truly involved with the body (in Plotinus she seems far less engaged). A consequence of this was greater emphasis on the bodily aspects of human life, on the practical life,[62] on bodily purification and on religious rites,

Egyptian, Chaldaean, and Orphic. Hierocles (who taught in Alexandria in the fifth century) and Proclus also discussed the themes of practical wisdom, the practical syllogism, and the relation between freedom, providence, and fate.[63] Simplicius, commenting on Epictetus' *Handbook* in the early to mid-sixth century, deals with the practical life, how to lead a morally good life, integrating Stoic ethics in the framework of the Platonist scale of virtues.[64] He writes in a climate of oppression: The Emperor Justinian's anti-pagan policies were making life very difficult for pagan philosophers. Simplicius suggests how those for whom he writes may nevertheless stay true to their philosophical principles and live a morally good life in the midst of what he considered to be generalized moral corruption and depravation.

NOTES

1. A parallel development in research has recently taken place in the domain of natural philosophy, in which it has also been thought (wrongly) that these "otherworldly" Platonists could not have had any interest; see now, for example, Chiaradonna & Trabattoni (2009).
2. Plotinus (204–70) studied philosophy in Alexandria and led an unofficial philosophical school in Rome from about 244 to 269. These Platonists of Late Antiquity are often labeled today as "Neo-Platonists," but they regarded themselves simply as Platonists.
3. See Kalligas (2014) 162–64.
4. 3, 22–26; Song (2009a) 67–71 refers to the relevant passages in Aristotle, where the homonymy of "good" is used as an argument to refute the supposed synonymy of Plato's Good.
5. *Nicomachean Ethics* I. 2. 1094a22; I. 7. 1097a29, b7, 15.
6. A short introduction to Plotinus' metaphysics can be found in O'Meara (1993).
7. *Nicomachean Ethics* X. 7. 1177b26–1178a8.
8. IV 8, 8, 1–6.
9. On his doctrine see Remes (2007); Song (2009a) 75–76 (on I 4).
10. In this section Plotinus speaks of the human being (*anthrôpos*), not of *men* in particular. However I will use the grammatical masculine, since it is also in the Greek.
11. 4, 23–31, trans. Armstrong, slightly modified (as in the following quotations from Plotinus).
12. The Plotinian good person (*spoudeios*) has been studied in depth by Schniewind (2003).
13. 16, 20–29.

14. See O'Meara (1999).

15. 1, 5–6; in I 8, 6, 10–12, Plotinus points out that the "flight" in Plato's text does not mean leaving earth, but being virtuous on earth, fleeing vice.

16. Alcinous, *Didaskalikos*, ch. 28, 181, 41–45.

17. On the precise place of bodily desires (*epithumiai*) and spirit (*thumos*) in soul's relation to the body, see Karfík (2014) 120–4.

18. See the analysis proposed by Kalligas (2014) 136, and, on the example of fire, Emilsson (2007) 27.

19. See Plato *Laws* 716C.

20. 3, 23–24 and 31; 6, 14–15. Soul can become good or evil (4, 14) and thus can have good and bad dispositions (virtue and vice), whereas divine Intellect remains what it is: purely good.

21. Circumstances will necessitate virtuous actions–war requiring bravery, injustice requiring just acts – but virtue itself would prefer not to have to act, just as a doctor would prefer not to have to use his art (i.e. would prefer that there would be no sickness needing a cure) (VI 8, 5, 4–20).

22. They are, in the chronological order of the treatises, numbers 19 (*Enn.* I 2) and 20 (*Enn.* I 3).

23. 6, 14–24; see II 9, 15, 15–17 (the chapter as a whole shows the importance Plotinus gives to virtue); Aristotle, *NE* VI, 13.

24. On concern for others in Plotinus, see Schniewind (2005), Remes (2006), Song (2009a) ch. 5; in Porphyry, Tuominen (forthcoming).

25. Plotinus has been referring earlier in the chapter to magical spells, but he widens the idea to cover more generally coming under the power of another.

26. Compare I 4, 4, 23–31 (quoted above, Section 1); in VI 8, 6, 10–18, we read: "But when necessary (*anagkaiôn*) passions and actions come in the way, it [virtue] has not, in its supervision [of soul], wished that they should occur, but all the same even among these it will keep its independence by referring back to itself even here; for it will not follow the lead of what happens (*pragmasi*), for instance by saving the man who is in danger, but, if it thinks fit, it will sacrifice him and command him to sacrifice his life and property and children and even his fatherland, having in view its own excellence (*to kalon*) and not the existence of what is subject to it." Plotinus stresses here the priority of the morally good (*to kalon*) to the necessities of material existence; this does not mean that the good person will, in general, have no care for these necessities, for his life and those of others.

27. See Chapter 10.

28. Plotinus uses the image of souls as each other's "sisters" (IV 3, 6, 13; II 9, 18, 16–20).

29. VI 4, 4, 35–44; IV 8, 3, 16–19; see Bene (2013) 152–3; O'Meara (2016).

30. On the theme of friendship in Plotinus and later Platonists in late Antiquity, see now the full treatment in Schramm (2013).

31. The image is found in I 6, 8, 16–27; see V 1, 1 and VI 4, 4, 43 (alienation).

32. The principle has its origin in Plato, of course, who held that those who are good (humans and gods) will do good, not evil. See O'Meara (1993) 63 for Plotinus; in O'Meara (2003) 73–81 I have applied the principle to the case of the philosopher's care for others in Plotinus and in later Platonists.

33. See Song (2009b) 38–42.

34. IV 8, 5, 24–32; see Remes (2006) 19; Song (2009b) 36–38.

35. See I 3, 1, 1–6; Schniewind (2003) 185–89. Proclus, in his *Commentary on the Alcibiades*, interprets Socrates as just such a soul which seeks the moral reform of the young Alcibiades (40, 17–41, 15; 53, 19–54, 24).

36. See Wildberg (2009).

37. Chs. 2–3. However both the first cause, the One, and the very last product, matter, are exceptions: the One is above (prior to) knowledge and matter is bereft of any determination such as is involved in knowledge.

38. 4, 30–47; 5, 1–6. Wilberding (2008), 375–78 thinks that action relates to weakness in knowledge (1), whereas production relates to fulfilled knowledge (2). However this contrast is misleading: Plotinus relates both (1) and (2) to action *and* production (4, 39–40), not distinguishing between action and production in respect to his argument about the priority of knowledge (see 3, 1–6).

39. See also ch. 6. In her critique of my position, Stern-Gillet (2014) ignores (414) the second way in which action relates to knowledge (as an expression of knowledge, not as a substitute due to weakness) and does not see that action is the area where "political" virtues are involved.

40. Smith (2005b).

41. On the theory of double activity, see Emilsson (2007) ch. 1. I take this as applying in the first place to action as an expression of knowledge, rather than to action as a poor substitute for knowledge.

42. This thesis is attributed incorrectly to me and others by Wilberding (2008) 373.

43. On this Epicurean term and its use in Plotinus, see Schniewind (2008).

44. I 3, 6, 6–14 (on this difficult passage see O'Meara (2012) 55).

45. *NE* II, 1. Plotinus can, however, allude to a phrase in Plato's *Republic* (518E1–2: *ethesi kai askêsesin*). Bene (2013) 154–56 argues that Plotinus distinguishes between theoretical and practical wisdom (*sophia* and *phronêsis*) in a way that differs from Aristotle. Certainly the dependence of practical wisdom on theoretical wisdom in Plotinus is un-Aristotelian. In some places, notably in I 2, Plotinus seems to use *sophia* and *phronêsis* as synonyms, but this reflects Plato's language when defining the cardinal virtues of *Rep*. IV.

46. See VI 8, 3, 20–6 (*tas enteuthen protaseis*). The Aristotelian idea of the practical syllogism may be present here; it certainly emerges clearly in later Platonists, in Iamblichus and Proclus; see O'Meara (2003) 137, Bene (2013) 156–57.

47. See IV 4, 44, 7 (*hai tou pathous protaseis*): irrational fear, for example (44, 13), may give rise to false opinions motivating action. As regards the premises coming "from above," they may express themselves as premises in practical wisdom, but their ultimate source is Intellect. In VI 8, 1, 39–41, Plotinus appears to distinguish between knowledge of particular circumstances ("this man is my father") and knowing a general rule (not to kill). The general rule, as a premise "from above," we can speculate, may derive from the principle of goodness and its implicit requirement for the care of others' lives (see Section 3).

48. Compare V 3, 6, 35–39, where Plotinus distinguishes between theoretical intellect, which is turned to itself, and practical intellect, which is turned to what is "outside" and has knowledge of it.

49. On freedom in Plotinus, see Collette-Dučić (2014).

50. See O'Meara (2013) 133–36 for the mixing of autonomy and heteronomy in Plotinus and in Proclus.

51. Porphyry's *Life of Plotinus* is still published today at the beginning of complete editions of the *Enneads*.

52. See Song (2013).

53. On this see Smith (1999) 229.

54. Quoted above at p. 248.

55. 9, 18–20; see II 9, 9, 44–45; I 4, 15, 21–25; Remes (2006) 11.

56. See O'Meara (2003) 74–76. The (top-down) providential desire of the philosopher which might take political (legislative) form should not be confused with the (bottom-up) lust for office and power which Plotinus rejects (above 248).

57. See above 252.

58. See already Plotinus I 1, 10, 11–13 (quoting Plato, *Rep.* 518E). On education in the "ethical" and "political" virtues in Iamblichus and Proclus, see van den Berg (2014).

59. Full information on the later Platonist scale of virtues can be found in Saffrey and Segonds' introduction to their edition of Marinus' *Life of Proclus*.

60. See Saffrey and Segond's notes in their edition.

61. See O'Meara (2006).

62. See Remes (2014), 464–68. Porphyry's arguments, in *On Abstinence*, against eating animals also involve interesting and important moral issues concerning justice and the concern for others, not just humans (see Tuominen (forthcoming)).

63. See Schibli (2002); Adamson (2014).

64. See I. and P. Hadot (2004); Vogel (2013); Remes (2014).

v   Themes

14 Ancient Eudaimonism and Modern Morality

Julia Annas

Often when we are comparing ancient with contemporary ideas we find that it is the ancient idea which appears difficult to bring into focus, while the contemporary one strikes us, with probably misleading force, as obvious and clear. Ancient eudaimonism, however, is relatively easy for us to understand, whether or not we find it convincing or even plausible, whereas when we turn to get a grasp of modern morality, we find from the start a nest of problems as well as tendencies in a number of quite different directions. In the interests of clarity I shall start with the easier term, ancient eudaimonism, and I will lay it out in a way which I hope will make fruitful contrasts with contemporary thinking in as straightforward a way as possible.

ANCIENT EUDAIMONISM

Eudaimonism is the structure of all ancient ethical theories, with only one notable outlier. It wobbles into view in the pre-Socratic Democritus in the fifth century BC, and the neo-Platonist Plotinus is in the third century AD still working out his own version of it via criticisms of his predecessors. The only outliers are the minor school of Cyrenaic philosophers.[1]

In the ancient way of thinking about ethics, the entry point for ethical reflection is one which an adult will most likely take up at some point in his or her life: thinking about her life as a whole. It will start from questions such as: How is my life going? Clearly such a question can only be posed by someone who already has a life – who has been brought up by particular parents and educators in a particular culture, functioning in a particular language and so on. Eudaimonist theories do not set out to convince some philosophical skeptic that it is worthwhile to think ethically, but rather to enable us all to improve in doing something we are already and unavoidably doing, namely living our lives.

Few if any of us are satisfied with our lives the way they are. Dissatisfaction may come from factors such as lack of talent, a society hostile to our ideals, or shaky health. This leads to reflection as to how we might deal better than we are with those or other challenges. Eudaimonist theories present themselves as systematic ways to think about your life and your sources of satisfaction and dissatisfaction, and then rethink your ways of living towards doing better, living a better life.

Underpinning this ordinary way of thinking is the implicit idea of a *final end*. This is emphatically not the idea of an already fixed end or life plan, towards attaining which your life should be organized. The thought is rather that you can think of your life, as it proceeds, in two ways. There is the everyday way, made salient to us by the demands of daily life: You do first this and then that, till the time (hour, day, lifetime) is used up. There is also the way that becomes apparent as a way to think about your *life* when you first ask yourself *why* you are doing what you are doing. Thinking about the action you are performing now, you ask yourself *why* you are doing it. The answer here is given by the goal you have in doing it. Many of your goals reveal themselves to be important only in the light of other, larger goals of yours. You shop to get food, to eat, to keep going, for example. You study to understand the subject, to get a job (let us say), to earn money, to maintain a higher standard of living than mere survival. Thought about the ways your goals hang together makes it clear that you have several large-scale goals: to have a satisfying job, to make money, to have a family life, perhaps to travel and so on. You have several goals you are set to achieve in your life.

But – you have only one life. All these goals have to be achieved in one temporal stretch. You might try to achieve only one, hoping that after that you can take care of the others (in some kind of "bucket list," for example). You might give some up when you think about the difficulty, or perhaps impossibility, of achieving them in a way compatible with your achieving other, more important, goals. Whatever you do, you have to organize your goals *somehow* into the living of a single life. If you give up on this, life will just do it for you, and you will be left with regrets that you didn't order things better while you still had options.

In thinking of your life as the single life in living which you have to organize and integrate your various goals, you have implicitly recognized your *final end* – the goal which is overarching in that you achieve it in achieving your goals, whatever they are, in a coherent way which enables you to live a better life than you would have done had you given the issue no thought. An implicit such end whose pressure is unconsciously felt is a *hupotelis*, but ancient thinkers are, disappointingly for us, not much concerned with the pre-conscious roots of ethical thinking, and the final end is nearly always discussed as your *telos*, your explicitly recognized final end.

Your final end is not a fixed point, since so far you have little or nothing determinate to say about it. It is simply the goal you are trying to achieve in your life as a whole, the goal that all your other goals are means to or help constitute. But this means that, in the ancient world, your final end is *eudaimonia*, happiness. For in the ancient world, obviously in Greek but transferable to Latin, happiness is what you aim for in everything you do, while you do not aim for anything further in aiming at happiness. We shall return to the point that this is not our only contemporary idea of happiness. This is the point, however, at which ancient eudaimonist theories meet ordinary thinking – the point where everyday thinking becomes more theoretical. For, as Aristotle says, everyone agrees that their final end is happiness, but they disagree as to what happiness is.[2] This is the point, then, at which someone trying to live a good life is able to become not only more reflective but more intelligently enquiring. For different theories offer different specific answers to the question of how to live a better life. Instead of thrashing about on your own, you can get practical help from philosophy. This is still possible, even though at this point our society offers self-help books as the obvious guide rather than philosophical theories.[3]

The idea of a final good is where ordinary thinking meets philosophy. Our everyday reflection gets us to see that we have been thinking in these terms all along, and that we need philosophy for us to get any further, since it is philosophical theories which offer us more worked-out accounts of what we are doing and what we need to do to become better at what we are doing – namely, living the only life we have.

This way of thinking, particularly the way that ordinary thinking finds the need for more specialized help at this point, is also freely available to people in the modern world, as can readily be seen by looking at the range of self-help books available in most bookstores and online. They start to offer help of various kinds at exactly this point of reflection. Some are moving in the direction of philosophy.

Another distinctive aspect of ancient eudaimonism is that our final end, although it is what I aim at in my life, you in yours, and so on, is not a merely prudential end. In ancient eudaimonism my practical thinking is not about *my* interests *as opposed to* those of others; it is about how best to live my life as a mother, soldier, son, relative, employee, employer, and so on. Concern for others is already built in to my concern for my *eudaimonia*. There is a question how far it is to extend, but the idea that I might have *no* concern for *anyone* but myself is never an assumption in ancient thinking. We find the idea introduced in a few places – as the position of Plato's Thrasymachus, for example – but it is always regarded as a deliberately provocative position to be refuted, not a serious ongoing challenge everybody makes. Moreover, even Thrasymachus does not think of his position as one where the agent cares for *nobody* else; it is a position where the agent rejects the constraints of a society which enforces justice, rather than relationships to everybody else. He will have a family to favor unfairly, for example.

This foregrounds the central point in ancient eudaimonism that it is common property among philosophers and ordinary people that happiness, *eudaimonia*, cannot be achieved without virtue. We should note the fact that many people nowadays find this to be implausible or even absurd in any version; this is due to the fact that since the early nineteenth century "happiness" has been used for feelings of pleasure, and this association is still uppermost with many people. We will return below to this point.

In the ancient world, *eudaimonia* is what everyone converges on when first asked to specify their final end, and so the point of common sense where philosophical thinking starts to specify what *eudaimonia* is and what is needed to achieve it. Because there are many divergent theories about this there are several views of what it means to claim that *eudaimonia* can't be achieved without virtue. As we see from Aristotle's account of everyday views in his *Rhetoric*,[4] most people thought that virtue must have some part in a life well lived, but did not have clear views as to how important that part was, nor how it related to other things also regarded as requisite parts of a *eudaimon* life, such as money or status. Nearly all philosophers agreed that virtue could not merely be one part or aspect of a *eudaimon* life along with others; it must in some way be the dominating aspect. Virtue is accordingly necessary (but not sufficient) for Aristotle, and necessary and sufficient for the Stoics. These positions engendered a lasting and subtle debate about the relation of virtue to other aspects of *eudaimonia*.[5] The outliers are the Cyrenaic school, whose focus on present experience made virtue unlikely to help in its acquisition, and Epicurus, whose hedonism forces him to regard virtue as having instrumental value for *eudaimonia*, though at times he speaks as though it is also partly constitutive of it.

Eudaimonia is, as already noted, an indeterminate end which becomes more determinate as a result of the choices we make and their implications for life as a whole. What does it mean to say that virtue is crucial for this? The claim is that you will not succeed in living a *eudaimon* life if the virtues do not have priority in the way you live your life. Money-grubbing, for example, will not lead to *eudaimonia*, but neither will a lofty indifference to money. We all deal with money in our lives (and similarly for status, power, and many other such things). We learn from our parents and culture to deal with it in some ways and not others, and at some point we start to reason for ourselves about it. Some of us are brought up to be honest with money, others not; and some of each kind endorse their upbringing while others reject it. We cannot avoid dealing with money, but it is up to us and the choices about it that we make whether we deal with it honestly or not. The claim most ancient philosophers make is that only dealing with money (and status and so on) virtuously, rather than viciously or indifferently, will form part of a *eudaimon* life.

We cannot avoid this kind of choice in the way we deal with money, status, and other aspects of life – in our relationships with others, for example. We have to deal with these things in some or other way, as that is just what it is to live a life in the society and culture in which we find ourselves; so we cannot escape choosing to deal with them virtuously or not, where this will require endorsing or rejecting parts of our upbringing. This, incidentally, shows the mistake in the claim that thinking in terms of virtue will tend to endorse the standards one has learnt and so be conservative. This does not appear to be true on the level of ordinary ethical living, and it is wildly false of ancient philosophers, whose claim that you need to live virtuously to achieve *eudaimonia* was, over a wide range of time and different societies, standardly quite at odds with the culture of the day.

I have given a bare sketch of the main features of ancient eudaimonism – enough, I hope, to make its structure fairly clear. One striking thing about it is the extent of the convergence of ancient ethics on a common framework, agreement on which goes so deep that it doesn't have to be discussed; it is not an object of contention, unlike the nature of virtue and the relation of virtue to happiness, both of which produce ongoing dispute and debate over hundreds of years.

MODERN MORALITY

In clear contrast, *modern morality* is a strongly contested idea, as is the wider idea of *morality* itself. I shall not attempt a definition, which I take to be a hopeless task, but will proceed in a more complicated way. I will first give an extremely brief account of the emergence of ways of thinking that are regarded as *moral*, as they emerged as competitors to eudaimonism. I will then discuss a widespread, but mistaken, way of drawing the contrast between eudaimonism and these competitors. Then I will briefly discuss various contemporary ways of characterizing morality. The result does not give us a unified subject to discuss, so I will then turn to characterizing various aspects in which ancient eudaimonism is commonly thought to contrast with morality. Since the result still does not indicate a single unified subject of morality, I should preface the discussion with two remarks. One is that there is a perfectly good use of the term *morality* in which it is just used as a general way of indicating the field which can also be referred to as ethics. I am concerned with *morality* in a narrower sense, in which it is held to contrast with ancient eudaimonism (and with contemporary forms of ethics which have a similar structure). This is a common use of the term.[6] The other remark is that what follows is not an attack on theories of morality. There are many of these, and, as we would expect of philosophical theories, they produce consistent and unified accounts of what, in the theory, morality is. Such accounts can be criticized only by criticizing the theory, and it would be too huge a task to criticize every theory of morality which has been produced. I am here dealing with morality as it is understood by those who hope to produce theories of it.

Eudaimonism as a structure for ethical thinking has had a very long life, in a variety of forms. In the West, it survived as the default form for ethical thinking in the Middle Ages in the theistic form whose grandest version is found in Aquinas. From the early modern period onwards it continued on, partly in the Aristotelian forms persistently taught in universities and partly in less overtly religious but still theistic forms such as those we find in the so-called "British Moralists." Eudaimonism was challenged as a default way of thinking ethically by the rise of two competitors: Kantian theory and utilitarianism.[7] Neither tradition has much use for virtue, which figures in both in a minor role, and both are actively hostile to *eudaimonia* as a final end that we seek in everything we do, and of which philosophy gives us a better and more determinate account. Both, though in other respects quite distinct, think of happiness in a determinate way as pleasure, or the fulfillment of desires, and hence misunderstand eudaimonism. Kant takes it to be at root a version of hedonism, while utilitarians have contrasted it unfavorably with their own determinate interpretations of happiness. Both have gone so far as to accuse eudaimonism of confusion in taking virtue to be in some way required for *eudaimonia*. Indeed, if *eudaimonia* is taken to be happiness understood as pleasure, the place of virtue in it will appear at best high-minded optimism. It is not surprising that eudaimonism was from the late eighteenth century onwards ignored as a serious subject for ethical discussion, both virtue and happiness being regarded as minor parts of a theory whose role would be obvious once the main work was done elsewhere.

One way of thinking of the fundamental contrast between ancient eudaimonism and Kantianism and utilitarianism has become influential. This view, formulated by the utilitarian Sidgwick, holds that ancient eudaimonism relied on "attractive" concepts, while since the emergence of the competitors we think of morality in terms of "imperative" concepts. This view might look persuasive at first, since ancient ethics gives prominence to the good and to *eudaimonia*, and generally to goals which we find attractive to achieve. And Kant does see morality in terms of imperatives, oughts, and obligations, and utilitarians think that the greatest good presents itself to us as something that we *must* bring about. The contrast, however, does not do justice to ancient eudaimonism, which does not rely just on "attractive" notions such as *good*, but also on "repulsive" notions such as *bad* and *shameful*. If something is bad or shameful, it does not just fail to be good and attractive; it is positively repulsive and to be avoided, without yet bringing in any imperatives or obligations. Furthermore, eudaimonism does make full use of imperative ideas like *should, ought,* and *must*, but in characteristically different roles from the ones they have in Kantianism or utilitarianism.[8] It is a mistake to think that any framework for ethical thinking could consist of attractive or imperative notions alone.

What of contemporary understandings of morality? I have distinguished four aspects of morality which are to be found in ethical writings of the present day. A more refined analysis would distinguish more types than the one I offer.

Morality is sometimes understood as essentially concerned with other people (sometimes other sentient beings) as opposed to oneself. This is characteristic of utilitarianism, most versions of which hold that the ideal that a moral person should aim at is that of regarding yourself as merely one among others, giving no special weight of any kind to your own point of view. Correspondingly, thinking in ways that give any kind of weight to your own point of view cannot, on this view, be moral; it is egoistic, which is defined in opposition to being moral. This demand leads to moral requirements which stand in such contrast to our ordinary ways of thinking that often bridging positions are introduced to make moral thinking and acting feasible for us.[9]

Morality is also characterized as what characterizes our reason as opposed to our desiring and emotional side, and hence as what characterizes rational planning as opposed to short-term gratifications. In some versions morality is characterized as reasoning which can oppose and override *all* our other motivations, including long-term ambitions and aims as well as desires. In these versions, typified by Kant, reason has to be seen as a deeply different and special kind of motivation, one not appealing to anything in our motivational repertoire. It then becomes deeply mysterious, and philosophers in this tradition have diverged greatly in their responses to this.

In contrast, morality is also sometimes characterized as what emerges from our social and cultural systems when we start to co-operate with others in order to live more peaceably, and so is seen as a constraint on our more competitive and individualistic tendencies. This type of theory has been found in Hume, and there are contemporary versions of it which appeal to interpretations of human evolution. This interpretation of morality stresses the force and resources of our emotional side, in contrast to the rationalist interpretation, and relies heavily on our capacities for empathy. Morality on this view is like a set of shared conventions for co-operation, one grounded on facts about our nature as beings who share certain basic character traits such as ability to empathize with others and to share in bringing about joint enterprises.

It is clear that while the second understanding of morality sees it as a constraint against aspects of our nature as humans which need to be subdued or overridden, the third takes morality to be a development, rather than a repression, of that nature.

Morality is also conceived of as a set of rules or principles, that is moral rules and moral principles, which we are all capable of recognizing, and of responding to their authority, which is that of duty or obligation. One influential version of this insists that these rules and principles do not form a unified system capable of precise application in every case; rather, in our lives as moral agents we apply various rules which tell us what is our duty *prima facie*, and so there is a role for the agent's judgment in assessing which rules are relevant to the situation and, given their differing salience, what the ultimate judgment about duty or obligation should be.

While these thumbnail accounts are brief and highly general, they bring out the point that it is hard to find between them a unified or readily unifiable notion of morality. Debates about morality, its nature and importance, and how we are to live according to it, continue.

The idea that we do not, in the West in the twenty-first century, have available to us a unified notion of morality is not new; it was pointed out over thirty years ago by Alasdair MacIntyre.[10] Nor is the idea that the very notion of morality itself no longer has the robust support in and from our other beliefs that it did in the past; that was pointed out fifty years ago by Elizabeth Anscombe.[11] But these points are worth underlining here, because eudaimonism, in either its ancient or its contemporary forms, is often contrasted with morality, and it makes a great difference what it is being contrasted with, as we cannot assess a contrast until we are clear which interpretation of morality is in view. Different contrasts with, and sometimes objections to, ancient eudaimonism can come from different sources. Because of this, I will not attempt to set out in general terms what major contrasts are to be found between ancient eudaimonism and modern morality. Rather, I will look at some ways in which eudaimonism has been seen as contrasting strongly with morality, and will explore the issue separately in each case. This is unsystematic, but at present it is the best we can do.

ANCIENT EUDAIMONISM AND MODERN MORALITY

The commonest objection to eudaimonism, in both its historical and contemporary forms, is that it is in some way egoistic. It is worth noting that this is a comparatively recent objection, current since the rise of Kantian and utilitarian ethics, and it is a moot point, as yet unexplored, whether it has a footing in our ordinary beliefs about ethics.[12] Those who press it strongly are often motivated by the thought that morality is by definition about others in a way which, insofar as I am moral, detaches me from anything special about my own viewpoint, but it is also seen as a problem by those whose conception of morality does not make other-concern a defining feature of morality.

Eudaimonism takes its start from the thought that in every action we aim at some good, and so at some good overall; so in the end the reason we do anything is to achieve our own good, *eudaimonia*. But doesn't it pretty much amount to a definition of selfishness, to be doing everything for your own good?

Any form of eudaimonism rules out organizing your life round selfish goals where these are just particular ends that you aim at. If you try to live your life aiming simply at having a good time, you are ignoring eudaimonism rather than displaying it, since you are ignoring the circumstances of your, or anyone's, life and focusing on one part at the expense of thinking of the whole, and of how your present pursuit could fit into that. So eudaimonism not only does not support, but rules out, ordinary forms of selfishness.

The objection holds, then, only against positions which can be argued to be selfish in their view of what we should aim at in our lives as wholes. Here we need to distinguish between different forms of eudaimonism. It is possible, as already stated, for a theory to be eudaimonist in form and to set up a final end which is self-concerned, in that the agent's character is such that all her actions, whatever their kind (helping others, for example) are undertaken ultimately for an aim which is an aim of hers, as opposed to an aim which also includes the concerns of others. As mentioned above, Epicurus has a theory of this type; it has the same form as Aristotle's, but urges us to achieve *eudaimonia* by aiming to secure (a sophisticated form of) pleasure.[13]

However, this is an outlying position; most types of eudaimonism, and particularly the Aristotelian kind most prominent in contemporary discussions, think that living virtuously is at least necessary for achieving *eudaimonia*, and so eudaimonism, in any realistic discussion, is the idea that, while we ultimately do everything to achieve *eudaimonia*, this is achieved by becoming and actively remaining virtuous. The argument now becomes one from *egoism*, not ordinary selfishness, and is aimed at a particular conception of our final end. I am acting virtuously in order to achieve *eudaimonia*, goes the argument, so this is an egoistic end: What I do is done for my own good, not that of others. This first point rests on an obvious misunderstanding: For me to be virtuous *is* for me to care about others, since otherwise I wouldn't be *virtuous*. To be brave is to struggle or endure for what is worthwhile – *not* what is worthwhile *for me*. The virtuous person is thus clearly not egoistic in aiming at *eudaimonia* in all she does.

At this stage the argument retreats to a more theoretical position. Eudaimonism is not egoistic in the sense of having a final end to my life as whole which is self-concerned or self-focused in content. Indeed, virtuous people are the least self-focused since, being virtuous, they act in ways that are generous, patient, brave, and so on, and so spend less time and energy on their own concerns than others do. If they are to be found egoistic, it must be in a different sense; "formal egoism" and "fundamental egoism" are some of the terms for this. This is the claim that, however unself-concerned is the content of the virtuous life you lead as a way of achieving *eudaimonia*, you are still in a sense egoistic, because the *eudaimonia* you are seeking to achieve is *yours*.

It is not clear what exactly is meant by this that could be a problem for a eudaimonist. There is a sense in which it is just trivial that the *eudaimonia* I seek is mine, since it is what I'm seeking in my life, and I can live only my life, not anyone else's. (Of course, I seek to improve the conditions of life for other people, to enable them to do more to seek their own *eudaimonia*; but I can hardly do *that* for them.) But it is true of anyone aiming to live their life ethically according to any theory that they are living their *own* life. The objection must be that there is some deeper problem lurking in the fact that I seek *eudaimonia* in seeking to live virtuously, given that logically the only *eudaimonia* I can seek is mine. What could this problem be?

The form in which it is usually posed is that eudaimonia, as my final end, must have some motivational force for me to be seeking it in everything I do. However, if I am motivated to seek my *eudaimonia* in being virtuous, this compromises the virtue, since a further aim is driving me to be brave, generous, or whatever, whereas an action cannot have such a further aim if it is to be virtuous. And if I am not partly motivated, in acting virtuously, by seeking my *eudaimonia*, then the latter is playing no role in my motivation, which is problematic. This alleged dilemma rests on an unsophisticated position about virtue. It assumes that every time someone performs a virtuous act, some thought about virtue must be actively and consciously motivating them, and that in a eudaimonist framework this must be joined by an actively and consciously motivating thought about *eudaimonia*. This, however, ignores the way that virtue is learned, and the way its connection to *eudaimonia* is learned. As with other practical dispositions like skills, what is first consciously learned becomes internalized in ways that allow it to motivate, in intelligent and discriminating ways, without the need for a consciously motivating factor.[14]

The basic forms of the egoism objection, then, either simply claim that eudaimonism is egoistic without argument, or rest on mistaken assumptions. It is worth looking at additional assumptions which could make the manifestly mistaken egoism assumption look plausible, as it does to many philosophers.

The egoism objection is aided by a tendency to think of *eudaimonia* simply as happiness, without realizing how complex and disputed the contemporary idea of happiness is. Firstly, happiness is often in contemporary discussions thought of as something determinate, whether a feeling of pleasure or a broader mood. Some philosophers even follow psychologists who call it an emotion. It is taken to be something which can be explored and better understood before we try to achieve it. Indeed, a lot of modern self-help books engage in discussions of happiness to produce an account which will indicate why their preferred strategy is the right one to achieve that. But, as we saw above, it is crucial to *eudaimonia* in a eudaimonist account that it is initially indeterminate. It is simply the overall goal in life. That is why it is always taken to be important to improve your understanding of it, in order to achieve it by making it more determinate in good and fruitful ways, rather than creating a life for yourself that will have built-in problems and weaknesses. There is an apparent convergence between ancient and contemporary popular appeals to change your life so as to achieve happiness, which you are failing to do at the moment. But this often conceals a wide difference in the way happiness is conceived, whether as a goal you can be better steered towards or as something that you can help to bring about for yourself as you change your life and hence make more determinate your conception of what *eudaimonia* is. In philosophical terms, contemporary discussions often take your change of life and strategies to be instrumental to becoming happy, whereas eudaimonism takes your change of life to be constitutive of what it is to achieve happiness when done thoughtfully and reflectively.

Not only is happiness often taken in contemporary discussions to be already determinate, it is often discussed in oddly narrow terms. Sometimes it is discussed in terms of a peculiar categorization: Theories of happiness (or more broadly well-being) are supposed to think of it in terms of *either* pleasure (hedonism) *or* getting what you want (desire-satisfaction) *or* "the objective list theory," according to which happiness requires getting various things that are valuable (health, success, etc.).[15] This arbitrary categorization simply ignores eudaimonism, so it is not surprising that debates in terms of it have been completely unhelpful.

Better categorizations at least recognize that happiness involves thinking about your life as a whole, and so are quite distinct from focusing on particular feelings or cases of getting what you want, or particular goals. Getting to grips with eudaimonism sometimes still fails here because many contemporary ways of thinking about your life as a whole distinguish sharply between "prudential" reasoning and "moral" reasoning. This returns us, of course, to the problem of distinguishing a sense here for "moral." It might be thought that we do do it here since "prudential" is supposed to be the easier term to understand; it is the way of thinking which concerns you and your concerns as opposed to those of everyone else. This idea, however, cannot be applied to eudaimonism, where the point is to achieve *eudaimonia* by living in ways that concern you *and* other people. The circumstances you live in do not isolate you in a bubble; you start thinking in terms of family, friends, social and political context, and so on. For eudaimonism there is nothing basic or easy about the idea that you think about yourself in isolation from all these concerns (or in a way which reduces other-concern to a kind of self-concern); it is a distinct theoretical position, not one that has a place in eudaimonist thinking about how to live.

As is clear, eudaimonism does not fit neatly into many contemporary ways of thinking about how to live, even ones that take the basic point that we think about our lives overall. Better understanding will hopefully come from rising familiarity with eudaimonism as a kind of theory.

A second basic objection, again with many aspects, is the idea that eudaimonism fails as an ethical theory because it does not provide "action guidance," does not direct us to act when we are unsure what we should do. This is a conception of an ethical theory as a provider of answers to ethical questions and problems, and this differs from what eudaimonism offers, namely a way of thinking about the ethical life. Because each person must think about ethical matters in and from the perspective of their own life, which is embedded in various cultural and social contexts, eudaimonism does not provide answers of a one-size-fits-all kind. Eudaimonists can agree with everyone else that it is useful for children at an early stage to learn general rules such as "Don't lie" and the like, but these are not capable of being developed into rules that can be applied by adults without a great deal of complication (is *this* a lie? This is a lie, but should I go ahead?). Further, people will not grow in ethical understanding until they get some idea of *why* lying shouldn't be done in *these* circumstances. This understanding is what is provided by virtue terms – it would be *dishonest, deceptive,* and so on. Thinking in terms of the virtues enables each of us to deliberate well in our own circumstances, but this is something each of us has to learn to do for ourselves. This is a point shared by all eudaimonist positions, whatever line is taken on the role of virtue in *eudaimonia*.

This position is sometimes criticized by opponents of virtue, on the grounds that direction given us by virtue terms will be too vague. Often it is assumed that virtue terms can do no more than indicate how to do what we should do, not what we should do itself. We should act honestly, for example, but what should we do that is honest? A fuller account of virtue would make clear the intuitive point that terms like "honest" are more specific and helpful than rules like "Don't lie," which cannot be applied without a great deal of extra work and information, and so provide only the sketchiest direction as to what to do in order to do the right thing.

Behind this objection there lies a broader point: Eudaimonism is being thought of as a way of thinking which inspires us to follow attractive goals, but does not really *direct* us in the way that *moral* direction requires.[16] This kind of objection is rooted in the approaches to morality which stress moral rules and principles, and also those which stress morality's *force*, thought of as overriding all our other sources of motivation. (It has less appeal to those who think of morality as a co-operative mechanism among empathic individuals.) The thought here is that morality is *demanding*, that it has claims on us which are properly expressed in forcefully directive terms, telling us what we *must* do. Sometimes this thought takes the form of a complaint that eudaimonism does not provide the force required for *duty* and *obligation*. Eudaimonism, the thought goes, tells us to seek *eudaimonia* in the best way we can, reflectively and hence virtuously, but where are the duties that we *have* to perform? Eudaimonism does show us what we ought to do, what we should do and what it is right to do, but can this amount to more than advice as to how best to achieve *eudaimonia*? Further, since we do this best when we are whole-hearted about it, how can we find in eudaimonism the obligations that we must fulfill even when doing this goes against all our desires and other aims?

To meet this basic thought, which underlies a number of different complaints that eudaimonism does not provide the kind of action guidance we need, all that is needed is to point out that virtue *is* demanding in the way it leads us to *eudaimonia*. For us to achieve a life which is happy and flourishing, we need direction by virtue, which functions not by making polite requests of us but by making *demands* on us. The notions of duty and obligation function differently in eudaimonism from the way they do in other kinds of theory. In eudaimonism, virtue provides the demands needed in most of our deliberations. Duties and obligations are what we have insofar as we are acting within a role defined by some institutions. If I am a soldier, for example, this role provides duties that I have to perform regardless of any of my motivations. (This is not, of course, to say that such duties might not conflict with virtues, just that their source is distinct.) Some contemporary theories assume that if an action is what we ought to do or should do, or it is right for us to do, then it must be a duty, because they take it, rightly, that if we should or ought to do something, there is a demand that we do it, but then also think, wrongly, that demand can come only from duty.

The answer to many objections about action guidance, then, springs from pointing out that, while it gives us ideals, eudaimonism is not simply an idealistic theory which points the way and assumes that we will be motivated by aspiration to virtue alone. Rather, it involves demand, the demand made by virtue. This is not the kind of demand that can be expressed in general rules about what to do and not do; that is too vague. It is a demand to act virtuously in ways that produce learning and education towards having a virtuous character, and so it is a demand for constant learning and active improvement. The kind of strong demand made by duty and obligation are not part of this; they enter as the specific demands made by roles understood in terms of institutions.

Examining these two types of objection to eudaimonism, both of which are clusters of different but related worries, indicates that eudaimonism is, indeed, a radically distinct kind of theory, one whose advantages cannot be obtained by inserting parts of the theory into other ethical theories (requiring virtue in utilitarianism, for example). The increasing appeal of forms of eudaimonism in contemporary society as well as contemporary ethical philosophy indicates a weakening of the idea that other contemporary theories are the best we can do, or all that we have.

This discussion has been on an abstract level, because of the wealth of detail about ancient theories of ethics to be found in the other contributions. We can of course study ancient ethical theories in their own right without worrying about contemporary forms of ethics and whether or not the ancient forms might provide an alternative, perhaps a preferable one. This is a fully philosophical way to proceed. Still, it is worth reflecting on the actual ethical alternatives that we are aware of, so as to treat the ancient texts with proper respect and not try to force them into Procrustean molds, or to come up with anachronistic blame (or praise). I have tried to indicate some reasons for being cautious when we approach ancient forms of eudaimonism and trying, as of course we do, to see them as ethical theories that might be available to us. To do this well we need to be aware of how the theories we have grown up with are more than slightly different from the ancient theories we get to know.

NOTES

1. I argue that Democritus can on balance be regarded as a eudaimonist in Annas (2002). Plotinus' essay on happiness is *Enneads* I, 4. On the Cyrenaics, who hold that our aim should be the maximum pleasure of the present, see Annas (1993) 227–36.
2. *Nicomachean Ethics* I, 7.
3. An interesting example of a book which uses ancient eudaimonism in an intelligent and attractive way is Evans (2012).
4. *Rhetoric*, I 5.
5. See Brad Inwood (2014). The issue is discussed incisively by Daniel Russell in (2012) part 2.
6. Bernard Williams has influentially characterized morality as making *obligation* central, "Morality, the Peculiar Institution," ch. 10 in (1985).
7. This implicitly challenges the claim of Jerome Schneewind (1990) that virtue suffered "misfortunes" earlier, in thinkers like Grotius, a challenge which cannot be adequately taken up here.
8. This important point is forcefully pointed out by White in (1992). It has not had the influence which it should have had.
9. For example, the theory recommends the following of rules or having characters justified by the theory, rather than living according to the theory. This is a highly unstable solution, ultimately unsuccessful.
10. MacIntyre (1970).
11. Elizabeth Anscombe (1958), very frequently reprinted.
12. This issue is complicated, however, when *eudaimonia* is regarded as happiness in a restricted contemporary use of the word: see below, p. 276.
13. It is interesting to compare Epicurus' theory, which at least aims to be eudaimonist, with the theories of the hedonist Cyrenaics, who urge us to aim at pleasure as a momentary end, and some of whom explicitly discount taking *eudaimonia* into account.
14. This is necessarily a very compressed account of objections to eudaimonism which rest on the character of virtue. For a fuller account see Annas (2011) 152–63 and Annas (2008).
15. This classification comes from Parfit (1986) appendix I, 493–502. I have no idea why it has acquired authority in discussions of happiness and a good life, since it ignores any form of eudaimonism.
16. This is the basis of Sidgwick's mistake (see note 8 above).

15 Partiality and Impartiality in Ancient Ethics

Richard Kraut

I WHO SHOULD SURVIVE? THE CONCEPT OF IMPARTIALITY

Suppose you are involved in a boating accident. You and another person are struggling to survive in the water. Nearby is a floating wooden plank large enough to assure the survival of only one of you. The two of you are equidistant from that plank. What should you do? Try to get it for yourself? Let the other person have it? If you and the other swimmer could flip a coin or choose randomly in some other way, would that be the best alternative?

I begin with this example as an illustration of what will be meant here by the notions of partiality and impartiality. If you and the other person could somehow flip a coin, that would certainly be one way of acting impartially. Neither of you would be exhibiting a bias in your own favor. You would not be acting on this sort of thought: "Jones is the one who should survive, because I am Jones." If, however, you were to swim as fast as you can to secure the plank for yourself, simply because you want to survive more than you want the other person to survive, clearly that would be an expression of partiality to yourself. That we all sometimes exhibit such partiality is no doubt true. Whether we are justified in doing so is another matter.

My example is derived from the work of a Stoic philosopher, Hecaton, as reported in the third book of Cicero's *De Officiis*. But Hecaton's discussion has a layer of complexity that I have omitted. Here is the relevant portion of Cicero's text: "Suppose there is one plank and two sailors, both of them wise men. Would each of them grab it for himself, or would one give in to the other?" Hecaton replies: "One should give in to the other, that is, to the one whose life most matters for his own or the republic's sake." The questioner continues: "And what if such considerations are equal for both?" Hecaton replies: "There will be no contest, but one will give in to the other as if losing by lot, or by playing odds and evens" (III.89–90).[1]

Notice that Hecaton is advocating impartiality in both of his responses – that is, not only when he proposes (in his second reply) that one individual should sacrifice himself as though he had lost a game of chance, but also when he offers a basis for saying that one of them ought to have the plank rather than the other. He says that A should let B have the plank if B is the one "whose life matters most for his own or the republic's sake" (and vice versa). A, being wise, will recognize that there is a stronger reason why B should have the plank. Hecaton's response also implies that A should be the one who has the plank, if the reason why *he* should survive is stronger than the reason why B should. If A takes the plank for himself on these grounds, he would not be doing so because his desire to survive has greater force than his desire that B survive. Rather, he would be taking the plank for himself on impartial grounds: He believes that the person whose survival is better supported by reasons is the one who should survive; as it happens, he is that person. So, it is possible to take something you desire for yourself, preventing someone else who wants it from having it, and to do so on impartial grounds. Impartial deliberation about what one should do can lead one to take some scarce resource for oneself.

With this explanation of what is meant by partiality and impartiality, let us now investigate how large a role these ideas play in Greek and Roman moral philosophy. I will argue (a) that Stoic ethics is a thoroughly impartial way of thinking; (b) that the case for reading Plato's ethics in this way is almost as strong; (c) that impartiality also plays an important role in Aristotle's thinking; (d) but that Epicureanism is an ethics of partiality.[2]

That in one's relationship with others one should deliberate from an impartial perspective is an idea that plays an important role in nearly every leading figure of the modern period – Spinoza, Hume, Smith, Bentham, Kant, Mill, Sidgwick, Moore, Rawls, Nagel, and Parfit, among others. But we would have a distorted picture of the history of moral philosophy if we thought that impartiality is of little or no significance in Greek and Roman thinkers. It would be no less a mistake to suppose that modern ethics is uniformly impartialist. Nietzsche, for example, is no fan of impartial ethics or of any of the philosophers just mentioned. Even Sidgwick endorses partiality: He says that both hedonistic self-interest and the adoption of the "point of view of the universe" are rational methods of ethics.[3] In recent times, Bernard Williams has sought to set a limit to the authority of impartial moral claims.[4] The history of ethics from Plato to the present is no simple progression from an era of partiality to one of impartiality. A better way to read it is to recognize that impartiality has been present from the beginning, with strong minority dissenters scattered here and there.

2   STOIC IMPARTIALITY

The passage discussed above, from Cicero's *De Officiis*, is one of many in which the impartiality of Stoic ethics is apparent. The Stoics conceive of the universe as a "perfectly organized society" governed by an all-pervasive divine fire or breath that guides and governs it in accordance with reasonable and universal law. This material force can be called by various names: "god," "intelligence," "fate," "Zeus." Our highest calling as human beings is to act and think in cooperation with this intelligent force.[5]

The idea is given poetic expression by Cleanthes, the second head of the Stoa, in his "Hymn to Zeus":

> You have so welded into one all things good and bad that they all share in a single everlasting reason. It is shunned and neglected by the bad among mortal men, the wretched, who ever yearn for the possession of goods and neither see nor hear god's universal law, by obeying which they could lead a good life in partnership with intelligence ... For neither men nor gods have any greater privilege than this: to sing forever in righteousness of the universal law.[6]

From Diogenes Laertius we have the report that our ultimate end is to live

> in accordance with the nature of oneself and that of the whole,
> engaging in no activity wont to be forbidden by the universal law,
> which is the right reason pervading everything and identical to Zeus,
> who is this director of the administration of existing things ...
> The virtue of the happy man and his good flow of life are ... always
> doing everything on the basis of the concordance of each man's
> guardian spirit with the will of the administrator of the whole.[7]

The Stoic god, unlike Yahweh, has no "chosen people." No nation or person is the favorite of Zeus, picked out for special treatment because he happens to like them, or because they have flattered, or honored, or sacrificed to him in the right way. To put this point in a different way: It is no more important or valuable to god that one human being fare well than that another fare well. We human beings should bear that in mind as we carry out our plans and give shape to our lives. I should of course want my own life to go well and should strive to achieve that goal. But I should also recognize that from a god's-eye perspective, my well-being does not make the universe a better place than does the well-being of some other human being.

This does not mean that we ought to care about and help every human being to the same extent. Nature inclines us to procreate and to love our children; just as animals give special care to their offspring, so should we. "Even among animals the power of nature is self-evident. When we observe the effort they devote to breeding and rearing, it is as though we hear nature's very own voice. Thus our impulse to love what we have generated is given by nature herself as manifestly as our aversion to pain" (*De Fin.* III. 62). Similarly, nature leads us to enter larger communities. "We are fitted by nature to form associations, assemblies, and states" (III.63). Just as each human being is but one small part of the divinely governed universe, so too is the citizen in relation to the political community. "That is why a preparedness to die for one's country is so laudable – it is right and proper that we love our homeland more than our very selves" (III.64).

Is there a contradiction, or at least a tension, lurking in these ideas? The Stoics propose that we view and act in the world from both an impartial and a partial perspective. A parent is to give his children more attention than he gives to the children of strangers, and yet when he looks at the universe from a god's-eye perspective, he should acknowledge that the good of his child is no more valuable than the good of any other. If the well-being of every human being is equally valuable, why should one's own children receive so much more of one's love than do other children?

Another way to raise this question is to imagine a Hecaton-style scenario in which only one person can survive an accident. Suppose a parent is in the water with two children, one his own, the other a stranger. Should he rescue his own child and let the other drown? Were he to decide randomly between them, he would violate a plausible and common assumption about the love and protection a parent owes his children. But if he saves his child and lets the other die, he makes some other parent and child suffer what he and his child would have suffered. Why is that any better than the death of his own child? Since his own family is no more important than the other family, shouldn't he choose randomly?

Should we accuse the Stoics of having accepted conflicting ideas, or can we find a way to acquit them of this charge? The answer is that they are innocent. We can say, on their behalf, that when we look at the universe from an impartial perspective, we find reasons for arranging human society in a way that charges us to favor certain people over others. The human community is best served, in other words, if we do not all aim to give equal attention to all of its members, but specialize in attending to the well-being of this or that group or individual.[8]

This idea is one that has been exploited by rule utilitarians. They tell us that we should act in accordance with that set of rules whose general acceptance would lead to the best state of the universe. To achieve this result, we are not to consider each act on its own, in isolation from other acts of that same type, asking whether *it* is the one most likely to lead to the best state of the universe. Rather, we must ask which *rules* are most likely to do so, and then we abide by those rules. To illustrate: In order to decide whether a parent should save his own child or another's, ask what would be the best generally recognized and observed rule governing such situations. Now, a rule that told parents to randomize, choosing indifferently between their own child and the child of a stranger, would obviously lead to great insecurity within the family. Children would know that when they are in danger their parents will be as likely to save a total stranger as them. The trust and security that are essential to good family life would be endangered. We can see from an impartial perspective – one that looks to the common good of all – that the best rules sometimes require us to be partial to certain people. A parent who saves his child in such a situation is not licensed by Stoic ethics to think that his child is in some way superior to others, or that his duty to love his child takes priority over some other parent's similar duty. Rather, the Stoic will say that he ought to give an impartial justification for choosing the survival of his child over that of another.[9]

This should not be taken to mean that the Stoics are the first rule utilitarians in the history of philosophy. They do not have the idea that, when we decide how to act, goods and harms should be amalgamated into a single "score" – one that sacrifices the good of some for the sake of achieving the greatest sum total of good. They think that the world is already well governed (by the gods), and is already in the best possible condition. By contrast, utilitarians assume that it is up to human beings to do their share in making the world a better place.

But although these are major differences, there are some themes that at least some Stoics have in common with at least some rule utilitarians. Stoics think that the gods govern the universe by means of laws: long-lasting general principles (even if they admit of exceptions) rather than an ongoing series of edicts, each of which fits one situation only. Their ethics is in this sense rule-centered. Furthermore, those rules are to be observed by *all*; there is not one set of laws for this people or nation, another set for others; for we are all part of a single world order. These rules are not esoteric but widely recognized, as they are accessible to common human reason. As examples, we should, as a general rule, help strangers in need; contribute to the common good of fellow citizens; refrain from theft and lying; keep our promises; prefer health to sickness, pleasure to pain, survival to death. It is through the observance of these rules that the state of the world is as it should be. Similarly, like some rule utilitarians, some Stoics believe that it is appropriate for us to devote more attention to certain people (our children, friends, fellow citizens) than others. Like rule utilitarians, their justification for this preferential treatment is that the state of the universe is better when we concentrate our efforts in this way rather than disperse it by giving equal attention to every human being we encounter.[10]

It is compatible with this way of reading the Stoics to see them, in addition, as accepting one of the fundamental tenets of Aristotle's ethics: that there is a single and most final aim that each human being should strive to achieve, namely *eudaimonia* (happiness, well-being, flourishing). In the vast anthology compiled by Stobaeus in the fifth century AD, we are told that according to the Stoics "being happy is the end, for the sake of which everything is done, but which is not itself done for the sake of anything. This consists in living in accordance with virtue."[11] Now, if my ultimate goal is *my own* well-being – a condition in which *I* am virtuous – does that mean that I ought always to view my social world from my own perspective (*my* well-being) rather than act from a god's-eye perspective? Not at all, for the two ways of thinking can be combined. I do what is best for myself by acting virtuously; and acting virtuously consists in taking an impartial stance to the rest of the world. For the Stoics, there is a harmony in the universe that keeps my self-interest from coming into conflict with the interest of other human beings. They do not claim that looking at the world from the impartial perspective of the gods is a stance that can be justified *only* by showing that it is good for me to do so. After all, it would be the grossest form of megalomania to suppose that what makes the world well arranged and governed is that it is good for me that it be so constructed and ordered.

Sidgwick pointed out, in the final chapter of *The Methods of Ethics*, that utilitarianism and egoism can yield the same conclusions about how one is to act, provided that the universe is governed by a benevolent deity. So too, according to the Stoics, when one thinks about what one ought to do by first looking at oneself from a god's-eye perspective on how the universe should be governed, and then from the far narrower perspective of one's own ultimate end, the same way of life will be justified.

Suppose you are aspiring to Stoic wisdom and are told by a soothsayer with infallible knowledge of the future that tomorrow either you or someone else will succeed in becoming a sage (but not both). Tomorrow you will be happy or someone else will be. Must the Stoics say that you ought to be neutral – that you should not hope that it will be you rather than this other person? No. In fact, their impartialism allows them to say not only that you *may* but also that you *ought* to have this preference. If your highest hope is to succeed at the task of self-perfection, and everyone else has this kind of aspiration for himself, and if these emotional orientations are more productive of a world full of sages than any other psychological dispositions, then such partiality for oneself has an impartialist justification – just as each parent's loving his own children above others is an attitude that is best from a god's-eye point of view. (We will meet this mode of argument again when we turn to Aristotle in Section 5.) What the Stoics must condemn is not this sort of preference for oneself, but rather the thought: "Let A be the one who is happy rather than B, for no reason other than that I am A." To think that this self-interested orientation is not only correct but that it stands in no need of justification, because self-interest is the sole self-evident foundation of practical philosophy; it is the hallmark of an ethics of partiality. As we will see, this is a minority view in the Greek and Roman world.[12]

3 PLATONIC IMPARTIALITY

At the beginning of Book IV of the *Republic*, Adeimantus asks Socrates how he will respond to the complaint that those in charge of the ideal city will not be very happy, because they are required to live like soldiers in a camp. They are fed and sheltered by the city, but are not allowed to possess their own gold, silver, land, houses, and money (416E–419A). Socrates replies: "in establishing our city, we are not looking to make any one group in it outstandingly happy, but to make the whole city so far as possible" (419BC, Reeve). His aim is to construct a city in which each citizen does his and her job well; each will have some "share of happiness" (421C) and so theirs will be a happy city. But each will have only as much happiness as is compatible with the city being well organized.

Socrates, in other words, is impartial in his treatment of the different classes that make up the city with respect to their happiness. Neither soldiers, nor farmers, nor craftsmen nor any other group is singled out for favored treatment. He does not say that it does not matter whether *anyone* in this ideal city is happy – that somehow the city could be happy even if no citizen is. The well-being of the citizens matters to him, but there is no portion of the citizenry whose well-being matters *more* to him than that of the others. As it turns out, it is the philosophical rulers who have the best lives. But that is because philosophy is the most worthwhile activity, not because the ideal city's constitution makes their good a higher priority than anyone else's.

Not only is this Kallipolis *constructed* from an impartial standpoint, it must be *governed* impartially as well. Plato does not make this point explicitly, but no other interpretation of him is plausible. It would sabotage the impartial nature of the constitution if those who govern the city were to single out this or that group of farmers, or artisans, or soldiers for special treatment simply because they happen to like them more. In fact, Socrates constructs the ideal city in a way that minimizes the kind of partiality that is accepted in ordinary social life – the partiality by which parents favor their children over others, and friends give each other better treatment than more distant members of the community. The rulers do not know who their biological children are, and their "marriages" are temporary devices for the production of offspring rather than life-long relationships in which husband and wife have special responsibilities and affection for each other. This is to be a community in which, so far as possible, citizens treat each other impartially. So, if a farmer were to set aside some portion of his produce for a group of friends, so that they will be better nourished than others, that would be a violation of the community-minded ethos of the city. Each citizen does the job for which he is best suited because in so doing he makes a contribution to the well-being of all of the citizens, not some portion of the city. And this attentiveness to the common good is accompanied by an emotional responsiveness to the well-being or misfortunes of all others: When any one individual feels some pleasure or pain, so too do all others, out of sympathy for their fellow citizen (462A–466A). Of course, we must not take equal concern for all to be the only form of impartiality there is. As we saw in our discussion of the Stoics, an impartial justification can be given of loving the members of one's family more than others. But in Kallipolis impartiality is achieved by egalitarian measures: the abolition of the traditional family among the ruling class, the requirement that each citizen work at some task for the benefit of all, and the fostering of strong emotional bonds among all citizens.

It might be thought that the impartiality that characterizes the construction, governance, and daily life of Kallipolis has no implications for how life should be lived by people in ordinary cities. Although these model citizens treat each other impartially, it does not immediately follow that the rest of us must follow suit, for we live in non-ideal cities – cities in which these forms of impartiality are not the accepted norms. If we do not have a strong emotional bond with most members of our political world, if we pay more attention to our own family than to strangers, if we choose our spouses simply on the basis of our erotic inclinations, we are not violating anyone's expectations – as citizens of Kallipolis would be. Even so, if we agree with Plato that this would be the best city, our attitudes towards our familiar institutions ought to change. If one believes that the family is a defective institution because it detracts from one's relationship with others, that ought to have some bearing on one's attitude to the prospect of getting married and having children in *any* community. Admitting that there could be better ways of organizing our emotional attachments – ways that are less exclusive and more evenly spread over the whole community – would make one less than fully enthusiastic about the arrangements of our non-ideal world.

It is not only in the *Republic* that Plato presents a model of a more impartial way of life. Several of his shorter works give us a rich characterization of Socrates as a human being, and in doing so they put before us a model of how life can be lived from a god's-eye perspective on the world. The *Apology* is where this portrait is most fully drawn. In his defense speech, Socrates describes himself as someone whose devotion to the reform of Athenian society is commanded by "the god" (21A–23B). He has abandoned his household (36B) in order to serve the human community at large. It so happens that Athens is where his service is located, but he says that if the jury decided to punish him by exiling him from Athens, he would go from one city to another, winning a following among the young people in all of them (37CE). If, when he dies, he finds himself in Hades, he will examine whomever he meets there, to see whether that person is really wise (41AB). In Athens, he is as ready to talk to outsiders as he is to citizens (23B, 30A). So, he is impartial in his choice of which individuals he seeks to benefit with his philosophical cross-examinations. That is because the unexamined life is not to be lived by *any* human being (38A). The human community at large, one might say, is his adopted family: He neglects his own affairs in order to address others "like a father or an elder brother" and persuade them "to care for virtue" (31B). Socrates has an impartial orientation towards the human community that is similar to that of the philosopher-ruler towards Kallipolis. We do not have to wait for the establishment of a utopian community in order to live our lives from the same sort of god's-eye perspective. To see the world as "the god" sees it, we need only treat all human beings impartially, provoking citizens and strangers alike to become more devoted to what is really good rather than what seems so.

So, a radical form of impartiality is available to us here and now: We need only take Socrates as our model and spend our lives persuading others to take virtue and the condition of their souls more seriously. That would in fact be the happiest way for us to live; we would not be sacrificing our own well-being in order to serve humanity. But – to repeat a point made earlier – our grounds for doing so need not be that "self-interest is the sole self-evident foundation of practical philosophy." We could instead justify the Socratic way of life as Socrates himself does when he defends himself before the jury: this is what a god would choose for human beings (he believes a god *has* made this choice), because this is what is best for them.

Turning to the *Crito*, we find another passage in which an impartial perspective is adopted for deliberative purposes. In this work, Socrates' friend Crito offers him an opportunity to avoid the death penalty that was recently imposed; Crito can bribe the jailor and arrange for his escape from Athens. During the first part of the dialogue, Socrates and Crito are the sole interlocutors, but at a crucial point their interchange is replaced by a long speech delivered by the personified Laws of Athens, who argue that were Socrates to escape he would be doing his city and its laws a great injustice. The plan proposed by Crito is, at this point in the dialogue, evaluated from the perspective of a hypothetical agent who has no particular attachment to Socrates and is free from personal or partisan loyalties to him. The implicit suggestion is that *this* is the point of view from which each of us should decide whether to undertake *any* action. Of course, this is not a cosmic perspective – it is the city's point of view that is occupied, not "the point of view of the universe" (in Sidgwick's phrase). Even so, the entry of the Laws into the dialogue is noteworthy because it proposes that we deliberate by asking, not "what would be best for me?" or "what would be best for my friends?", but "what would a representative of the whole community think about my action?"

That general perspective is made especially salient when the Laws ask Socrates: "Do you think it possible for a city not to be destroyed, if the verdicts of its courts have no force but are nullified and set at naught by private individuals?" (50B, Grube). In effect, the Laws are telling Socrates that his action can be justified only if, when he imagines other people making relevantly similar decisions, that *general pattern* of behavior is justified.

The Laws insist that what a citizen owes his city always takes priority over his obligations to his family (51AB). Two of Crito's reasons for urging Socrates to escape – if Socrates dies, he (Crito) will be losing a great friend (44B) and his (Socrates') children will become orphans (45CD) – are thus portrayed as having too narrow an orientation. Crito is not portrayed as a bad man, but the narrowness of his perspective is an illustration of how the emotional bonds that attach friends and family to each other can keep them from deliberating properly. Blinded by their affection, they ignore the fact that the whole community would be harmed if people generally acted in the same way. Here in the *Crito*, as in the *Republic*, there is a concern that friendship often obscures or occludes the proper point of view, which is not that of a partisan, but of the whole community.

In the *Symposium*, we encounter, in the speech of Diotima, a metaphysical framework in which even someone who deliberates from the point of view of his city has not yet achieved a sufficiently general perspective, because he is not yet looking at the human condition from a yet wider point of view. A human body can be appreciated for its beauty, but it is better to recognize what all such bodies have in common. It is better still to appreciate the greater beauty of the soul, and to recognize what unites all beauty of soul. Next in the order of value are: the beauty of laws and customs; the beauty of the sciences and their objects; and finally the form of beauty itself (210A–211A). Just as it would be a mistake to become so passionate about one individual that one fails to see that there is greater reason to care about the laws of one's community, so one would be constrained in one's appreciation of reality if one failed to recognize the beautiful order of mathematics and other subjects, and the beauty that all of these beautiful things have in common. Diotima's speech must be read as a reply to Aristophanes' portrait of eros as a force that brings two individuals together so tightly that they meld together into a self-sufficient unit oblivious to everyone and everything outside of itself (192BE). Such a couple would say: "If we had to choose between the survival of ourselves as a unified couple and the survival of a whole city full of happy people, it is our own loving relationship that we would select."

Like the Stoics, Plato conceives of the created cosmos as an orderly whole that is supervised by gods who care about human life. In the *Timaeus*, he shows how the present state of the observable world could have been the outcome of a rational process in which a benevolent demiurge decides to impose harmony and beauty on originally disorderly materials. Our highest goal is to approximate in our own lives this divine governance of the cosmos (*Theaetetus* 176AB).[13] That does not mean that we are to take earth, air, fire, and water and make a miniature physical cosmos somewhat like the one we inhabit. Rather, what we ought to do is give shape to the parts of our souls and, if possible, do our share in making the political community to which we belong a well-ordered whole. (Socrates did this in his own unique manner, but that is not the only way.) In striving to be godlike, we should bear in mind what a small part of the whole universe each human being is, and remember that it does not exist or operate for us, but we for it (*Laws* 903BE). Although one will never go wrong if one makes decisions by finding the correct answer to the question, "What would be best in terms of my own well-being?", we should never be tempted to think that one's own well-being is the only or the best standpoint from which to view and act within the universe.

4   EPICUREAN PARTIALITY

Epicurus and his school have at least this much in common with the Stoics: They hold that only one thing is good for us, and only one is bad. For the Stoics, these are virtue and vice; for the Epicureans, pleasure and pain. This does not mean that, according to the Epicureans, qualities of mind like wisdom, justice, and courage have no value at all. They do not want to depart so radically from common sense. What they claim is that these familiar virtues merely have *instrumental* value. There are gentle and long-lasting pleasures to be had by the just person: He need never be disturbed by a fear of punishment.[14] A tranquil soul – a state of mind in which one is confident that one's life has been and will continue to be painless – is the greatest pleasure of all. To achieve this, one should stay clear of the troubled world of politics, and confine one's social milieu to a small circle of trustworthy friends with whom one enjoys simple and easily attained mental and physical pleasures.

Against Plato and the Stoics, the Epicureans hold that there is no divine providence at work in the world. On one interpretation of their philosophy of religion, the gods exist in a remote region of space where they live eternally pleasant lives, having nothing to do with the governance of the universe or the affairs of human beings. A different reading holds that their existence is entirely a product of human thought – they are our images of an ideal and eternal community.[15] In either case, they have no causal power and no desire to govern the world. They can agree with Plato that we should strive to be godlike, but since gods do not govern, neither should we.

Let us ask how an Epicurean would respond to a question similar to the one raised above in Section 2. Suppose he is told by someone who knows the future that tomorrow A will have a most pleasant day but B will be in great pain. One of them will be he, but he is not told which. What would he choose or hope for? The Epicurean might respond: "That depends on whether the individual who is not me is a friend of mine. If he is, then I am indifferent. But if he is a stranger, then I would choose to be the person who experiences pleasure rather than pain." We might attribute such a reply to the Epicurean on the basis of Cicero's discussion of this school in *De Finibus*, where he attributes to them the idea that "the wise man will ... have just the same feelings towards his friend that he will have towards himself and he will work as much for his friend's pleasure as he would for his own."[16]

So interpreted, the Epicureans make some room for impartiality: One should be neutral with respect to the well-being of a friend and one's own well-being, and have an equal concern for both. But they must pay a heavy price for restricting their impartiality so severely. They present themselves as upholders of justice and other virtues, but because they regard everyone outside their circle of friends with indifference or as a mere means to their own ends, they are forced to accept conclusions at odds with plausible and widely held ethical assumptions. For consider what they must say about the example with which we began in Section 1: A boating accident has occurred, and two people are in the water struggling to survive. Let us now suppose that one of them is an Epicurean and the other a stranger to that Epicurean. The stranger has been lucky: A plank floats in his direction and it will enable him to survive. The Epicurean, however, is going to suffer painfully in the water for many days until he dies – unless he takes that plank away from the stranger. If he does so, no one will ever know that he survived by bringing about the stranger's death.

Unfortunately, Epicureanism has no resources for explaining why one should not cause a stranger's death in these circumstances. The Epicurean might say that someone who survives by these methods will suffer the pains of remorse for the rest of his days. But what if he does not? In any case, why *should* he feel remorse, if his ultimate goal, pleasure, is the right one, and he has done exactly what was needed to achieve it?

The Epicurean does not seek his own well-being (or that of a friend) because from a god's-eye point of view it is best that he do so. An impartial perspective on the state of the universe is not available to him. He does not ask which rules are such that their general observance would produce the best results. Like an Aristophanic lover, he says: "Let these people, not those, be the ones who are going to fare well rather than suffer, for no reason other than that these people happen to be me and my friends." They believe, absurdly, that the "sole self-evident foundation of practical philosophy" is the well-being of this small group.

5 ARISTOTELIAN IMPARTIALITY

Unlike Plato and the Stoics, Aristotle does not view the universe as a divinely governed whole in which all things are arranged, so far as possible, for the best. His god, the "unmoved mover," is not a practical thinker or an active ethical force at work in the world. Instead, it reflects – eternally, unchangingly, and with great pleasure – on scientific truths. Since Aristotle does not view all of humanity as united together in a single project or community, the kind of impartiality that accompanies this picture, which is present in Plato (*Laws* 903BE) and more fully so in the Stoics, is not available to him. Nonetheless, there is an important element of impartiality at work in his writings, and its range is more extensive than is the case for the Epicureans.

Aristotelian impartiality takes this form: The good of the whole political community to which one belongs is a worthwhile goal, and whatever one does as a citizen of this community must be justified in terms of the happiness of that larger whole. For the good of a single citizen is not as weighty a reason for action as the good of the political community to which he belongs. This is what I take him to mean when he announces, in the second chapter of Book I of the *Nicomachean Ethics*, that the topic under investigation is not so much the highest good of one individual as that of the city to which he belongs. "For even if the good is the same for the city as for an individual still the good of the city is apparently a greater and more complete good to acquire and preserve" (1094b7–10).

A comparison between Aristotle and Cicero will be helpful for our purposes: For Cicero, the political life is the best there is (De Off. I.153–8), and, as we saw earlier, he holds that we should be prepared to die for our country, because it is "right and proper that we love our homeland more than our very selves" (De Fin. III.64). Aristotle agrees that we should be willing to face death on the battlefield, but he argues that philosophy is a better activity than politics (NE X.7–8), and that one should love oneself most of all – provided that one does so in the right way, namely, by seeking to surpass others in ethical achievement (IX.8). His thought, as I understand it, is that when there is someone who shows the most practical wisdom in the assembly, or who is most courageous on the battlefield, others cannot reasonably complain that they have been harmed or mistreated by him. "When everyone strains to achieve what is kalon [beautiful, fine, noble] and concentrates on the actions that are most kalon, everything that is right will be done for the common good, and each person individually will receive the greatest of goods, since that is the character of virtue" (1169a8–11).

Here there seems to be a line of thought similar to one that I discussed earlier, in Section 2. To repeat: "The human community is best served ... if we do not all aim to give equal attention to all of its members, but specialize in attending to the well-being of this or that group or individual." Aristotle's parallel thought in this passage is that the political community is best served if one strives to be its most virtuous member. When everyone's self-love takes this form, everyone will benefit. Aristotle is justifying this form of self-love by asking what would happen if there were a rule that told us to love ourselves in this way.

This is the kind of impartiality that, as we saw, is at work in the Crito and Plato's other dialogues, as well as many Stoic writings. Individual actions are justified by bringing them under a general rule whose operation can be approved when one looks at its results from the perspective of the whole community. What Sidgwick hopes is true – that what is best for an individual will coincide with what ought to happen from the point of view of the universe – is close to something about which Aristotle is confident (if one thinks in terms of the common good of the polis rather than the point of view of the universe). The common good and an individual's good will coincide: Whatever serves the one will also serve the other.

Let us come full circle and imagine once again a boating accident, with two men in the water struggling to survive. They are, let us suppose, strangers to each other, and equally good citizens of different but equally good political communities. Are any of Aristotle's doctrines incompatible with saying that there is no greater reason why one of them should survive than the other, and that each of the two can and ought to recognize this symmetry? I believe he can accept this point without difficulty. It *must* be accepted, because by hypothesis nothing of ethical relevance distinguishes one from the other. We know that Aristotle would say that each should love himself more than he does the other. His justification would be that if each loves himself more than strangers, that will be better *for everyone*. Like Cicero, he makes room for partiality towards oneself by incorporating it within a larger framework of impartiality to all. Aristotle's polis-centered outlook can in this way be enlarged. It allows one to look at political communities in general, standing outside of them and evaluating them impartially on the basis of their merits.

NOTES

1. Here and throughout, translations of *De Officiis* are those of E.M. Atkins. See Cicero, *On Duties* (1991). Translations of Aristotle are those of Terence Irwin, see Aristotle (1999).
2. According to Julia Annas, "impartiality does not figure in Aristotle" but is "introduced by the Stoics." See Annas (1993) 450. At p. 265 n. 68, a kind of impartialism in Plato's *Republic* is acknowledged. On my reading, impartiality plays a much larger role in ancient ethics than this.
3. Sidgwick (1907) 382.
4. See his essay in Smart and Williams (1973), Williams (1981) and Williams (1995).
5. Texts expounding this aspect of Stoic physics are gathered in Long and Sedley (1987) 274–80. On the world as a "perfectly ordered society," see Aristocles (G, p. 276). On the several names of the divine force, see Diogenes Laertius (B, p. 275). Henceforth I will refer to this sourcebook and commentary as LS.
6. LS (I, p. 327).
7. LS (C, p. 395).
8. Here my understanding of Stoicism differs from that of Julia Annas, who says that they give "no distinctive ethical role" to friends and family. See Annas (1993) 265.
9. For a recent defense of this idea, see Parfit (2011). See especially p. 385, where he argues that "the optimific principles" allow one to save one's child rather than five strangers.

10. Katja Vogt argues that according to the Stoics the law is simply what the reason of a sage decides upon in this or that particular situation; they prescribe no "body of rules." See Vogt (2008) 162, and throughout ch. 4. If she is right, my suggestion that the Stoics can justify duties to friends and families in the two-stage manner of rule utilitarianism must be rejected. Vogt's argument seems to rest on a questionable inference: "what is appropriate is determined, in each given occasion, by the perfect judgment of the sage"; hence "there *can* be no rules" (p. 190, her emphasis). I think the Stoics are more plausibly read as accepting a sizable body of *defeasible* rules, for example, that it is generally part of nature's plan that human beings be healthy rather than sick. In saying that rules play an important role in their thinking, I follow several scholars against whom Vogt argues. (David Sedley, for example, writes: "to every proper action there corresponds a verbalizable rule recommending that action" (cited on p. 190, n. 74).

11. LS (A, p. 394).

12. Warning: This way of understanding ancient ethics is controversial. Nearly all scholars label these philosophers as "eudaimonists," meaning by this that self-interest (one's own *eudaimonia*) and only self-interest is the ground of all practical justification. For doubts about reading Plato this way, see Kraut (2017).

13. See Sedley (2000) 309–28.

14. LS (A, B, p. 125).

15. See LS, pp. 144–49, for a discussion of these two readings.

16. LS (O, p. 132). There is considerable uncertainty about how to understand the Epicurean account of friendship. The interpretation I have adopted here is only one possibility. For discussion, see Mitsis (1988) 98–128.

16 Elitism in Plato and Aristotle

Christopher Bobonich

I INTRODUCTION

It is an old and persistent complaint about ancient ethics that it is unjustifiably elitist, that is, that it restricts the possibility of virtue to too narrow a group. And since ancient ethics tightly links happiness to virtue, the possibility of happiness is similarly restricted. This basic charge can take many forms and the various schools of ancient philosophy differ in their kinds and degrees of elitism. In this chapter, I consider some important aspects of Plato's and Aristotle's ethics that are relevant to the charge of elitism.

The central notions of Greek ethics are those of excellence or virtue (*aretê*) and happiness (*eudaimonia*). A basic point about both is that they are optimizing notions. An *aretê* is an excellence; in particular, it is the best psychic condition in the relevant domain. For example, in the *Republic* the virtue of wisdom is knowledge of what is best for each part of the soul and the whole soul in common (442C4–7). As knowledge, it is better than any form of belief (506C6–9). Being happy is, very roughly and with the caveat that different philosophers have distinctive conceptions of happiness, the attainment and correct use of the human goods or living the best possible (or at any rate, the superlatively choiceworthy) life for you.

Simply by being optimizing notions, virtue and happiness are unlikely to be attained by most people. But ethical excellence's rarity is not, in itself, an especially problematic form of elitism. (Or if problematic, it is not uncommon). Kant thinks that one can never know if she (or others) have acted from duty, so it is possible that only a few people have ever performed actions having moral worth. It is hardly uncommon in the Judeo-Christian tradition to think that moral or spiritual excellence is very rare and even Rawlsian "purity of heart" may be hard to find.[1]

More troubling than such differences in moral attainment are more basic differences in moral capabilities. According to Jerome Schneewind, a major development in early modern moral thought was the rise of a morality of self-governance. On this view, "all of us ... have an equal ability to see for ourselves what morality calls for and are in principle equally able to move ourselves to act accordingly."[2] Both Plato and Aristotle reject this claim. In Section 2, I focus on the cognitive demands that Plato makes on the virtuous agent since these demands, when combined with differing intellectual capabilities among people, are a main source of Plato's elitism. I argue that Plato's views about people's ethical capabilities undergo important changes in the late dialogues and I sketch their nature and sources. In Section 3, I turn to Aristotle. Despite his rejection of the morality of self-governance, Aristotle holds that, at least in principle, a wide range of people are capable of attaining full virtue. In the rest of Section 3, I consider whether this claim is undermined by some of Aristotle's other views on ethical virtue and practical wisdom.[3]

2   PLATO

The Middle Period

Plato imposes rigorous conditions on the virtuous person's non-rational motivations. I shall, however, here concentrate on the cognitive demands he makes on virtue, since these are both great and foreign to us. I begin with middle-period Plato.[4] In the *Phaedo*, Plato holds that all non-philosophers lack genuine virtue and can, at best, have a "façade" of it containing "nothing healthy or true" (69B7–8). Their choices cannot be virtuous because they are neither guided by nor aim at wisdom (69AC). Wisdom here involves knowledge of Platonic Forms. The *Republic* also denies genuine virtue to non-philosophers and offers an implicit judgment of their happiness in its description of the attitude of the philosopher outside the Cave to all non-philosophers who remain within it:

> When he reminds himself of his first dwelling place and what passed for wisdom there, and of his fellow prisoners, do you not think that he would count himself happy because of the change and pity the others? ... Would he not feel with Homer that he would greatly prefer to 'work the earth as a serf to another, one without possessions' and go through any sufferings, rather than share their beliefs and live their life?[5]
>
> (*Rep. 516C4-D7*)

Drawing on the rest of the *Phaedo* and the *Republic*, we can fill out Plato's middle-period position.

(1) Only philosophers can be virtuous.

(2) (1) is true because virtue requires knowledge and only philosophers can have knowledge.

(3) The knowledge required for virtue is knowledge of Platonic Forms. This is not simply justified true belief about what is good for humans. What is required is explicit knowledge of the relevant Forms, e.g., the Forms of Justice and the Good.

(4) Only philosophers can have happy lives, since happiness requires virtue and virtue is by far its most important component.

(5) Non-philosophers are badly off with respect to virtue and happiness.

To begin, the knowledge required for virtue is an understanding of Forms and this is extremely intellectually demanding. Knowing a Form requires knowing its real definition and grasping its place within a complex explanatory structure in which more fundamental Forms explain the natures of less fundamental ones. But the cognitive demands on the virtuous person are even higher than this may suggest, since ethical properties do not form a separate, self-contained system. Indeed, the Form of the Good plays a fundamental explanatory role with respect to all other Forms.[6] More generally, although it is not fully explicit in the *Republic*, Plato thinks that quasi-mathematical principles of order and structure are, as such, both value properties and the properties that make intelligible whatever is intelligible.[7] Thus the intellectual demands of genuine virtue are high because genuine understanding requires grasping both (i) a wide interrelated field of items, and (ii) the explanatory relations among these items.

Virtue and happiness are thus radically restricted to the few capable of mastering such a theory. But (5) goes further and commits Plato to there being a wide gap between philosophers' and non-philosophers' virtue and happiness. We tend to think of ethics as largely concerned with how we treat others (along, perhaps, with some imperfect duties of self-improvement). It thus seems implausible to us that people who are concerned with others' welfare, but lack a sophisticated understanding of ethical theory, are significantly ethically defective. It is even less plausible that those lacking a sophisticated grasp of reality fail to be virtuous.

We can, however, better appreciate Plato's position by starting with his understanding of human nature. At least while embodied, human souls are a composite of the Reasoning part, the Spirited part (the home of anger, the desire for honor and other self-assertive desires and emotions), and the Appetitive part (the home of desires for food, sex, and drink). Although embodied people are not identical with their Reasoning parts, they are to identify themselves with it and its good condition is a central component of their happiness (*Rep.* 588C–590D). Having the lower parts of the soul in a good condition is essential for being just. But since their good condition is not a way of knowing the truth about reality, it is a much lower good.

The Reasoning part's distinctive virtue, wisdom (*sophia*), is characterized in Book 4 as knowledge of what is good for the whole soul (442C). The Reasoning part's primary motivations are seeking its own good, that is, happiness, and thus seeking knowledge as a great good (e.g. *Rep.* 611B–612A). It also desires to bring about, on the basis of its knowledge, good states in others (*Symp.* 206B–212B and *Tim.* 29D–30A). What unites these activities is reason's orientation towards objective value. First, it seeks to grasp fully the truth about non-sensible principles of value and order. Second, it is part of its own nature to love the truth and the good. Third, reason seeks to instantiate genuine goodness in itself and in others, bringing itself and others into the appropriate relation to genuine value. Given this conception of the Reasoning part, it cannot be in an excellent or virtuous condition without attaining knowledge of Forms in general. In particular, without knowledge a person must lack wisdom and since Plato accepts the Reciprocity of the Virtues – a person has one virtue if and only if she has all the virtues – she lacks all the virtues.[8]

The above line of thought only shows that philosophical knowledge is necessary for virtue and, given virtue's centrality in happiness, necessary for happiness. (Less than fully accomplished philosophers who grasp only some of the relevant Forms will more or less closely approximate full virtue and happiness.) It does not yet show how badly off non-philosophers must be. Even if they fall short of knowledge, they might approximate it and thus approximate genuine virtue. Yet Plato's characterization of a virtuous Reasoning part constrains the nature of such approximation. What is needed for a good approximation is a partial grasp of the correct objective, non-sensible value properties. This is precisely what Plato denies to non-philosophers: Their second-best motivations are not a close second-best. In the *Phaedo*, non-philosophers think that nothing is real except what is bodily (83C) and thus do not recognize the existence of Forms. The *Republic*'s lovers of sights and sounds understand the fine (*kalon*) in terms of various sensible property-types, e.g., colors and shapes (476B4–C7).[9]

Non-philosophers thus have a double misfortune: (a) They entirely fail to value what is genuinely good or fine in itself, and (b) what they do value, sensible properties, are never good or fine in themselves. Non-philosophers are thus cut off from any appreciation of genuine value. As we have seen, it is precisely such an appreciation of value that Plato thinks is essential to virtue. Aiming at it is a basic aspect of our nature as rational creatures, so its frustration is a deep failure to realize our own nature. Given these views, Plato's endorsement of (5) is reasonable. We might disagree with Plato over whether there are objective and intrinsic values and, if so, what they are, but if they exist, it must be a serious defect in a valuing agent to fail to value what is valuable and to value what is lacking in value.

The Later Period

I have argued elsewhere that in the later dialogues Plato offers a more positive view of non-philosophers' capacities to attain valuable character states and thus a kind of happiness.[10] In the *Laws*, Plato's last dialogue, he advocates the innovation of attaching "preludes" to the laws.[11] All previous lawgivers have erred in treating citizens as slaves by giving them commands backed up by the threat of force without attempting to persuade them (722BC). What the lawgiver in Magnesia (the *Laws'* best city) does by means of preludes is described as "teaching," that is, giving the citizens reasons and explanations for what the law commands and leading them to "learn" (718CD, 723A, and 888A). In the best case, these arguments will "come close to philosophizing" (857CE). The lawgiver, both via preludes and other means, is supposed to teach the citizens about what is fine, just, and good (858DE). Indeed, Plato expects non-philosophical citizens to accept that virtue is good in itself and that it is necessary for benefitting from anything else.

But the education of Magnesia's non-philosophers is not limited to what we would think of as the purely ethical. Although the preludes are not cast in quasi-mathematical terms, non-philosophers' education is arranged so that they come to grasp value properties in much wider contexts. At the lowest level, they are to appreciate the order and structure of the music in which they take pleasure (*Laws* 653D–654A, 664E). But they are also to learn of non-sensible mathematical properties, both by grasping the orderly and thus good motions of heavenly bodies (822AC) and by recognizing the existence of incommensurable magnitudes (820B). In addition, they receive a version of the cosmological argument for self-moving souls as ultimate sources of motions (893A–899D).

The mathematical cast of their education should be unsurprising, since the late dialogue, the *Philebus*, provides the most direct statement in the dialogues of the idea that value properties are quasi-mathematical properties that structure reality in general. Here Plato characterizes fineness and virtue simply in terms of measure (*metriotês*) and proportion (*summetria*) and gives an account of the good itself in terms of fineness, proportion, and truth (*alêtheia*, 64D–65A). Near the end of the *Philebus*, Plato considers the value of various kinds of knowledge. Those having the greatest accuracy (*akribeia*), purity (*katharotês*), clarity (*saphêneia*), and truth are both the best simpliciter and the best for their possessor (55C–62B). This ranking reflects the degree to which the kinds of knowledge grasp their subject in mathematical terms.[12] So if ethical knowledge is to be highly valuable in itself to us, it will have to grasp its subject matter in mathematical or quasi-mathematical terms.[13]

So why has Plato come to think that non-philosophers are capable of a better approximation of virtue and happiness? The answer lies in his epistemology and psychology. As we saw, non-philosophers' primary defect in the middle period was that their value concepts were based solely on sense-experience and thus they could not grasp the correct non-sensible value properties. In the middle period, Recollection required an explicit recognition that what was recollected was a Form and was thus limited to philosophers. In the later period, Recollection is much more widely embedded in human thought. For example, the ability to judge that "x is F" requires contact with the non-sensible property of being. Such contact does not require that the person recognize the property of being as such or its non-sensible nature, but nevertheless the person is drawing on non-sensible resources in making such judgments.[14]

Magnesia's education of non-philosophical citizens is designed so that they come to recollect, albeit partially and indistinctly, non-sensible properties of value and order. This is clearest in their mathematical and astronomical studies where they are explicitly thinking of mathematical properties, but it is plausible that Plato thought that those whose ethical judgments had a rational basis (even without full philosophical explanation) were recollecting, to some degree, perfectly general principles of value and order. In the middle period, non-philosophers' second-best motivations were not a close second-best precisely because they had no appreciation of genuine value properties. In the later period, at least some non-philosophers can achieve a closer approximation because they have a partial and indistinct grasp of the same principles that philosophers grasp fully and distinctly.

So how elitist is Plato in the later period? To begin, Magnesia contains philosophers who understand the definitions of the virtues (*Laws* 964A–966A), the truth about the gods (966BC) and mathematics and its relations with other sciences (967DE, cf. *Rep.* 531C, 537C). In sum, like the *Republic*'s philosophers, they have comprehensive knowledge of value and reality and so know Platonic Forms. Although Plato is not fully explicit, it is reasonable to assume that because of this knowledge they surpass the other citizens in virtue and happiness. Those capable of attaining such knowledge will be, for familiar reasons, very few, so Plato still restricts the highest forms of virtue and happiness to an intellectual elite.

What of the rest of the citizens? There is a wide range in Magnesia, but let us consider the best of them. It seems clear that they lead lives that are well worth living and have a good approximation of philosophers' higher virtue and happiness. Although their education is primarily ethical, they also receive some education in matters that Aristotle would count as falling under wisdom, such as astronomy and the cosmological argument of Book 10. Even though they may not come to recognize Forms explicitly, their mathematical education should make them familiar with non-sensible properties and entities. Plato does not suggest that only a eugenic elite can attain such a level. Given the proper early training in pleasures and pains and the rest of the prescribed Magnesian education, it seems reasonable to expect that such a kind of virtue and happiness can be widely shared.

3   ARISTOTLE

Aristotle, in contrast to Plato, sharply distinguishes the intellectual virtue required for ethical success from knowledge of reality in general. He bipartitions the rational part of the soul. One part, that concerned with scientific understanding (*epistêmonikon*), reflects upon necessary and eternal objects (*N.E.* 1139b20–24). The other part, the deliberative part (*bouleutikon*), reflects upon things that can be otherwise (1139a8). Since these parts have different objects, they also have different virtues: The scientific part's primary virtue is wisdom (*sophia*), while the deliberative part's primary virtue is practical wisdom (*phronêsis*).

As the deliberative part's primary virtue, practical wisdom enables its possessor to deliberate well about the good life in general (*N.E.*

1140a25–8). While wisdom is concerned only with universals, practical wisdom "is not concerned with universals only, it must also know particulars, since it is concerned with action and action is concerned with particulars" (1141b14–16).[15] Practical wisdom and the ethical virtues (e.g. courage and moderation) which belong to the non-rational part of the soul are interentailing: Aristotle accepts the Reciprocity of the Virtues (1144a29–b1, 1144b14–32, 1145a1–2). Practical wisdom and the ethical virtues together comprise full virtue which can be had without possessing wisdom.

Wisdom is comprehension (nous) of the explanatory first principles of the highest things and scientific understanding (epistêmê) of the consequences of these first principles (N.E. 1141a18–20). Comprehension, however it is ultimately spelled out, is a grasp of first principles as such. Scientific understanding requires more than correct deduction from true premises: the premises must be explanatory of the conclusion, and the deduction must display the correct explanatory link between the premises and the conclusion. It is clear that acquiring such a proper grasp of first principles and of the explanatory connections that they have with their consequences across an entire field of study would be an immensely difficult intellectual accomplishment.

Given this understanding of wisdom, Aristotle has a strongly elitist position about the best form of happiness (N.E. 10.7–8). This sort of happiness requires – as at least a prominent component – philosophical contemplation, which is an activity of wisdom. So the best form of happiness is restricted to a small elite because of the intellectual demandingness of wisdom. This is a point of partial agreement with Plato, who also thinks that because the best sort of happiness requires wisdom in the form of philosophical knowledge, it is restricted to a few, but – unlike Aristotle – also includes within wisdom knowledge of ethical values.

Aristotle, however, recognizes a secondary form of happiness (N.E. 1178a9–10) which, although less good than the philosophical kind, is still a form of happiness. Secondary happiness consists of the full actualization of the ethical virtues and practical wisdom, especially in political activity. Full virtue is thus far less demanding than complete Platonic virtue, since the former does not require wisdom, but we must consider how demanding it is in other respects.

Aristotle thinks that full virtue is rare (although wisdom is rarer, since philosophers are a small subset of virtuous people).

Virtuous people, however, even if a small minority, are found in Greek cities (e.g. *Pol.* 1301a39–41). But despite their actual rarity, Aristotle suggests that virtue and happiness are, at least in principle, much more widely attainable:

> [Happiness] will also be something available to many (*polukoinon*); for it will be possible for it to belong, through some kind of learning (*mathêseôs*) and practice (*epimeleias*), to all those who are not handicapped with respect to virtue.[16]   (N.E. 1099b18–20)

The most natural reading of this passage is that those who are not handicapped with respect to virtue are all normal Greek males.[17] Women and non-Greeks are handicapped because of innate deficiencies.[18] Manual workers (*banausoi*) are handicapped because of their way of life, not – if they are normal Greek males – because of some innate feature.

So it is possible for all normal Greek males to engage successfully in the practice and learning that results in full virtue and happiness. (I shall call this the "possibility thesis.") In society as it is, few realize these capacities and attain full virtue. But in the *Politics'* best city, this possibility is realized. The ideal city assumes the best possible circumstances, but no impossibilities, and, in particular, takes human nature as it is. There all full citizens are virtuous, and we can thus infer that there are no innate barriers preventing some within the group of normal Greek males from attaining virtue and happiness.[19] The *Politics* thus supports our reading of the above passage.

We might, nevertheless, think that the *Nicomachean Ethics* contains other lines of thought that should lead us to revise these judgments. So let us turn to three specific worries: two concerning the ethical virtues and one concerning practical wisdom.

The Ethical Virtues

The first worry is that essential precursors of the ethical virtues may be innate so that the fully virtuous turn out to be a eugenic elite. This concern gains force when we remember that Aristotle thinks that non-Greeks' biological characteristics render them incapable of full virtue.[20] In Book 6 of the *Nicomachean Ethics* Aristotle says:

> For everyone thinks that each of the various sorts of character traits belongs to us in some sense by nature – because we are just, and

disposed to moderation, courageous, and the rest from the moment we are born... For natural dispositions belong to children and animals, but without intelligence to accompany them they are evidently harmful ... just as a powerful body when moving without sight may stumble badly ... But if a person acquires intelligence it makes a difference to his actions; and his disposition, which was merely similar to virtue in the strict sense, will then be that virtue.[21]

(1144b4–14)

This passage seems to suggest that the natural virtues together with practical wisdom comprise full virtue so that in someone with practical wisdom (the *phronimos*) the natural virtues are sufficient (and perhaps necessary, N.E. 1144b14–17) for ethical virtue. If only a few are so fortunate as to possess all the natural virtues (the Reciprocity thesis does not apply to natural virtues, 1144b31–1145a2), Aristotle would have a strongly elitist view about full virtue.

We should, however, resist this interpretation. Indeed, shortly after this passage, Aristotle allows that either natural or habituated virtue can combine with practical wisdom to comprise full virtue (N.E. 1151a15–19), so natural virtue is not necessary for ethical virtue. But we can go further. It is one of Aristotle's deepest commitments that ethical virtue arises by habituation, not by nature:

[E]thical virtue results from habituation... This makes it quite clear that none of the virtues comes about in us by nature; for no natural way of being is changed through habituation ... In that case, the virtues develop in us neither by nature nor contrary to nature, but because we are naturally able to receive them and are brought to completion by means of habituation.
(N.E. 1103a17–26)

Since the ethical virtues are produced by a long process of habituation that we are naturally capable of undergoing, natural virtue is not necessary for ethical virtue; habituated virtue is sufficient. Indeed, habituation is presented here as the only route to ethical virtue, so unhabituated natural virtue combined with practical wisdom should not be sufficient for ethical virtue.[22] This is what we should expect given natural virtue's limitations. As befits their child-like origin, natural virtues are undiscriminating and are at their best in stereotypical circumstances: In novel situations, they lead their possessor to a fall. In any case, by the time that practical wisdom develops, long habituation will have extensively reworked whatever innate dispositions there were.

What, then, should we make of the natural virtues? We can think of them as innate dispositions to act and feel in ways that significantly resemble those of a virtuous person. But this initial resemblance in itself is not their ethically most important feature, since it does not prevent the naturally virtuous from stumbling. What is more important is that having a natural virtue makes it easier to lead one to ethical virtue via habituation (cf. *Pol.* 1327b18–38). So even if all are capable of proper habituation, not all are *equally* capable of such habituation. For some, it will be easier. Nevertheless, the presence of natural virtue neither renders habituation unnecessary nor guarantees its success, nor does its absence guarantee its failure.

In sum, there is nothing in Aristotle's discussion to suggest that either

(1) some normal Greek males are incapable of being properly habituated given the right training, or
(2) the naturally virtuous, after habituation, have a higher kind or degree of ethical virtue.[23]

Our first elitist worry was that one's virtues were innate. Our second elitist concern is that once one's character has been acquired, it is unchangeable. Since most people have been brought up badly, society will consist of a few good people, while the rest have permanently bad characters and have irrevocably lost their capacity for virtue.

There are grounds for such a worry. Ethical virtue arises from proper habituation and leads one to take pleasure in the appropriate objects; misdirected pleasures tend to destroy one's ability to see the correct goals of action.

> For the first principles of things done are the goals sought. But once someone is corrupted through pleasure or pain, he fails to see the first principle, and to see that one should choose everything, and act, for the sake of this, and because of this – for vice is corruptive of the first principle.   (N.E. *1140b16–20, cf. 1144a34–6 and 1151a15–19*)

Arguments are of little use with those who have not been brought up with good habits. The many live, pursuing bodily pleasure, by their passions: "What argument, then, would change the rhythm of their lives? For it is not possible, or not easy, for argument to dislodge what has been long absorbed in one's character" (*N.E.* 1179b16–18).

Finally, once an unjust character has been acquired, it is not clear that it can be reformed:

But if someone does, not in ignorance, the things that will result in his being unjust, he will be unjust voluntarily – and yet he will not stop being unjust, and be just, merely if he wishes it. For no more will the sick person be healthy merely by wishing it . . . Previously, then, he had the option not to be ill, but once he has let himself go, he no longer has it . . . So too at the beginning the unjust person and the self-indulgent one had the option not to become like that, and hence they are voluntarily unjust and self-indulgent; but once they have become like that, it is no longer possible for them not to be. *(N.E. 1114a12–21)*

So how elitist is Aristotle's position on character? To begin, even if the bad are eventually incurable, Aristotle argues that since their character arises at least in part from their actions and they knew (or should have known) this when acting, they are responsible for their character and thus are voluntarily bad (*N.E.* 1114a3–31). But we also have good grounds for denying the strict unchangeability of character. Even a virtuous person can lose his virtue (1165b13–22) and the *Categories* holds that if a bad person is led into better ways of living and talking, he can make gradual progress with each step facilitating the next so that he might eventually become virtuous (13a23–31). Finally, even *N.E.* 1114a12–21 quoted above seems primarily to stress that a bad person cannot utterly change his character in a moment simply by wishing to do so. Change in character might be possible – after all, not all sick people are incurable – but it would require a long process of counter habituation, as the *Categories* suggests, and mere arguments would not suffice.[24] But neither are all sick people capable of recovering and other passages in the *Nicomachean Ethics* hold that at least some bad people are incurable, for example, self-indulgent people who have no regrets and thus no internal motivation to change (1150b29–36, cf. 1165b13–22).

But even granting these qualifications, Aristotle's view of actual society is highly elitist. It will be composed of a few virtuous people, the continent and the incontinent, and a great majority with varying degrees of bad character. This majority, the many, even if they are not extremely unjust, have highly defective characters. They have no notion of the fine and are typically motivated by pleasure and pain and thus avoid wrongdoing from fear of the penalty (*N.E.* 1179b11–16). They never think that the virtuous act is worth doing for its own sake.[25] (Our own common sense psychology is more willing to allow that occasional moral motivation can co-exist with generally predominant motivations for other things and that it can sometimes move the agent to act even if it usually does not.)

Reformation of some of those with bad character is possible, but difficult. Since pleasure corrupts one's judgments of goodness and grasp of the end, such reformation must change what the person finds pleasant. (Since the good, the fine, and the pleasant coincide for the good person, it will also involve changing his judgments of the fine.) It would require reproducing in the adult the process the properly habituated child underwent to develop the appropriate pleasures (or bringing about its functional analogue). Even without working out the details, such a process would clearly be lengthy and prone to failure.

So in actual societies, the capacities that all normal Greek males had at birth to be properly habituated and educated will, in the great majority of cases, simply go unrealized. Significant improvement can only come – as Aristotle observes (N.E. 1179b30ff) after remarking about arguments' uselessness in reforming bad character – via a system of good laws that prescribe the appropriate habituation and education from birth onwards. Yet despite his pessimism about the characters that most people develop, we have found nothing that calls into question Aristotle's commitment to the idea that, at least within the group of normal Greek males, there are no innate barriers to the success of habituation. Given the depth of his pessimism about actual outcomes, it would not have been surprising for him to attempt to explain them by positing corresponding natural inequalities (as the *Republic* did, for example, in the myth of the metals). That he did not is a sign of how committed he is to both the power of habituation and the possibility thesis.

Practical Wisdom

Finally, let us turn to practical wisdom. This topic has generated enormous controversy and I must be brief and dogmatic here. I shall focus on two aspects of practical wisdom:

(1) it grasps a conception of happiness (N.E. 1142b31–2, 1140b11–19), and
(2) it discovers the action that the agent can take in his circumstances that best furthers his happiness.

Let us begin with (1). So where does the *phronimos'* conception of happiness come from?[26] The lectures comprising the *Nicomachean Ethics* aim at helping us become good (1103b26–9). Their topic is political science (e.g. 1095a2–4) and political science is the same psychic disposition as practical wisdom, although they differ in definition (1141b23–4). So it is plausible to infer that these lectures help us improve with respect to practical wisdom. The most important thing that they provide is a definition of happiness in the famous function argument of *Nicomachean Ethics* 1.7 that is elaborated in the later books. Knowing what happiness is has "great weight" in life (1094a23); it gives the individual a target to aim at in all his actions (1094a23–24) and, by having a target, he is more likely to hit it.[27] Once the definition is established, practical wisdom can then use it in deliberation.

I shall discuss two worries about practical wisdom and the possibility thesis. First, since the *phronimos*' ultimate end is happiness, his deliberation must take into account (or at least track) all the considerations relevant to his happiness. Could more than a few ever do this? Second, if the *phronimos* has acquired his conception of the good from the *Nicomachean Ethics*, how deep must his grasp of the *Nicomachean Ethics* be? In particular, if practical wisdom is the same disposition as political science, must the *phronimos* have scientific understanding of political science?

Before taking up these issues, however, we must be clear about what standard the virtuous person sets. Are the deliberative and non-rational parts of his soul in the best possible condition?[28] If so, the possibility thesis faces a very high bar. But Aristotle may be more accommodating, since he explicitly recognizes degrees of virtue (*N.E.* 1173a16–22, cf. 1117b9–11 and 1172a10–14), although he does not tell us how to cash out the idea. Presumably it will involve some suboptimal functioning in at least of one of the parts of the soul that is not serious enough to render the person continent or incontinent. In any case, this gives us grounds for still counting as virtuous those who fall short of perfection.

Let us turn to the first worry. Practical wisdom arises mostly through teaching (*N.E.* 1103a14–16). Much of this will be non-systematic: The younger will receive piecemeal advice from the older (1143b11–13). But Aristotle himself offers several general rules for hitting the mean (2.9) and this practice could be further developed. The teaching that conduces to practical wisdom, however, need not be limited to formal matters. The role of principles in practical deliberation is controversial: Some scholars think that Aristotle did not believe in general ethical principles (except as summaries of particular perceptual ethical judgments) and gave normative priority to perceptual judgments, while others think that he gave normative priority to general principles and gave them a prominent place in deliberation.[29] I am in the latter group, but cannot argue the point here.

But if using correct principles is a major part of good practical deliberation, this should in general be within the capacities of the properly habituated and educated. Principles seem to be teachable and having principles to rely on, ceteris paribus, makes deliberation easier (e.g. they tell us what considerations are important and how to weigh them). Greater use of principles would make deliberation more tractable for more people.

This is, however, only part of the story. First, principles must be applied and this requires that the agent be sensitive to all the features of a situation that are relevant to them (and, ultimately, to the agent's happiness).[30] Such sensitivity will, at least in large part, be the product of successful habituation. Second, principles will typically hold only for the most part – when principles, as in spelling, are exceptionless, there is no need for deliberation (*N.E.* 1112a34-b8) – so practical wisdom must determine when there is an exception and work out what to do in those cases in which there is no further decisive guidance from any principles.[31] Third, ethical generalizations are often inexact and do not specify what actions are to be done (1104a5–11) and fully exact specifications are either impractical or impossible (1109b18–23 and 1126a35-b4). In all of these cases, the *phronimos* "perceives" what (type of) action in these circumstances best furthers his end (1142a23–30, 1143a32-b5).[32] But even in cases in which principles are not available or are inexact, the *phronimos'* perception is not unconstrained. He may well, for example, have identified with the aid of principles some range of responses within which his action must fall.

Given this conception of practical wisdom, how does the possibility thesis fare? Aristotle strongly associates experience with the ability to hit upon the right action in cases not fully covered by rules (*N.E.* 1143b6–14). Although Aristotle does not give much detail, experience provides, for example, the nascent doctor with a grasp of the various causal powers of particulars along with an ability to recognize such particulars in complicated circumstances.[33] The *phronimos* will, via experience, have such a grasp of ethical particulars. Such familiarity seems to be exactly what he needs to find the right action that constitutes his happiness in cases in which the principles run out, clash, or are too general to be action guiding in the circumstances. If a number of old people who are not *phronimoi* can develop this ability to a high degree (1143b11–13), it is not unreasonable to think that a better habituated and educated nascent *phronimos* could, with sufficient dedication and practice, also develop to a high degree the abilities needed.

Finally, let us consider how much knowledge of the *Nicomachean Ethics* or political science the *phronimos* needs. Since this inquiry's aim is practical, it aims at our "becoming good" and knowledge's value is purely instrumental to becoming virtuous (*N.E.* 1103b26–29, cf. 1179a35-b4). This suggests that the nascent *phronimos* coming to the *Nicomachean Ethics* need not grasp the material as a philosopher would. He will need an intelligent appreciation of the text, but not the sort of deeper engagement with it that would lead him to write his own ethical treatises. It is not unreasonable to hold, I think, that in good circumstances the properly habituated and educated are capable of such an appreciation of the *Nicomachean Ethics'* main aspects.

Does this require grasping other parts of Aristotle's philosophy? If, for example, the function argument depends on theses from Aristotle's metaphysics and psychology, must the student also grasp these? Aristotle's answer here seems to be no. Such exactness (*akribeia*) is simply not needed for an ethical inquiry (*N.E.* 1098a26–33).[34] This is consistent with the citizens' education in the *Politics*, which does not include metaphysics, natural science, or anything more than a basic acquaintance with any of the branches of wisdom.

The claim, however, that practical wisdom is the same disposition as political science raises more difficult issues (*N.E.* 1141b23–4). Aristotle here treats practical wisdom as a genus with three species: (1) practical wisdom which is concerned with one's own good, (2) household management, and (3) political science which subdivides into (4) legislative science, which is architectonic, and (5) political science which subdivides into (6) deliberative science and (7) judicial science. If (1) requires grasping (2)–(7), this will increase substantially the intellectual demands on the *phronimos*.[35] Still, this is not especially surprising, since the best expression of full virtue is political activity (1094b7–10). Although the nascent *phronimos* must know more, the difference is one of degree, not of kind, and it is not clear that it is beyond the capacities of the well-habituated and educated normal Greek male with adequate leisure. We must remember how intensely motivated such a person is: There is nothing that he cares more about than gaining practical wisdom.

But there is a further point to consider. C.D.C. Reeve has argued that ethics or political science can be a demonstrative science for Aristotle.[36] Ethical generalizations may typically hold only for the most part (*hôs epi to polu*), but so do the generalizations of the natural sciences and we can have scientific knowledge of the latter. Thus the fact that ethical generalizations hold only for the most part does not disqualify them from scientific knowledge. So, on this view, if practical wisdom is the same disposition as political science and has the same body of knowledge, then, once political science becomes a demonstrative science, in order to have practical wisdom one would have to possess an Aristotelian science as set out in the canonical *Posterior Analytics* form.[37] This would, I think, be more than one might reasonably expect from the normal Greek male. Nor is it obvious that it is impossible to develop political science into such a form. The possibility thesis, it seems, is thus contingent upon none of the sciences that are identified with practical wisdom developing into an Aristotelian science.

Here it may be better to abandon or at least weaken our understanding of the identification of practical wisdom and political science. Aristotle can still stress the important similarities between them in that both aim at happiness and can still hold that since the *phronimos* wants to improve others he should learn the relevant parts of legislative science. But this does not entail that for his practical purposes he must learn or possess these truths as a series of explanatory syllogisms meeting the criteria of the *Posterior Analytics*. For his practical purposes, it is enough to have the relevant thats without the corresponding whys (*Meta.* 993b20–4). This seems to satisfy Aristotle's motivations for requiring the *phronimos* to learn legislative science without having the radical consequence that only one who grasps an Aristotelian science has practical wisdom.[38]

Finally, let me close by noting one crucial difference between Plato and Aristotle that opens out onto broader issues. We saw that for Plato the basic reasons behind his middle-period elitism were:

(1) the genuinely virtuous agent must have full and complete knowledge of the fundamental goodmaking and finemaking properties, and
(2) the fundamental goodmaking and finemaking properties are theoretically deep so that coming to know them is an extraordinary intellectual accomplishment.[39]

As we also saw, in the late period, Plato relaxed condition (1), but still retained the basic idea that a virtuous agent must have an appropriate grasp of the nature of value properties.

Aristotle, however, does not accept (1). His ethical lectures will answer certain why-questions in terms of the agent's happiness, but it is not part of ethics to trace the grounding of this conception of happiness to Aristotle's psychology and metaphysics, and such knowledge is not required of the virtuous agent. Similarly, the notion of the fine (*kalon*) plays an important role in the *Nicomachean Ethics* since the virtuous agent is frequently described as acting for the sake of the fine (e.g. 1115b2, 1120a23–4). Moreover, the fine seems susceptible of a theoretically deep analysis.[40] Nevertheless, within the *Nicomachean Ethics* itself there is no analysis of the fine nor any suggestion that the virtuous person needs one. Aristotle seems to think that such an understanding would be a theoretical excellence rather than the sort of correct appreciation of value that is necessary for having the right motivation for one's action. Thus to grasp this difference between Aristotle and Plato more fully, we would need a deeper understanding of the contrast that Aristotle draws between the theoretical and the practical and of why Plato does not draw such a contrast. The question of elitism thus leads beyond itself and back into some of the fundamental issues in Plato's and Aristotle's conception of philosophy and philosophical inquiry.

NOTES

1. Rawls (1971) 587.
2. Schneewind (1998) 4.
3. One aspect of Plato's and Aristotle's elitism that I lack space to discuss are their views on the ethical capacities of women, non-Greeks and *banausoi* (roughly, workers in the arts and trades). The following discussions are a start on the literature. For Plato, see Kamtekar (2002), Okin (2013), and Taylor (2012). For Aristotle, see Deslauriers (2003), Karbowski (2012), Leunissen (2012), (2013), and Nielsen (2015). Both Plato and Aristotle hold that *banausoi* are less capable than leisured Greeks. For Aristotle, this seems to be because of their way of life (*Pol.* 1328b39–41) rather than their nature insofar as they are normal Greek males. Cf. Kraut (2002) 215–17. In the *Republic*, *banausoi* have an inferior innate capacity for virtue; its eugenics is muted in the later dialogues, see *Pol.* 310A-311A and *Laws* 772E-773E.
4. My interpretation of middle-period Plato is controversial; for other views, see Kamtekar (1998), Kraut (2010), Wilberding (2009), and Devereux's contribution to this volume (Chapter 3).
5. Translations of Plato draw on Cooper (1997). This is not merely a judgment of their cognitive condition as opposed to their happiness, since for Plato one's cognitive condition is a primary determinant of one's happiness.
6. On the Good, see Denyer (2007) and Sedley (2007b).
7. Burnyeat (1987) and (2000) are seminal discussions.
8. Bobonich (2002) 43.

9. The auxiliaries' musical education does not give them a grasp of non-sensible value properties, see *Rep.* 522A4-B1 and Bobonich (2002) 47–48 and 58–66.

10. Bobonich (2002).

11. My interpretation of the preludes is controversial; for other views, see Annas (2011) and Laks (1990).

12. Bobonich (2002) 168–79.

13. It is hard for us to imagine such a theory. But, as a beginning, we might think of good character states as the result of imposing ratios of naturally concordant numbers on an appropriate qualitative continuum, e.g., of harshness and gentleness. On naturally concordant ratios, see Burnyeat (2000) 47–56 and Robins (1995).

14. Bobonich (2002) 298–331.

15. Translations from the *Nicomachean Ethics* draw on Broadie and Rowe (2002); other Aristotle translations draw on Barnes (1985).

16. A similar point is made at *E.E.* 1215a12–19, especially a13–14; also see *Pol.* 1324a23–5.

17. "Handicap" (*pêroô, pêrôsis*) is a strong term and occurs only five other times in the *N.E.*, three times with respect to bestial vice: 1145a31, 1148b17, and 1149b29; the other two are bodily defects: 1114a25 and 1131a8. For Aspasius, the handicapped are "the foolish" from birth or those who are "handicapped from bad pursuits and become incurable" (25, 5–6). He does not suggest that the latter have an innate tendency to bad pursuits. Eustratius thinks that virtue and happiness are possible for anyone who "wishes for them and is suitably serious" in their pursuit (commentary on 1099b18). *Pol.* 1316a9–10 allows that some people cannot be made good by education, but the context suggests that they are few.

18. On non-Greeks, see *Pol.* 1327b18–38; on women and natural slaves, see *Pol.* 1260a12–14. Cf. fn. 3. Both women and slaves have virtues (*Pol.* 1259b34–1260b7), but these differ from those of free men in kind, not merely by "more or less," and are inferior to them. *Pol.* 1327b33–6 is the only passage I know of where Aristotle suggests that some Greeks share the one-sided nature of barbarians disqualifying them from virtue.

19. Slaves and banausics are not citizens; women are less than full citizens since they lack political authority. I agree with Kraut (2002) 197–202, 224–29 and Ober (2015) that all adult citizens are (more or less) equally virtuous in the best city and that their state education does not include philosophical studies or more than a basic study of natural science. See Leunissen (2013) for how some biological characteristics facilitate ethical development.

20. See Leunissen (2012) on the interactions between innate and environmental factors.

21. Cf. *E.E.* 1234a2–3, *HA* 588a18-b3, and *MM* 1197b36–1198a9.

22. The natural virtues that combined with practical wisdom suffice for full virtue have been reworked by habituation. They are still distinct from habituated virtues not originating in natural virtue.

23. *Pol.* 1332a38–b3 emphasizes habituation's superiority over what comes by nature because habituation can change it. Hertig is helpful on natural virtue.

24. Cf. Di Muzio (2000).

25. See Garrett (1993).

26. For persuasive criticisms of the claim that the conception of happiness is determined by (i) deliberation, see Reeve (1992) 79–84; or by (ii) comprehension, see Broadie (1998). Both the deliberative and the comprehension accounts show considerable optimism about people's ability to get the account of happiness right (including the role of external goods, the good of others, and the relative value of virtue and virtuous activity) unaided by something like Aristotle's lectures. The student must bring to the lectures a rudimentary but largely correct conception of happiness and comprehension may help furnish this.

27. Happiness need not always enter explicitly into the individual's deliberation, but correct choice (*prohairesis*) must hit upon what constitutes happiness in one's circumstances.

28. For a provocative discussion, see Curzer (2005).

29. I draw on Irwin (2000) here.

30. Deliberation may seem very complex if we imagine the agent weighing and comparing goods in each possible option. Deliberation is simplified by the fact that the option that optimally contributes to my happiness is the most virtuous option and that identifying this option is standardly a matter of determining the relevant mean.

31. This is the case whether or not an exceptionless set of principles is theoretically possible.

32. Typically, the *phronimos* has narrower objectives than happiness, but this is his ultimate end in all his actions and his choice is correct only if it optimally advances his happiness. I omit here the details of the relations among practical wisdom, practical perception, and practical comprehension.

33. The key texts are *Meta.* 1.1 and *Post. An.* 2.19. Hasper and Yurdin (2014) is a helpful discussion.

34. See also *N.E.* 1102a23–32, 1178a20–23. For the "that" at *N.E.* 1095b6–7, the "why," i.e. the definition of happiness, is made clear, but this stays within the ethical. I here agree with Scott (2015) 123–67.

35. 1142a9–10 suggests that practical wisdom requires a grasp of (2)–(7). I am considering (1)–(7) as nascent sciences which is all they were when Aristotle wrote. Below I consider treating political science as a finished science.

36. Reeve (1992) and (2012), cf. Henry (2015) and Winter (1997).

37. See Reeve (1992) 73–79 and Cooper (2010) 227n18. Weaker interpretations of being the same disposition will demand less of practical wisdom.

38. Also *N.E.* 1141b9–10 holds that practical wisdom concerns things that it is possible to deliberate about. But no one can deliberate about the theorems of legislative or ethical science.

39. As opposed, e.g., to coming to grasp that pleasure is the only ultimate goodmaker because this how it pre-reflectively seems.

40. For a beginning on this issue, see *Meta.* 1078a30–b6 and the different views expressed in Cooper (1999c), Irwin (2011), Lear (2004), and David Charles' contribution to this volume (Chapter 6). Even if fineness cannot be defined or reductively analyzed, the notion of fineness may be theoretically elucidated by grasping this fact about it as well as its connections with other concepts. Such elucidation may also be unnecessary for the virtuous person as such.

17 Becoming Godlike

David Sedley

THE PHYSICAL BACKGROUND

In Plato's world as described in his *Timaeus*, there are numerous divine, self-sufficient spherical beings. The world itself is one, but others are the earth, sun, moon, planets, and stars. All of them rotate on their own axes, thereby blissfully enjoying their own everlasting (because eternally recurrent) thoughts of eternal truths or entities.

Why then can't we ourselves be spheres, and enjoy that same intellectual fulfillment? In a sense, spheres are just what we are. When the gods created mankind, according to Timaeus, initially humans were merely heads. The approximately spherical human head, imperfectly mimicking the perfectly spherical heaven, was designed to house the individual human rational soul, itself a less pure version of the divine world soul. Thus inside our round heads the proper motions of our rational souls, when our intellects are fully functional, are a miniature version of the perfect rotations that the world soul enjoys. To that extent, the intellectually fulfilled human being is godlike.

It is tempting to suppose that, inside our heads, there are no *literally* circular motions, and that the processes of pure thought, with their ability to dwell endlessly on knowledge of unchanging truths, are merely *analogous* to circular motions. But the *Timaeus* is a work on physics, and the text leaves no doubt that the motions are spatial ones in the head just as much as they are in the heaven, which the head mimics at the microcosmic level. Indeed, if the motions in our heads were not literally circular, there would be no need for our heads to be (approximately) round.[1]

The reason why we could not retain our simple sphericity is merely practical. As Plato carefully explains (*Ti.* 44D–45A), an autonomous spherical head trying to roll around from place to place and deal with the necessities of life would have little chance of survival. So to enable human beings to live a life long enough to provide a realistic prospect of intellectual progress, the gods who made us appended a variety of additional equipment, such as the neck, the trunk, the legs,

Warmest thanks to Frisbee Sheffield for searching comments on an earlier draft of this chapter, and to Chris Bobonich for helpful editorial interventions.

and arms – indeed, a complete transport, nutrition, and defense system: the very appendages which the world sphere itself had been mercifully spared, thanks to its complete self-sufficiency. And this added substructure brought with it new obstacles to the smooth functioning of our brains, above all bodily appetites, which violently disrupt the intellectual endeavors going on up above in our heads, and sense-perception, whose short-lived rectilinear motions disrupt the naturally circular motions of pure thought. Hence the task of re-establishing the dominance of the intellect within the human body is a difficult and protracted one, to which only philosophers can aspire. The highest achievement of a human life, Timaeus explains, is to stop thinking of yourself as the entire amalgam of body and soul parts, and instead identify exclusively with the spherical thinking-hub perched on top of this complex vehicle. By doing so, you can concentrate on restoring the circular motions in your head to match those of the world soul, and hope to achieve a truly godlike existence, in so far as that is possible for a human being (90C).

GOD AS PARADIGM

Plato's famous formula for the goal of human life was *homoiōsis theōi kata to dunaton*, "becoming like god so far as is possible."[2] The same goal was inherited by his pupil Aristotle, albeit without ever using the identical formulation. It will therefore be fruitful to consider the two philosophers together, albeit with occasional attention to their differences.

There are five attributes of god in respect of which, according to Plato and Aristotle, humans may realistically seek to resemble this ideal being: (1) immortality, (2) happiness, (3) goodness, (4) wisdom, and (5) self-sufficiency. Most of these had been accepted as basic attributes of god by the preceding religious tradition. An exception is (3), the assumption of god's moral goodness, which had not been an obvious part of literary or cultic depictions of gods. Here it is safer just to say that god's intrinsic goodness was at any rate an established *philosophical* postulate.

As early as the sixth century BC Xenophanes had criticized the authoritative poets Homer and Hesiod for depicting gods as prone to human wrongdoings. Socrates, seemingly influenced by many aspects of Xenophanes' theology, developed this critique into a positive thesis of divine moral goodness.[3] And the same thesis reappears prominently in Plato's dialogues, in the mouth not only of Socrates but of others too; for example, Timaeus: God is an essentially good being.

Indeed, in what must be among the earliest occurrences, or anticipations, of the becoming-like-god theme in Plato's dialogues, god's moral goodness is given full centrality. In Books 2–3 of the *Republic*, the main speaker, Socrates, constructing an educational system for an idealized city, is narrowing down what myths can appropriately be taught to the young. In particular, the way gods are portrayed to them is likely to prove morally formative, for better or worse. For this reason it is vital that gods should be portrayed as entirely lacking in badness and hence – by appeal to the Platonic principle that like causes like – as never being the cause of bad, that is, of harm, either to each other or to human beings (377D–380D). If they inflict punishments, those must be corrective punishments, benefiting rather than harming the wrongdoer.

Importantly, Plato's concern here has little to do with establishing truths about the gods. The morally beneficial myths prescribed by Socrates are seen by him as deliberate falsehoods, crafted for educational purposes. So although we meet here Plato's initial engagement with the idea of gods as role models for human emulation, and although this is the passage in which the concept of "theology" (*theologia*, 379A) makes its very first recorded appearance, the focus is at least as much on educational expediency as on theological truth.

Fully coherent with this focus is the fact that, among the misrepresentations of the gods that Socrates goes on to catalogue and outlaw, there is no mention of anthropomorphism. As noted above, for Plato the scientifically true shape of divinity is the sphere, the asymmetric human frame being an expedient necessitated precisely by our lack of divine self-sufficiency. If he did not insist on that here in the *Republic*, it was not because he had not yet arrived at his rejection of anthropomorphism, a rejection which after all had been entrenched in the philosophical tradition since Xenophanes. Rather, it is because envisaging gods as human in form is an educationally benign error; indeed, probably one that actively encourages the young to emulate their divine role models.

The *Republic* passage's constant emphasis on divine goodness, by contrast, involves no tension at all between theological truth and educational expediency: It is precisely the fact that gods are essentially good that makes them appropriate role models for the young.

TRUTH

One further example of the *Republic*'s motif of gods as moral paradigms is Socrates' insistence (381E–383A, cf. 389BD) that they must not be represented as practicing deceit. The "lie in the soul" – believing false-hoods – is hateful to everyone, he maintains; outward verbal deceit, in contrast, *can* have positive value, as a remedy (*pharmakon*) for unfavorable circumstances, but these turn out to be circumstances in which gods could never find themselves. Note how this argument implicitly bears on the regular motif that the human goal is to become like god "so far as is possible." In Book 3, in an explicit resumption of the Book 2 argument about falsehood, we learn that even the best citizens of Socrates' ideal city, its expert rulers, must sometimes resort to deceit (389BD) as a political "remedy." And near the end of Book 3 (414B–415D), Socrates will present a "noble lie" about the city's origins which all citizens must somehow be made to believe, for the sake of civic cohesion.

On a possible reading of this, the need for selective deceit is one area in which human godlikeness is ruled out. If so, we should expect humans to fall short of the divine model, not because to seek complete equality with god would be impious (although it may be), but simply because it exceeds what is humanly attainable. On an alternative reading, however, the incompleteness in question is inevitable only in the context of a *political* life, of which these rulers are an idealized exemplar. Later in the *Republic*, in the aftermath of Book 7's celebrated cave simile, we will learn the following (519C9–520E). For those who have left the cave – who have, that is, achieved enlightenment by gaining intellectual access to the intelligible world – the preferred choice is to lead a contemplative life, remaining outside the cave. True, they will nevertheless usually opt for a political life, but that is a second-best choice to which they are committed by law, and which it is readily conceded will bring them less happiness than the superior life of pure contemplation would have done (519D–520A).[4] If they could instead somehow remain non-political contemplators, there is every reason to assume that their life would be one fully focused on truth. If so, the life of contemplation properly lived is the most nearly godlike, and, for that reason among others, superior to the political life.

The discussion of falsehood in *Republic* 2–3 permits both readings, but for reasons which will become clearer in the remainder of this chapter, it is the latter that goes to the heart of Plato's thinking.

CONTEMPLATION

To see why, we can usefully start from Aristotle, then work back to Plato.

In *Nicomachean Ethics* 10.7–8 Aristotle makes his definitive comparison between the contemplative life and the political or civic life. Contemplation, the pure exercise of knowledge for its own sake, is the happiest activity available to humans, being in fact the one we can confidently attribute even to god. It is supremely enjoyable. It is the most final and complete of all activities, in that its value does not depend on any further ends it might serve. And it brings us close to god's self-sufficiency: It requires only a minimum of material resources, and can be done even in complete isolation from others. Even its non-inclusion of the exercise of civic virtues like justice and courage – comparable to Plato's philosophers while they are still outside the cave[5] – is a divine characteristic. For gods likewise cannot plausibly be credited with moral virtues: Justice among them would imply that they are, discreditably, bound by contractual relations with each other; courage would imply that they can face dangers; and so on (1178b7–21).

Many scholars[6] have been reluctant to admit that Plato and Aristotle considered a purely intellectual life superior to one that includes moral or civic activity, but the combined meaning of *Republic* 7 and *Nicomachean Ethics* 10 should leave little room for doubt. Moreover, we may suspect an autobiographical undercurrent in these texts. In *Republic* 7 the obligation to take part in running the city is incurred by the philosophers only because they owe their philosophical education to the city, and it is conceded (520B) that in current, non-ideal cities philosophers have no such obligation. This exclusionary clause may contain an oblique biographical allusion to Socrates and Plato, both of whom, in their pursuit of philosophy at Athens, had adopted a politically minimalist life.

Aristotle's case is somewhat different. At Athens he had the status of a metic – a non-citizen, with seriously curtailed civic rights.[7] To lead a civic life, he would have had to stay on in his native Stagira. But Athens was the philosophical hub of the Greek world, and in moving there at the age of seventeen to pursue a philosophical career in Plato's Academy he was effectively sacrificing a civic life in favor of one devoted to intellectual fulfillment. That he should nevertheless spend nine of the ten books of the *Nicomachean Ethics* strongly recommending the life of civic virtue as the proper fulfillment of human nature is unsurprising, especially when one bears in mind that many of his students were from elite families in other Greek cities, to which they would eventually return to take part in government. But if Aristotle had himself forsaken such a life by leaving

Stagira for Athens, the reason was that he had himself opted for an even higher mode of activity, one that, rather than merely fulfilling human nature, altogether transcends it, raising someone to the level of the divine.

Like Plato, Aristotle is nevertheless careful to say that this ideal human life is no more than an approximation to the divine (e.g. 1178b25–7). What god does uninterruptedly, namely contemplate, a human contemplator can do only intermittently, punctuated by unavoidable human activities, and presumably also limited by the span of a human life. For this reason, Aristotle's choice of phrase is surprising: such a life enables one "so far as it can be done, to achieve immortality" (*eph' hoson endechetai athanatizein*; 1177b33). The contemplator's activity may be supremely fulfilling *while* it is taking place, but the gods' immortality – understood as everlasting duration – seems to be exactly what it lacks. To see why Aristotle has chosen this unexpected phrase, we must turn to Plato.

According to Plato's *Timaeus*, as mentioned above, the human head, housing the rational part of the soul, is approximately spherical because it is modeled on the perfectly spherical heaven. The astronomical rotations of the spherical world-god along its soul's two constituent circles, that of the Same and that of the Different, are quite literally that cosmic god's acts of thinking. And if we ourselves practice mathematical astronomy to a high enough standard and internalize those motions we will be replicating the world-god's thoughts in our intellects. Nor is this achievement of expertise in astronomy an end in itself; rather, it is the route to philosophy, the greatest of all blessings available to humans (47AB).

The *Timaeus* is Plato's one dialogue devoted to physics, and in keeping with that it tells us about the attainment of happiness from a physical point of view. Specifically, you become happy by harmonizing your intellect, housed in your head, with the world-god's intellect, located in the spherical heaven. Now another part of this dialogue's physics concerns the physiology of the human soul, which, as in the *Republic*, has three parts. The soul's rational part is found in the head, and is immortal. The two irrational parts of the soul have locations below the neck – the spirited or competitive part in the chest, the appetitive part in the midriff – and both, being intimately linked to the body's functioning, share its mortality.

It is in the light of this physiology that Timaeus characterizes the choice of lives[8] (90BC):

Hence if someone has devoted all his interest and energy to his
appetites or to competition, all his beliefs must necessarily be mortal
ones, and altogether, so far as it is possible to become *par excellence*
mortal, he will not fall the least bit short of this, because it is the
mortal part of himself that he has developed. But if someone has
committed himself entirely to learning and to true wisdom, and it is
these among the things at his disposal that he has most practiced, he
must necessarily have immortal and divine wisdom, provided that he
gets a grasp on truth. And so far as it is possible for human nature to
have a share in immortality, he will not in any degree lack this. And
because he always takes care of that which is divine, and has the
daimôn that lives with him well ordered [*eu kekosmêmenon*], he will
be pre-eminently happy [*eudaimôn*].

This is a crucial passage. Every human being, indeed every animal,
possesses an immortal component, the rational soul, but that is not
enough to make every human being immortal. Godlikeness is an aspiration for a complex being, consisting of a body and three soul-parts, to
pursue during an incarnate existence. That is when each of us has to
decide which soul-part is our real self. Those who pursue self-indulgent
bodily pleasures have identified with the appetitive soul; and competitive types, like the military class in Plato's *Republic*, have identified
with the spirited part of the soul. In doing so, both types are locating their
identity in something mortal and transient. In complete contrast, those
who have chosen an intellectual path are identifying their real self with
their one divine and immortal component, the rational soul, and in doing
so they have attained as great a degree of immortality as is available to an
embodied human.

   This brings us back to Aristotle's description of the intellectual life
as "so far as it can be done, to achieve immortality." The key to its
interpretation seems to lie in the very strong continuity between
Plato's thought and his own. For Aristotle, like Plato, not only considers
the intellect (*nous*) to be a divine component of the human being; in
On the soul he declares it (*de An.* 1.4, 408b18–19), or at least its active
aspect (3.5, 430a23), to be immortal. Hence Aristotle's phrase "so far as it
can be done, to achieve immortality" accurately reproduces the meaning
and theoretical presuppositions of Plato's "becoming like god so far as is
possible," despite the fact that it reproduces none of its wording.
To understand Aristotle here, we have to remind ourselves that he is in
many respects a Platonist. For him as for Plato, the highest degree of

immortality attainable in a human life lies in making the intellectual component of your soul the core of your being.

A further correspondence between Plato and Aristotle lies in the fact that each is here making his formal pronouncement on the highest form of *eudaimonia*, "happiness." In the case of Plato the point is reinforced with a suggested etymology. The human intellect, housed in the topmost part of our body and thus nearest to its heavenly origin (90A), is our own resident *daimôn* or "divinity." And the prefix *eu-*, "well," added to *daimôn*, yields *eudaimonia*, taken to mean having your own internal divinity – your intellect – in a well-ordered state.

In the cited passage Aristotle is explicitly talking about the contemplative life, here contrasted with the political life founded on the exercise of moral virtue. He accepts that in practice the contemplator will at times be required to act morally (1178b5–7), but he never so much as hints that this moral activity confers any additional value on the godlike life of contemplation.

In Plato's case, some scholars[9] have challenged the assumption that the godlike life extolled in the *Timaeus* is purely intellectual, and not also moral. The assumption can, however, be defended from the text. Consider Timaeus' description of such a life (90CD):

> Now for everybody there is one way to care for every part, and that is to grant to each part its own proper nourishments and motions. For the divine element in us, the motions which are akin to it are the thoughts and revolutions of the whole world. Everyone should take a lead from these. We should correct the corrupted revolutions in our head concerned with becoming (*genesis*), by learning the harmonies and revolutions of the whole world, and so make the thinking subject resemble the object of its thought, in accordance with its ancient nature; and, by creating this resemblance, bring to fulfillment (*telos*) the best life offered by the gods to mankind for present and future time.

The best and happiest human life is attained by aligning our microcosmic rational rotations, the thoughts inside our heads, with the macrocosmic rotations of the divine world-soul, seen in the heavens. Astronomy is thus a bridge-discipline that can make our own thoughts godlike.[10] Similarly in *Republic* 7 astronomy was one of the five bridge-disciplines that can liberate our souls from their focus on the world of "becoming" (*genesis*) and help replace it with a focus on pure being (*ousia*). Hence it is highly credible that the above translation, "We should correct the corrupted revolutions in our head concerned with becoming [*genesis*]," is right, where others have preferred to translate "We should correct the revolutions in our head which were corrupted around the time of our birth [*genesis*]." If I am right, this confirms that the goal of becoming intellectually godlike involves leaving behind the sensible world of "becoming" and instead focusing our thought on the pure "being" that Plato typically associates with the unchanging world of Forms, such as is symbolized by the realm of truth outside the cave.

Some have responded that, when we are invited to imitate the revolutions of the world-soul, those revolutions must include not only its pure understanding of eternal entities, but also its beneficent thoughts in administering the world whose soul it is. Hence, it is inferred, a human being's godlike thinking will be moral as well as intellectual in character.[11]

But although Plato does often speak of divine benefactions, he never explicitly says that the god who is their source is or includes the world or world-soul. True, the world-soul's thinking is said to include not only pure understanding of intelligibles, but also "opinion" (*doxa, pistis*) about perceptible entities (*Ti.* 37BC). The most this can show, however, is that the world-soul is aware of what is going on in the world-body it animates. Neither this passage nor any other in the *Timaeus* supplies evidence that the world-soul actually governs the world, in the sense of determining how it or its inhabitants should be regulated.[12]

There is also positive evidence for the same point. As seen above, at the end of the *Timaeus* our cerebral imitation of the world's celestial rotations is the privileged route to happiness, *eudaimonia*. Much earlier in the dialogue (34B), the Demiurge's initial creation of the rotating heaven was summed up as follows:

> [H]e set it up as one single heaven, able thanks to its virtue to associate
> with itself and in no need of another, but satisfied with its own
> acquaintance and friendship. Thanks to all these things, he created it
> a happy (*eudaimôn*) god.

This description sums up the perfect, divine "happiness" – that of the world god – to which human happiness is at the end of the dialogue described as an approximation. Our world, an intelligent living being, is the only thing in the universe (31AB), and hence has (comic as the idea may sound) no social or political life at all: There are no neighboring fellow-beings for it to interact with. Yet despite that lack of opportunities for quasi-civic moral interaction it is a paradigm of happiness, enjoying its internal rotations of thought in splendid isolation. In other words, our world's well-being is the happiness of a solitary contemplator, exercising intellectual rather than moral virtue. And that in turn confirms that those of us who attain happiness by replicating its revolutions inside their own heads will likewise be becoming contemplators, rather than socially or politically virtuous beings.

Compare Aristotle's gods in *Nicomachean Ethics* 10.8. As we saw, they have no moral virtues, not because they necessarily lack fellow gods with whom to interact morally, but because even if they do have fellow gods they do not need anything like contractual relations with them. One might ask why Aristotle's gods do not nevertheless need moral virtues, namely for their interactions not with other gods but with us humans, to whom they might behave with justice and practical wisdom. Presumably because moral relations are essentially relations with members of one's own kind and one's own society.[13] Even if gods were hypothesized to adopt attitudes of beneficence towards humans, that would be beneficence by a higher towards a lower being. It would be analogous to humans' own kindness towards their dogs, and to that extent not properly moral at all. Plato is assuming much the same view with regard to the morality of a world-god: such a morality would have to be expressed, if at all, towards other members its own kind; but there are none. Even if the world-god were somehow to act benevolently towards the world's internal inhabitants such as ourselves (and, to repeat, there is no evidence that it does), it is doubtful that Plato would think of such internal regulation as a model of moral activity.

Is there then no moral component to godlikeness? Not according to Book 10 of Aristotle's *Nicomachean Ethics*, at any rate, where godlikeness is precisely what distinguishes the contemplative life from the merely human moral life. And not according to Plato's *Timaeus* either.

JUSTICE

To say this is not by any means to deny the positive value assigned to moral goodness in the *Timaeus*, just to keep it separate from the theme of becoming like god. A key text for this is Timaeus' first description of the transmigration of souls, at 41D–42E. There we learn of the rule that those who overcome the obstacles presented by embodiment thereby live "with justice" (*dikêi*; 42B2), and are after death permitted to return to their own assigned star, to enjoy a "happy (*eudaimôn*; 42B4) life." Living "with justice" is here undoubtedly a moral more than an intellectual kind of fulfillment, and it is duly rewarded with an appropriate kind of happiness. However, there is no hint that this happiness consists in "becoming like god so far as is possible,"[14] which Plato views rather as an attainment within an incarnate human life. Instead, the reward is here one that the rational soul is offered *after death*, when detached from the human body. In other words, Plato by no means intends to devalue moral self-fulfillment, any more than Aristotle does, but he does in the *Timaeus* firmly distinguish it from the godlike state to which an elite of high-achieving humans can aspire during their incarnate lives.

Despite this alliance between Plato's *Timaeus* and Aristotle in equating human godlikeness with strictly intellectual attainment, the story is not quite so simple. We saw earlier that, at least in *Republic* 2–3, Plato had undoubtedly represented the gods as moral exemplars. Was this no more than a local expedient, absent from the rest of his corpus? Presumably not, because what in antiquity became the most celebrated Platonic passage on "becoming like god" includes a distinctly moral thread. This is *Theaetetus* 176A.

The context is a critique of relativism. By 172A the main speaker, Socrates, has shown that a global relativism of the kind espoused by Protagoras, with his celebrated "Man is the measure of all things," cannot survive scrutiny. It cannot be successfully applied either to matters depending on expertise, or to itself. But, Socrates adds, there is a reduced relativism, adopted by those who do not go all the way with Protagoras (172B), namely a relativism of certain values. What is beneficial is, they accept, not a matter of which everyone is the measure; but they distinguish a second, culture-relative tier of values for which humans are indeed the sole measure of truth: these are justice, lawfulness, beauty, and holiness, values widely believed to differ radically from city to city according to the local culture.

Socrates' aim in the "digression" that follows (172C–177C) is to show that even these values – and notably justice, the example on which he concentrates – are in reality absolute, not relative. He does so by portraying the apparent relativity of justice as an artifact of the civic environment, especially the law courts, where the prevalence of rhetoric and the time-restraints on arguments leave no room for absolute justice. By way of contrast, the true philosopher is a seeker of truth, detached from this civic context, and unconstrained by either time limits or narrow personal perspectives. The culmination of his detachment is when the philosopher's intellect escapes from the corrupt civic environment and gravitates towards the divine realm. In doing so it becomes maximally godlike (176A). One might have thought that this escape from the political and juridical world to the divine realm corresponded to the transition from political to intellectual virtue. We are, however, in for a surprise (176AB):

> But it is not possible for evils to be eliminated, Theodorus – there must always exist some opposite to good – nor can evils be established among the gods. Of necessity, it is mortal nature and our vicinity that are haunted by evils. And that is why we should also try to escape from here to there as quickly as we can. To escape is to become like god so far as is possible, *and to become like god is to become just and holy*, together with wisdom [emphasis mine].

So the escape to godlikeness, far from being an abandonment of the paradigmatic civic virtue justice, is precisely how true justice is attained. What can this mean? As Socrates goes on to observe (176BC):

> God is not at all in any respect unjust, but as just as can be; and there is nothing more like him than any one of us who becomes in his own turn as just as possible.

But how can the philosopher's "justice" lie in self-distancing from the law courts and similar civic institutions? In context, the answer must be linked to Socrates' quest in the *Theaetetus* digression, namely to rid justice of the taint of relativism. In the civic context what is just for one party, from one perspective, or in one society is bound to be unjust for another party, from another perspective, or in another society. This relativization satisfies a basic principle of Platonic metaphysics, according to which in the sensible world every property that has an opposite is compresent with that opposite. Normally we would expect Plato, when asked how we can escape this relativization, to point to the *Form* of justice as the paradigm of absolute justice. But in the *Theaetetus* digression, for reasons too complex or unclear to delay us now,[15] the Forms are absent, and the status of moral paradigm is instead assigned to god, viewed as perfectly just from every point of view. As the main speaker in the later dialogue the *Laws* says (4.716C), in an unmistakable authorial reference to the *Theaetetus* digression, "It will be god who is, *par excellence*, the measure of all things, rather than, as is claimed, some man or other." Plato's specific point in the case of justice, we may conjecture, is that true justice requires complete impartiality, which can never be attained from within the civic environment, but requires the detachment that god alone fully possesses.

The difficulty that now faces us is that of determining whether human "justice," thus understood, is still a moral virtue at all, or has now become essentially an intellectual virtue. The philosopher who attains godlikeness is described in the digression as utterly unworldly. Not only does he not know his way to the law courts or the assembly, he does not even know that he does not know it (173CE). He barely notices whether or not his neighbor is a human being, so intent is he on the purely theoretical question "What is a human being?" (174B). Nor is he interested in the practical question "What injustice am I doing you, or you me?", we are told, but rather in the definitions of justice and injustice themselves (175C).

Clearly this degree of detachment from the material and social world he inhabits would make it hard for such a philosopher to discharge any administrative role in the city. He is, in fact, unmistakably like the ex-prisoner in *Republic* 7's Cave simile, able to see clearly in the world of Forms outside the cave but thereby rendered useless when he returns to the city, represented by the fire-lit world inside the cave. On the other hand, we are assured in *Republic* 7 (520C) that the escaped prisoner can eventually readjust his eyes to the inside of the cave, and will then be genuinely useful in government.

What we should say about the godlike philosopher in the *Theaetetus* digression is, then, the following. At present, on the one hand, his godlike state of "justice" is essentially one of perspective-free intellectual understanding, with no direct application to political reality. On the other hand, like the ex-prisoner returning to the cave, he is, at least in theory, capable of applying his justice to political questions; and in doing so he would be calling into service his godlike impartiality, an impartiality that the inextricably relativized "justice" found in the city could never have taught him. Godlikeness remains a primarily depoliticized, intellectual state, but Plato does not want us altogether to lose sight of its potential moral applications, if not in the Athens of Socrates and Plato then at any rate in an ideally good city.

BACK TO IMMORTALITY

One reason why truly godlike justice requires the philosopher to detach himself from the city is that, as emphasized in the *Theaetetus* digression, orators are always hampered by time constraints, thanks especially to the use of water-clocks in the law courts. Philosophers, by contrast, free from any such limitation, have all the time they need to follow each argument to its conclusion. Although the point is not made explicit, we may conjecture that god's immortality functions as a paradigm of this same freedom from time constraints. He has, quite literally, all the time in the world to think things through.

Be that as it may, we have already seen ample reason to link the ideal of godlikeness to the imitation of god's immortality in particular. *Timaeus* 90BC and *Nicomachean Ethics* 10.7 both suggested a respect in which the contemplator attains immortality, namely by identifying his real self with his immortal intellect rather than with the mortal parts of his soul. But there is another way of seeking immortality, well summed up by Aristotle when he writes (*de An.* 2.4, 415a26-b7):

> The most natural function for living things ... is to produce another like themselves – an animal an animal, a plant a plant – in order that they may partake of the everlasting and the divine in the respect in which they are able to do so. For that is what they all strive towards, and all their behavior is naturally for its sake ... Hence, since they are unable to partake in the everlasting and the divine by continuous existence, given that nothing perishable can remain numerically one and the same, they partake in it in the way that each of them is able, some to a greater extent some to a lesser, and they remain, not that individual itself, but like that individual – not numerically one, but one in form.

Aristotle is ready to trace the striving for godlikeness downwards through the natural hierarchy, well below the human level: not only to lower animals, but even to plants, and elsewhere, yet further down, to the cyclical changes of the four simple bodies earth, water, air, and fire. In nature, *everything* is somehow, in however attenuated a form, imitating divine everlastingness. This coheres with Aristotle's view of god's causal powers, namely as an object of love who *inspires* cyclical change, as an approximation to his own eternal actuality (*Metaphysics* Lambda 7).

Plato does not fully anticipate Aristotle in this, but in his *Symposium* he does anticipate him with regard to the specific theme explained in the passage just quoted, that *biological* reproduction is a mode of attaining a degree of immortality. Plato's speaker here is the priestess Diotima, quoted as addressing Socrates (207D–208B):

> Mortal nature seeks so far as is possible to exist always and to be immortal. It can achieve this in only one way, by generation, in that it

always leaves another behind, a new one to replace the old ... It is in this way that everything mortal is preserved, not in virtue of always being absolutely the same one, as in the case of the divine, but in virtue of the fact that whatever is lost and whatever grows old leaves behind another such as it was. It is by this device Socrates ... that what is mortal – both body and everything else – partakes of immortality. What is immortal does so in a different way.

Before turning to the broader implications of these words, we should examine their familiar proviso, that for mortal nature reproduction is the biological means of achieving immortality "so far as is possible." Of course, to a considerable extent the proviso is elucidated in the text by the explanation that each item "leaves behind *another such as it was*" – what Aristotle refers to as remaining in perpetuity one in form, but not numerically one. However, a further puzzle remains: Why does Diotima say nothing about the immortality of the soul, a doctrine that Plato was passionately defending in a dialogue probably close in date, the *Phaedo*? If at least humans, and probably other animals too, are likely to have an immortal soul, what can it mean to say that procreation is the *only* way in which they can, to a limited degree, attain immortality?

The anomaly has led some to speculate whether soul's immortality might be, for whatever reason, absent from Diotima's speech in the *Symposium*.[16] But this is unnecessary. Compare *Timaeus* 90BC. There, as we saw, the nearest approximation to immortality is said to be by contemplating; yet there is no doubt whatsoever that in the same dialogue the individual rational soul has, regardless of its eventual intellectual attainments, been immortal all along, in the literal sense that it will never die. The explanation of the apparent anomaly is as follows. "Becoming like god so far as is possible" is, as has been emphasized throughout this chapter, a recipe for achieving happiness, in the form of an attenuated kind of immortality, *in our present incarnate life*. What may or may not become of the soul after this human life is over is an important question for Plato, but an entirely separate one. The same distinction applies as much to the *Symposium* as to the *Timaeus*. The capacity of what is mortal to become immortal is that of a flesh-and-blood living being, a soul-body composite.

I now return to the comparison with Aristotle. The dominant idea of immortalization in the passage just quoted from the *Symposium* differs in one important respect from the other Platonic accounts of godlikeness that we have met: Much as in Aristotle's biological account of immortality through procreation, this kind of immortalization is not limited to humans, but extends all the way down the scale of living things, to include lower animals, and even, so far as one can tell, plants. All of them alike, albeit in different degrees, strive by means of reproduction to perpetuate their form, which is the nearest they can come to individual immortality.

However, this universal truth about the natural world permits a progression which turns the focus back to specifically human godlikeness. In some humans, Diotima continues, the goal of their erotic passion is to perpetuate themselves, not in the crude biological sense, but by attaining immortal fame (208CE). Pregnancy in the soul is superior to bodily pregnancy, and seeks to give birth to virtue, to perennial works of art, and to enduring law codes (208E–209E). So far there is a substantial ethical and political content to the products through which these individuals aspire to perpetuate themselves. But when Diotima proceeds to the "higher mysteries" (209E–212A), the ultimate ascent to human self-immortalization, the distinction between intellectual and moral activity becomes harder to maintain. The highest achiever "generates true virtue" (212A) of such a kind that, being loved by the gods, "to him if to anyone it belongs to become immortal." Whether this "true virtue" is moral or intellectual is left unclear, but one must suspect the latter, since it is portrayed not as any kind of civic or interpersonal attainment, but as the outcome of a series of intellectual advances which culminate in direct engagement with a Form, the Beautiful itself. Although there remains much here that defies easy interpretation,[17] it is tempting to conclude that this highest kind of human self-immortalization depends on a progression from moral to intellectual virtue. That would not be altogether unlike the *Theaetetus*, where godlikeness seemed to be primarily intellectual in character, yet was identified as the culmination of "becoming just." The moral and intellectual paths towards godlikeness, that is, need not be branching, alternative paths, even if it is only the intellectual ascent that takes one to the very pinnacle of human achievement.

MORAL GODLIKENESS

This "convergence" model of godlikeness, as we might call it, offers a promising template for uniting Plato's many references to "becoming like god so far as is possible." As one ascends towards, and converges on, the pinnacle of godlikeness, moral considerations take second place, and intellectual self-fulfillment becomes dominant; but lower down the scale a lesser degree of godlikeness may be attained by less intellectual means.[18]

For there is no doubt that Plato does in some cases – what I take to be non-paradigmatic cases – refer to a moral kind of godlikeness, a well-known example being *Republic* 10.613AB, "For the gods, at any rate, never neglect someone who is willing to strive to become just and who, by practicing virtue, becomes as like god as possible." It is important, however, to take into account that this is said in support of the dialogue's strictly supplementary and secondary aim of showing that justice is desirable for its consequences or "rewards" (612AB) as well as for its own sake. A comparable example from the *Symposium* is the attainment of a degree of immortality through creating a law code. Much further down the scale we find the immortality attained by biological reproduction, a kind which is neither intellectual nor moral, but merely existential.

The myth in Plato's *Phaedrus* is another case in which a non-paradigmatic level of moral godlikeness is illuminated. There (252C–253C), very unusually for Plato, different gods are portrayed as presenting different paradigms of character. Each lover is said to have a character imitative ("so far as is possible," of course) of the particular god he follows. Followers of Ares, for example, are typically vengeful, Zeus inspires philosophy and leadership, and Hera is a model of "royal" character. This religious symbolism is here used by Socrates to explain erotic choices: Each lover seeks a beloved who is such as to follow and cultivate the same god as he himself does. That we are here, with the probable exception of Zeus' inspiration of a "philosophical" nature, operating below the highest level in the hierarchy of godlikeness is already suggested by the primarily moral and largely non-intellectual character of the imitation, and is further confirmed by the myth's readiness to distinguish different gods as representing differing and even competing moral ideals – an idea coherent with the religion of the classical era and memorably showcased in Euripides' *Hippolytus*, but in considerable tension with Plato's philosophical commitment to the homogeneity of divine goodness.[19]

THE LIFE OF A PHILOSOPHER

Plato and Aristotle differed on many questions, but one substantial area of agreement between master and pupil was godlikeness. While both advocated the virtuous civic life as a primary route to human happiness, both saw even greater value in their own alternative chosen life, the pursuit of philosophical understanding. Their decision to extol this latter life as divine might look like an undignified display of self-conceit, but that impression is at least mitigated by their constantly asserted proviso, that one must not aspire to be god's equal, just to resemble him "so far as is possible." Nor should we overlook the reasons for their appeal to the ideal of godlikeness, which lay in the combination of two profound convictions that they shared. The first was that the pure exercise of intellectual understanding is the most fulfilling of all activities. The other was that this exercise of the intellect makes minimal use of what is distinctively human about us – our bodies, our appetites, our interdependence with fellow members of our society – and instead assigns maximum value to attributes associated with the divine, especially wisdom and self-sufficiency. By criteria widely endorsed in ancient Greek theological thinking, their life was indeed an approximation to that of the gods.

NOTES

1. See further Sedley (2000) 317–19.
2. The rapidly expanding literature on this theme, in Plato and beyond, includes Annas (1999), Sedley (2000), Russell (2004), Baltzly (2004), Armstrong (2004), Lavecchia (2006), and Silverman (2010a), (2010b).
3. Sedley (2007a) ch. 3.
4. At *Rep.* 7.521B9–10 the contemplative life is explicitly "a life better than the political one."
5. Cf. *Rep.* 7.518D, where one lesson of the Cave simile is the superiority of wisdom over moral virtues.
6. For Plato, most notably Mahoney (1992) and (2008). But the same inclination is widespread in the literature on Aristotle's ethics.
7. See Whitehead (1975).
8. This corresponds to the choice among the pleasures of intellect, spirit, and appetite in *Rep.* 9.580D–587E. As for the Aristotelian choice between the lives of civic and contemplative virtue, note that civic virtue, analyzed in *Republic* 4 as a harmonious relation among the three soul parts, was treated briefly at *Ti.* 89E3–90A2, immediately *before* Timaeus turned to the godlikeness and pre-eminent happiness of the purely intellectual life. For a sensitive reading of Plato along these lines, cf. Plotinus 1.2.
9. E.g. Russell (2004), Armstrong (2004), Mahoney (2008), and Silverman (2010a), (2010b).

10. Although the dialogue's paradigmatic means to true happiness is astronomy, this can be broadened to include the study of divine causality more generally, 68E–69A.

11. Notably Mahoney (2005) 87–91. Both Mahoney and Silverman (2010a) and (2010b) also speak of assimilation to a higher god, the divine Creator, but nothing in the *Timaeus* suggests that he is the god we should aim to become like, and at 68D we are warned, in one particular regard (experimental science), *not* to try to imitate his work.

12. Indeed, at 41E–42D it emerges that the major administrative outcomes, namely the promotions and demotions of transmigrating souls, have been in effect automated by an original decree of the Creator.

13. Cf. Xenophanes B11: "Homer and Hesiod have attributed to the gods all those things which are matters of censure and blame for humans: stealing, committing adultery, and deceiving one another." No mention of gods wronging humans.

14. Nor, *pace* Russell (2004) 242–43, is the incarnate life of justice here itself associated with godlikeness.

15. My own view on this is argued in Sedley (2004).

16. The suggestion of Hackforth (1950). Further discussion in Guthrie (1975) 387–92, Sheffield (2006) 147–48, Sedley (2009) 158–60.

17. See e.g. extended discussion in Sheffield (2006) ch. 4.

18. Cf. Lear (2004), who attractively interprets Aristotle as making the merits of a political life consist precisely in its degree of approximation to a contemplative life.

19. This is a strong implication of the *Euthyphro*, not contradicted by any other Platonic passage I can recall.

18 Horace and Practical Philosophy

Terence Irwin

PUTTING PHILOSOPHY INTO PRACTICE

A moderately attentive student of the Hellenistic moral philosophers would have to notice that they offered advice on how to live one's life. But even a serious student might find it difficult to put philosophical advice into practice. Three difficulties among others might arise:

(1) Each of the main philosophical schools offers advice that claims to rely on the basic principles of that school, which differ sharply from the basic principles of all the other schools. Each school holds that no one can live correctly without having decided on fundamental questions of philosophy. But most people have neither time nor inclination nor capacity to weigh all the relevant arguments and to decide on these fundamental questions.

(2) But even if we were to decide in favor of one philosophical outlook by reflection on its foundations and their consequences, we might find it difficult to live the life that it recommends. The Cynics and Cyrenaics argue for radical rejection of pursuits that most people take seriously. Even the ostensibly more moderate Stoics and Epicureans hold counter-intuitive views that separate the philosopher from common-sense morality. The serious acceptance of philosophical ethics seems to force us into social isolation.[1]

(3) Even if we accept the consequences of living by a system of philosophical ethics, we may not want to live our lives in a constant state of reflection and self-examination. We may find the effort of constant philosophical assessment paralyzing, and hence self-defeating. If we want to live by the virtues, as we conceive them, we may find it difficult to get on with living if we are always thinking about it.

Some of these questions about the ancient philosophical schools may be less applicable to recent ethical theory. Opposed ethical theories may not all rely on opposed fundamental philosophical principles. But at least the second and the third questions still apply. Critics of utilitarian and Kantian views often allege that the sort of life that they

I have benefited from acute and helpful comments on this chapter by Barnaby Taylor.

338

require would not be ethically appealing. Dickens in *Hard Times* criticizes not only the substance of utilitarian views (as he conceives them), but also the constantly calculating attitude that he takes to be necessary for the application of such views to one's life. One critic who has presented a more sophisticated version of the Dickensian objection is Bernard Williams.[2] Similar objections have been raised to the obsessively conscientious outlook that is supposed to result if one takes Kant seriously.[3]

These questions about the practical import of ethical theory may help to introduce some discussion of Horace. Though he does not address these questions explicitly, he deals with them implicitly, and he offers a distinctive answer to some of them. The first book of his *Epistles* professes to be a series of letters to actual people on practical problems that fall within the scope of moral philosophy. These letters belong to "ancient ethics" both because they are about the Socratic question, "How ought we to live?" and because they draw on the theories of the different philosophers who have offered answers to this question. Horace sometimes represents himself and his friends discussing ethical questions as though they mattered to them:

> Then conversation arises, not concerning other people's villas and
> houses, nor whether Lepos dances well or not, but we debate on what
> matters more to us and it is bad not to know: Are people happy because
> of wealth or because of virtue? What leads us into friendships –
> advantage, or the right? [4]
> (Satires ii 6. 71–6)

These questions about happiness, virtue, and friendship are central questions in ancient moral philosophy. Horace seems to take them seriously and to answer them.

HORACE'S ATTITUDE TO THE PHILOSOPHICAL SCHOOLS

A serious concern to put moral philosophy into practice is not unusual among the surviving sources for ancient philosophy; Epictetus and Seneca, for instance, display this concern. But, despite the apparent aim of the *Epistles*, attempts to ascribe serious philosophical ambitions of this sort to Horace face some apparently serious obstacles.[5]

He does not adhere to any of the main philosophical schools, but describes himself as being attracted to one or another philosophical outlook in different circumstances:

> And in case you might happen to ask under what leader, in what house
> I enter – I am enrolled to swear to the words of no teacher, but wherever
> the weather carries me away, I am borne off as a visitor. Now I become
> active, and am submerged in the waves of civic life, a guardian and
> unbending dependent of true virtue. Now I slip back unnoticed into
> Aristippus' precepts, and try to adapt things to myself, not myself to
> things.   (Epistles i 1.13–19)

What does he mean by this profession of philosophical non-alignment?

It may appear to express an eclectic attitude. But philosophical
eclectics are non-aligned for a reason that Horace does not mention.
They suppose that different doctrines of various philosophical schools
are defensible, and that they can be separated from the less defensible
views maintained by these schools.[6] We might call this approach "critical eclecticism." It may not be obvious whether a particular eclectic
project will succeed, and a decision requires philosophical argument.

If we are attracted to some Stoic and to some Peripatetic doctrines,
but we would rather avoid the hard work of seeing whether they can be
consistently or plausibly combined, we might prefer "lazy eclecticism"
to critical eclecticism. Lazy eclectics prefer to follow the views that
appeal to them, without worrying about whether they make a coherent
outlook. One might argue that in moral philosophy lazy eclecticism is
the best way to make sense of our intuitive convictions, and that it is
misguided to be too concerned about their systematic integration. If this
is right, laziness is not an intellectual vice in this case. Horace does not
argue like a critical eclectic. He seems more like a lazy eclectic who
picks and chooses the appealing bits from different schools without
worrying about the cumulative effect of his choices.

But he differs from a lazy eclectic on one significant point. Lazy
eclectics look for a collection of views to be held all at once; but Horace
follows his variable preference for one philosophical outlook after
another. He is not inconsistent, since he does not hold incompatible
views at any one time. He is inconstant, because he accepts incompatible
views in succession.

But if he vacillates between a Stoic, an Epicurean, a Cynic, and
a Cyrenaic outlook, has he made a bad choice? Since each philosophical
school prescribes not just a set of propositions to be believed, but a whole
life lived through the training of habits and emotions, acceptance of
a philosophical outlook is not like putting on a new suit today, changing
it for another tomorrow, and putting it on again the next day. Trying to be

a Stoic today, an Epicurean tomorrow, and a Cyrenaic the next day sounds about as sensible as training to be a marathon runner today, a sprinter tomorrow, and a ballet dancer the next day. We will make very little progress in any school. Moreover, progress in one direction may impede progress in another direction.

The appearance of capricious vacillation may suggest to us that Horace is indifferent to the content of philosophical theories and does not take them very seriously. He may view them as suitable material for his literary purposes, but perhaps he is not concerned to maintain the truth of any specific philosophical doctrines, or to explore the questions that bear on their truth.

USES FOR MORAL PHILOSOPHY

The argument from vacillation to indifference is open to doubt, however, if Horace's transitory preferences still allow him to take moral philosophy seriously. To see how he might take it seriously, we may return to the questions (quoted earlier) that begin Horace's after-dinner conversations. Perhaps these questions, rather than any definite answers to them, are the aspect of philosophy that matters to him.[7]

This allegedly Socratic attitude conflicts with some prominent features of the earliest accounts of Socrates, by Plato, Aristotle, and Xenophon. In Socrates' view, it is better to suffer injustice than to do injustice, virtue is sufficient for happiness, and knowledge is sufficient for virtue. These are controversial philosophical doctrines on the basis of which Socrates is willing to live and die. He does not agree that the questions matter and the answers do not matter.

Whatever Horace might or might not have thought about Socrates, the feature of Socrates that I have just mentioned also shows that Horace does not regard moral philosophy simply as a source of worthwhile questions for discussion in civilized company.[8] When he refers to moral philosophy, he treats it as a source of answers about how to live and what to do, and he sometimes speaks as though we ought to act on these answers.

But how and why does he care about the answers? We might look at the different philosophical schools as doctrinal systems that direct our lives, but this is not the only way to look at them. We might prefer to treat the works of the philosophers, or popular expositions of their views, as sources of useful maxims that remind us of things we should keep in mind when we make various decisions. Their role might be similar to the role of proverbs and fables. If we are in a hurry to finish a task, and notice that we are making many mistakes, we may recall Augustus' advice "Festina lente," or the equivalent "haste makes waste." Someone might benefit from remembering the advice "Go to the ant, thou sluggard," or from a fable of Aesop or La Fontaine.[9]

Maxims, proverbs, and old saws may be useful whatever their source. The advice "To thine own self be true" and so on may be useful to us even if we forget that Polonius says it, or that it comes from *Hamlet*, or from Shakespeare. Nor does it matter if two maxims seem to give opposite advice. "Many hands make light work" and "Too many cooks spoil the broth" are both true, but they may seem to pull us in opposite directions if we are wondering whether to help with this particular task or stay out of the way. The apparent opposition does not make the maxims useless. Each maxim is often relevant and worth considering, though further judgment is needed to decide whether and how either of them fits this occasion. We may get used to applying each maxim on different occasions, without stopping to ask whether they are really consistent, or whether there are some occasions to which both maxims apply and we have to decide which one to follow. This might be a reasonable way to use moral philosophy. The different philosophical schools may sometimes offer good advice, even if they maintain conflicting doctrines. We may be able to use them apart from the systems they belong to, just as we can use Polonius' advice without reference to *Hamlet*.

If Horace treats philosophy as a source of useful maxims, his use of it is intelligible. Readers remember his epigrammatic formulation of ethical doctrines, and he probably intends these short statements to be striking and memorable. Different maxims suit different circumstances. If we are involved in public life, the upright integrity of the Stoic reminds us of what we need to do. But in other circumstances we should not be taking things too seriously, and we should not worry too much about tomorrow; Cyrenaic advice should help us to relax. Relaxation will not turn into dissipation if we take Epicurean advice to seek stable and enduring pleasure. Nor will we be too disappointed at the ups and downs of life if we remember the Cynic advice to cultivate self-sufficiency. Each philosophy can contribute something to the anthology of maxims that we collect for different stages and circumstances of our lives.

PHILOSOPHY AS MORAL CRITICISM

This approach to philosophy explains some features of Horace's treatment, but it does not explain everything. Proverbs characteristically remind us of something we already believe, or are inclined to believe. The maxims about the many hands and the cooks recall for us the sorts of situations in which one of the two maxims applies. The fact that they sum up familiar beliefs and assumptions is their whole point.

We do not normally expect maxims and proverbs, therefore, to change our minds about basic principles and assumptions. On the contrary, something is suitable as a maxim because it sums up something we already accept. Since maxims are isolated pieces of good advice, they do not examine, or argue, or draw conclusions from other principles or beliefs. If, then, Horace uses philosophy as a source of maxims, he should use it not to argue, but to remind us of the familiar.

Now admittedly this contrast between reminding and arguing is too simple. We may use a maxim in an argument to show that someone has overlooked something that should have been remembered. Though we may have been tempted to let things slide, we should have remembered that a stitch in time saves nine. The characteristic form of criticism through a maxim is a reminder of something familiar. If the considerations that are recalled by the maxim are not in fact familiar to us, the maxim loses its practical impact.

Horace does not always treat philosophy simply as a source of maxims. Though some of his philosophical remarks might be described as reminders of familiar assumptions and beliefs, the same is not true of his use of philosophy in general. The moral philosophers whom Horace cites and uses sometimes attack conventional morality, though they attack it to different degrees and in different ways. Sometimes he seems to agree with the critical attitude. He argues that conventional morality has a basically mistaken attitude to life.

To expose this mistaken attitude, Horace describes a sharp choice between the philosophical pursuit of virtue and the Roman pursuit of wealth:

> The primary virtue is to flee vice, and the primary wisdom is to have got rid of folly.[10] You see with what toil of mind and head you avoid those things which you believe to be the greatest evils, a small fortune and a shameful repulse. A tireless merchant, you hurry to the furthest Indies, fleeing poverty through sea, through rocks, through flames. Are you unwilling to learn, and hear, and believe a better person telling you not to care about the things that you foolishly admire and wish for?
>
> (Ep. i 1.41–8)

Aristotle makes a similar comment on common views about virtue and happiness. Most people, in his view, think virtue is all right in its place, but that it has to take second place to the accumulation of external goods.

> Some think that any limited degree of virtue is all they need, but seek increase of wealth, property, power, reputation, and the like, without limit. *(Pol. 1323a36–8)*

These are ordinary respectable people who are not opposed to or indifferent to morality, but do not attach to it the importance that it deserves. Aristotle tries to change their mind through philosophical argument.

Horace seems to have a similar aim in mind. He suggests that he is swimming against the tide, because the leaders of respectable opinion will not agree with him.

> "Citizens, citizens, money is to be sought first; virtue after riches."
> This is what Janus teaches from one end to the other; young men and old repeat these maxims ... But boys at play cry, "You will be king, if you act rightly." Let this be our bronze wall, to be conscious of no ill, to turn pale with no fault ... Does he advise you best, who says, "Make a fortune – by acting rightly if you can, but if you cannot, by whatever means"– ... or he who stands by you to exhort and enable you to stand free and upright with an answer to willful fortune? *(Ep. i 1.53–69)*

These people are respectable, not unscrupulous. They agree it is preferable to make a fortune honestly. But they give honesty lower priority, and if it gets in the way of making a fortune, honesty has to be sacrificed. The teaching of Janus is not the unqualified voice of common sense. Horace mentions the boys at play who shout: *"Rex eris, si recte facies"* ("Right royal, if you do right"). Respectable people know this familiar maxim as an encouragement to virtue, but they do not treat it as an objection to their attitude towards virtue and wealth.

The philosophers whom Horace discusses, however, agree that respectable people who follow Janus are mistaken; for these philosophers all reject "virtue after money" (virtus post nummos). Horace recommends Stoic integrity as a preferable alternative to excessive respect for wealth. The Cynics go further than the Stoics. Epicureans give the same advice as the Stoics give about excessive concern with accumulation. The Cyrenaics agree, on different grounds. They do not accept accumulation as an appropriate long-term aim, because they do not approve of long-term aims in general. They prefer a flexible and present-oriented pursuit of pleasure, and so reject the assumption that accumulation of wealth is necessary for a good life.

This example of wealth, therefore, shows how Horace can take philosophy seriously without belonging to any philosophical school. Even if he wavers, as he appears to, between Stoics, Epicureans, and Cyrenaics, he has no reason to waver on the advice about wealth that is common to all these schools. He might reasonably argue that if philosophers disagree about so much, but agree in their rejection of the conventional attitude to wealth, their agreement deserves some attention.

The different schools disagree on whether wealth is a genuine instrumental good, because they disagree on whether the ends to which wealth is a means are genuine non-instrumental goods. The Stoics and Cynics answer no, for different reasons. Peripatetics, Epicureans, and Cynics answer yes, for different reasons. But they agree that it is not important enough to justify the importance that many people attach to it. Their view is not a commonplace; many people act as though they do not believe it. Hence it seems to be something that we learn from moral philosophy. In this case, then, Horace gives serious and non-trivial advice on the basis of philosophical theory.

REASONABLE VACILLATION?

Our explanation of this example, however, does not answer the questions that arise from Horace's apparent vacillation between different schools. His vacillation is not an effort to find consensus. He does not say that he changes his mind from day to day about who is right, or that he can never make his mind up. His description of his philosophical vacillation treats it as a passive process; he is carried from one to the other as if he were drifting on an open sea, "wherever the prevailing wind carries me off" (quo me cumque rapit tempestas). We might suppose that this drifting will result in hopeless confusion of thought.

Some of Horace's moral beliefs are exempt from this drifting, because he does not derive them primarily from the philosophical schools. On some questions he finds Homer a better guide than the philosophers:

> While you, Lollius Maximus, declaim at Rome, I at Praeneste have read over again the writer of the Trojan war; who says more manifestly and better than Chrysippus and Crantor, what is beautiful,[11] what is base, what is useful, and what is not.
> (Ep. i 2.1–4)

Does this praise of Homer show that Horace does not take the work of moral philosophers to be very important after all?[12] This would be an unwarranted inference.[13] In Horace's view, Homer gives us clear examples of people who act well or badly. We do not need to work out what a virtuous person does from the philosophers' conceptions of virtue and happiness, and if we did try to work this out from their theories, we would get much less evident examples than we get from Homer. But it does not follow that every question that moral philosophy answers is answered better or more clearly by Homer. Horace does not say, for instance, that Homer tells us why we should live one way or another, or about what the place of virtue should be in relation to other goods; but these are questions to which the philosophers give answers that interest Horace. His references to Homer give us no reason to take his engagement with moral philosophy less seriously.

Perhaps Horace's drifting from one philosophy to another is an aspect of his literary persona. He sometimes presents himself as prone to change his mind, and to abandon his considered resolution on a momentary impulse.[14] But this is not a sufficient explanation. Drifting may be a sign of lack of purpose, or indecision, or weak will; but it need not be. If I do not know where I want to go, but I believe that the tide might carry me to some dangerous places, it is unwise to drift. But if I want to reach the shore, and I know the tide is coming in, it may be reasonable to drift in on the tide. Similarly, Horace's passive vacillation is consistent with serious attachment to philosophy if he has some plausible reason for it.

He might have such a reason if he can explain why different philosophical outlooks are appropriate for people in different situations and circumstances. If we are attracted to them, and repelled by them, in sequence, part of the reason for the attraction and repulsion may be our recognition that they do or do not suit us in our various circumstances. Does Horace say anything to support this suggestion?

AN EPICUREAN EXPLANATION: THE RIGHT PLACE FOR STOICISM

We can find a possible theoretical basis for Horace's position if we consider some of his comparative judgments on the Stoic and the Epicurean outlook.[15]

Stoicism appeals to Horace because it emphasizes the paramount importance of moral virtue and the relative unimportance of external circumstances that are not in one's control. These points of emphasis might reasonably seem especially relevant for someone who is engaged in arduous public service where the opportunities for avoiding one's obligations are tempting. If we undertake public service in the first place, it is reasonable to keep in mind the arguments for believing it is worthwhile and not to be shirked in favor of an easy life, or perverted for the sake of rewards that undermine our devotion to the task at hand.

But while these Stoic attitudes in these circumstances are admirable, the Stoic theory has some unwelcome results. The result that Horace attacks is the Stoic doctrine that all moral errors are equal. We know it is sensible to go easy on the relatively minor faults of our friends. We do not want to lose good friends by excessive fault-finding on minor matters; and we should always avoid plucking out the mote from our friend's eye while overlooking the beam in our own eye. But a sensible attitude to the faults of our friends implies that, contrary to the Stoics, not all faults are equal.

> Those who have maintained that all errors are more or less equal get into difficulty when one comes to the truth of the matter: good sense and good conduct oppose them, and utility itself, nearly the mother of what is just and fair.
> (Satires i 3.96–8)

If the Stoics were right, we could not discriminate among faults, and we would soon lose all our friends. Cicero includes this Stoic doctrine in his list of the absurd views that Cato endorses by being a Stoic (*Pro Murena* 61).

This criticism allows Horace to generalize about the Stoics' mistake. He argues that it leads them to neglect the place of utility in morality. What the Stoics neglect the Epicureans emphasize, and so Horace turns to the Epicurean account of the origins of justice and social morality. He describes the historical development of norms of justice.

> When they crawled out as animals on the newly-formed earth, the mute and foul herd fought with nails and fists for their acorn and caves, afterward with clubs, and finally with weapons that experience had forged: till they found out words and names, to indicate their utterances and thoughts. From then on they began to abstain from war, to fortify towns, and establish laws prohibiting anyone from being a thief, a robber, or an adulterer ... You must admit, if you are willing to turn over the ages and records of the world, that laws were invented from fear of injustice. Nor can nature separate what is unjust from

what is just, in the same way as she distinguishes goods from the opposite, and things to be avoided from those to be sought, nor will reason prevail on us to agree that someone who breaks down the cabbage-stalk in his neighbor's garden makes as great an error as someone who steals by night things consecrated to the gods. Let there be a standard to impose punishments that fit the crimes ... For I am not afraid that you will only beat with a stick someone who deserves greater punishment; for you assert that pilfering is as great a crime as highway robbery, and you threaten to prune with the same hook both small and great things, if people were to allow you sovereignty over them. [16]   *(Sat. i 3.99–124)*

Stoic doctrine, according to Horace, opposes the necessary and useful gradation of offences and punishments, and advocates an unrealistically and harmfully strict standard.

Now that he has explained the conflict between utility and Stoic doctrine, Horace adds a little ridicule of the Stoic sage. The uncompromising Stoic is a social misfit, who looks absurd to other people.

If the one who is wise is rich, and a good shoemaker, and the only one who is handsome, and a king, why do you still wish for what you have?
He answers: "You don't understand what father Chrysippus says: the wise man never made himself shoes nor slippers, but still the wise man is a shoemaker." ...
The wild boys pull your beard, and unless you keep them off with your stick, you'll be pushed by a crowd gathered all round you.

(Sat. i 3.124–35)

The extremes of Stoic doctrine do not have the salutary effect of encouraging us to observe a higher moral standard than we otherwise would. They simply make Stoicism as a whole look ridiculous.

One might protest that Horace has misunderstood the Stoic position. The extremes that he attacks are his own invention, not genuine implications of the Stoic view.[17] To say that all errors that manifest the same mistaken state of mind are equal in that respect (Diogenes Laertius vii 120) is not to say that they are all equal in every respect. The Stoic analogy between fools and drowning men is applicable (Cicero, *De Finibus* iii 48). If the sage is the only one with his head above water, everyone else is drowning, and none is drowning any less than any other, but it does not follow that they are equally far under water, or that it is not worth their while to try to get closer to the surface.

We misunderstand the Stoics if we suppose that they recognize no morally significant differences between actions that are – in one respect – equally good or equally bad.

Horace does not consider this defense of the Stoics. He may not see that he misinterprets them. But even if he saw it, he might not mind. He cares about whether people are likely to interpret the Stoics as holding the paradoxical doctrine that he ascribes to them. If they accept these paradoxical views on Stoic authority, Horace chooses to attack the views rather than to ask whether the Stoics really hold them.

He commends Epicurus' recognition of the place of utility in justice. In his view, Epicureans take the right "external" attitude to justice and social institutions. The external attitude is not the attitude of the just person, but the attitude of someone who asks whether and why anyone, the questioner or other people, should be just. We can ask this question if we are not yet committed to justice. Epicurus undertakes to persuade us that justice is in our interest. He argues that self-interested people have reason to favor just practices and institutions because they are in everyone's interest. When we reflect on justice, it is appropriate to ask Epicurus' question, and Horace suggests that we should accept his answer.

A utilitarian[18] explanation of justice may be found surprising, because rules of justice do not overtly appeal to utility; on the contrary, they are characteristically applied without reference to utility. But these features of justice do not count against Epicurus' utilitarian explanation; for he is not trying to describe the outlook of the just person, but explaining why we have institutions and rules that require such an outlook. Once we see what Epicurus is trying to do with justice, we can also see that the same sort of explanation may be applied to social rules, practices, roles, and institutions that are not about justice, narrowly understood. Epicurean utility may justify outlooks that are not Epicurean.

If Horace grasps this aspect of Epicurean utilitarian explanation, he can readily use it to show why Epicurean questions about utility should often not be prominent in the mind of some public servants. It may be unwise to ask the Epicurean question if we are politicians, judges, or soldiers who face some onerous task for the common good. It might be difficult to satisfy ourselves that it is in our interest to fulfill our obligation, and the mere asking of the question may reduce our enthusiasm for our immediate task. Stoicism may be the right view for the participant, and we might reasonably want participants to think like Stoics rather than Epicureans. In fact, Epicurean reflection may assure us that the Stoic attitude is the right one for participants; for the Stoic attitude helps just institutions and practices to flourish, and if they flourish, we all benefit. The Epicureans take the right external attitude, but the Stoics take the right internal attitude.

THE RIGHT PLACE FOR CYRENAIC HEDONISM

If this is the right way to combine partial acceptance of Stoicism with partial acceptance of Epicureanism, a similar argument may explain why Horace sometimes supports Aristippus' Cyrenaic views.[19] He imagines a debate between Aristippus and a Cynic.

> [Cynic:] If Aristippus could put up with a dinner of vegetables, he would never frequent [the tables] of the great.
>
> [Aristippus:] If my critic knew how to live with the great, he would scorn his vegetables.
>
> Tell me whose words and actions you approve. Or, since you are my junior, hear the reason why Aristippus' view is preferable.
>
> (Ep. i 17.13–17)

Horace argues that when the Cynic rejects the pleasures and comforts that appeal to other people, he is really less adaptable than the Cyrenaic.

> For in this way, it is said, Aristippus outwitted the snapping Cynic: "I play the fool for my own advantage, but you do it with an eye on other people. What I do is more correct and far more honorable. I do what is required so that a horse can carry me and a great man feed me. But you beg for refuse, an inferior to the [poor] giver; though you pretend you are in want of nothing."
>
> Aristippus found that every complexion of life, every position in society and every degree of prosperity was equally suitable, since he aimed for greater things, but was satisfied with his present condition. By contrast, I will be amazed if a change in his way of life would suit the Cynic, whom endurance clothes with a folded rag. Aristippus will not wait until he is clothed in a purple robe, but will pass through the most frequented places wearing anything at all, and without awkwardness will keep up either role. But the Cynic will be more anxious to avoid a Milesian cloak than to avoid a dog or viper. He will die of the cold, unless you give him back his rags. So give them back to him, and let him live his fool's life.
>
> (Ep. i 17.17–32)

The Cynic professes to be indifferent to external advantages, but his practice implies that he is excessively concerned about them. He goes to great lengths to show that he can do without them, but, if they are as unimportant as he says they are, why does he make such a display of renouncing them? Aristippus shows that he is more detached from them than the ostentatious Cynic is, because he enjoys them when they are available, and does not regret their loss if he is deprived of them.[20]

The Cynic might answer that the Cyrenaic attitude is unrealistic. We cannot simply switch our desires on and off when the opportunities are present and absent. When we enjoy things, we also desire them, and the desire does not go away when we cannot satisfy it. We are bound to suffer pain and regret at the loss of goods that were sources of enjoyment, and we are bound to face the future with less confidence if we cannot expect them in the future. The Cynic advises us, therefore, to get rid of the desire in the first place, so that it does not persist and harm us with its after-effects.

The Cyrenaic may reply that the Cynic attaches too much importance to his past and future, and therefore subjects himself to regret for the past and fear for the future if he cannot satisfy the desires he used to be able to satisfy. Cyrenaics reject concern for a continuing self, and so they free themselves from regrets about what they did in the past and from fears about what will happen to them in the future. This is an easy way to achieve the detachment from external goods and harms, and easier than Cynic renunciation of all concern for external goods and evils.

Perhaps this defense of the Cyrenaic attitude to external goods explains why Horace, in some circumstances at least, prefers the Cyrenaic to the Cynic attitude. But we may still be puzzled by his sympathy for the Cyrenaic view in the light of his Epicurean sympathies. It is difficult to see how Cyrenaic hedonism can be combined with Epicurean hedonism; indeed, Epicurus sets out to refute the view that a hedonist should be a Cyrenaic. He argues that if we think about maximizing our pleasure over our lives as a whole, we will not follow the Cyrenaic policy of pursuing the pleasure that seems greater here and now. Our impressions about the greater immediate pleasure are distorted because we do not consider the future as clearly as we consider the present, and so we do not count the more remote pleasures and pains. We cannot consistently be both Epicureans and Cyrenaics about the same pleasures in the same circumstances.

If, then, we aim to be consistent Epicureans and Cyrenaics, we need to apply the different doctrines to different pleasures, or to the same pleasures in different circumstances. The idea of an internal and an external point of view may be relevant here too. If we are thinking about what kind of life to live, Epicurean prudence is the guide we need. If we decided a question that affects our whole lives, but we did not stop to think about the impact of our actions on our whole lives, we would be likely to regret our rashness and blindness. But we are not always asking ourselves how we ought to live, or what the shape of our lives as a whole should be. We also face shorter-term questions about what to do here and now, how to spend this day, these next few hours, and so on. In these circumstances, long-term Epicurean calculation may be possible, but none the less ill-advised. We may prefer to act on our immediate impulse, and to take advantage of what is offered to us now, without bothering to work out whether this is the best thing to do all things considered. This spontaneous pursuit of immediate pleasure is the Cyrenaic attitude. It prompts us to adapt ourselves to the present circumstances, and not to worry about longer-term questions. If our pursuit of this pleasure today costs us something tomorrow, we are ready to face this consequence.

This division between situations that allow Cyrenaic spontaneity and those that require Epicurean reflection is too simple. Moreover, the question of which type of situation we are in cannot itself be a matter of Cyrenaic spontaneity or of Epicurean reflection. If we leave the decision to the Cyrenaics, they will get us into situations we will regret. Horace illustrates this point through the story of the insufficiently cunning little vixen who grew too fat for her own safety.

> A thin vixen happened to creep through a narrow chink into a chest of grain; and, after stuffing herself, she tried in vain to get out again, with her body now full up. A weasel called to her from a distance "If you want to get out of there, be thin when you come back to the narrow hole that you got into when you were thin."   (Ep i 7.29–34)

The vixen got into trouble because she was too Cyrenaic; she was so spontaneous that she did not consider the consequences. But if we leave all such judgments to Epicureans, they will always detain us with reflection until it is too late to enjoy spontaneous pleasures.

If neither the Cyrenaic nor the Epicurean outlook is wholly reliable in every situation, Horace apparently has to occupy a third point of view, neither Epicurean nor Cyrenaic, in order to decide when an Epicurean approach or a Cyrenaic approach is better. If that is so, his treatment of the different schools includes some basic assumptions that are undefended and unexplained.

One might reply, however, that this conclusion misses a point about Epicurus. In this respect, his views are not simply the opposite of Aristippus' views. Cyrenaics do not advise us on how to think about our lives as a whole, because they reject concern for one's whole life. Epicurus, however, offers us advice for our lives as a whole, and so he answers questions that the Cyrenaics refuse to ask. But he does not necessarily advise us to think about our lives as a whole all the time and in every situation. Realistic Epicureans are capable of seeing that excessive reflection on the past and the future may fill us with regret and fear, take away our enjoyment of the present, and therefore leave us with less pleasure to recall in the future. Epicurus, therefore, should not tell us to think about long-term consequences all the time, since that would be a way to lose the best long-term consequences.

If this is the right account of the Epicurean position, Horace's degree of sympathy with the Cyrenaic attitude is similar to his degree of sympathy with Stoicism. In both cases, we may say that Epicurus takes an external point of view that makes room for another philosophical outlook as an internal point of view. The internal point of view tells us how we ought to think and choose here and now in this particular situation. An Epicurean tells us that sometimes we ought to think like a Stoic, and at other times we ought to think like a Cyrenaic. The Epicurean view is to be preferred because it incorporates the plausible elements in these other views.

THE COHERENCE OF HORACE'S POSITION

The conclusion that we have reached about Horace's treatment of the Stoic and Cyrenaic outlooks is consistent with Horace's profession of non-alignment ("*nullius addictus* ..."). He shows more sympathy to Stoicism and to Cyrenaic hedonism than a wholehearted Epicurean would show, but his sympathy is limited. His non-aligned attitude does not rest on an arbitrary selection from these different philosophical views. Sometimes he defends Epicurean utility as the basic standard, and his sympathy with other views can be explained as sympathy for them as internal points of view within an Epicurean external point of view. Though he is non-aligned, he is, in the ways I have tried to explain, fundamentally Epicurean, since Epicureanism provides the fundamental external point of view that justifies non-Epicurean internal points of view. Horace is indeed "a pig from the herd of Epicurus."[21]

If Horace distinguishes an external from an internal point of view, he agrees with recent moral philosophers who have discussed questions about morality and alienation. By "alienation" they mean that the appropriate immersion in particular roles or relations (e.g., friendship) is undermined by the asking of questions that moral theories require us to ask. They answer this objection by arguing that (e.g.) an objective consequentialist (who wants to maximize good consequences) will not necessarily be a subjective consequentialist (who constantly thinks about how to maximize good consequences). If we recognize that a moral outlook can reasonably place some limits on the extent to which we think about it, some objections of the form "A utilitarian can't be a real friend" collapse. Something similar can be said about deontological moral theories.[22] This is the sort of position I have attributed to Horace through the suggestion that he distinguishes external from internal points of view, and takes Epicureanism to give the right external view within which internal points of view that are not subjectively Epicurean may be justified.

This statement of Horace's position may make it seem more explicit than it really is. My references to internal and external points of view, and to the different roles of different philosophical doctrines, go beyond anything he says. They may also go beyond, and even against, what he believes or implies. Even if he accepted the Epicurean external view in the Satires, we may doubt whether we can legitimately import it into the much later Epistles, where he does not repeat it.[23] Perhaps we should not suppose that the Epicurean explanatory framework that he endorses in the Satires really lies behind his attitude to different philosophical views in his later works. We might be better advised to say that Horace relies on his intuition that each of the three favored schools (Epicurean, Stoic, Cyrenaic) is right about something and worth listening to in some situations, but has no view about why this is so. In speaking of an "intuition" here I simply mean that he does not hold this view as a result of philosophical theory or argument, but none the less relies on it. He may have no view on why this intuition is reliable, or on whether it commits him to inconsistent conclusions. Perhaps he simply finds himself selectively attracted to these different views at different times, and does not try to explain or to justify the selective attraction.

I am not sure that this explanation accounts for all the evidence quite as well as my more theoretical explanation accounts for it. Horace's rather elaborate defense of the Epicurean appeal to utility suggests a basic standard for evaluating ethical doctrines and practical principles. It is reasonable to infer that this is the role Horace intends for it. At any rate, it allows a defense of other doctrines as internal points of view. Even if Horace were indifferent to questions about the consistency of his outlook, we would have good reason to affirm its consistency.

But lack of explicitness may not simply result from Horace's failure to make his basic assumptions clear. He might have a different reason – again, perhaps not wholly explicit – for choosing not to state the Epicurean framework within which his apparent vacillation is defensible. I mentioned the problem of alienation, and the solution that appeals to internal and external points of view. But we may find this solution too easy. If we cannot be wholehearted friends (e.g.) if we are always thinking about good and bad consequences, is it clear that we can be wholehearted friends if we recognize that we value friendship on objective consequentialist grounds? The fact that we do not always think about consequences when we are doing what friends do may not answer the objection about wholeheartedness; for do we not take an inappropriately calculating attitude to friendships when we consider whether they have an objective consequentialist justification?[24]

If this is a good objection to an objective consequentialist solution to the problem of alienation, Horace could offer a philosophical reason for his failure to advertise his fundamental Epicureanism. We may decide it is better to recognize the external and internal points of view without trying to articulate them in an explicit theory that might undermine our wholehearted attachment to the various internal points of view. If Horace reaches a similar conclusion, he has a theoretical reason to avoid an explicit exposition of the framework of internal and external points of view. Perhaps he is inexplicit not because he does not bother to think through his theoretical assumptions, but because he sees the questions we have raised about alienation and wholeheartedness. Perhaps he is right to present himself as drifting rather than executing a deliberate policy of adopting different outlooks in different circumstances.

Though this defense of inexplicitness deserves consideration, I doubt whether it succeeds; for I do not believe that we should be moved by the concerns about alienation and wholeheartedness. Moreover, a more explicit statement of Horace's outlook would have usefully led to the question whether he is right to assume that the Epicurean view is the right external point of view. We can perhaps see why the Cyrenaic and Cynic views are unsuitable for this role. But what about Stoicism? It would be a bad guide to many situations in life if it told us to think only about what virtue requires, and told us that nothing except virtue is worth considering. But this is not what Stoicism tells us. Stoic doctrines about value, selection, and preferred and non-preferred indifferents give us a good reason to attend to other valuable things besides virtue, on the right occasions, and do not tell us that we should always be thinking about what virtue requires of us.

Why does Horace not see this way in which Stoicism, no less than Epicureanism, provides an external view that justifies different internal points of view in different situations? His interpretation of Stoicism explains why he thinks it needs to be regulated by an Epicurean external point of view that puts utility first. He does not consider any argument to show that Stoic theory might have the appropriate regulative role.

NOTES

1. These four Hellenistic schools are the ones I will discuss, because these are the ones that Horace refers to most explicitly and most often. But they are not the only philosophical sources for Horace's views. McGann (1969) ch.1 discusses the influence of Panaetius and Democritus, inter alios.

2. A well-known statement of this sort of objection to utilitarian and Kantian views is Williams (1981).

3. See, e.g., Blackburn (1998) Preface.

4. I have provided a rather dull and literal translation of the quotations from Horace (based on the Loeb).

5. Recent students have disagreed about the extent to which Horace is serious about the philosophical topics he discusses. Among those who take him to be serious are Fraenkel (1957), 308; Macleod (1979); Moles (2002) and (2007). Among those who reject this view, to some degree, are Rudd (1993) and Mayer (1986).

6. An "eclectic" attitude to philosophy is defended by Diderot in the Encyclopaedia, and in antiquity it is defended by Galen. See Donini (1985) and Hatzimichali (2011) 15–20. Hatzimichali takes Horace to be an implicit eclectic in this sense.

7. This is the view of Brower (1959) 173; Mayer (1986).

8. The possible extent of Horace's knowledge of Socratic discourses is discussed by Sedley (2014) 104–6.

9. Morgan (2007) chs. 2–4 offers a detailed and informative discussion of proverbs, fables, and gnômai (which are roughly what I have called "maxims"). In ch. 11 she compares them with philosophy.

10. "Virtus est vitium fugere et sapientia prima/ stultitia caruisse." I follow Mayer ad loc. in taking "prima" apo koinou, with both "virtus" and "sapientia." "Prima" might mean "most important" or (more probably) "the first step."

11. Horace prefers *"pulchrum"* to Cicero's *"honestum"* as a rendering of the Greek *"kalon."*

12. See Mayer (1994) ad loc: Rudd (1993) 70.

13. At *Ep.* ii 2.41–5 Horace mentions both Homer and Greek philosophy as parts of his education.

14. See, e.g., *Odes* i 34; *Satires* ii.7. Griffin (1993) 18 discusses this aspect of Horace's self-presentation.

15. Here I develop a suggestion by Rudd (1993) 75.

16. Since the passage fits its context, it has the appropriate elements of ridicule (which is perhaps also present in 106–10). These are emphasized by Gowers (2012) 138, 141. But these features of the passage do not affect the clear and coherent statement of Epicurean doctrine.

17. I have discussed some of the relevant questions in Irwin (1990).

18. I use "utilitarian" simply to describe the features of Epicurus' position that I have mentioned in the previous paragraph. I do not mean that he maintains a utilitarian position, as it has been understood since the 19th century.

19. The importance of Cyrenaic views in Horace is emphasized by Traiana (2009).

20. This passage is mentioned by Lampe (2015) 72, with further evidence of Cyrenaic claims of adaptability. Warren (2014) 190–96 offers a different account of Cyrenaic attention to the present.

21. *"Epicuri de grege porcum,"* *Ep.* i 4.16. This playful phrase is not represented as a serious statement of Horace's philosophical views. But it may none the less be a convenient summary of one part of them.

22. Railton (1984) provides a clear statement of this answer to alienation, and a persuasive argument for it.

23. *Satires* i was published in 36–35, *Epistles* i in 20–19.

24. Railton (1984) 150–51 replies to this objection.

Bibliography

PRIMARY SOURCES

Collections

CPF I.1*	*Corpus dei Papiri Filosofici Greci et Latini* I.1* (Florence: Olschki) 1989
CPF I.1***	*Corpus dei Papiri Filosofici Greci et Latini* I.1*** (Florence: Olschki) 1999
SSR	Giannantoni, G., 1990 *Socratis et Socraticorum Reliquiae*, vols. 1–4 (Naples: Bibliopolis)
SVF	von Arnim, H. (ed.) 1921–24 *Stoicorum Veterum Fragmenta*, 4 vols. (Leipzig: Teubner)

Inwood, B. and Gerson, L., 2008 *The Stoics Reader: Selected Writings and Testimonia* (Indianapolis: Hackett)

Long, A.A. and Sedley, D., 1987 *The Hellenistic Philosophers*, 2 vols. (Cambridge: Cambridge University Press)

Wachsmuth, C. and Hense, O. (eds.), 1884–1912 *Ioannis Stobaei Anthologium*, 4 vols. (Berlin: Weidmannsche Buchhandlung)

Alcinous

Didaskalikos. Edition and French translation in J. Whittaker and P. Louis (eds.), 1990 *Alkinoos. Enseignement des doctrines de Platon* (Paris: Les Belles Lettres). English translation in J. Dillon (ed.), 1993 *Alcinous: The Handbook of Platonism* (Oxford: Clarendon Press)

Aquinas

Litzinger, C.I., 1964 *Commentary on the Nicomachean Ethics by Thomas Aquinas*, 2 vols. (Washington, D.C.: Henry Regnery Company)

Aristotle

Barnes, J. (ed.) 1985 *The Complete Works of Aristotle*, 2 vols. (Princeton, NJ:Princeton University Press)

Broadie, S. and Rowe, C., 2002 *Aristotle Nicomachean Ethics* (Oxford: Oxford University Press)

Bywater, L. (ed.), 1894 *Aristotelis Ethica Nicomachea* (Oxford: Clarendon Press)

Inwood, B. and Woolf, R. (eds.), 2013 *Aristotle: Eudemian Ethics* (Cambridge: Cambridge University Press)

Irwin, T., 1999 *Aristotle: Nicomachean Ethics*, 2nd edn. (Indianapolis: Hackett)

Walzer, R.R. and Mingay, J.M. (eds.), 1991 *Aristotelis Ethica Eudemia* (Oxford: Clarendon Press)

Aspasius

Heylbut, G. (ed.), 1892 *In Ethica Nicomachea quae supersunt commentaria* (Berlin: Reimer)

Konstan, D. (ed.), 2006 *Aspasius: On Aristotle Nicomachean Ethics 1–4, 7–8* (London: Bloomsbury)

Cicero

Atkins, E.M., 1991 *Cicero: On Duties* (Cambridge: Cambridge University Press)

Damascius

Life of Isidore. Edition and English translation in P. Athanassiadi, 1999 *Damascius: The Philosophical History* (Athens: Apamea Cultural Association)

Eustratius

Heylbut, G. (ed.), 1892 *Eustratii et Michaelis et Anonyma in Ethica Nicomachea Commentaria* (Berlin: Reimer)

Hierocles

Commentary on the Golden Verses: edition by W. Köhler, 1974 (Stuttgart: Teubner); English translation and commentary in Schibli, H., 2002 *Hierocles of Alexandria* (Oxford: Oxford University Press)

Iamblichus

Letters: edition and English translation by J. Dillon and W. Polleitchner, 2009 *Iamblichus of Chalcis: The Letters* (Atlanta, GA: Society of Biblical Literature); edition, Italian translation and commentary by D. Taormina and R. Piccione 2010 *Giamblico I frammenti dalle epistole* (Naples: Bibliopolis)

On the Pythagorean Life: edition by L. Deubner, 1937 *Iamblichi De Vita Pythagorica Liber* (Leipzig: Teubner); English translation by G. Clark, 1989 *Iamblichus: On the Pythagorean Life* (Liverpool: Liverpool University Press)

Marinus

Life of Proclus: edition and French translation by H. Saffrey and A. Segonds, 2001 *Proclus, ou sur le Bonheur* (Paris: Les Belles Lettres); English translation by M. Edwards, 2000 *Neoplatonic Saints. The Lives of Plotinus and Proclus by their Students* (Liverpool: Liverpool University Press)

Plato

Burnet, J. (ed.), 1900–07 *Platonis Opera*, 5 vols. (Oxford: Clarendon Press)
Cooper, J. (ed.), 1997 *Plato: Complete Works* (Indianapolis: Hackett)
Duke, E.A., Hicken, W.F., Nicoll, W.S.M., Robinson, D.B. and Strachan, J.C.G. (eds.) 1995 *Platonis Opera* vol. I (Oxford: Clarendon Press)
Slings, S.R. (ed.) 2003 *Platonis Respublica* (Oxford: Clarendon Press)

Plotinus

Henry, P. and Schwyzer, H.-R., 1964–82 *Plotini Opera* (editio minor) (Oxford: Clarendon Press)
Armstrong, A., 1966–1988 *Plotinus: Enneads*, 7 vols. (Cambridge, MA: Harvard University Press)

Porphyry

To Marcella: edition and French translation by É. Des Places, 1982 *Porphyre Vie de Pythagore, Lettre à Marcella* (Paris: Les Belles Lettres); English translation by K. O'Brien Wicker, 1987 *Porphyry the Philosopher To Marcella* (Atlanta, GA: Society of Biblical Literature)
On Abstinence: edition and French translation by J. Bouffartigue and M. Patillon, 1977–1979 *Porphyre. De l'Abstinence* (Paris: Les Belles Lettres); English translation by G. Clarke, 2000 *Porphyry. On Abstinence from Killing Animals* (London: Bloomsbury)
Sentences: edition by F. Lamberz, 1975 *Porphyrius Sententiae* (Leipzig: Teubner); French translation and commentary by L. Brisson et al., 2005 *Porphyre Sentences* (Paris: Vrin) (includes English translation by J. Dillon).

Proclus

Commentary on Plato's Alcibiades: edition and French translation by A. Segonds, 1985–1986 *Proclus sur le premier Alcibiade de Platon* (Paris: Les Belles Lettres); English translation by W. O'Neill, 1965 *Proclus: Alcibiades I* (The Hague: Martinus Nijhoff)

Simplicius

Commentary on Epictetus' Handbook: edition by I. Hadot, 1996 *Simplicius Commentaire sur le Manuel d'Epictète* (Leiden: Brill); English translation by T. Brennan and C. Brittain, 2002 *Simplicius. On Epictetus' Handbook 1–26* (London: Duckworth) and T. Brennan and C. Brittain, 2002 *Simplicius. On Epictetus' Handbook 27–53* (London: Duckworth)

SECONDARY SOURCES

Ackrill, J.L., 1974 "Aristotle on *Eudaimonia*," *Proceedings of the British Academy* 60: 339–59

Adam, J., 1902 *The Republic of Plato*, 2 vols. (Cambridge: Cambridge University Press)

Adamson, P., 2014 "Freedom, Providence and Fate," in Remes and Slaveva-Griffith (eds.) pp. 437–52

Adkins, A.H., 1960 *Merit and Responsibility. A Study in Greek Values* (Oxford: Clarendon Press)

  1963 "'Friendship' and 'Self-Sufficiency' in Homer and Aristotle," *Classical Quarterly* 30:30–45

Alberti, A., 1995 "The Epicurean Theory of Law and Justice," in A. Laks and M. Schofield (eds.), *Justice and Generosity* (Cambridge: Cambridge University Press), pp. 161–90

Algra, K., 1997 "Chrysippus, Carneades, and Cicero: The Ethical *Divisiones* in Cicero's *Lucullus*," in B. Inwood and J. Mansfeld (eds.), *Assent and Argument: Studies in Cicero's Academic Books* (Leiden: Brill), pp. 107–39

Allen, J., 1994 "Academic Probabilism and Stoic Epistemology," *Classical Quarterly* 44:85–113

Annas, J., 1982 "Plato's Myths of Judgment," *Phronesis* 32:119–43

  1988 "Self-Love in Plato and Aristotle," *The Southern Journal of Philosophy* 27:1–18

  1992 *Hellenistic Philosophy of Mind* (Berkeley: University of California Press)

  1993 *The Morality of Happiness* (Oxford: Oxford University Press)

  1998 "Doing without Objective Values: Ancient and Modern Strategies," in S. Everson (ed.), *Companions to Ancient Thought 4: Ethics* (Cambridge: Cambridge University Press), pp. 193–220

  1999 *Platonic Ethics Old and New* (Ithaca, NY: Cornell University Press)

  2002 "Democritus and Eudaimonism," in V. Caston and D. Graham (eds.), *Presocratic Philosophy: Essays in Honor of Alexander Mourelatos* (Aldershot, Hants: Ashgate), pp. 169–80

  2007 "Carneades' Classification of Ethical Theories," in A. Ioppolo and D. Sedley (eds.), *Pyrrhonists, Patricians, Platonizers: Hellenistic Philosophy in the Period 155–86 BC* (Naples: Bibliopolis), pp. 189–223

  2008 "Virtue Ethics and the Charge of Egoism," in P. Bloomfield (ed.), *Morality and Self-Interest* (Oxford: Oxford University Press), pp. 205–21

  2010 "Law and Virtue in Plato," in Bobonich (ed.) pp. 71–91

  2011 *Intelligent Virtue* (Oxford: Oxford University Press)

Annas, J. and Barnes, J., 1985 *The Modes of Scepticism: Ancient Texts and Modern Interpretations* (Cambridge: Cambridge University Press)

  2000 *Sextus Empiricus: Outlines of Scepticism*, 2nd edn. (Cambridge: Cambridge University Press)

Anscombe, E., 1958 "Modern Moral Philosophy," *Philosophy* 33:1–19

Armstrong, J.M., 1997 "Epicurean Justice," *Phronesis* 42:324–34

  2004 "After the Ascent: Plato on Becoming Like God," *Oxford Studies in Ancient Philosophy* 26:171–83

Arpaly, N., 2003 *Unprincipled Virtue: An Inquiry into Moral Agency* (Oxford: Oxford University Press)

Ausland, H., 1989 "On the Moral Origin of the Pyrrhonian Philosophy," *Elenchos* 10: 359–434

Balansard, A., 2001 *Technê dans les Dialogues de Platon* (Sankt Augustin: Academia Verlag)

Baltzly, D., 2004 "The Virtues and 'Becoming Like God': Alcinous to Proclus," *Oxford Studies in Ancient Philosophy* 26:297–322

Bandini, M. and Dorion, L.A., 2000 *Mémorables: Introduction Générale*, vol. I (Paris: Les Belles Lettres)

Barnes, J., 1982 "The Beliefs of a Pyrrhonist," *Proceedings of the Cambridge Philological Society* 28:1–29

1990 *The Toils of Scepticism* (Cambridge: Cambridge University Press)

Barney, R., 2010 "Note on Plato on the *Kalon* and the Good," *Classical Philology* 105: 363–77

Beckwith, C., 2011 "Pyrrho's Logic: A Re-examination of Aristocles' Record of Timon's Account," *Elenchos* 23:287–327

Beierwaltes, W., 2002 "Das Eine als Norm des Lebens. Zum Metaphysischen Grund neuplatonischer Lebensform," in Kobusch and Erler (eds.) pp. 121–51

Belfiore, E., 2012 *Socrates' Daimonic Art: Love for Wisdom in Four Platonic Dialogues* (Cambridge: Cambridge University Press)

Bene, L., 2013 "Ethics and Metaphysics in Plotinus," in Karfík and Song (eds.) pp. 141–61

Beriger, A., 1989 *Die aristotelische Dialektik: ihre Darstellung in der Topik und in den Sophistischen Widerlegungen und ihre Anwendung in der Metaphysik M 1–3* (Heidelberg: C. Winter)

Betegh, G., 2014 "Pythagoreans, Orphism and Greek Religion," in C.A. Huffman (ed.), *A History of Pythagoreanism* (Cambridge: Cambridge University Press), pp. 149–66

Bett, R., 1989 "Carneades' Pithanon: a Reappraisal of its Role and Status," *Oxford Studies in Ancient Philosophy* 7:59–94

1994 "Sextus' *Against the Ethicists*: Scepticism, Relativism or Both?," *Apeiron* 27: 123–61

1997 *Sextus Empiricus: Against the Ethicists* (Oxford: Clarendon Press)

2000 *Pyrrho, His Antecedents, and His Legacy* (Oxford: Clarendon Press)

2005 *Sextus Empiricus: Against the Logicians* (Cambridge: Cambridge University Press)

2011 "How Ethical Can an Ancient Sceptic Be?," in D. Machuca (ed.), *Pyrrhonism in Ancient, Modern, and Contemporary Philosophy* (Dordrecht: Springer), pp. 3–17

2012 "Can an Ancient Greek Sceptic Be *Eudaimôn* (or Happy)? And What Difference Does the Answer Make to Us?," *Journal of Ancient Philosophy* 6:1–26

Blackburn, S., 1998 *Ruling Passions: A Theory of Practical Reasoning* (Oxford: Oxford University Press)

Bobonich, C., 1991 "Persuasion and Compulsion in Plato's *Laws*," *Classical Quarterly* 41:365–88

2002 *Plato's Utopia Recast: His Later Ethics and Politics* (Oxford: Clarendon Press)

2007a "Plato on *Akrasia* and Knowing Your Own Mind," in C. Bobonich and P. Destrée (eds.), *Akrasia in Greek Philosophy from Socrates to Plotinus* (Leiden: Brill), pp. 41–60

2007b "Why Should Philosophers Rule? Plato's *Laws* and Aristotle's *Protrepticus*," *Social Philosophy & Policy* 24:153–75. Reprinted in D. Keyt and F. Miller (eds.), *Freedom, Reason, and the Polis: Essays in Ancient Greek Political Philosophy* (Cambridge: Cambridge University Press), pp. 153–75 (ed.) 2010a *Plato's Laws: A Critical Guide* (Cambridge: Cambridge University Press)

2010b "Socrates and Eudaimonia," in Morrison (ed.) pp. 293–332

Bollack, J., 2003 *Empédocle. Les Purifications. Un projet de paix universelle* (Paris: Points)

2006 *Parménide, de l'étant au monde* (Paris: Verdier)

Bolton, R., 1989 "Nature and human good in Heraclitus," in K. Boudouris (ed.), *Ionian Philosophy* (Athens: International Association for Greek Philosophy and International Center for Greek Philosophy and Culture), pp. 49–57

Boys-Stone, G., 2004 "Phaedo of Elis and Plato on the Soul," *Phronesis* 49:1–23

Boys-Stone, G. and Rowe, C., 2013 *The Circle of Socrates* (Indianapolis: Hackett)

Brancacci, A., 1985–1986 "La Théologie d'Antisthène," *Philosophia* 15–16:218–29

1990 *Oikeios Logos: La Filosofia del Linguaggio di Antistene* (Naples: Bibliopolis)

2005a "The Double *Daimôn* in Euclides the Socratic," in Destrée and Smith (eds.) pp. 143–54

2005b "*Epistêmê* and *Phronêsis* in Antisthenes," *Methexis* 18:7–28

2011 "Antisthene e Socrate in una Testimonianza de Filodemo (T 17 Acosta Méndez-Angeli)," *Cronache Ercolanesi* 41:83–91

2015 "The Socratic Profile of Antisthenes' Ethics," in Zilioli (ed.) pp. 43–60

Brennan, T., 1996 "Reasonable Impressions in Stoicism," *Phronesis* 41:318–34

1998 "Pyrrho on the Criterion," *Ancient Philosophy* 18:417–34

2005 *The Stoic Life: Emotions, Duties and Fate* (Oxford: Oxford University Press)

2012 "The Nature of the Spirited Part of the Soul and Its Object," in R. Barney, T. Brennan and C. Brittain (eds.), *Plato and the Divided Self* (Cambridge: Cambridge University Press), pp. 102–27

Brickhouse, T. and Smith, N.D., 1994 *Plato's Socrates* (Oxford: Oxford University Press)

2010 *Socratic Moral Psychology* (Cambridge: Cambridge University Press)

Brink, D., 1999 "Eudaimonism, Love and Friendship and Political Community," *Social Philosophy and Policy* 16:252–89

Brittain, C., 2005 "Arcesilaus," in E. Zalta (ed.), *The Stanford Encyclopedia of Philosophy* https://plato.stanford.edu/archives/fall2008/entries/arcesilaus/

2006 *Cicero. On Academic Scepticism* (Indianapolis: Hackett)

Broadie, S., 1991 *Ethics with Aristotle* (Oxford: Oxford University Press)

1998 "Interpreting Aristotle's Directions," in J. Gentzler (ed.), *Method in Ancient Philosophy* (Oxford: Clarendon Press), pp. 291–306

Brower, R. A., 1959 *Alexander Pope: The Poetry of Allusion* (Oxford: Oxford University Press)

Brown, E., 2002 "Epicurus on the Value of Friendship (*Sententia Vaticana* 23)," *Classical Philology* 91:68–80

Brown, L., 2014 "Why is Aristotle's Virtue of Character a Mean? Taking Aristotle at His Word (*NE* iii 1–5)," in R. Polansky (ed.), *The Cambridge Companion to Aristotle's Nicomachean Ethics* (Cambridge: Cambridge University Press), pp. 64–80

Brunschwig, J., 1984 "Hippias d'Elis, Philosophe Ambassadeur," in K. Boudouris (ed.), *The Sophistic Movement* (Athens: Athenian Library of Philosophy), pp. 269–76

1986 "The Cradle Argument in Epicureanism and Stoicism," in M. Schofield and G. Striker (eds.), *The Norms of Nature: Studies in Hellenistic Ethics* (Cambridge: Cambridge University Press), pp. 206–32

1994 "Once again on Eusebius on Aristocles on Timon on Pyrrho," in J. Brunschwig, *Papers in Hellenistic Philosophy* (Cambridge: Cambridge University Press), pp. 190–211

1999 "Pyrrho," in K. Algra, J. Barnes, J. Mansfeld and M. Schofield (eds.), *The Cambridge History of Hellenistic Philosophy* (Cambridge: Cambridge University Press), pp. 241–51

2003 "Stoic Metaphysics," in B. Inwood (ed.), *The Cambridge Companion to the Stoics* (Cambridge: Cambridge University Press), pp. 206–32

Burkert, W., 1985 *Greek Religion* (Cambridge, MA: Harvard University Press)

Burnyeat, M., 1980 "Can the Sceptic Live His Scepticism?," in M. Schofield, M. Burnyeat and J. Barnes (eds.), *Doubt and Dogmatism* (Oxford: Clarendon Press), pp. 20–53

1982 "Idealism and Greek Philosophy: What Descartes Saw and Berkeley Missed," *Philosophical Review* 91:3–40

1987 "Platonism and Mathematics: A Prelude to Discussion," in A. Graeser (ed.), *Mathematics and Metaphysics in Aristotle* (Bern: Haupt), pp. 213–40

1997 "Antipater and Self-Refutation: Elusive Arguments in Cicero's *Academica*," in B. Inwood and J. Mansfeld (eds.), *Assent and Argument: Studies in Cicero's Academic Books* (Leiden: Brill), pp. 277–310

2000 "Plato on Why Mathematics Is Good for the Soul," in T. Smiley (ed.), *Mathematics and Necessity: Essays in the History of Philosophy* (Oxford: Oxford University Press), pp. 1–82

2006 "The Truth of Tripartition," *Proceedings of the Aristotelian Society* 106:1–23

Burnyeat, M. and Frede, M. (eds.), 1997 *The Original Sceptics* (Indianapolis: Hackett)

Bussanich, J. and Smith, N.D. (eds.), 2013 *The Bloomsbury Companion to Socrates* (London: Continuum)

Cajolle-Zaslawsky, F., 1990 "Étude Préparatoire à une Interprétation du Sens Aristotélicien d'*Epagôgê*," in D. Devereux and P. Pellegrin (eds.), *Biologie, logique, et métaphysique chez Aristote* (Paris: CNRS), pp. 365–87

Carone, G., 2001 "Akrasia in the *Republic*: Does Plato Change His Mind?," *Oxford Studies in Ancient Philosophy* 20:107–48

Castagnoli, L., 2010 *Ancient Self-Refutation: The Logic and History of the Self-Refutation Argument from Democritus to Augustine* (Cambridge: Cambridge University Press)

(forthcoming)a "*Aporia* and Inquiry in Ancient Pyrrhonism," in V. Politis and G. Karamanolis (eds.), *The Aporetic Tradition in Ancient Philosophy* (Cambridge: Cambridge University Press)

(forthcoming)b "Dialectic in the Hellenistic Academy," in T. Bénatouïl and K. Ierodiakonou (eds.), *Dialectic in the Hellenistic Academy: Proceedings of the 13th Symposium Hellenisticum on Dialectic in Hellenistic Philosophy* (Cambridge: Cambridge University Press)

Charles, D., 2010 "Some Issues Concerning Potentiality and Actuality," in J. Lennox and R. Bolton (eds.), *Being, Nature and Life in Aristotle* (Cambridge: Cambridge University Press), pp. 168–97

2012 "Teleological Causation," in C. Shields (ed.), *Oxford Handbook of Aristotle* (Oxford: Oxford University Press), pp. 227–66

2015 "Aristotle on the Highest Good," in J. Aufderheide and R.M. Bader (eds.), *The Highest Good in Aristotle and Kant* (Oxford: Oxford University Press), pp. 60–82

Chiaradonna, R. and Trabattoni, F. (eds.), 2009 *Physics and Philosophy of Nature in Greek Neoplatonism* (Leiden: Brill)

Chroust, A.-H., 1952 "Socrates in Light of Aristotle's Testimony," *New Scholasticism* 26: 327–65

Claus, D., 1981 *Toward the Soul* (New Haven, CT: Yale University Press)

Cleary, J., (ed.), 1999 *Traditions of Platonism. Essays in Honour of John Dillon* (Aldershot, Hants: Ashgate)

Collette-Dučić, B., 2014 "Plotinus on founding Freedom in *Ennead* VI 8 [39]," in Remes and Slaveva-Griffith (eds.) pp. 421–36

Cooper, J., 1984 "Plato's Theory of Human Motivation," *History of Philosophy Quarterly* 1:3–21

1999a "Aristotle on the Forms of Friendship," in J. Cooper, *Reason and Emotion: Essays on Ancient Moral Psychology and Ethical Theory* (Princeton, NJ: Princeton University Press), pp. 312–35

1999b "Pleasure and Desire in Epicurus," in J. Cooper, *Reason and Emotion: Essays on Ancient Moral Psychology and Ethical Theory* (Princeton, NJ: Princeton University Press), pp. 485–514

1999c "Reason, Moral Virtue, and Moral Value," in J. Cooper, *Reason and Emotion: Essays on Ancient Moral Psychology and Ethical Theory* (Princeton, NJ: Princeton University Press), pp. 253–80

2004 "Arcesilaus: Socratic and Sceptic," in J. Cooper, *Knowledge, Nature, and the Good* (Princeton, NJ: Princeton University Press), pp. 81–103

2010 "Political Community and the Highest Good," in J. Lennox and R. Bolton (eds.), *Being, Nature, and Life in Aristotle* (Cambridge: Cambridge University Press), pp. 212–64

2012 *Pursuits of Wisdom* (Princeton, NJ: Princeton University Press)

Corcilius, K. and Perler, D. (eds.), 2014 *Partitioning the Soul. Debates from Plato to Leibniz* (Berlin: De Gruyter)

Couissin, P., 1983 "The Stoicism of the New Academy," in M. Burnyeat (ed.), *The Skeptical Tradition* (Berkeley: University of California Press), pp. 31–63 [First published as P. Couissin, 1929 "Le Stoïcisme de la Nouvelle Académie," *Revue d'histoire de la philosophie* 3:241–76

Crisp, R., (ed.), 2013 *The Oxford Handbook of the History of Ethics* (Oxford: Oxford University Press)

Crisp, R., 2014 "Nobility in the *Nicomachean Ethics*," *Phronesis* 59:231–45

Curzer, H., 2005 "How Good People Do Bad Things: Aristotle on the Misdeeds of the Virtuous," *Oxford Studies in Ancient Philosophy* 28:233–56

Deman, T., 1942 *La Témoignage d'Aristote sur Socrate* (Paris: Les Belles Lettres)

Demont, P., 2007 "Démocrite, l'Atomisme, l'Éthique et les Atomes de l'Âme: Quelques Remarques," *Philosophie Antique* 7:179–87

Demos, R., 1964 "A Fallacy in Plato's *Republic*," *Philosophical Review* 73:395–98

Denyer, N., 2007 "Sun and Line: The Form of the Good," in G.R.F. Ferrari (ed.), *The Cambridge Companion to Plato's Republic* (Cambridge: Cambridge University Press), pp. 284–309

Deslauriers, M., 2003 "Aristotle on the Virtues of Slaves and Women," *Oxford Studies in Ancient Philosophy* 25:213–31

Destrée, P., and Smith, N.D. (eds.), *Socrates' Divine Sign: Religion, Practice, and Value in Socratic Philosophy* (Berrima, NSW: Academic Printing and Publishing)

Devereux, D., 1992 "The Unity of the Virtues in Plato's *Protagoras* and *Laches*," *Philosophical Review* 101:765–89

    1995 "Socrates' Kantian Conception of Virtue," *Journal of the History of Philosophy* 33:381–408

    2004 "The Relationship between Justice and Happiness in Plato's *Republic*," *Proceedings of the Boston Area Colloquium in Ancient Philosophy* 20:265–305

Di Muzio, G., 2000 "Aristotle on Improving One's Character," *Phronesis* 45:205–19

Dillon, J., 1996 "An Ethic for the Late Antique Sage," in Gerson (ed.) pp. 315–35

Dillon, J. and Dixsaut, M. (eds.), 2005 *Agonistes. Essays in Honour of Denis O'Brien* (Aldershot, Hants: Ashgate)

Donini, P. L., 1985 "The History of the Concept of Eclecticism," in J. Dillon and A.A. Long (eds.), *The Question of 'Eclecticism'* (Berkeley: University of California Press), pp. 15–33

Döring, K., 2010 "The Students of Socrates," in Morrison (ed.) pp. 24–47

Dorandi, T., 2015 "Epicureanism and Socraticism: The Evidence on the Minor Socratics from the Herculaneum Papyri," in Zilioli (ed.), pp. 168–91

Dorion, L.-A., 2010 "The Rise and Fall of the Socratic Problem," in Morrison (ed.) pp. 1–23

    2012 "The Nature and Status of *Sophia* in the *Memorabilia*," in F. Hobden and C. Tuplin (eds.), *Xenophon: Ethical Principles and Historical Inquiry* (Leiden: Brill), pp. 455–75

El Murr, D., 2014 "*Philia* in Plato," in S. Stern-Gillet and G.M. Gurtler (eds.), *Ancient and Modern Concepts of Friendship* (Albany, NY: SUNY Press), pp. 3–34

Emilsson, E., 2007 *Plotinus on Intellect* (Oxford: Oxford University Press)

Edelstein, L. and Kidd, I.G. (eds.), 1989 *Posidonius: The Fragments* (Cambridge: Cambridge University Press)

Evans, J., 2012 *Philosophy for Life and Other Dangerous Situations: Ancient Philosophy for Modern Problems* (Novato, CA: New World Library)

Evans, J.D.G., 1977 *Aristotle's Concept of Dialectic* (Cambridge: Cambridge University Press)

Evans Jr., J.W., 1970 "Heraclitus and Parmenides as Moral Philosophers," unpublished PhD thesis (New Haven, CT: Yale University)

Evans, M., 2004 "Can Epicureans be Friends?," *Ancient Philosophy* 24:407–24

Everson, S., 1990 "Epicurus on the Truth of the Senses," in S. Everson (ed.), *Companions to Ancient Thought 1: Epistemology* (Cambridge: Cambridge University Press), pp. 161–83

    1998 "Aristotle on Nature and Value" in S. Everson (ed.), *Companions to Ancient Thought 4: Ethics* (Cambridge: Cambridge University Press), pp. 77–106

Fine, G., 2003 "Sextus and External World Scepticism," *Oxford Studies in Ancient Philosophy* 24:341–85

Ford, A.L., 2008 "The Beginnings of Dialogues: Socratic Discourses and Fourth-Century Prose," in S. Goldhill (ed.), *The End of Dialogues* (Cambridge: Cambridge University Press) pp. 29–44

2010 "Sôkratikoi Logoi in Aristotle and the Fourth-Century Theories of Genre," *Classical Philology* 105:221–35

Fraenkel, E., 1957 *Horace* (Oxford: Oxford University Press)

Frede, D., 2012 "The *Endoxon* Mystique: What *Endoxa* Are and What They Are Not," *Oxford Studies in Ancient Philosophy* 43:185–215

Frede, M., 1983 "Stoics and Sceptics on Clear and Distinct Impressions," in M. Burnyeat (ed.), *The Skeptical Tradition* (Berkeley: University of California Press), pp. 65–94

1987 "The Sceptic's Beliefs," in M. Frede, *Essays in Ancient Philosophy* (Minneapolis: University of Minnesota Press) [English version of M. Frede, 1979 "Des Skeptikers Meinungen," *Neue Hefte für Philosophie, Aktualität der Antike* 15–16:102–29]

1996 "Introduction," in M. Frede and G. Striker (eds.), *The Skeptical Tradition* (Berkeley: University of California Press), pp. 1–28

1999 "Stoic Epistemology," in K. Algra, J. Barnes, J. Mansfeld and M. Schofield (eds.), *The Cambridge History of Hellenistic Philosophy* (Cambridge: Cambridge University Press), pp. 295–322

2001 "On the Stoic Conception of the Good," in K. Ierodiakonou (ed.), *Topics in Stoic Philosophy* (Oxford: Oxford University Press), pp. 71–94

Freudenburg, K. (ed.), 2009 *Horace: Satires and Epistles* (Oxford: Oxford University Press)

Fuhrer, T. and Erler, M. (eds.), 1999 *Zur Rezeption der hellenistischen Philosophie in der Spätantike* (Stuttgart: Franz Steiner Verlag)

Garrett, J., 1993 "The Moral Status of 'the many' in Aristotle," *Journal of the History of Philosophy* 31:171–89

Gera, D.L., 2007 "Xenophon's Socrateses," in M. Trapp (ed.), *Socrates from Antiquity to the Enlightenment* (Farnham, Sr.: Ashgate) pp. 33–50

Gerson, L. (ed.), 1996 *The Cambridge Companion to Plotinus* (Cambridge: Cambridge University Press)

(ed.), 2013 "Platonic Ethics in Late Antiquity," in Crisp (ed.), pp. 129–46

Gigon, O., 1959 "Die Sokratesdoxographie bei Aristoteles," *Museum Helveticum* 16: 174–212

Gili, L., 2013 "Antishenes [sic] and Aristotle on Socrates's Dialectic: A New Appraisal of the Sources," in de Luise and Stavru (eds.) pp. 321–28

Gill, C. 1998 "Altruism or Reciprocity in Greek Ethical Thought," in C. Gill, N. Postlethwaite and R. Seaford (eds.), *Reciprocity in Ancient Greece* (Oxford: Oxford University Press), pp. 303–28

Glassen, P., 1957 "A Fallacy in Aristotle's Argument About the Good," *Philosophical Quarterly* 7:319–22

Gosling, J.C.B. and Taylor, C.C.W., 1982 *The Greeks on Pleasure* (Oxford: Clarendon Press)

Gowers, E. (ed.), 2012 *Horace, Satires Book I* (Cambridge: Cambridge University Press)

Graver, M., 2002 *Cicero on the Emotions: Tusculan Disputations 3 and 4* (Chicago: University of Chicago Press)

2007 *Stoicism and Emotion* (Chicago: University of Chicago Press)

Gray, V. (ed.), 2010 *Xenophon* (Oxford: Oxford University Press)

Grgić, F., 2006 "Sextus Empiricus on the Goal of Skepticism," *Ancient Philosophy* 26: 141–60

Griffin, J., 1993 "Horace in the Thirties," in Rudd (ed.), pp. 1–22

Guthrie, W.K.C, 1975 *A History of Greek Philosophy* vol. 4 (Cambridge: Cambridge University Press)

Hackforth, R., 1950 "Immortality in Plato's *Symposium*," *Classical Review* 64:43–5

Hadot, I. and Hadot, P., 2004 *Apprendre à philosopher dans l'Antiquité. L'enseignement du Manuel d'Epictète et son commentaire néoplatonicien* (Paris: Poche)

Halperin, D., 1985 "Platonic Eros and What Men Call Love," *Ancient Philosophy* 5:161–204

Hankinson, R., 1994 "Values, Objectivity and Dialectic: The Sceptical Attack on Ethics: Its Methods, Aims, and Success," *Phronesis* 39:45–68

   1995 *The Sceptics* (London: Routledge)

   2010 "Aenesidemus and the Rebirth of Pyrrhonism," in R. Bett (ed.), *The Cambridge Companion to Ancient Scepticism* (Cambridge: Cambridge University Press), pp. 105–19

Hansen, M.H., 1991 *The Athenian Democracy in the Age of Demosthenes* (Oxford: Blackwell)

Hasper, P. and Yurdin, J., 2014 "Between Perception and Scientific Knowledge: Aristotle's Account of Experience," *Oxford Studies in Ancient Philosophy* 47:119–50

Hatzimichali, M., 2011 *Potamo of Alexandria* (Cambridge: Cambridge University Press)

Henry, D., 2015 "Holding for the Most Part: The Demonstrability of Moral Facts," in D. Henry and K. Nielsen (eds.), *Bridging the Gap Between Aristotle's Science and Ethics* (Cambridge: Cambridge University Press) pp. 169–89

Hertig, M., "Wise Is Clever? An Elitist Requirement about Aristotle's Practical Wisdom," www.academia.edu/3128711/Wise_is_Clever_An_elitist_requirement_about_Aristotles_practical_wisdom

De Heer, C., 1969 *Makar-Eudaimôn-Olbios-Eutychês* (Amsterdam: Adolf H. Hakkert)

Hiley, D., 1987 "The Deep Challenge of Pyrrhonian Scepticism," *Journal of the History of Philosophy* 24:185–213

Huffman, C., 2009 "The Pythagorean Conception of the Soul from Pythagoras to Philolaus," in D. Frede and B. Reis (eds.), *Body and Soul in Ancient Philosophy* (Berlin: De Gruyter), pp. 21–43

   2013a "Plato and the Pythagoreans," in G. Cornelli, C. Macris, and R. McKirahan (eds.), *On Pythagoreanism* (Berlin: De Gruyter), pp. 237–70

   2013b "Reason and Myth in Early Pythagorean Cosmology," in J. McCoy (ed.), *Early Greek Philosophy: The Presocratics and the Emergence of Reason* (Washington, D.C.: Catholic University of America Press), pp. 71–98

Hursthouse R., 1999 *On Virtue Ethics* (Oxford: Oxford University Press)

Inwood, B., 1985 *Ethics and Human Action in Early Stoicism* (Oxford: Oxford University Press)

   2014 *Ethics After Aristotle* (Cambridge, MA: Harvard University Press)

Inwood, B. and Gerson, L., 2008 *The Stoics Reader: Selected Writings and Testimonia* (Indianapolis: Hackett)

Ioppolo, A., 1986 *Opinione e scienza: il dibattito tra Stoici e Accademici nel III e nel II secolo a. C.* (Naples: Bibliopolis)

Irwin, T., 1975 "Aristotle on Reason, Desire, and Virtue," *Journal of Philosophy* 73: 567–78

1980 "The Metaphysical and Psychological Basis of Aristotle's Ethics," in A.O. Rorty (ed.), *Essays on Aristotle's Ethics* (Oxford: Oxford University Press), pp. 35–53

1986 "Socrates the Epicurean?," *Illinois Classical Studies* 11:85–112

1988 *Aristotle's First Principles* (Oxford: Clarendon Press)

1990 "Virtue, Praise, and Success: Stoic Criticisms of Aristotelian Virtue," *Monist* 73:59–79

1995 *Plato's Ethics* (Oxford: Oxford University Press)

1998 "Kant's Criticisms of *Eudaimonism*," in J. Whiting and S. Engstrom (eds.), *Aristotle, Kant, and the Stoics: Rethinking Happiness and Duty* (Cambridge: Cambridge University Press), pp. 63–101

2000 "Ethics as an Inexact Science: Aristotle's Ambitions for Moral Theory," in B. Hooker and M. Little (eds.), *Moral Particularism* (Oxford: Oxford University Press), pp. 130–56

2007 *The Development of Ethics. Volume 1: From Socrates to the Reformation* (Oxford: Oxford University Press)

2011 "Beauty and Morality in Aristotle," in J. Miller (ed.), *Aristotle's Nicomachean Ethics: A Critical Guide* (Cambridge: Cambridge University Press), pp. 239–53

2012 "Conceptions of Happiness in the Ethics," in C. Shields (ed.), *Oxford Handbook of Aristotle* (Oxford: Oxford University Press), pp. 495–528

Jaeger, W., 1936 *Paideia. Die Formung des griechischen Menschen*, 3 vols. (Berlin: De Gruyter). English trans. 1944–1945 *Paideia. The Ideals of Greek Culture* (Oxford: Oxford University Press)

1928 "Über Ursprung und Kreislauf des philosophischen Lebensideal," *Sitzungsberichte der Preussischen Akademie des Wissenschaften zu Berlin* 390–421, repr. in W. Jaeger, 1960 *Scripta Minora*, vol. 1 (Rome: Edizioni di Storia e Letteratura). English trans. "On the Origin and Cycle of the Philosophic Ideal of Life," in W. Jaeger, 1948 *Aristotle: Fundamentals of the History of His Development*, trans. R. Robinson (Oxford: Clarendon Press), pp. 426–61

Johansen, T., 2008 *Plato's Natural Philosophy: A Study of the Timaeus-Critias* (Cambridge: Cambridge University Press)

2012 *The Powers of Aristotle's Soul* (Oxford: Oxford University Press)

Johnsen, B., 2001 "On the Coherence of Pyrrhonian Skepticism," *Philosophical Review* 110:521–61

Jones, R., 2013 "Wisdom and Happiness in *Euthydemus* 278–282," *Philosophers' Imprint* 13:1–21

Kahn, C., 1960/1994 *Anaximander and the Origins of Greek Cosmology* (Indianapolis: Hackett)

1981 "Aristotle on Altruism," *Mind* 90:20–40

1987 "Plato's Theory of Desire," *Review of Metaphysics* 41:77–103

1994 "Aeschines on Socratic Eros" in Vander Waerdt (ed.) pp. 87–106

1996 *Plato and the Socratic Dialogue: The Philosophical Use of Literary Form* (Cambridge: Cambridge University Press)

1998 "Pre-Platonic Ethics," in S. Everson (ed.), *Companions to Ancient Thought 4: Ethics* (Cambridge: Cambridge University Press), pp. 27–48

2003 "On Platonic Chronology," in J. Annas and C. Rowe (eds.), *New Perspectives on Plato, Modern and Ancient* (Cambridge, MA: Harvard University Press), pp. 93–127

Kalligas, P., 2014 *The Enneads of Plotinus. A Commentary*, vol. 1 (Princeton, NJ: Princeton University Press)

Kamtekar, R., 1998 "Imperfect Virtue," *Ancient Philosophy* 18:315–39

2002 "Distinction Without a Difference? Plato on 'Genos' vs. 'Race'," in J. Ward and T. Lott (eds.), *Philosophers on Race: Critical Essays* (Oxford: Blackwell), pp. 1–13

2005 "The Profession of Friendship: Callicles, Democratic Politics and Rhetorical Education in Plato's *Gorgias*," *Ancient Philosophy* 25:319–39

2016 "The Soul's (After-)life," *Ancient Philosophy* 36:1–18

forthcoming *Plato's Moral Psychology: Intellectualism, the Divided Soul, and the Desire for Good*

Karbowski, J., 2012 "Slaves, Women, and Aristotle's Natural Teleology," *Ancient Philosophy* 32:323–50

Karfík, F., 2014 "Parts of the Soul in Plotinus," in Corcilius and Perler (eds.) pp. 107–48

Karfík, F. and Song, E. (eds.), 2013 *Plato Revived. Essays on Ancient Platonism in Honour of Dominic J. O'Meara* (Berlin: De Gruyter)

Kerferd, G.B., 1981 *The Sophistic Movement* (Cambridge: Cambridge University Press)

Kobusch, T. and Erler, M. (eds.) 2002 *Metaphysik und Religion. Zur Signatur des spätantiken Denkens* (Munich: K.G. Saur)

Konstan, D., 2010 "Socrates in Aristophanes' *Clouds*," in Morrison (ed.) pp. 75–90

Korsgaard, C., 2008 "From Duty and for the Sake of the Noble: Kant and Aristotle on Morally Good Action" in C. Korsgaard, *The Constitution of Agency: Essays on Practical Reason and Moral Psychology* (Oxford: Oxford University Press), pp. 174–206

Kosman, A., 1976 "Platonic Love," in W.H. Werkmeister (ed.), *Facets of Plato's Philosophy* (Assen: Van Gorcum), pp. 53–69

2010 "Beauty and the Good: Situating the *Kalon*," *Classical Philology* 105:341–57

Kraut, R., 1973 "Egoism, Love and Political Office in Plato," *Philosophical Review* 82: 330–44

1989 *Aristotle on the Human Good* (Princeton, NJ: Princeton University Press)

2002 *Aristotle: Political Philosophy* (Oxford: Oxford University Press)

2010 "Ordinary Virtue from the *Phaedo* to the *Laws*," in Bobonich (ed.) pp. 51–70

2017 "Eudaimonism and Platonic Eros," in P. Destrée and Z. Giannopoulou (eds.), *Plato's Symposium: A Critical Guide* (Cambridge: Cambridge University Press), pp. 239–52

Laks, A., 1990 "Legislation and Demiurgy: On the Relationship Between Plato's *Republic* and *Laws*," *Classical Antiquity* 9:209–29

2008 "Le Génie du Rapprochement et les Limites de la Similitude: à propos de l'Anaximandre de Vernant," *Agenda de la Pensée Contemporaine* 10:113–27

2010 "Hystéron Protéron. Des *Origines* aux *Purifications*," in C. König and D. Thouard (eds.), *La Philologie au présent. Pour Jean Bollack. Cahiers de Philologie* (Villeneuve d'Ascq: Presses Universitaires du Septentrion), pp. 19–26

Laks, A. and Most, G.W., 2016 *Early Greek Philosophy*, 9 vols., Loeb Collection (Cambridge, MA: Harvard University Press)

Laks, A. and Saetta-Cottone, R. (eds.), 2013 *Socrate et les Présocratiques dans les Nuées d'Aristophane* (Paris: Éditions Rue d'Ulm)

Lampe, K., 2015a *The Birth of Hedonism* (Princeton, NJ: Princeton University Press)
  2015b "Rethinking Aeschines of Sphettus," in Zilioli (ed.) pp. 61–81

Lane, M., 2007 "Virtue as the Love of Knowledge in Plato's *Symposium* and *Republic*," in D. Scott (ed.), *Maieusis: Essays in Ancient Philosophy in Honour of Myles Burnyeat* (Oxford: Oxford University Press), pp. 44–67

Laursen, J., 2004 "Yes, Skeptics Can Live Their Skepticism and Cope with Tyranny as Well as Anyone," in J.R. Maia Neto and R. Popkin (eds.), *Skepticism in Renaissance and Post-Renaissance Thought: New Interpretations* (Amherst, NY: Humanity Books), pp. 201–34

  2006 "Plato on Learning to Love Beauty," in G. Santas (ed.), *The Blackwell Guide to Plato's Republic* (Malden, MA: Blackwell), pp. 104–24

Lavecchia, S., 2006 *Una via che conduce al divino. La "homoiosis theo" nella filosofia di Platone* (Milan: Vita e Pensiero)

Lear, G., 2004 *Happy Lives and the Highest Good* (Princeton, NJ: Princeton University Press)

Lennox, J., 1997 "Material and Formal Natures in Aristotle's *De Partibus Animalium*," in W. Kullmann and S. Föllinger (eds.), *Aristotelische Biologie* (Stuttgart: Franz Steiner Verlag), pp. 163–81

  2010 "*Bios* and Explanatory Unity in Aristotle's Biology," in D. Charles (ed.), *Definition in Greek Philosophy* (Oxford: Oxford University Press), pp. 329–55

Leunissen, M., 2012 "Aristotle on Natural Character and Its Implications for Moral Development," *Journal of the History of Philosophy* 50:507–30

  2013 "'Becoming Good Starts with Nature': Aristotle on the Moral Advantages and the Heritability of Good Natural Character," *Oxford Studies in Ancient Philosophy* 44:99–127

Lévy, C., 1992 *Cicero Academicus: Recherches sur les Académiques et sur la Philosophie Cicéronienne* (Rome: École française de Rome)

Lévystone, D., 2005 "La figure d'Ulysse chez les Socratiques: Socrate polutropos," *Phronesis* 50:181–214

Long, A.A., 1986 *Stoic Studies* (Cambridge: Cambridge University Press) repr. 2001 (Berkeley: University of California Press)

  1988 "Socrates in Hellenistic Philosophy," *Classical Quarterly* 38:150–71

  1996 "Dialectic and the Stoic Sage," in A. Long *Stoic Studies* (Cambridge: Cambridge University Press), pp. 85–106

  2004 "Eudaimonism, Divinity, and Rationality in Greek Ethics," *Proceedings of the Boston Area Colloquium in Ancient Philosophy* 19:123–43

  2011 "Socrates in Later Greek Philosophy," in D. Morrison (ed.), *The Cambridge Companion to Socrates* (Cambridge: Cambridge University Press), pp. 355–80

Long, A.A. and Sedley, D., 1987 *The Hellenistic Philosophers*, 2 vols. (Cambridge: Cambridge University Press)

Lorenz, H., 2006 *The Brute Within: Appetitive Desire in Plato and Aristotle* (Oxford: Clarendon Press)

Lories, D. and Rizzerio, L. (eds.), 2008 *Le jugement pratique. Autour de la notion de Phronèsis* (Paris: Vrin)

Ludwig, P., 2002 *Eros and Polis: Desire and Community in Greek Political Theory* (Cambridge: Cambridge University Press)

de Luise, F., and Stavru, A. (eds.), 2013 *Socratica III* (Sankt Augustin: Academia Verlag)

Machuca, D., 2006 "The Pyrrhonist's *ataraxia* and *philanthropia*," *Ancient Philosophy* 26:111–39

MacIntyre, A., 1970 *After Virtue* (London: Duckworth)

Macleod, C. W., 1979/2009 "The Poetry of Ethics: Horace, *Epistles* I" in Freudenburg (ed.), repr. from *Journal of Roman Studies* 69:16–27

Mahieu, W. de, 1963/1964 "La doctrine des athées au Xe livre des *Lois* de Platon: Essai d'analyse," *Revue Belge de Philologie et d'Histoire* 41:5–24 (I. "Essai d'analyse") and 42:16–47 (II. "Etude des sources")

Mahoney, T., 1992 "Do Plato's Philosopher-Rulers Sacrifice Self-Interest to Justice?," *Phronesis* 37:265–82

2008 "Moral Virtue and Assimilation to God in Plato's *Timaeus*," *Oxford Studies in Ancient Philosophy* 28:77–91

Mallet, J.-A., 2013 "The Notion of *theia moîra* in Aeschines of Sphettus' Fragments," in de Luise and A. Stavru (eds.), pp. 225–32

Mansfeld, J., 2011 "Anaximander's Fragment: Another Attempt," *Phronesis* 56: 1–32

Martin, R., 1993 "The Seven Sages as Performers of Wisdom" in C. Dougherty and L. Kurke (eds.), *Cultural Poetics in Archaic Greece: Cult, Performance, Politics* (Cambridge: Cambridge University Press), pp. 108–28

Mayer, R.G., 1986 "Horace's *Epistles* I and Philosophy," *American Journal of Philology* 107:55–73

(ed.), 1994 *Horace: Epistles I* (Cambridge: Cambridge University Press)

McCaskey, J., 2007 "Freeing Aristotelian *Epagôgê* from *Prior Analytics* II.23," *Apeiron* 40:345–74

McDowell, J., 1979 "Virtue and Reason," *The Monist* 62: 331–50

McGann, M. J., 1969 *Studies in Horace's First Book of Epistles* (Brussels: Latomus)

McNamara, C., 2009 "Socratic Politics in Xenophon's *Memorabilia*," *Polis* 26:223–45

McPherran, M., 1989 "*Ataraxia* and Eudaimonia in Ancient Pyrrhonism: Is the Skeptic Really Happy?" *Proceedings of the Boston Area Colloquium in Ancient Philosophy* 5:135–71

1990 "Pyrrhonism's Arguments against Value," *Philosophical Studies* 60:127–42

2007 "Socratic Epagôgê and Socratic Induction," *Journal of the History of Philosophy* 45:347–65

2010 "Socratic Religion," in Morrison (ed.) pp. 111–37

Menn, S., 1995 "Physics as a Virtue," *Proceedings of the Boston Area Colloquium in Ancient Philosophy* 11:1–34.

Mikalson, J., 1983 *Athenian Popular Religion* (Chapel Hill: University of North Carolina Press)

Miller, J. (ed.), 2012 *The Reception of Aristotle's Ethics* (Cambridge: Cambridge University Press)

Mitsis, P., 1988 *Epicurus' Ethical Theory: The Pleasures of Invulnerability* (Ithaca NY: Cornell University Press)

Modrak, D., 1987 *Aristotle, The Power of Perception* (Chicago: University of Chicago Press)

Moles, J., 2002/2009 "Poetry, Philosophy, Politics, and Play," in Freudenburg (ed.). Repr. from D. Feeny and A.J. Woodman (eds.), *Tradition and Contexts in the Poetry of Horace* (Cambridge: Cambridge University Press), pp. 141–57

2007 "Philosophy and Ethics," in S.J. Harrison (ed.), *The Cambridge Companion to Horace* (Cambridge: Cambridge University Press), pp. 165–80

Moller, D., 2004 "The Pyrrhonian Skeptic's Telos," *Ancient Philosophy* 24:424–41

Mondolfo, R., 1956 "Natura e Cultura alle Origini della Filosofia," repr. in W. Leszl (ed.), 1982 *I Presocratici* (Bologna: Società ed. il Mulino), pp. 223–55

Moore, C., 2013 "Socrates Psychagôgos (*Birds* 1555, *Phaedrus* 261a7)," in de Luise and Stavru (eds.) pp. 41–55

Morgan, T. J., 2007 *Popular Morality in the Early Roman Empire* (Cambridge: Cambridge University Press)

Morison, B., 2011 "The Logical Structure of the Sceptic's Opposition," *Oxford Studies in Ancient Philosophy* 40: 265–95

Morrison, D., 2010 "Xenophon's Socrates on Sophia and the Virtues," in Rossetti and Stavru (eds.) pp. 227–39

2010 "Xenophon's Socrates as Teacher," in Gray (ed.) pp. 195–227

Morrison, D. (ed.), 2010 *The Cambridge Companion to Socrates* (Cambridge: Cambridge University Press)

Moss, J., 2008 "Appearances and Calculations: Plato's Division of the Soul," *Oxford Studies in Ancient Philosophy* 34:36–68

2012 *Aristotle on the Apparent Good: Perception, Phantasia, Thought and Desire* (Oxford: Oxford University Press)

2014 "Right Reason in Plato and Aristotle: On the Meaning of Logos," *Phronesis* 59:181–230

Mourelatos, A.G.P., 2013 "Xénophane et son 'astro-néphologie' dans les *Nuées*," in Laks and Saetta-Cottone (eds.) pp. 32–60

Nagel, T., 1972 "Aristotle on Eudaimonia," *Phronesis* 17:252–59

Natali, C., 2006 "Socrates' Dialectic in Xenophon's *Memorabilia*," in L. Judson and V. Karasmanis (eds.), *Remembering Socrates: Philosophical Essays* (Oxford: Clarendon Press), pp. 3–19

Natorp, P., 1893 *Die Ethika des Demokritos* (Marburg: Olms), repr. 1973 (New York: Hildesheim)

Nehamas, A., 2010 "Aristotelian Philia, Modern Friendship?," *Oxford Studies in Ancient Philosophy* 39:213–47

Nielsen, K., 2015 "The Constitution of the Soul: Aristotle on Lack of Deliberative Authority," *Classical Quarterly* 65:572–86

Nikolsky, B., 2001 "Epicurus on Pleasure," *Phronesis* 46:440–65

Nussbaum, M., 1986 *The Fragility of Goodness* (Cambridge: Cambridge University Press)

1991 "Skeptic Purgatives: Therapeutic Arguments in Ancient Skepticism," *Journal of the History of Philosophy* 29:1–33

O'Connor, D.K., 2010 "Xenophon and the Enviable Life of Socrates," in Morrison (ed.), pp. 48–74

O'Keefe, T., 2001a "Is Epicurean Friendship Altruistic?," *Apeiron* 34:269–305

2001b "Would a Community of Wise Epicureans be Just?," *Ancient Philosophy* 21: 133–46

O'Meara, D., 1993 *Plotinus. An Introduction to the Enneads* (Oxford: Clarendon Press)

1999 "Epicurus Neoplatonicus," in Fuhrer and Erler (eds.), pp. 83–91

2003 *Platonopolis. Platonic Political Philosophy in Late Antiquity* (Oxford: Clarendon Press)

2006 "Patterns of Perfection in Damascius' Life of Isidore," *Phronesis* 51:74–90

2012 "Aristotelian Ethics in Plotinus," in Miller (ed.), pp. 53–66

2013 "Moral Virtue in Late Antique Platonism. Some Elements of a Background to Ethics in Early Arabic Philosophy," *Mélanges de l'Université Saint-Joseph* 65:47–61 (Beirut)

2016 "Souls and Cities in Late Ancient Platonic Philosophy," *Chôra (Revue d'études anciennes et médiévales)* 14:15–28

Obdrzalek, S., 2010 "Moral Transformation and the Love of Beauty in Plato's *Symposium*," *Journal of the History of Philosophy* 48:415–44

2013 "*Eros Tyrannos*: Philosophical Passion and Psychic Ordering in the *Republic*" in N. Notomi and L. Brisson (eds.), *Dialogues on Plato's Politeia* (Sankt Augustin: Academia Verlag), pp. 215–20

Ober, J., 2010 "Socrates and Democratic Athens," in Morrison (ed.) pp. 138–78

2015 "Nature, History, and Aristotle's Best Possible Regime," in T. Lockwood and T. Samaras (eds.), *Aristotle's Politics: A Critical Guide* (Cambridge: Cambridge University Press), pp. 224–43

Okin, S., 2013 *Women in Western Political Thought* (Princeton, NJ: Princeton University Press)

Pangle, T., 1994 "Socrates in the Context of Xenophon's Political Writings," in Vander Waerdt (ed.), pp. 127–50

Pappas, N., 2016 "Plato's Aesthetics," in E. Zalta (ed.), *The Stanford Encyclopedia of Philosophy* https://plato.stanford.edu/archives/fall2016/entries/plato-aesthetics

Parfit, D., 1986 *Reasons and Persons* (Oxford: Oxford University Press)

2011 *On What Matters*, vol. I (Oxford: Oxford University Press)

Parker, R., 1996 *Athenian Religion: A History* (Oxford: Oxford University Press)

Parry, R., "Episteme and Techne," in E. Zalta (ed.), *The Stanford Encyclopedia of Philosophy* https://plato.stanford.edu/archives/fall2014/entries/episteme-techne/

Patzer, A., 1993 "Die Wolken des Aristophanes als philosophiegeschichtliches Dokument," in P. Neukam (ed.), *Klassische Sprachen und Literatur* Bd. 27 (Munich: Bayerischer Schulbuch Verlag), pp. 72–93

1994 "Sokrates in den Fragmenten der Attischen Komödie," in A. Bierl and P. von Möllendorff (eds.), *Orchestra: Drama Mythos Bühne* (Leipzig: Teubner), pp. 50–81

2010 "Xenophon's Socrates as Dialectician," in Gray (ed.), pp. 228–56

2012 "Sokrates als Philosoph: Das Gute," *Studia Socratica* (Tübingen: Gunter Narr Verlag), pp. 8–31

Patzer, A., (ed.), 1985 *Der historische Sokrates* (Darmstadt: Wissenschaftlicher Buchgesellschaft)

Penner, T. and Rowe, C., 1994 "Desire for Good: Is the *Meno* Inconsistent with the *Gorgias*?," *Phronesis* 39:1–25

2005 *Plato's Lysis* (Cambridge: Cambridge University Press)

Perin, C., 2010 *The Demands of Reason: An Essay on Pyrrhonian Scepticism* (Oxford: Oxford University Press)

Pietsch, C. (ed.), 2013 *Ethik des antiken Platonismus* (Stuttgart: Franz Steiner Verlag)

Polito, R., 2004 *The Sceptical Road: Aenesidemus' Appropriation of Heraclitus* (Leiden: Brill)

2014 *Aenesidemus of Cnossus: Testimonia* (Cambridge: Cambridge University Press)

Prauscello, L., 2014 *Performing Citizenship in Plato's Laws* (Cambridge: Cambridge University Press)

Price, A., 1997 *Love and Friendship in Plato and Aristotle* (Oxford: Clarendon Press). Originally published in 1989; reissued with changes in 1997.

Prince, S., 2015 *Antisthenes of Athens* (Ann Arbor: University of Michigan Press)
(forthcoming)a "Antisthenes and the Short Route to Happiness"
(forthcoming)b "Virtues and Their Ontology in the Socratic Banter of Xenophon's *Symposium*"

Purinton, J., 1993 "Epicurus on the Telos," *Phronesis* 38:281–320

Railton, P., 1984 "Alienation, Consequentialism, and the Demands of Morality," *Philosophy and Public Affairs* 13:134–71

Ranocchia, G., 2012 "The Stoic Concept of Proneness to Emotion and Vice," *Archiv für Geschichte der Philosophie* 94:74–92.

Rapp, C., 2006 "What Use Is Aristotle's Doctrine of the Mean?" in B. Reis and S. Haffmanns (eds.), *The Virtuous Life in Greek Ethics* (Cambridge: Cambridge University Press), pp. 99–126

Rawls, J., 1971 *A Theory of Justice* (Cambridge, MA: Harvard University Press)

Reeve, C.D.C., 1992 *Practices of Reason: Aristotle's Nicomachean Ethics* (Oxford: Clarendon Press)

2012 *Action, Contemplation, and Happiness* (Cambridge, MA: Harvard University Press)

Remes, P., 2006 "Plotinus' Ethics of Disinterested Interest," *Journal of the History of Philosophy* 44:1–23

2007 *Plotinus on Self. The Philosophy of the "We"* (Cambridge: Cambridge University Press)

2014 "Action, Reasoning and the Highest Good," in Remes and Slaveva-Griffith (eds.), pp. 453–70

Remes, P. and Slaveva-Griffith, S. (eds.), 2014 *The Routledge Handbook of Neoplatonism* (London: Routledge)

Robins, I., 1995 "Mathematics and the Conversion of the Mind: *Republic* VII 522c1–531e3," *Ancient Philosophy* 15:359–92

Roochnik, D., 2007 *Of Art and Wisdom: Plato's Understanding of Technê* (Pennsylvania State University Press)

Rossetti, L., 2010 "I Socratici 'primi filosofici' e Socrate 'primo filosofo,'" in Rossetti and Stavru (eds.), pp. 59–70

Rossetti L., and Stavru, A. (eds.), 2010 *Socratica 2008* (Bari: Levante)

Rowe, C., 2006 "The *Symposium* as a Socratic Dialogue," in J. Lesher, D. Nails, and F. Sheffield (eds.), pp. 9–22

Rudd, N., 1993 "Horace as a Moralist" in Rudd (ed.), pp. 64–88

Rudd, N. (ed.), 1993 *Horace 2000: A Celebration* (London: Duckworth)

Russell, D., 2004 "Virtue as 'Likeness to God' in Plato and Seneca," *Journal of the History of Philosophy* 42:241–60

2012 *Happiness for Humans* (Oxford: Oxford University Press)

Santas, G., 1964 "The Socratic Paradoxes," *Philosophical Review* 73:147–64

1966 "Plato's *Protagoras* and Explanations of Weakness," *Philosophical Review* 75:3–33

Sassi, M., 2007 "Ordre cosmique et << isonomia >> En repensant *Les origines de la pensée grecque* de Jean-Pierre Vernant," *Philosophie Antique* 7:190–218

Schibli, H., 2002 *Hierocles of Alexandria* (Oxford: Oxford University Press)

Schneewind, J., 1990 "The Misfortunes of Virtue," *Ethics* 101:42–63

1998 *The Invention of Autonomy* (Cambridge: Cambridge University Press)

Schniewind, A., 2003 *L'éthique du sage chez Plotin. Le paradigme du spoudaios* (Paris: Vrin)

2005 "The Social Concern of the Plotinian Sage," in Smith (ed.), pp. 51–64

2008 "'La phronèsis est une sorte d'epilogismos . . . '. À propos d'un concept épicurien chez Plotin, *Ennéade* I 3, 6, 8–14," in Lories and Rizzerio (eds.), pp. 199–214

Schofield, M., 1984 "Ariston of Chios on the Unity of Virtue," *Ancient Philosophy* 41:83–96

1999 "Academic Epistemology," in K. Algra, J. Barnes, J. Mansfeld and M. Schofield (eds.), *The Cambridge History of Hellenistic Philosophy* (Cambridge: Cambridge University Press), pp. 323–51

2012a "Injury, Injustice, and the Involuntary in the *Laws*," in R. Kamtekar (ed.), *Virtue and Happiness: Essays in Honour of Julia Annas*, Oxford Studies in Ancient Philosophy supp. vol. pp. 103–14

2012b "The Neutralizing Argument: Carneades, Antiochus, Cicero," in D. Sedley (ed.), *The Philosophy of Antiochus* (Cambridge: Cambridge University Press), pp. 337–49

2013 "Friendship and Justice in the *Laws*," in G. Boys-Stones, D. El Murr and C. Gill (eds.), *The Platonic Art of Philosophy* (Cambridge: Cambridge University Press), pp. 283–97

Schramm, M., 2013 *Freundschaft im Neuplatonismus. Politisches Denken und Sozialphilosophie von Plotin bis Kaiser Julian* (Berlin: De Gruyter)

Scott, D., 2007 "Eros, Philosophy, and Tyranny," in D. Scott (ed.), *Maieusis: Essays in Ancient Philosophy in Honour of Myles Burnyeat* (Oxford: Oxford University Press), pp. 136–54

2015 *Levels of Argument* (Oxford: Oxford University Press)

Sedley, D., 1998 "The Inferential Foundations of Epicurean Ethics," in S. Everson (ed.), *Ethics, Companions to Ancient Thought 4* (Cambridge: Cambridge University Press), pp. 129–50

2000 "The Ideal of Godlikeness," in G. Fine (ed.), *Plato 2: Ethics, Politics, Religion, and the Soul* (Oxford: Oxford University Press), pp. 309–28

2004 *The Midwife of Platonism: Text and Subtext in Plato's Theaetetus* (Oxford: Oxford University Press)

2007a *Creationism and Its Critics in Antiquity* (Berkeley: University of California Press)

2007b "Philosophy, the Forms, and the Art of Ruling," in G.R.F. Ferrari (ed.), *The Cambridge Companion to Plato's Republic* (Cambridge: Cambridge University Press), pp. 256–83

2009 "Three Kinds of Platonic Immortality," in D. Frede and B. Reis (eds.), *Body and Soul in Ancient Philosophy* (Berlin: De Gruyter), pp. 145–61

2014 "Horace's Socraticae Chartae," *Materiali e Discussioni per l'Analisi dei Testi Classici* 72:97–120

Sharples, R. and Sorabji, R. (eds.), 2007 *Greek and Roman Philosophy 100 BC – 200 AD. Bulletin of the Institute of Classical Studies. Supplement 94* (London: Institute of Classical Studies)

Sheffield, F.C.C., 2006 *Plato's Symposium: The Ethics of Desire* (Oxford: Oxford University Press)

2011 "Beyond Eros: Plato on Friendship in the *Phaedrus*," *Proceedings of the Aristotelian Society* 111: 251–73

2012 "*Eros* Before and After Tri-Partition," in R. Barney, C. Brittain and T. Brennan (eds.), *Plato and the Divided Self* (Cambridge: Cambridge University Press), pp. 211–37

Sider, D., 2013 "Heraclitus' Ethics," in D. Sider and D. Obbink (eds.), *Doctrine and Doxography: Studies on Heraclitus and Pythagoras* (Berlin: De Gruyter), pp. 331–44

Sidgwick, H., 1907/1981 *Methods of Ethics*, 7th edn. (Indianapolis: Hackett)

Silverman, A., 2010a. "Contemplating the Divine Mind," in A. Nightingale and D. Sedley (eds.), *Ancient Models of Mind* (Cambridge: Cambridge University Press), pp. 75–96

2010b. "Philosopher Kings and Craftsman Gods," in R. D. Mohr and B. Sattler (eds.), *One Book, the Whole Universe* (Las Vegas, NV: Parmenides Publishing), pp. 55–67

Singpurwalla, R., 2013 "Why Spirit Is the Natural Ally of Reason," *Oxford Studies in Ancient Philosophy* 44: 41–65

Smart, J.J.C. and Williams, B., 1973 *Utilitarianism: For and Against* (Cambridge: Cambridge University Press)

Smith, A., 1999 "The Significance of Practical Ethics for Plotinus," in Cleary (ed.), pp. 227–36

2005a (ed.) *The Philosopher and Society in late Antiquity* (Aldershot, Hants: Ashgate)

2005b "Action and Contemplation in Plotinus," in Smith (ed.), pp. 65–72

2005c "More Neoplatonic Ethics," in Dillon and Dixsaut (eds.), pp. 235–39

Smith, N., forthcoming "Aristotle on Socrates," in F. de Luise and A. Stavru (eds.), *Socrates and the Socratic Dialogues* (Milan: Limina Mentis)

Snyder, C., 2014 "The Socratic Benevolence of Arcesilaus' Dialectic," *Ancient Philosophy* 34:341–63

Song, E., 2009a *Aufstieg und Abstieg der Seele. Diesseitigkeit und Jenseitigkeit in Plotins Ethik der Sorge. Hypomnemata 180* (Göttingen: Vandenhoeck and Ruprecht)

2009b "The Ethics of Descent in Plotinus," *Hermathena* 187:27–48

2013 "Ashamed of Being in the Body? Plotinus versus Porphyry," in Karfík and Song (eds.), pp. 96–116

Stern-Gillet, S., 1995 *Aristotle's Philosophy of Friendship* (Albany: SUNY Press)

2014 "Plotinus on Metaphysics and Morality," in Remes and Slaveva-Griffin (eds.), pp. 396–420

Stokes, M. C., 1995 "Cicero on Epicurean Pleasures," in Powell, J.G.F. (ed.), *Cicero the Philosopher* (Oxford: Oxford University Press), pp. 145–70

Stopper, M., 1983 "Schizzi Pirroniani," *Phronesis* 28:265–97

Striker, G., 1980 "Sceptical Strategies," in M. Schofield, M. Burnyeat and J. Barnes (eds.), *Doubt and Dogmatism: Studies in Hellenistic Epistemology* (Oxford: Clarendon Press), pp. 54–83

    1990 "Ataraxia: Happiness as Tranquillity," *Monist* 73: 97–110

    1991 "Following Nature: A Study in Stoic Ethics," *Oxford Studies in Ancient Philosophy* 9:1–73

    1996a "Epicurean Hedonism," in Striker (1996c) pp. 196–208

    1996b "Epicurus on the Truth of Sense-Impressions," in Striker (1996c) pp. 77–91

    1996c *Essays on Hellenistic Epistemology and Ethics* (Cambridge: Cambridge University Press)

Tarrant, H., 2007 "Moral Goal and Moral Virtues in Middle Platonism," in Sharples and Sorabji (eds.), vol. II, pp. 419–29

Taylor, C. C. W., 1980 "'All Perceptions Are True'," in M. Schofield, M. Burnyeat and J. Barnes (eds.), *Doubt and Dogmatism: Studies in Hellenistic Epistemology* (Oxford: Clarendon Press), pp. 105–24

    2012 "The Role of Women in Plato's *Republic*," in R. Kamtekar (ed.), *Virtue and Happiness: Essays in Honour of Julia Annas*, *Oxford Studies in Ancient Philosophy* supp. vol. pp. 75–87

Taylor, D., 2014 "Pyrrhonian Skepticism, Value Nihilism and the Good of Knowledge," *Ancient Philosophy* 34: 317–39

Thom, Johan C., 2013 "The Pythagorean *Akousmata* and Early Pythagoreanism," in G. Cornelli, C. Macris and R. McKirahan (eds.), *On Pythagoreanism* (Berlin: De Gruyter)

Thorsrud, H., 2003 "Is the Examined Life Worth Living? A Pyrrhonian Alternative," *Apeiron* 36:229–49

    2009 *Ancient Scepticism* (Durham: Acumen)

Traina, A., 2009 "Horace and Aristippus: the Epistles and the Art of Convivere," in Freudenburg (ed.), pp. 287–307

Tsouna, V., 2002 "Is There an Exception to Greek Eudaemonism?," in P. Pellegrin and M. Canto (eds.), *Le Style de la Pensée* (Paris: Les Belles Lettres), pp. 464–89

    2009 "Epicurean Therapeutic Strategies," in J. Warren (ed.), *The Cambridge Companion to Epicureanism* (Cambridge: Cambridge University Press), pp. 249–65

Tuominen, M., (forthcoming) *Justice for the Living: On Porphyry's Ethics of On Abstinence*

van den Berg, R., 2014 "Proclus and Iamblichus on Moral Education," *Phronesis* 59: 272–96

Vander Waerdt, P., 1987 "The Justice of the Epicurean Wise Man," *Classical Quarterly* 37:402–22

    1989 "Colotes and the Epicurean Refutation of Skepticism," *Greek, Roman and Byzantine Studies* 30:225–67

Vander Waerdt, P. (ed.), 1994 *The Socratic Movement* (Ithaca, NY: Cornell University Press)

Vernant, J.-P., 1962 *Les Origines de la Pensée Grecque* (Paris: Presses Universitaires de France), repr. in Vernant 2007, vol. I, pp. 155–238. English trans. 1982 *The Origins of Greek Thought* (Ithaca, NY: Cornell University Press)

1968 "Structure Géométrique et Notions Politiques dans la Cosmologie d'Anaximandre," *Eirene* 7: 5–23, repr. in Vernant 2007, vol. I, pp. 436–54

2007 *Œuvres. Religions, Rationalités, Politique,* 2 vols. (Paris: Seuil)

Vlastos, G., 1981a "The Individual as Object of Love in Plato," in Vlastos (1981b), pp. 3–42

1981b *Platonic Studies* (Princeton, NJ: Princeton University Press)

1981c "The Unity of the Virtues in the *Protagoras,*" in Vlastos (1981b), pp. 221–69

1991 *Socrates, Ironist and Moral Philosopher* (Ithaca NY: Cornell University Press)

1995a "Equality and Justice in Early Greek Cosmologies," in Vlastos and Graham (ed.) (1995), pp. 57–88

1995b "Physics and Ethics in Democritus," in Vlastos and Graham (ed.) (1995), pp. 328–50

Vlastos, G. and Graham, D.W. (ed.) 1995 *Studies in Greek Philosophy I: The Presocratics* (Princeton, NJ: Princeton University Press)

Vogel, C., 2013 *Stoische Ethik und platonische Bildung. Simplicius' Kommentar zu Epiktets Handbüchlein der Moral* (Heidelberg: Universitätsverlag Winter)

Vogt, K., 2008 *Law, Reason, and the Cosmic City: Political Philosophy in the Early Stoa* (Oxford: Oxford University Press)

2010 "Scepticism and Action," in R. Bett (ed.), *The Cambridge Companion to Ancient Scepticism* (Cambridge: Cambridge University Press), pp. 165–80

2012 *Belief and Truth: A Skeptic Reading of Plato* (New York: Oxford University Press).

2014 "I Shall Do What I Did: Stoic Views on Action," in R. Salles, P. Destrée and M. Zingano (eds.), *What Is Up To Us? Studies on Agency and Responsibility in Ancient Philosophy* (Sankt Augustin: Academia Verlag), pp. 107–20.

Warren, J., 2002 *Epicurus and Democritean Ethics: an Archaeology of Ataraxia* (Cambridge: Cambridge University Press)

2004 *Facing Death. Epicurus and His Critics* (Cambridge: Cambridge University Press)

2014 *The Pleasures of Reason in Plato, Aristotle, and the Hellenistic Hedonists* (Cambridge: Cambridge University Press)

Waterfield, R., 2013 "The Quest for the Historical Socrates," in Bussanich and Smith (eds.), pp. 1–19

White, F., 2004 "Virtue in Plato's *Symposium,*" *Classical Quarterly* 54:366–78

White, M., 2003 "Stoic Natural Philosophy (Physics and Cosmology)" in B. Inwood (ed.), *Cambridge Companion to the Stoics* (Cambridge: Cambridge University Press), pp. 124–52

White, N., 1992 "The Attractive and the Imperative: Sidgwick's View of Greek Ethics," in B. Schultz (ed.), *Essays on Henry Sidgwick* (Cambridge: Cambridge University Press), pp. 311–30

Whitehead, D., 1975 "Aristotle the Metic," *Proceedings of the Cambridge Philological Society* 201:94–9

Whiting, J., 1988 "The Function Argument: A Defense," *Ancient Philosophy* 8: 33–48

1991 "Impersonal Friends," *The Monist* 74:3–29

2002 "Locomotive Soul: the Parts of the Soul in Aristotle's Scientific Works," *Oxford Studies in Ancient Philosophy* 22:141–200

2006 "The Nicomachean Account of *Philia*," in R. Kraut (ed.), *The Blackwell Guide to Aristotle's Nicomachean Ethics* (Oxford: Oxford University Press), pp. 276–304

2012 "Psychic Contingency in the *Republic*," in R. Barney, T. Brennan and C. Brittain (eds.), *Plato and the Divided Self* (Cambridge: Cambridge University Press), pp 174–208

Wiggins, D. 1980 "Deliberation and Practical Reason," in A.O. Rorty (ed.), *Essays on Aristotle's Ethics* (Berkeley: University of California Press), pp. 221–40

Wilberding, J., 2008 "Automatic Action in Plotinus," *Oxford Studies in Ancient Philosophy* 13:331–45

2009 "Plato's Two Forms of Second-Best Morality," *The Philosophical Review* 118: 351–74

Wildberg, C., 2002 "Pros to telos: Neuplatonische Ethik zwischen Religion und Metaphysik," in Kobusch and Erler (eds.), pp. 261–78

2009 "A World of Thoughts: Plotinus on Nature and Contemplation (*Enn*. III.8.[30] 1–6)," in Chiaradonna and Trabattoni (eds.), pp. 121–43

Wilkerson, K., 1988 "Carneades at Rome: a Problem of Sceptical Rhetoric," *Philosophy and Rhetoric* 21:131–44

Williams, B., 1981 "Persons, Character, and Morality," in B. Williams *Moral Luck* (Cambridge: Cambridge University Press), pp. 1–19

1985 *Ethics and the Limits of Philosophy* (London: Fontana)

1993 *Shame and Necessity* (Berkeley: University of California Press)

1995 "The Point of View of the Universe: Sidgwick and the Ambitions of Ethics" in B. Williams, *Making Sense of Humanity* (Cambridge: Cambridge University Press), pp. 153–71

Williamson, T., 1994 *Vagueness* (London: Routledge)

Winter, M., 1997 "Aristotle, *hôs epi to polu* Relations, and a Demonstrative Science of Ethics," *Phronesis* 42:163–89

Wolf, S., 2007 "Moral Psychology and the Unity of the Virtues," *Ratio* 20:145–67

Wolfsdorf, D., 2003 "Socrates' Pursuit of Definitions," *Phronesis* 48:271–312

2004a "Interpreting Plato's Early Dialogues," *Oxford Studies in Ancient Philosophy* 27:15–41

2004b "Socrates' Avowals of Knowledge," *Phronesis* 49:75–142

2004c "The Socratic Fallacy and the Epistemological Priority of Definitional Knowledge," *Apeiron* 37:35–67

2008 "Hesiod, Prodicus, and the Socratics on Work and Pleasure," *Oxford Studies in Ancient Philosophy* 35:1–18

2013a *Pleasure in Ancient Greek Philosophy* (Cambridge: Cambridge University Press)

2013b "Socratic Philosophizing," in Bussanich and Smith (eds.), pp. 35–65

Woodruff, P., 1988 "Aporetic Pyrrhonism," *Oxford Studies in Ancient Philosophy* 6: 139–68

Woolf, R., 2004 "What Kind of Hedonist Was Epicurus?," *Phronesis* 49:303–22

2009 "Pleasure and Desire," in J. Warren (ed.), *The Cambridge Companion to Epicureanism* (Cambridge: Cambridge University Press), pp. 158–78

Zilioli, U. (ed.), 2015 *From The Socratics to the Socratic Schools: Classical Ethics, Metaphysics and Epistemology* (London: Routledge)

Index

Academic skeptics, 214, 219, 220–22,
    225–28, 233
action
    eudaimonism and action guidance, 277–79
    and knowledge (Plotinus), 250–53
    possibility of in skepticism (agency),
        225–26, 235–36
    Stoic account of, 204–5
        and emotion, 209
        selection, 205–6
active principle (Stoic physics), 189, 201
activity, in Aristotelian function argument,
    107–8
Aenesidemus, 219, 222, 224, 230, 234
Aeschines, 40–41, 43
Against Colotes (Plutarch), 225–26
Against the Ethicists (Sextus Empiricus), 222
agency, in skepticism, 225–28, 230–31, 235–36
akratic actions, 72–73
    see also unwilling actions
Alcibiades (Aeschines), 40–41, 87
Alcibiades (Plato), 256
Alexander of Aphrodisias, 192
alienation, 354, 355
anatomy, human *see* physiology
Anaxagoras, 19, 20
Anaximander, 22–23
anger, 82–83, 84, 207
    see also emotions
animals
    arguments from natural instincts, 166,
        284, 332
    capacity for happiness, 241
    divided soul, 107–8, 127–28, 129, 130
        immortal component, 325, 333
    goals of, 110, 113–14, 141n
    natural virtue, 134
    reincarnation (Plato), 84–85
    sacrifice and consumption of, 24–25, 261n
    Stoic account of, 189, 201–3
Annas, Julia, 156, 296, 296n
Anscombe, Elizabeth (G. E. M.), 1, 273
Antigonus of Carystus, 229

Antiochus of Ascalon, 219
Antiphon, 28n
Antisthenes, 39, 41
Apelles, Pyrrhonist parable of, 234–35, 236
Apology (Plato), 12–13, 53, 84, 289–90
aporia, 219, 234, 236
appearances
    imaginative *(phantasiai)*, 127, 130
    perceptual *(phainomena)*, 74, 225, 230–31
    see also perception
appetites
    in Aristotle, 125, 127
    in Plato, 74, 78, 82–83, 84, 320
        and physiology, 81–82
    see also desire
appropriation *(oikeiôsis)*
    Plotinus, 248–49
    Stoics, 189–90
apraxia charge, 225–26
    Academic responses, 225–28
    Pyrrhonist responses, 230–31, 232–33
Aquinas, Thomas, 141, 270
Arcesilaus, 219, 220–21, 233
    answer to *apraxia* charge, 225–27
Aristippus, 40, 350–51
Aristo, 185, 191
Aristophanes
    as character in *Symposium*, 291–92
    Clouds, 20, 30, 38
Aristotle, 105–23
    biographical information, 31, 323–24
    on contemplative *vs.* political life, 322–24,
        335–36
        and immortality, 324
        and moral activity, 326
    elitism *see* elitism: Aristotle
    and "ethics" as field, 35
    eudaimonism, 267, 268
        egoism objection, 274–75
    evidence for Pre-Socratic thought in, 11, 16
    on friendship *(philia)*, 143–58
        commonplace beliefs, 146–48, 150,
        156–57

Other Volumes in The Series of Cambridge Companions

(*continued from page ii*)